Robot Sex

Robot Sex

Social and Ethical Implications

John Danaher and Neil McArthur

The MIT Press
Cambridge, Massachusetts
London, England

This book was set in ITC Stone Sans Std and ITC Stone Serif Std by Toppan Best-set Premedia Limited. Printed and bound in the United States of America.

Library of Congress Cataloging-in-Publication Data is available.

ISBN: 978-0-262-03668-9

10   9   8   7   6   5   4   3   2   1

Contents

Acknowledgments

It is an old cliché to say that books are never solo efforts, but that is truer in the present instance than in most. This book was not the product of one author in either conception or execution. We, the editors, would like to sincerely thank each of the contributors for dedicating their time and energy to their chapters. By adding a diversity of perspectives they have greatly enhanced the quality and depth of the insights that have been brought to bear on this topic. We would also like to thank the editors and reviewers at the MIT Press for their feedback and help at all stages of the production process.

John Danaher: I would like to thank my coeditor Neil McArthur for proposing the idea of this edited collection to me and for feedback on my draft chapters. I am grateful as well to my colleagues at Keele University and NUI Galway for helpful conversations and feedback about the ideas contained within this book. I would also like to thank my partner Aoife Lynch for her help and support. I know it hasn't always been easy putting up with my odd research interests and my propensity to discuss them at social functions, but you have always done so with remarkable patience and good humor.

Neil McArthur: Thanks are due to my coeditor, John Danaher, for feedback on various drafts of my chapter. My colleague Rhonda Martens and her students read an early version and invited me to discuss it in class. Markie Twist of the University of Wisconsin, Stout, invited me to present my ideas in a public lecture at her institution, and I benefited greatly from the discussion that followed.

I   Introducing Robot Sex

Sexbots are coming. But many people consider the very idea of sex with a robot perverse or bizarre. The opening chapter, by Danaher, tries to explain what a sex robot is, whether any currently exist, and why this is a topic worth taking seriously right now. The second chapter, by Migotti and Wyatt, looks at the nature of sexual activity and asks whether it is possible to have sex with a robot. In the process of doing so, they argue that there is a distinct good involved in sexual activity as an exercise of shared agency.

1 Should We Be Thinking about Robot Sex?

John Danaher

The fourth skinjob is Pris. A basic pleasure model—the standard item for military clubs in the outer colonies.
—*Blade Runner*

1.1 Introduction

There is a cave in the Swabian Alps in Germany. It is called the Hohle Fels (rough translation "hollow rock"). Archaeologists have been excavating it since the late 1800s and have discovered there a number of important artifacts from the Upper Paleolithic era. In June 2005, they announced a particularly interesting discovery. They announced that they had unearthed the world's oldest dildo.

The object was 20 cm long and 3 cm wide. It was estimated to be 28,000 years old. It was made from highly polished stone. It was, as Professor Nicholas Conard of the dig team remarked, "clearly recognizable" as a phallic representation. The fact that its size and shape were reasonably lifelike led some to speculate that it may have been used for sexual stimulation and not just for religious or symbolic purposes.[1]

Of course, we can never know for sure. The past is often unrecoverable. But artifacts for sexual stimulation have long been a staple in human life. Dildos have been found in ancient cultures in both the East and West. And the technology of sex has advanced over the centuries. In 1869, the American physician George Taylor invented the first steam-powered vibrator. It was used at the time as a treatment for women suffering from hysteria. The first electrical vibrator for consumer sale was produced by the company Hamilton Beach in 1902.[2] At around the same time, the first manufactured sex dolls became available, though the idea of the sex doll has a much longer history—one that can be traced back to the myth of Pygmalion and to Dutch sailors' *dames des voyages* in the 1700s.[3] Since the early part of the twentieth century there have been further developments in the technology of sex, from artificial vaginas to lifelike silicone dolls to teledildonics.

This book is about another development in the technology of sex, namely: the creation of advanced sex robots. It features papers from a diverse set of contributors, each of whom focuses on a different aspect of the philosophical, social, and ethical implications that might arise from the creation of such devices. The contributions are speculative and analytical in nature. They are intended to raise questions and provoke answers. Some do so by taking a strong view on the topic, but all are written in the shadow of an uncertain future.

I do not wish to recapitulate or summarize what the contributors have to say in this opening chapter. Instead, I want to set the stage for the remainder of the book by asking and answering a few preliminary questions: What are sex robots? Do any exist right now? Why should we care about their creation? I take each question in turn.

1.2   What Are Sex Robots?

"Robot" has become a familiar term and robots have become a familiar concept. The term was first used in Karel Čapek's play *R.U.R.* (*Rossum's Universal Robots*). Čapek used the term robot to describe an artificial humanoid being made from synthetic organic matter. The term was quickly adopted by scientists and science fiction writers, perhaps most famously by Isaac Asimov in his *Robot* series of short stories and novels. In the process, the concept evolved away from what Čapek originally intended. It was no longer used to describe humanoid artificial beings. It was, instead, used to describe virtually any embodied artificial being. The most common real-world examples of robots are to be found in industrial manufacturing processes. The International Federation of Robotics defines an industrial robot as "an automatically controlled, reprogrammable, multipurpose, manipulator programmable in three or more axes, which may be either fixed in place or mobile for use in industrial automation applications."[4]

Obviously, sex robots are not quite the same as industrial robots. In previous work I have proposed a definition of "sex robot" that brings us back a little bit closer to Capek's original intention.[5] The definition holds that a "sex robot" is any artificial entity that is used for sexual purposes (i.e., for sexual stimulation and release) that meets the following three conditions:

Humanoid form, i.e., it is intended to represent (and is taken to represent) a human or human-like being in its appearance.

Human-like movement/behavior, i.e., it is intended to represent (and is taken to represent) a human or humanlike being in its behaviors and movements.

Some degree of artificial intelligence, i.e., it is capable of interpreting and responding to information in its environment. This may be minimal (e.g., simple preprogrammed behavioral responses) or more sophisticated (e.g., human-equivalent intelligence).

Defined in this manner, sex robots are different from existing sex toys and sex dolls. Most existing sex toys do not have a humanoid form. They are, typically, representations of discrete body parts or orifices. These partial representations may have some humanlike movement, but they do not have much in the way of artificial intelligence (although this is certainly changing with the rise of "smart" tech and the Internet of Things). Sex dolls, on the other hand, do have a humanoid form, but are passive, inanimate, and unintelligent. Sex robots have more going on.

Though most of the contributors to this volume accept the preceding definition of "sex robot," the three conditions can be disputed. For instance, there is no particular reason why robots that are intended for sexual stimulation and release have to take on a humanoid form or be humanlike in behavior. One could imagine (if one's imagination is willing) sex robots that take on an animal form. Indeed, there are many sex toys for sale that already do this. Nevertheless, the conditions of being humanlike seem important for two reasons. The first is that one presumes the major drive behind the development of sex robots will be the desire to create an artificial substitute (or complement) to human-to-human sexual interactions. In other words, it is plausible to think people will be interested in creating sex robots because they want something that is close to the "real thing." The second reason is that many of the most interesting philosophical and ethical issues arise when the robots take a humanoid form. The representative and symbolic properties of sex robots are often alluded to in the debate about their social acceptability.[6] That debate tends to focus on what the development of sex robots says about our attitudes toward our fellow human beings. It is only when the robots have humanlike form and behavior that these debates are typically enjoined.

The definition is also agnostic on one important issue: whether the robots are embodied or not. Certainly the paradigmatic sex robot would tend to be an embodied animatronic agent, like Pris the "pleasure model" in the movie *Blade Runner*. But the definition could encompass virtual beings too. With the emergence of virtual reality technologies, like Oculus Rift and Google Cardboard, and haptic technologies (i.e., technologies that replicate and transmit touchlike sensations via a network), it is possible to have immersive sexual experiences in virtual reality. The pornography industry has already developed films (using real human actors) in VR.[7] And the Dutch company Kiiroo already sells haptic dildos and artificial vaginas for use by couples in long distance relationships. At the moment, neither of these developments would involve sex robots as we define them—they both involve real human actors or couples engaging in sexual interactions remotely (although they probably should not be called "interactions" in the case of VR pornography due to the asymmetrical nature of the relationship). However, if someone used the same technology to enable sexual interactions with a virtual being, it would fit the definition.

1.3   Do Any Sex Robots Exist Right Now?

The simple answer is "yes"—with the caveat that those in existence right now are relatively crude and unsophisticated. There are plenty of humanoid robots in existence, and many of them have been designed with gendered and highly sexualized characteristics. Most of these, however, are not designed or used for sexual purposes. There are only two intentional sex robots that I know of that are currently in existence: TrueCompanion's Roxxxy/Rocky and RealDoll's prototype models. I will discuss both in some detail in order to convey a sense of what is currently out there and how the technology might develop.

TrueCompanion's Roxxxy robot was first unveiled to the public at the 2010 AVN Adult Entertainment trade show in Las Vegas. The Roxxxy robot was the invention of Douglas Hines and was billed as "the world's first sex robot." It received a good deal of attention at the time of its unveiling.[8] If you are so inclined, you can easily locate videos of Roxxxy online, including several videos from the manufacturer that demonstrate some of her features.[9] She takes the form of a human female and is customizable in several ways. You can choose among different faces and hairstyles, and different behaviors and personalities. Roxxxy comes in two basic models: RoxxxySilver and RoxxxyGold.[10] The "silver" model—priced at $2995 at the time of this writing—can engage in "sex talk." The "gold" model—priced at $9995 at the same time—has preprogrammed personality types and can "hear" you when you talk. The personality types include "Frigid Farah," "Wild Wendy," "S&M Susan," "Young Yoko," and "Mature Martha"—all names rich in sexual overtones and innuendo.

From video demonstrations, the degree of artificial intelligence seems limited. Roxxxy can initiate preprogrammed verbal responses to environmental stimuli, but does not learn and adapt to the user's behavior. Nevertheless, the user can program the robots' personalities and "swap them online" with others. The manufacturers claim that this is "the same as wife or girlfriend swapping without any of the social issues or sexual disease related concerns!"[11] Roxxxy's movements are also too limited to be considered humanlike. She can gyrate and move "her private areas inside"[12] when being used. She can swivel her head and move parts of her face when talking. But she cannot walk unassisted or move her limbs. According to the webpage, she has a heartbeat and circulatory system, and her visual appearance is certainly humanlike, though no one would ever confuse her for a real human being. There is apparently a male version of the robot too, called *Rocky*, though no pictures are available of him.

I should mention that some people are skeptical about Roxxxy. As best I can tell, TrueCompanion does genuinely offer her for sale from their website, and actively seeks interested investors in the technology. Also, the manufacturer clearly does have some kind of prototype that was demonstrated at the 2010 expo and in the associated online videos. Yet, despite this, it seems that, in the seven years since her launch, no real-world purchasers or users have surfaced, and one of the leading figures in the world of robots and sex (David Levy) has written an article that disputes the credibility of the claims made by Douglas Hines.[13] Since I have not attempted to purchase Roxxxy/Rocky, and since I know of no one who has, I remain agnostic on this issue.

The other candidate for sex robot status is the prototype currently being developed by RealDoll. RealDoll is a product made by Abyss Creations, a company that was founded in 1995 by the artist and musician Matt McMullen. It specializes in sculpting lifelike silicone sex dolls, complete with fully articulable limbs. RealDoll is a successful business.[14] It sells these dolls for more than $5,000 each, with prices often much higher if the customer wants to customize it to meet their own preferences. It caters overwhelmingly to a male audience. According to McMullen fewer than 10% of the customers are female. The vast majority of the dolls exhibit stereotypical, porn-star-esque features (indeed RealDoll has a deal with Wicked Entertainment whereby it recreates some of their stars in doll form). But it does make dolls for more diverse tastes, including male dolls and transgender dolls. This is interesting insofar as the preference profile of RealDoll customers could well be something that carries over into the sex robot era. In other words, we might expect the sex robot market to cater to a majority male audience and for the robots to match certain stereotypical norms of beauty/sexuality. This could provide fodder for critics of the technology, something discussed in more detail in several of the contributions to this book.[15]

RealDoll is currently developing a robotic prototype it hopes to start selling sometime in 2017. McMullen has already previewed the prototype in several documentary films.[16] The plan is to create a model with a moving head and face, which can talk to the user through an AI personality. Following the lead of Apple's *Siri*, Microsoft's *Cortana*, and Google's *Assistant*, RealDoll's AI will be cloud-based and will learn and adapt to its user's preferences. This suggests a more significant and serious engagement with the latest AI technologies than is apparent from TrueCompanion's robot. Nevertheless, McMullen's current plans are modest. He is not developing a version of RealDoll with moving limbs. Robots with humanlike motor skills are being developed by other companies (the best known probably being Boston Dynamics), but we are still some distance away from a robot that integrates those movement features with humanlike appearance and touch, and advanced AI.

From these two examples, it is apparent that humankind has taken its first steps toward sophisticated, humanlike sex robots. The visions of science fiction authors and moviemakers are still beyond the horizon. Nevertheless, we can expect the technology to develop further and for converging advances in animatronics and AI to be utilized for sexual purposes. The current trend for single-use sex robots may not continue. I suspect that it won't and that the future will be more akin to that depicted in the Channel 4 TV series *Humans*,[17] where domestic robots are used for multiple purposes, including on occasion sexual purposes. How prevalent and ubiquitous the technology will become is up for debate. Some futurists make strong predictions, suggesting that sex robots are poised to take over the adult sex work industry,[18] or that they will be "everywhere" by 2050.[19] This may happen, but as other contributors to this volume point out there are several hurdles that stand in the way. These hurdles are probably not technological in nature—the technological advances are likely to continue; they are, rather, psychological, sociological and normative. It is these hurdles that form the focus for the remainder of this book.

1.4 Why Should We Care?

Is it worth taking the development of this technology seriously? Or should we just laugh it off as some outlandish fantasy that, even if it does become a reality, is likely to appeal to a small minority?

Obviously I and the other contributors to this book think that the subject is worthy of serious consideration. We would not have invested so much time and energy in this book if we did not. We think there are issues of genuine philosophical and practical interest arising from the development of sex robots. These issues range from the analytical and metaphysical to the ethical and sociological. Many of them are assessed in greater depth in the individual chapters that follow. Here, I simply wish to sketch some of the terrain in which those chapters are located.

One of the first issues raised by the prospect of sophisticated sex robots is the analytical nature of sex itself. Does one "have sex" through autostimulation or must another individual be involved? Questions of this sort have fascinated philosophers and sexologists for quite some time. They are also questions of practical import. For better or worse, many cultures and religions hold the status of "virginity" in special regard.

For young people, their "first time" is a moment of personal and societal significance, and many try to carefully skirt the boundaries between "real" sex and other forms of sexual activity in order to avoid breaching religious or cultural norms. Consequently, figuring out whether or not sexual activity with a sex robot would count as "real" sex is going to be a matter of some importance to them. Of course, virginity is really more a social construct than it is a natural kind—something frequently used to police and shame—but that does not make the debate about the status of particular sexual activities any less significant. If we assume (as most of the contributors to this volume do) that sex robots are not going to be persons in the philosophically rich sense of the term "person," then engaging in sexual activity with a robot seems to occupy an interesting and contested territory: It is like autostimulation in some ways, but it also involves an interaction, possibly reciprocal, with a humanlike entity. So where on the spectrum does robot sex lie?[20]

Another issue raised by the prospect of sophisticated sex robots has to do with the connections between sexual intimacy and other forms of intimacy. Will it be possible for people to have a meaningful intimate relationship with a robot—one that goes beyond mere sex? The suspicion among many is that it will not. Meaningful relationships require some degree of emotional reciprocity. If a robot is a mere automaton—if it has no inner life of its own—then it cannot reciprocate in the appropriate way. But this, of course, raises important questions about the possibility of machine consciousness and what happens when the outward behaviors of robots are such that they can "pass" for humans. Spike Jonze's movie *Her* depicts an intense intimate relationship between a man and an unembodied AI. It seems odd from our present standpoint. But is this where our future lies? Will intimate relationships with robots come to be seen as something within the normal range of human sexuality? Hauskeller (chapter 11) and Nyholm and Frank (chapter 12) both touch upon these questions.

This is where philosophical speculation joins psychological reality. We already know that humans form intimate attachments in unusual ways. The objects and subjects of human affection are highly malleable. There is already a subculture that prefers "relationships" with sex dolls to those with human beings. Davecat, a nickname adopted by a Michigan-based man, is a well-known advocate for synthetic love.[21] He is a member of an online community of iDollators who view their dolls not merely as sex toys but as life partners. He has appeared in several documentaries about the lifestyle. Davecat owns two RealDolls: Sidore and Elena. He calls Sidore his "wife" and they wear matching wedding bands. Elena is his mistress. He shares an apartment with both and has constructed elaborate stories about how they came to meet and share their lives together. Some people find his expression of sexuality bizarre—the fetishising of an inanimate object. But Davecat says there is a much deeper connection between himself and Sidore:

It seemed perfectly normal for me to treat something that resembles an organic woman the same way I'd treat an actual organic woman ... With Sidore, her draw was instantaneous. There was never a moment when [she]—or any Doll, for that matter—was merely an object to me.

If people like Davecat are already forming what they take to be meaningful intimate relationships with inanimate dolls, imagine what will happen when the dolls can behave and interact in intelligent ways with their users. The chapters from Scheutz and Arnold (chapter 13), Carpenter (chapter 14), and Adshade (chapter 15) delve into some of these issues.

Of course, there may be psychological and sociological impediments to the widespread acceptance of this form of sexuality. Back in 1970, the Japanese roboticist Mashiro Mori developed the "uncanny valley" hypothesis. The gist of the hypothesis was that as robots became more humanlike in behavior and appearance, they would become more acceptable to humans. But only until they reached a point where they became so close to being humanlike that they started to be creepy. In other words, until they reached a point where they were "uncannily" humanlike but still obviously artificial. At that point, there would be a dip (or valley) in their acceptability.

If the uncanny-valley hypothesis is true, it could pose something of a dilemma for sex robot advocates and manufacturers. They will, no doubt, push for more and more humanlike devices. This should, initially, lead to more social acceptability, but then they could fall into the uncanny valley, turning people off and blocking their acceptability for some time. The question would then become how deep and wide the valley actually is. Would it be merely a temporary blip or something more prolonged?

For many years, Mori's hypothesis was little more than that: a hypothesis. There was some anecdotal support for it. The advent of humanlike CGI in films brought with it reports of negative reactions from audiences. The most infamous example of this being the human characters in Robert Zemeckis's 2004 film *The Polar Express*.[22] However, it is really only in the past decade that researchers have started to empirically test the hypothesis. Some initial studies supported its existence,[23] but, as is to be expected, the latest picture from the research is more complicated,[24] with some studies now disputing its existence, suggesting that it is a bundle of different phenomena, or that it can be overcome through repeated exposure or other psychological tricks.[25] This suggests that the uncanny valley might be less of a problem than previously thought. This does not mean, however, that the sex robots will be socially accepted. That depends on factors beyond the reaction of any individual user. Julie Carpenter discusses these factors in some detail later in this book.

When we turn to the question of social acceptability, the phenomenon's legal, ethical, and moral acceptability are also raised. And there is much to think about in this regard. Indeed, the majority of the papers in this volume take up one or more of the ethical problems that arise in relation to sex robots. These issues can be usefully lumped into three main categories: (1) benefits and harms to the robots; (2) benefits and harms to the users; and (3) benefits and harms to society.

The first category is the most speculative and outlandish. There is a possibility, however conceptually implausible or empirically distant it may seem, that robots themselves have a moral status that ought to be factored into their creation. Robots could be the beneficiaries of their sexual interactions with humans, but they could also be harmed by those interactions. Furthermore, if they do have moral status, what might the implications be of creating an underclass of robotic sexual slaves? Surely this is something we should avoid? The issue is not as clear-cut as it initially seems. Some roboticists argue that robots should always be slaves.[26] And some philosophers argue that there is nothing unethical about this, even if the robots themselves are moral persons.[27] Can these groups be right? The contributions from Goldstein (chapter 10) and Petersen (chapter 9) delve into some of these issues.

The second category shifts focus from the robot to the user. Can human beings be benefited or harmed by the interaction? Sex is an important human good. In addition to being intrinsically pleasurable, physical and mental health and well-being are often found to correlate with increased sexual activity. The importance of sexual activity in the well-lived life is now widely recognized in the emerging discourse on sex rights (see McArthur, chapter 3; and Di Nucci, chapter 5, in this volume). If sex robots can facilitate more sexual activity, we might be inclined to welcome them with open arms. But there can also be a dark side to sex. Some people worry that those who seek out sexual interactions with robots will withdraw from social interactions. This may prevent them from forming normal and healthy relationships with their fellow human beings. Since sociality and friendships are also commonly included in lists of basic human goods there could be a trade-off of human goods when it comes to the user of the sex robot.

This brings us then to the third category of ethical issues. This one has to do with the benefits and harms to society. "Society" can be interpreted broadly here to include the immediate family and friends of the sexbot user and then society-at-large (a more general and possibly abstract entity). One worry about sex robots has to do with the impact they will have on the other intimate relationships of the user. On the one hand, they could add variety and novelty to existing intimate relationships, perhaps solidifying them in the process. On the other, they might provoke jealousy and disaffection, causing breakdown and strife. The fallout for society at large then becomes a concern. Will the sexbot user be encouraged to adopt positive or negative behaviors toward their fellow human beings? Or will they come to adopt an objectified and instrumentalizing attitude wherein their fellow human beings are treated as obstacles to pleasure? This is where the symbolic properties of sex robots also become important. The earlier descriptions of Roxxxy/Rocky and the RealDoll prototype were replete with arguably sexist symbolism. The robots tended overwhelmingly to represent human females, to adopt stereotypical and gendered norms of beauty and behavior, and to perpetuate problematic attitudes toward women. The makers of TrueCompanion seem to revel in the idea of "wife or girlfriend swapping"; they preprogram their robot with loaded personality types ("Wild Wendy," "Frigid Farah," and so forth); the bulk of RealDoll's customers seek out the porn-star look; only a minority of the customers look for something more unusual. What consequences would this have for treatment of women in our society? Some people are very worried—and this is to say nothing of robots that cater to clearly unethical forms of sexuality such as rape fantasies or pedophilia. Litska Strikwerda (in chapter 8) and I (in chapter 7) take up these issues later in this volume.

1.5   The Sexbots Are Coming

In short, sex robots are worth taking seriously. They are robots with humanlike touch, movement, and intelligence that are designed and/or used for sexual purposes. They already exist in primitive and unsophisticated forms, and the technology underlying them is likely to develop further. They may eventually become widespread in society, with sexual functions being incorporated into general-purpose robots. Their creation raises important philosophical, social, and ethical questions for users and the broader society in which they live. I hope the brief synopsis of these issues in the preceding paragraphs and pages is enough to whet your appetite for this discussion. All of these issues are addressed in greater depth in the remaining chapters. If you wish to follow my coauthors and I down the rabbit hole, read on.

Notes

1. All details in this paragraph are taken from J. Amos, "Ancient Phallus Unearthed in Cave," *BBC News* (July 25, 2005), http://news.bbc.co.uk/2/hi/science/nature/4713323.stm.

2. Rachel P. Maines, *The Technology of Orgasm* (Baltimore: Johns Hopkins University Press, 2001).

3. Anthony Ferguson, *The Sex Doll: A History* (Jefferson, NC: McFarland, 2010).

4. http://www.ifr.org/industrial-robots.

5. John Danaher, "Robotic Rape and Robotic Child Sexual Abuse: Should They be Criminalized?" *Criminal Law & Philosophy* (December 2014): 1–25, doi:10.1007/s11572-014-9362-x.

6. For more on this topic, see chapter 7 of this volume.

7. For an informative overview of the technology and its prospects, we recommend the *VICE* documentary "The Digital Love Industry," http://www.vice.com/video/love-industries-digital-sex-669.

8. Brian Heater, "Roxxxy the 'Sex Robot' Debuts at AVN Porn Show," *PC World*, January 9, 2010; Joel Taylor,"Sex Robot with 'Personality' Unveiled," *Metro.co.uk*, January 11, 2010.

9. For information on Roxxxy's features, see http://www.truecompanion.com/shop/faq; for videos depicting these features, see the TrueCompanion YouTube channel: https://www.youtube.com/channel/UCwY5KmyS9ZI9Net9Hm-rgvA.

10. All information taken from the FAQ on TrueCompanion's webpage.

11. Ibid.

12. Ibid.

13. David Levy, "Roxxxy the 'Sex Robot'—Real or Fake?" *Lovotics* 1 (2013): 1–4, doi:10.4303/lt/235685; http://www.omicsonline.com/open-access/2090-9888/2090-9888-1-101.pdf?aid=15073.

14. All the information about RealDoll is taken from the following sources: the RealDoll webpage (https://www.realdoll.com); Cara Santa Maria, "Inside the Factory Where the World's Most Realistic Sex Robots Are Being Built," *Fusion: Real Future* (February 10, 2016), http://fusion.net/story/281661/real-future-episode-6-sex-bots; George Curley, "Is This the Dawn of the Era of Sex Robots?" *Vanity Fair* (April 16, 2015), http://www.vanityfair.com/culture/2015/04/sexbots-realdoll-sex-toys#13; and Curtis Silver, "The Future of Sex Could be AI Robot Sex Dolls," *Forbes* (August 19, 2016), http://www.forbes.com/sites/curtissilver/2016/08/19/realdoll-ai-sex-robot-head-ama/#44bccb852fd4.

15. In particular the chapters from Danaher, and Danaher, Earp, and Sandberg.

16. Cara Santa Maria, "Inside the Factory."

17. For further information see: http://www.channel4.com/programmes/humans.

18. David Levy, *Love and Sex with Robots* (London: Harper, 2008); and Ian Yeoman and Michelle Mars, "Robots, Men and Sex Tourism," *Futures* 44 (2012): 365–371.

19. Ian Pearson, "The Future of Sex Report: The Rise of Robosexuals," http://graphics.bondara.com/Future_sex_report.pdf.

20. See chapter 2 of this volume for more information.

21. Julie Beck, "Married to a Doll: Why One Man Advocates Synthetic Love," *The Atlantic* (September 6, 2013), http://www.theatlantic.com/health/archive/2013/09/married-to-a-doll-why-one-man-advocates-synthetic-love/279361.

22. Paul Clinton, "'Polar Express': a creepy ride," CNN.com (November 10, 2004), http://edition
.cnn.com/2004/SHOWBIZ/Movies/11/10/review.polar.express.

23. Karl F. MacDorman and Hiroshi Ishiguro, "The Uncanny Advantage of Using Androids in
Cognitive and Social Science Research," *Interaction Studies* 7, no. 3(2006): 297–337, doi:10.1075/
is.7.3.03mac. Karl F. MacDorman, "Subjective Ratings of Robot Video Clips for Human Likeness,
Familiarity, and Eeriness: An Exploration of the Uncanny Valley," Proceedings of the ICCS/
CogSci–2006: Toward Social Mechanisms of Android Science, (Vancouver, 2006): 26–29.

24. Tyler Burleigh, Jordan R. Schoenherr, and Guy Lacroix, "Does the Uncanny Valley Exist? An
Empirical Test of the Relationship between Eeriness and the Human Likeness of Digitally Created
Faces," *Computers in Human Behavior* 29, no. 3 (2013): 759–771, doi:10.1016/j.chb.2012.11.021.

25. The developments are rapid. For a reasonably up-to-date picture, see the *Frontiers* symposium
on the topic: *The Uncanny Valley and Beyond* available at: http://journal.frontiersin.org/
researchtopic/2385/the-uncanny-valley-hypothesis-and-beyond#articles.

26. Joanna Bryson, "Robots Should Be Slaves," in *Close Engagements with Artificial Companions:
Key Social, Psychological, Ethical and Design Issues*, ed. Yorick Wilks (Amsterdam: John Benjamins
Co., 2010).

27. Steve Petersen, "Designing People to Serve" in *Robot Ethics: The Ethical and Social Implications
of Robotics*, eds. Patrick Lin, Keith Abney, and George A. Bekey (Cambridge, MA: MIT Press, 2012).
See also chapter 9 of this volume.

2   On the Very Idea of Sex with Robots

Mark Migotti and Nicole Wyatt

Invention in aid of sexual satisfaction is not new. Archeologists have found dildos dating back to the Upper Palaeolithic,[1] and the history of pornography is in many ways a history of technological advances.[2] Nonetheless, the prospect of sophisticated and humanlike robots designed specifically for our sexual gratification has attracted a great deal of recent media attention.[3] Is this attention warranted—specifically, is the development of sex robots more significant for our sexual lives than the invention of dildos, cameras, vibrators, etc.? If our sexual relations with sex robots can be understood in just the same terms as our sexual relations with vibrators and RealDolls, it's unlikely that their impact on our experience and understanding of sex and sexuality will be deep. But if sex robots are something genuinely new and different, and in particular if they become possible sex *partners*, rather than sex toys, questions about how to relate to them and what to think about them will abound.

In this chapter, we focus on the simple sounding question: What is it to have sex? On the assumption that having sex is what you do with all and only your sexual partners, this offers a way of focusing the question: What would it take for a sex robot to be a sex partner? In order to understand the significance of the development of robots with whom (or which) we can have sex, we need to know what it is to have sex with a robot. And in order to know this, we have to know what it is to have sex, period. In the bulk of the chapter, we develop an account of shared sexual agency we think is a plausible precondition of genuinely having sex. In the final section, we remark briefly on the issue of what it would take to form a *sexual we* (as we call it) with a robot. For if we can do this, we can probably have sex with robots; but if we can't, we can't.

2.1   Having Sex

In the broadest of senses, we can have sex with lots of things. In this sense, you can be said to have sex with someone, or something, whenever you engage in sexual activity with them, be they vibrator, blow-up doll, sex robot, or whatever. Indeed, in this sense, shocking even himself, Alexander Portnoy once had sex with a slab of liver before it reached the dinner table! While it is no doubt true that, in this maximally broad sense, we can have sex with robots, it isn't interestingly true. A robot with which we can have sex in the same sense of having sex in which we can have sex with a slab of liver won't raise the sorts of issue to which this volume is a response. In particular, neither slabs of liver, nor Roombas, plausibly give rise to the sorts of challenges addressed by other contributions to this volume—it's unlikely, for example, that we feel any need to revise our ideas about relationships or worry about the impact on standards of consent in light of sexual activity with slabs of liver or Roombas. If these concerns and projects make sense—and we think that they do—then there must be another, narrower concept of having sex in the offing.

So, to echo what we said above, sex (in the interesting, exigent sense needed for these concerns about sex robots and robot sex to arise) is what you have with all and only your sexual partners. Some people will never have sex, some will have it with no more than one person in their lifetime, and others will have sex with lots and lots of people. If you have had more than one sexual partner, you may wish to know how many sexual partners you've had; and this means that you'll need to know how to go about establishing the correct number. Someone who counts among their partners everyone they have kissed or flirted with, for example, has an evidently mistaken idea of what it means to have sex. But so does someone who insists that only those with whom they have had penile-vaginal intercourse belong on the list.

Being a truism, it is of course true that having penile-vaginal intercourse is one way for people to have sex. But it is manifestly inadequate as a definition of what it is to have sex, rather than an exemplar of it. Your list of sex partners may well include people with whom you've done sexual things other than penile-vaginal intercourse.[4] It may also, however, legitimately not include all of those who (arguably) have had penile-vaginal intercourse with you. This claim needs argument, which will be provided in due course.

In the wake of l'affaire Clinton-Lewinsky, Kinsey Institute researcher Stephanie Sanders organized and interpreted a subset of the results of a 1991 survey of 600 students at a state university in the midwestern United States.[5] The original survey, of 102 items, was undertaken to collect data on "the prevalence and interrelationships among behaviors associated with sexually transmitted disease risk." Sanders excerpted eleven questions of the form "Would you say you 'had sex' with someone if the most intimate behavior you engaged in was [X]" and arranged them in order of the pre-theoretic plausibility of an affirmative response, from the least to the most plausible candidates.

Not surprisingly, virtually everybody said that they would say they had had sex with someone with whom they had had penile-vaginal intercourse, and virtually nobody said that they had had sex with someone with whom they had done nothing more than "deep kissing" or breast and/or nipple fondling. In between, however, there are surprises. Only 80% of respondents seem prepared to count anal intercourse as a way of having sex, and only 40% seem to think that you can have sex by having oral sex. Clearly, the penetration paradigm is alive and well among these college students, with fully one fifth of them apparently ready to subscribe to it in its virulent, to our mind evidently mistaken, heteronormative form.

In the present context, however, Sanders' data needs careful scrutiny. Survey subjects were asked to respond to questions that were doubly indexed to their personal experience and judgment; and, which, moreover, were directed, not at what they thought would be the case if … , but at what they would say if … . One the one hand, we have "would you say that in doing 'X, Y, Z' *you* would be having sex?" with no mention of what you would say about other people doing the same thing; and on the other hand, we have "would you *say* that in doing 'X, Y, Z' you would be having sex?," with the strong suggestion that we're concerned with the mastery of a linguistic idiom, rather than understanding the nature of an activity.

As we've said, the phrase "having sex" can apply to a broad range of activities, certainly including most of the entries on Sanders' survey, but also masturbation, phone sex, etc. Moreover, to echo *mutatis mutandis*, a point Alan Turing makes at the beginning of the article in which he put forward the so-called "Turing test" for intelligence,[6] if the answer to the question "can we have sex with robots?" is to be determined solely by examining how the expression "sex" is commonly used, it would seem that the answer could be arrived at via appropriate statistical surveys. But a critical examination of the Sanders survey shows that this approach is more likely to sow confusion than to settle the question. What we need is not simply information about acceptable linguistic usage, but, as it might be called, conceptual engineering.

In ordinary contexts, we deploy the concept of having sex without much trouble, and without much thought. But in the present, philosophical context, this lack of thought can lead to outright incoherence. If you, a practicing heterosexual, are not prepared to count oral or anal sex as sex for you, but also believe that men can have sex with men and women with women, you are in a familiar bind; what you are inclined to say here turns out to be incompatible with what you are inclined to say there.

To be sure, those of us happy to countenance oral, anal, and homosexual sex as ways of having sex avoid this self-contradiction. But to think that just because we don't fall into egregious error, we know perfectly well what it is to have sex would be to give us too much philosophical credit. If we are to get a handle on the differences between a robot that can be a full-fledged sex partner and one that is merely an extremely sophisticated sex toy, we need a better grasp of what sex is. Either way, we need help. And, as Socrates insisted, before we can surmount or circumvent a philosophical impasse, we need to examine the intellectual failure that led us to it.

2.2 Definition

Greta Christina's engaging Socratic meditation on our topic explains why clarity about the boundaries of this concept matters for personal, as well as philosophical, reasons: "I mean, you have to know what qualifies as sex, because when you have sex with someone your relationship changes. Right? Right?"[7] What we need, therefore, is an account of what it is to have sex that both locates having sex—in the interesting, exigent sense—within the general category of sexual activity, and also makes clear what purpose the concept serves, why it's of value to us. We need an account of having sex that illuminates our behavior in and attitudes toward sexual relationships and sexual partners, human or otherwise.[8]

In his probing commentary on Plato's *Theatetus*, Myles Burnyeat distinguishes "definition by analysis into elements" from "definition by classification." The first kind of definition seeks to break down a target phenomenon into its ultimate parts, the second to understand core "respects of sameness and difference" the target phenomenon bears to other higher and lower order phenomena in the conceptual neighborhood. This distinction helps clarify things in the present context as follows: while it's easy to take it for granted that having sex must be understood in terms of a multiplication of sex acts, we think that this is only one dimension of the phenomenon.[9] Instead of viewing having sex as a chapter in the larger story of engaging in sexual activity, we view it as a chapter in the larger story of people entering into sexual relations with one another.

Structurally, the change of focus we're proposing for our understanding of having sex is the same as the change of focus for inquiry into justice found in closing pages of Plato's *Euthyphro*. After a series of unsuccessful attempts to define what it is to be pious by ascertaining the relationship between this concept and the concept of being loved by the gods, Socrates needs to give his plodding interlocutor a helping hand: "See [Euthyphro] whether you think that all that is pious is necessarily just?" (11e). Euthyphro's agreement allows the discussion to continue for four more Stephanus pages before the problem of how being pious relates to being loved by the gods crops up again. But progress has been made. Until Socrates connects piety to justice, he and

Euthyphro have assumed that they are trying to find out what makes a human's relation to the gods pious (rather than impious). That avenue having led nowhere, they can now begin investigating what distinguishes justice between radical unequals (gods and humans) from justice between peers (humans and humans or gods and gods). At least, they might have begun such an investigation had Euthyphro not been in such a hurry. The *Euthyphro* ends in aporia because of Euthyphro's impatience, not because the approach Socrates suggested is doomed from the start.

As piety, according to Socrates, needs to be understood as a distinctive kind, or dimension, or context of justice, so, according to us, having sex needs to be understood as a distinctive exercise of shared sexual agency. And as Plato needed a much longer work than the *Euthyphro* to explain the concept of justice, so we would need a much longer paper than this to explain our higher order concepts of sexual agency and shared agency adequately.

For present purposes, it will do to say that agency is sexual when one of two things is true of it: either it pays the right sort of attention to sexual organs—taking for granted a rough and ready understanding of what counts as "the right sort of attention";[10] or it involves a self-conscious understanding of the domain of the sexual whose boundaries may be idiosyncratic.[11] Agency is shared when people do things together with others, as opposed to simply alongside them. To borrow an example of John Searle's, a gaggle of disparate picnickers running to shelter to avoid the rain may move in exactly the same ways as a performance art troop rehearsing a piece. But while the picnickers are not acting collectively (as a "we"), the performance artists are; the performers are doing something as a group, rather than just *en masse*.[12]

So: while having sex is, obviously, about sex, it is also about doing something together. This proposal makes clear immediately why sexual activity involving Roomba's and slabs of liver raises none of the concerns that sex robots potentially do. Whatever else is going on, Portnoy and the liver are not doing something together. Moreover, if the concerns about sex robots mentioned above are justified, it must be the case either that robots can exercise genuine sexual agency, or at least that they can approximate it, or successfully mimic it. Before getting to robots in their own right, however, we need a somewhat fuller account of the concept of shared sexual agency.

2.3 Conversation

Sometimes we do things together in order to get other things done; sometimes we do things together in order to get together. Sometimes the other things that we set out to do could be done without a we; sometimes not. When we gather to move a heavy log, we form a we that is both instrumental and dispensable: the aim is to move the log, and this could be done by a machine. But when we throw a party, we form a we that is by nature integral and by custom indispensable. You cannot have a get-together without getting together, and when a get-together is a party, it may be thrown for its own sake, rather than for an ulterior purpose.

Some things we do together we can only do together; some things we do alone we can only do alone; and some things can be done either together or alone. Getting married and having a reunion are examples of the first type; living as a hermit and doing things without help are examples of the second; and walking and talking, examples of the third. Alone or together, when we walk, we walk, and when we talk, we talk. But when we walk or talk together, we do so as a we; and you can't do something as a we by yourself. When we speak to each other, we turn speech into an activity that can only be done together. When we talk in suitable ways to each other we have a conversation; and when we do suitable sexual things with each other we have sex.

Our hypothesis, then, is that having sex can be understood as a an epitome of being sexual together in much the same way having a conversation can be understood as an epitome of what Paul Grice calls a "talk exchange."[13] As an exchange of backrubs will not by itself qualify as a case of having sex, so an exchange of words at an information booth does not amount to a conversation between the seeker and provider of information. Conversations can be formal or informal, but an interrogation, as of a witness on the stand, is not a conversation; conversations can be long or short, but each day brings new ones, and a ritualistic exchange of "good mornings" is not really a conversation. For conversation to occur, there must be a we conversing, not just a collection of I's talking; conversation requires people talking to, rather than at or independently of, each other. And for sex to be had—we maintain—there must be a sexual we having it.

If having sex requires shared sexual agency, it really does take (at least) two to tango; and this means that you can't have sex by—which is to say with—yourself. The opening sentence of Christina's essay makes the point with panache: "When I first started having sex *with other people*, I used to like to count them" (emphasis added). If, as Christina implies was true of her, you masturbate before you have sex with someone else, your first sexual partner apart from yourself does not become your second sexual partner in actual fact. And if you can't have sex without a sexual we, you can't have sex unilaterally; it can't be the case that you are having sex with someone who is not, *eo ipso*, having sex with you.

2.4   Masturbation

Familiar sex toys, such as vibrators and Fleshlights, are primarily seen as aids to masturbation. If having sex is the epitome of doing something sexual *together*, masturbation
does not count as having sex with oneself, and the addition of mere sex toys, whether
the familiar or the more exotic, cannot change that. In terms of the logic of relations,
to claim that you can't have sex either by yourself or unilaterally is to claim that having
sex is necessarily irreflexive and symmetrical, i.e., a relation you can't have to yourself,
and that you can only have with someone who is also having it with you. The irreflexivity supports the symmetry—because if you could have sex with yourself, you could
bring this about by fiat, so to speak. And if this were so, why couldn't you also bring
it about by fiat that you have sex with someone else, even if that person is not having
sex with you? But given that you can't make it the case that you're having sex all by
yourself, it follows that you can't make it the case that you're having sex with someone
else all by yourself.

When James Joyce (in *Ulysses*) makes mention of "one-handed adulterers," and
when Woody Allen cracks wise about masturbation being an example of "sex with
someone I love," their witticisms attest to the irreflexivity of having sex by being witticisms, not serious pronouncements.[14] Sanders's survey questions attest to the point
by not allowing yourself to qualify as a "someone" with whom you have engaged in
the various behaviors listed. Moreover, if masturbation[15] counts as having sex with
yourself, anyone who masturbates thereby has homosexual sex; and perhaps also
incestuous sex.[16]

Why can't you have sex with yourself? More precisely, why would it be worse
than pointless to revise our working concept of having sex (construed as a necessarily
symmetrical and irreflexive activity) so as to allow you to count as one of your own
sexual partners? The answer was suggested at the outset: because such a concept would
open the door to the idea that you can have sex with a Roomba or blow-up doll. We
already have a concept that allows this, the concept of having sex in the broadest
sense; so we don't need another one to do this job. More deeply, a concept intermedi-
ate between the exigent, interesting concept of having sex and the broadest possible
one would blur the distinction between a sex partner and a sex prop; and this would
be intellectually baleful. Sex props are mere objects; sex partners are also subjects in
their own right.

We don't deny that masturbation may play an important, or even central, role in
someone's sexual life, nor that mutual masturbation may be a way for two or more
people to have sex with each other. The point is simply that if sex robots are nothing

more than aids to masturbation (or for that matter to sex with a human partner), they are no different from the broad variety of sex toys already on offer, and so don't raise any distinctive social, ethical, or conceptual problems.

2.5   Sexual Assault

Turning from the (ir)reflexivity of having sex to its (a)symmetry, and returning to our guiding analogy of sex and conversation, it is undeniable that conversations must be undertaken together. No amount of haranguing can count as a conversation. For conversation to occur, interlocutors need to address each other. In the case of having sex, however, it's not clear that there's anything obviously amiss with saying that sexual abusers have sex with their victims, but not vice versa. It might be argued that is precisely because it involves having sex forced upon you that this kind of abuse is so heinous. Moreover, it's not clear that we can deal with this fact by appealing to our familiar distinction between sex in the broad sense and sex in the interesting, exigent sense.

Nevertheless, we maintain, it's true that you can only have sex with your partner(s) if your partner(s) is *eo ipso* having sex with you. There is an important, categorical distinction between doing something *to* somebody, and doing something *with* them. The reason having sex (in the interesting, exigent sense) must be symmetrical is of a piece with the reason that mugging can't be. In the case of mugging, it is evidently impossible to do together the same thing that a mugger does to his victim. And the same, we say, goes for what a rapist does to his victim.

From our perspective, it's important to distinguish outright rape and other forms of sexual assault from what Scott Anderson calls "sex under pressure."[17] Anderson argues that attention to the background context surrounding decisions to have sex, particularly the male-dominant gender hierarchy, reveals both why pressuring someone to have sex is worse than pressuring them to go bowling, and second why a man pressuring a woman to have sex is more problematic than vice versa.[18]

For example, Sarah Conly, to whom Anderson is responding, offers the following description of a man pressuring a woman to have sex:

The aggressor may implore and wheedle until the other feels guilt; he may tease her with jealousy, berate her for her coldness and immaturity, chastise her for the harm she does him, refute her reasoning when she tries to articulate her position, and subject her to a barrage of angry words. Ultimately she may find herself in a state of psychological exhaustion, feeling unable to resist in the face of what seems an implacable will.[19]

It strikes us that in such a case the psychologically exhausted woman does not have the usual participatory intention—she does not so much intend to have sex as intend simply to bring the unpleasant encounter to an end.[20] And as a result of the pressure he has applied, the man cannot reasonably assume that he and his victim/partner form a sexual we. Nonetheless, there is a participatory intention of a sort. Possibly this is neither a case of having sex, in the fully collective sense sketched here, nor a case of not having sex, and thus, perhaps, as Conly and Anderson suggest, falls short of counting as rape. This is not, we should emphasize, to suggest that the man is not morally culpable for his behavior.

2.6 Robots

So, if we're going to be able to have sex with robots (in the pertinent, exigent sense), they must be able to have sex with us, a point that is not lost on Matt McMullen, the founder and CEO of RealDoll. In a 2015 video interview for the New York Times, McMullen described his company's current goal as to develop artificial intelligence for the RealDolls that would allow them to "arouse someone on an emotional, intellectual level, beyond the physical." He added that: "I want people to actually develop an emotional attachment to not only the doll, but to the actual character behind it. To develop some kind of love for this being." McMullen is explicit that this requires interactivity, in particular for the doll to be able to converse with and respond to their partner.[21]

If sex robots are to instigate a revolution in our sexual relationships, it may be because they, in virtue of this interactivity, seem potentially capable of having sex with us, rather than merely serving as a passive aid to sexual gratification. Sex robots, as we naturally imagine them and as McMullen describes them, give at least an appearance of exercising the sort of agency required for someone to be our sexual partner, rather than a prop for our sexual imagination. A sex doll—whether the novelty blow-up variety or the expensive and realistic appearing RealDoll—differs most importantly from a sex robot in its inertness.

It is the prospect of sex robots capable of exercising sexual agency that gives rise to some of the challenges discussed in this volume. For sex robots to actually have sex with us, they will need full-fledged sexual agency. If they have agency, then the moral issues that arise in our sexual relations with other human beings will arise in our relations with them as well. The familiar questions related to consent, fidelity, religious sexual rules, pornography, sex work, and emotional bonds between sexual partners will be equally pressing.

On the other hand, sex robots with genuine agency will be unlikely to serve some of the purposes that their creators and advocates imagine for them. Commentators sometimes suggest (e.g., Neil McArthur in chapter 3 of this volume) that sex robots could serve to provide broad access to a universal good—sexual fulfillment—that is otherwise unevenly distributed. But sex robots with the agency required to genuinely have sex with us may equally well choose not to have sex with us. Their preferences will no doubt differ as widely as the sexual preferences of actual human beings, but there is no reason to think the result will be even distribution of sex partners. In short, there is a tension between the idea that sex robots have human sexual gratification as their *raison d'être*, and the idea that they can be genuine sexual partners for us.[22]

The distinction between having sex understood as an exercise in shared agency, and the broad category of sexual activity can help dissolve some of this tension. Given technological advances that (to quote McMullen again) create the "illusion that she's actually talking to you. That she's got sentience," combined with the anatomical detail and accuracy of the high-end sex doll bodies, does have the potential to make a certain range of sexual acts broadly available. This may well constitute a sexual good that is currently unevenly distributed and serve to make it more equally accessible. But if we are right, there is another sexual good—the good of having sex with another agent—that cannot be democratized in this way.

As McMullen's comments make clear, designers of sex robots are not in general aiming to create genuine agents, but instead to create the illusion of agency. They aim to create robots that are sufficiently humanlike for us to take the intentional stance toward them,[23] i.e., to attribute beliefs, desires, and experiences to them, and to develop affection toward them. It is perhaps notable that McMullen imagines his clients developing an emotional attachment to "the actual character behind [the doll]," suggesting that he imagines the attachment as similar to the one may people have to their favorite characters from novels, video games, films, and other forms of fiction. If that is the case, is there any important difference between sexual activity with a sex robot and sexual activity involving, for example, a vibrator and a healthy fantasy life? Is there something about the ease with which we project agency and desire upon such a sex robot that creates special problems?

Perhaps, then, sex robots will soon provide a broader access to genuine sexual fulfillment and other sexual goods than more primitive sex toys. Perhaps they will revolutionize our relationships, or at least throw some spanners into the works. This, however, might be largely because sexual fulfillment is not only found in partnered sex, in having sex in the important, exigent sense in which we've been exploring it. But if we are going to have sex with them, and they with us, in this sense, sex robots must develop agency and be able to engage in collective action. In the end, perhaps we will have to wait and see. However, we admit some skepticism. Certainly there are already some people who project sufficient degrees of agency onto existing sex toys to want to treat them as romantic partners, and those people will no doubt be gratified by technological advances that improve the illusion. Those numbers may increase slightly as the illusion becomes more compelling. But as long as it is an illusion—as long as the sex robots in question do not exercise real agency—then sexual relationships between human beings will continue to offer something that sexual activity involving sex robots does not.

Of course, some people might *prefer* have their sex robot-style, rather than with humans, in much the same way that some people now prefer masturbation to having sex. But there is no particular reason to think that this eventuality offers us any special philosophical challenges.

Notes

1. A. Marshack, *The Roots of Civilization* (New York: McGraw-Hill, 1972), 333.

2. *Pornography: The Secret History of Civilisation*, directed by Chris Rodley, Dev Varma, and Kate Williams (UK: produced by World of Wonder for Channel 4 Television Corporation, 1999); available on DVD from Koch Vision, Port Washington, NY, 2006.

3. The media attention is not limited to the tabloid press. Both the *Toronto Star* and *The Guardian* have run recent articles discussing moral, ethical, and legal issues raised by the technology (Sunny Freeman, "Sex Robots to Become a Reality: Advancements in Machines that Can Mimic Human Beings Are Raising a Host of New Ethical, Legal and Moral Questions," *Toronto Star* (June 4, 2016), https://www.thestar.com/business/2016/06/04/sex-robots-to-become-a-reality.html; Deborah Orr, "At Last a Cure for Feminism: Sex Robots," *The Guardian* (June 10, 2016), https://www.theguardian.com/commentisfree/2016/jun/10/feminism-sex-robots-women-technology-objectify; Eva Wiseman, "Sex, Love and Robots: Is This the End of Intimacy?," *The Guardian* (December 13, 2015), https://www.theguardian.com/technology/2015/dec/13/sex-love-and-robots-the-end-of-intimacy.

4. To anticipate a point that will be expanded upon later, if all of your sex partners are of the same sex as you, your list will contain *nobody* with whom you've have penile-vaginal intercourse!

5. Stephanie A. Sanders, "Would You Say You 'Had Sex' If …?," *Journal of the American Medical Association* 281 (1999): 275–277.

6. Alan Turing, "Computing Machinery and Intelligence," *Mind* 59 (1950): 433–60.

7. Greta Christina, "Are We Having Sex Yet or What?" in *The Erotic Impulse*, ed. David Steinberg, (New York: Tarcher/Penguin, 1992), 24–29.

8. This way of putting things is inspired in part by the discussion of concept analysis in science in C. Kenneth Waters, "What Concept Analysis in Philosophy of Science Should Be (and Why Competing Philosophical Analyses of Gene Concepts Cannot Be Tested by Polling Scientists)," *History and Philosophy of the Life Sciences* 26 (2004): 29–58.

9. Alan Soble favors the view that having sex is to be understood merely in terms of sex acts when he suggests that Christina's puzzlement about what counts as having sex could be dissolved by allowing that whatever else they are, the various encounters she considers are cases of sexual activity. He adds that we can "negotiate whether to add ... some of these activities to 'having sex' category" (17), including possibly solitary masturbation. See Alan Soble, "Activity, Sexual," in *Sex from Plato to Paglia* (Westport, CT: Greenwood Press, 2006), 15–25.

10. Perhaps one could circumscribe the right sort of attention negatively, by proposing a near-exhaustive list of kinds of attention that can be paid to sexual organs *without* thereby expressing sexual agency—as when doctors (*qua* doctors) examine their patients and painters (*qua* painters) contemplate their models, and so forth—and suggesting that any attention paid to sexual organs that doesn't fall into one of the listed categories probably counts as an expression of sexual agency.

11. Children who do not yet have a self-conscious understanding of the domain of the sexual may be credited with sexual agency in light of the first of these conditions; fetishists whose sexual activities may have little to do with their or anybody else's genitals may yet embody sexual agency in virtue of the second.

12. We do not here need to enter into too much detail as to the nature of collective action as such. We take for granted that participants in collective action have some intention of the sort "we will ..." or "we are ..."—what, following Kutz, we will call a *participatory intention*. But we will remain neutral as to whether this participatory intention should be taken as primitive as in Gilbert or understood reductively as in Bratman's intermeshing intentions approach. See Christopher Kutz, "Acting Together," *Philosophy and Phenomenological Research* 61 (2000): 1–31; Margaret Gilbert, "Walking Together: A Paradigmatic Social Phenomenon," *Midwest Studies In Philosophy* 15 (1990): 1–14; and Michael E. Bratman, "Shared Cooperative Activity," *Philosophical Review* 101 (1992): 327–341.

13. Paul Grice, *Studies in the Way of Words* (Cambridge, MA: Harvard University Press, 1989). Grice's maxims are meant to apply to any kind of talk exchange, not with conversation as such.

14. To put the point with pedantic exactitude, we note that Joyce's quip is about married onanists, not about married people with only one arm who cheat on their spouses.

15. More precisely, "sexually stimulating yourself all by yourself." According to the OED, masturbation, strictly speaking, is a matter of manual genital stimulation, with no specification of how many persons are involved or whose hands are stimulating which genitals.

16. We owe the latter point to Jack MacIntosh, but it's also found in Alan Soble's series of papers on masturbation, the most recent of which is Alan Soble, "On Jacking Off, Yet Again," in *The*

Philosophy of Sex (sixth edition), eds. Nicholas Power, Raja Halwani, and Alan Soble, (Lanham, Maryland: Roman & Littlefield, 2013), 77–100.

17. Scott A. Anderson, "Sex Under Pressure: Jerks, Boorish Behavior, and Gender Hierarchy," *Res Publica* 11 (2005): 349–369.

18. Or, one assumes, than pressure from one half of a same-sex couple, though Anderson does not mention this case.

19. Sarah Conly, "Seduction, Rape, and Coercion," *Ethics* 115 (2004): 96–121.

20. Victims of sexual assault are victims pure and simple. But people subjected to importunate sexual advances may react in a way that makes them, in the excellent phrasing of Alice Munro, at once "victim and accomplice" (Alice Munro, "Wild Swans," in *Who Do You Think You Are?* (Toronto: Penguin, 2006 [1978]), 63.

21. Zackary Canepari, Drea Cooper, and Emma Cott, "Sex Dolls that Talk Back," *Robotica*, episode 5 (New York Times Video, June 11, 2015), http://www.nytimes.com/2015/06/12/technology/robotica-sex-robot-realdoll.html.

22. In addition, at least part of what we value in a sexual encounter is the other agent's desire to have sex with us, which would be undermined if that agent is programmed to desire sex with any human being. The significance of mutual desire plays a central role in Thomas Nagel, "Sexual Perversion," *The Journal of Philosophy* 66 (1969): 5–17.

23. See Daniel C. Dennett, "Intentional Systems," *The Journal of Philosophy* 68 (1971), 87–106; and Daniel C. Dennett, *The Intentional Stance* (sixth printing) (Cambridge, MA: MIT Press, 2006 [1987]), among others.

II Defending Robot Sex

The advent of sophisticated sex robots intrigues many people and raises serious concerns for others. The chapters in this section make the case for developing sex robots, and try to address some of those serious concerns. McArthur starts in chapter 3 by arguing that the invention of sexbots will, on balance, be beneficial for society. He explains how sex robots can promote pleasure and well-being, distribute sexual experience more widely, and improve intimate human relationships. Danaher, Earp, and Savulescu then follow up in chapter 4 by looking at the recently launched Campaign Against Sex Robots. They argue that, although the Campaign raises some important issues, nothing they say is sufficiently serious to warrant all-out bans on this technology. Finally, in chapter 5, Ezio Di Nucci looks at the topic of sexual rights and disability, arguing that sex robots may be a good way to assist the severely disabled in exercising their positive sexual autonomy.

3 The Case for Sexbots

Neil McArthur

Sexbots will not just be life-sized sex toys. Some people do imagine them this way, and as a result are somewhat puzzled by the question of whether or not it should be legally or morally permissible to own them, given that we do not generally raise a similar question with more familiar sex toys. While there are certainly many parallels between sexbots and sex toys, a sexbot promises to provide a sexual experience that is significantly more realistic and intense than what can be obtained merely through the use of a sex toy. This is both because of its physical similarity to a human and due to the level of humanlike interaction it would (theoretically) provide. Sexbots will be qualitatively different from other kinds of sex toys, and this difference raises distinct philosophical issues.

The difference is reflected in public attitudes. People have strong reactions to the prospect of sexbots, ones that far exceed any reactions provoked by more familiar sex toys. In February of 2013, the polling firm YouGov conducted a poll, sponsored by the Huffington Post website, that asked people about their attitudes toward robots. It was a relatively large (one thousand adults), random sample. One question asked: "If it were possible, would you ever have sex with a robot?" Only nine percent said yes. Eleven percent said they were not sure, and the remaining eighty-one percent (figures were rounded by the polling firm) said no.[1] The poll also asked: "If it were possible for humans to have sex with robots, do you think that a person in an exclusive relationship who had sex with a robot would be cheating?" A total of 42 percent said yes, and 26 percent said they were not sure. Only 31 percent said no.[2] Other surveys have produced similar results. Overwhelming majorities consistently say they would not have sex with a robot.[3]

The polling data unfortunately does not give us any specific insights into why people answered the way they did. We do not know how many respondents have a considered moral objection to sex with robots, as opposed to those who simply consider it distasteful. And we do not know what, if any, rationales any of the respondents would provide for their negative attitudes. While I cannot offer any further insights on why people are as a matter of fact averse to sex with robots, I will identify several philosophical justifications that might be given for opposing sexbots. I will argue that these justifications are not sufficient, on balance, to establish that the development of sexbots should be viewed as harmful. On the contrary, we should view their development as something that should be welcomed and promoted, and we should actively combat any stigmas that exist against robot sex. In sum, I propose that the invention of sexbots will be a good thing, and that society on the whole will end up better off for it.

3.1 A Right to Sexbots?

There is a simple, rights-based argument in favor of sexbots that some people might consider decisive. According to this rights-based argument, sex with a robot is something that people will generally do in the privacy of their own homes, and it causes no direct harm to others. It is therefore covered by the more general right to privacy that people possess in a free society. The laws in nearly all liberal democracies now recognize a right to privacy that offers significant protections for private sexual behavior. For instance, in 2004, the United States Supreme Court, in a decision granting homosexuals the right to engage in consensual sex, commented that such a right "has been accepted as an integral part of human freedom" in numerous liberal-democratic jurisdictions around the world.[4] A 2008 federal court decision, which overturned Texas's law against "obscene devices" (sex toys), said of the Lawrence decision: "The right the Court recognized was not simply a right to engage in the sexual act itself, but instead a right to be free from governmental intrusion regarding 'the most private human contact, sexual behavior.'"[5] According to this line of reasoning, many of the arguments against sexbots are misguided from the outset, since they presume the legitimacy of something that is in fact illegitimate, the interference by society in the lives of individuals, in matters of strictly private concern. Defenders of the rights-based view appeal to a principle that many take to be at the basis of a liberal, democratic society: the harm principle. This principle was most famously formulated by John Stuart Mill. As he put it in his book *On Liberty*: "The only purpose for which power can be rightfully exercised over any member of a civilized community, against his will, is to prevent harm to others."[6]

A rights-based argument for sexbots faces challenges, however. First of all, individual rights are never absolute. It may be that sexbots have an impact on society that, on balance, outweighs the privacy interest of their owners. Not everyone will agree that the use of sexbots is an entirely private matter. It is worth remembering that sexbots involve commercial transactions, and it is generally thought that our right to privacy is much more limited once we enter the commercial sphere. We have laws and regulations governing many sorts of commercial transactions, even though they concern products that are meant to be used in private. Defenders of such laws point out that these products must be manufactured, marketed, and sold, and all of these activities take place in the public marketplace and involve other people in various ways. Even if people are not forbidden outright from owning sexbots, we might think that, like the products involved in other sorts of commercial transactions, sexbots would be potentially subject to various kinds of restrictions and regulations.

Second, I am interested not just in legal restrictions, but also in moral judgments. Few people think that the right to privacy is as stringent when it comes to morality. We have the legal right to engage in many activities that deserve no positive encouragement and that indeed may rightly be the subject of condemnation by others. Infidelity is a private matter, for instance, but we still make moral judgments concerning those who engage in it. If we want to defend sexbots, we must show that they can survive criticism on moral, as well as legal, grounds.

Third, even for those positively predisposed to the idea of sexbots, the conclusion established by the right to privacy is too limited. The right to privacy establishes only that we should tolerate sexbots, whereas I believe a case can be made for a stronger conclusion. I said at the outset that I believe the invention of sexbots will be not just morally neutral, but will in fact be, on balance, a positive good. I am advocating not just that we tolerate them, but that we actively encourage their development, support their distribution, and work to overcome stigmas associated with them. While an individual's right to sexual privacy is important, it cannot on its own establish this stronger conclusion. Indeed, the appeal to privacy is in one sense an admission of defeat. When we resort to it, we are effectively conceding that we cannot provide reasons in favor of the practice we are defending. But I believe that when it comes to sexbots, we can do just this.

3.2 Hedonic Arguments

One potential reason we should welcome the development of sexbots is that they promise to deliver direct hedonic benefits. Put more simply, people will enjoy having them, and there is reason to believe they will be happier on balance as a result. I take it as a premise that sexbots will offer people a realistic and intensely satisfying sexual experience, one that approximates at least in many ways sex with a human partner. And this will benefit them in various ways.

Other things being equal, sex is considered by most people to be a good rather than a bad thing. A life with more sex is generally preferable to one with less. And various studies have suggested that people generally get less sex than they would like, and would be happier if they had more. One study has concluded that for the average person, increasing the frequency of sexual intercourse from once a month to at least once a week offers as much additional happiness as an increase in salary of $50,000 per year.[7] It is reasonable to conclude that the possession of a realistic sexbot will, at least for many people, lead to an increase in the absolute quantity of sexual experiences. Sexbots thus have the potential to maximize both the amount of hedonic satisfaction, and, as a result, the level of overall happiness, in the world.

Greater levels of sexual satisfaction, on top of their impact on people's levels of happiness, contribute to better health outcomes. High levels of sexual activity correlate to weight loss, lower stress levels, better heart and blood-pressure outcomes, lower rates of prostate cancer for men, and better sleep. People who have more sex quite simply tend to live longer, healthier lives.[8] Some of these benefits can be achieved through solitary sex or the use of existing sexual aids. However, others are the result of the physical exertion required for sex with a partner, and the sense of psychological well-being that results from partnered sex. Research has shown that sex with a partner has certain psychological benefits that masturbation cannot achieve.[9] We do not fully understand the reasons for this, and so we cannot say whether robot sex will achieve the same benefits as partnered sex. However, I think it is plausible to say that sexbots will deliver at least some of these benefits. For instance, robots will require the same level of physical exertion as sex with a human partner. Indeed, they could be programmed to require more. And the touch and feel of another person seems to activate a certain sort of physical reaction in us that (at least as the technology develops) may be achieved with a robot. The full psychological experience of partnered sex may never be precisely imitated with a robot. Indeed, we may think this would be for the best. But it is reasonable to believe that robots can deliver health benefits that significantly exceed those available through the use of more familiar sex toys.

3.3 Anti-Hedonism

Such hedonic arguments may not convince many detractors. The appeal of these arguments depends crucially on a proposition that many people reject, which is that sex can be seen purely as a vehicle for hedonic satisfaction. There are several reasons why we might reject the idea that sex can ever be seen solely as a means of attaining physical pleasure. First of all, there are those who see the purpose of sex as necessarily procreative. According to procreationism (as it is sometimes called), any sexual activity that is inherently non-procreative, as sex with a robot must be, violates this natural purpose of sex, and is therefore immoral. Sex is, as John Finnis, puts it, "an instrumental good" that is meant to be "in the service" of procreation.[10] Such people do not generally insist that each individual sex act must be intended to produce children. Rather, they argue that acceptable sex acts must belong to the class of acts that could potentially be reproductive. Kant says that "natural sex" is that as a result of which "procreation of a being of the same kind is possible."[11] Using the language of natural law theory, Finnis says that sex is morally acceptable to the extent that it instantiates a "biological union" between a man and a woman. He defines such a union in this way: "Biological union between humans is the inseminatory union of male genital organ with female genital organ; in most circumstances it does not result in generation, but it is the behavior that unites biologically because it is the behavior which, as behavior, is suitable for generation."[12]

Strict procreationism has by now become a minority view, its adherents mostly motivated by religious reasons. However, there are two other approaches to sex that are not tied to religious faith, both of which give us philosophical reasons for opposing sexbots. I consider these to be of more concern for my own position. First, there are those who think that sex should be reserved for contexts where two people have an emotional bond with one another. David Benatar calls this the Significance View. As he presents this view: "for sex to be morally acceptable, it must be an expression of (romantic) love. It must, in other words, signify feelings of affection that are commensurate with the intimacy of the sexual activity. On this view a sexual union can be acceptable only if it reflects the reciprocal love and affection of the parties to that union."[13]

Second, there are those who adopt what we might call the Reciprocity View. Proponents of this view do not insist that sex express love, but they do require that sex acts should involve two people, and reflect a mutuality and reciprocity of desire between the parties involved. Jean-Paul Sartre offers an analysis of sexual desire based on what he calls "a double reciprocal incarnation": "I make myself flesh in order to impel the Other to realize for herself and for me her own flesh, and my caresses cause my flesh to be born for me in so far as it is for the Other flesh causing her to be born as flesh."[14] Thomas Nagel, taking Sartre's analysis as his point of departure, argues that sexual activity that does not include such reciprocal desire is a form of perversion:

I believe that some version of this overlapping system of distinct sexual perceptions and interactions is the basic framework of any full-fledged sexual relation and that relations involving only part of the complex are significantly incomplete. ... I believe that various familiar deviations constitute truncated or incomplete versions of the complete configuration, and may therefore be regarded as perversions of the central impulse.

In particular, narcissistic practices and intercourse with animals, infants, and inanimate objects seem to be stuck at some primitive version of the first stage. If the object is not alive, the experience is reduced entirely to an awareness of one's own sexual embodiment.[15]

Roger Scruton offers a similar analysis of desire and arousal to Sartre's: "Arousal is a response to the thought of the other, as a self-conscious agent, who is alert to me, and who is able to have 'designs' on me."[16] He says that to see sexual arousal and sexual pleasure as purely 'physical' is to reduce us to what two followers of Melanie Klein call, in a text Scruton cites, mere "desiring machines."[17] Like Nagel, he sees this as a form of perversion, or as a corruption of our character. Similarly, John Finnis objects to any act in which "one's body is treated as instrumental for the securing of the experiential satisfaction of the conscious self."[18]

People who adopt one of these anti-hedonic views of sexual activity might see sex with a robot as a particularly intense, and perhaps dangerously appealing, form of auto-eroticism. Many philosophical defenders of these views explicitly argue that masturbation is morally impermissible. For Roger Scruton, masturbation is immoral because it "involves a concentration on the body and its curious pleasures"—indeed, an "obsession … with the organs themselves and with the pleasures of sensation."[19] John Finnis also holds the Kantian view (which he draws from Aquinas and natural law theory) that masturbation entails a surrender to one's purely "physical self," and thus an abandonment of the "choosing self" that makes us human. It is, for this reason, a degradation of our nature.[20] It should be noted that all of these arguments are clearly ones that have some resonance among the public. There remains a high level of public concern regarding masturbation, and, while no liberal jurisdictions forbid masturbation per se, several states continue to make "obscene devices" (sex toys) illegal.

To dismiss all forms of masturbation as morally impermissible will, however, strike many people as extreme. I think there will be some people who are sympathetic to one or more of the anti-hedonist positions, but who construe them in a more moderate way, such that they are not troubled by masturbation, but still object to sex with robots. They will be disturbed not by the similarities of robot sex and autoeroticism, but precisely by the dissimilarities. They will think robot sex approximates partnered sex far too closely—but partnered sex of the most objectionable sort. This is to say, it is a form of casual sex totally devoid of any emotional connection, and indeed of the possibility of such a connection.

We might raise an objection here: Why, we might wonder, does robot sex count as "real," dyadic sex, rather than as mere physical release? One answer is, because people will tend to see it as such, because of the way in which they naturally view robots. We can look here at research on research by Sherry Turkle, who has argued that robots are different than other forms of technology because they are what she calls "relational artifacts."[21] Relational artifacts are non-living objects that are, or at least appear to be, sufficiently responsive that people naturally conceive themselves to be in a mutual relationship with them. They therefore affect our sense of self, our emotional well-being, and our relationships with other humans in ways that other forms of technology do not. Turkle has looked at studies of people interacting with robots in various settings, and this empirical work suggests that many of us have a natural, even irresistible, tendency to project human intentions and emotions onto such objects, to attribute to them some sort of soul or essence, and to form an emotional bond with them. She points to one study of human-robot interaction that observed a high percentage of their subjects attributing to robots some kind of "technological essence" (75% made this attribution), a "lifelike essence" (48%), mental states (60%), and social rapport (59%).[22]

If it is empirically true that people tend to see robots as a special kind of object, sex with a robot potentially becomes more than a mere autoerotic act. It includes an entity with which we may naturally, at least in our own minds, form a certain kind of relationship, and which is therefore distinct in kind from, and more dangerous than, other sorts of sex toys. We are having "real" sex with an entity with which we can never form a true, reciprocal bond, but which we can easily become deluded into thinking has some sort of genuine personhood.

On this view, what is objectionable about nonreciprocal sex is not that it treats sex as a mere physical release, but rather that it deploys an "Other" as an object for our own gratification. Sex with a robot is perverse in the way that, according to proponents of the Significance or Reciprocity Views, sex with a child or an animal is. In sex acts of this kind, we do not merely gratify ourselves, we do so by objectifying another being, one who can never be a proper subject equal to us—even if we do this only in our own mind. One of the wrongs of nonreciprocal sex is obviously that such objectification can harm the Other. But even if we do not think that the Other involved is capable of being harmed during a particular sex act, nonreciprocal sex makes sex itself into a vehicle for objectification, and it implicitly condones such objectification as morally legitimate. It can also generate an attitude toward objectification that can spill over into our human relationships. Kathleen Richardson argues that there is an inherent moral link between sexbots and the use of sex workers, and quotes from an author whose study of sex work concludes that: "… a denial of subjectivity occurs when the experiences and feelings of the 'object' are not recognized."[23] Robot sex thus in some way "enacts" an extreme form of sexual objectification. In psychoanalytic terms, sex with a robot allows us to indulge and foster our incomplete, narcissistic desires in a way that legitimates such desires.

It is at least partly an empirical question to what extent nonreciprocal sex will actually cause us to view our human sexual partners as less than full subjects in their own right. However, I do not think the people making this objection to sexbots have concerns that can be resolved on purely empirical grounds. There is also the explicitly moral question of what sorts of practices we as individuals and as a society condone, even if we do not indulge in them ourselves. The concern is that, by allowing or indeed encouraging sex with robots, we as a society are condoning sexual objectification more generally. This has both symbolic and practical importance. Practically speaking, people may become more likely to view their human partners simply as sex objects, and we may begin to weaken the power of sex to act as an expression of intimate, reciprocal connection between two partners.

Since the empirical question cannot yet be resolved, I do not think it is possible to offer decisive counterarguments against this view of robot sex. But I do think we can encourage those who are sympathetic to it to balance it against other considerations. I want to argue first of all that, in cases where sex is difficult or impossible to obtain, sex with a robot, even if it is less than ideal, is better than total deprivation. Second, far from harming our ability to have reciprocal or significant sexual encounters, robots may make people more able to engage in reciprocal, significant sex. They can thus have a positive effect on balance, by opening up the possibility of serious sexual relationships with fellow human beings.

3.4 Distributive Arguments

Inequality has become a key topic of concern among academics and policymakers. Yet few commentators have noted how uneven is the distribution of sexual satisfaction. It has been the great achievement of theorists such as Amartya Sen and Martha Nussbaum to point out that the list of basic goods, the distribution of which we should care about, goes beyond the satisfaction of people's rudimentary material needs. According to such modern egalitarians, we should try to ensure that everyone is able not just to feed and clothe themselves, but to access a variety of goods, such as education and leisure, which form key components of a flourishing human life.

If we accept that there is a plurality of basic human goods, we should, I think, be willing to acknowledge that some degree of sexual satisfaction belongs among them, and that it represents a significant hardship to deprive someone of this good unnecessarily. Sex is increasingly recognized as a basic human good. For instance the World Health Organization recently endorsed a "Declaration of Sexual Rights" drawn up by participants attending the 13th World Congress of Sexology in 1997. According to the Declaration:

> Rational and satisfactory experience of sexuality is a requirement for human development. ... Sexual pleasure, including autoeroticism, is a source of physical, psychological, intellectual, and spiritual well-being. It is associated with a conflict-free and anxiety-free experience of sexuality, allowing, therefore, social and personal development.[24]

My proposal is this: whether or not we see nonreciprocal sex as harmful to individuals and society, we should also be willing to recognize that enforced sexual deprivation is a harm worth attending to as well, and that this weighs heavily in favor of sexbots. Even if people would prefer a human partner, they might well prefer robot companionship to total celibacy. We should at least be willing to give them that choice. This is particularly true since sexual deprivation affects those who are most vulnerable to other forms of inequality as well.

There are a number of reasons why some people may face serious, even insuperable, obstacles in finding a companion. First of all, there is the challenge of demographics. Some societies, most notably China, possess dramatically uneven gender ratios overall, which leaves large numbers of straight men with little or no opportunity for sexual companionship. Simple mathematics dictates that where the gender balance of a society is uneven, significant numbers of heterosexual people will not be able to find serious relationships. Members of sexual minority communities are equally at the mercy of their demographic environment. There are many places, such as small towns, in which gays and lesbians have little opportunity to find relationships. The problem is often compounded by stigmas that make it difficult and even dangerous to seek out a partner.

There are also many people who are forced to live in single-sex environments, the majority of whom are heterosexual. First, there are prisons. The global prison population numbers around nine million people. Even those prisoners who are married often have difficulty obtaining private time with their spouses. Second, there is the military. Over twenty million people are currently in active service in the military. By no means are all of these military personnel entirely isolated from potential partners, but it is certainly more difficult for many of them to meet people to have sex with. They are often segregated by gender and cut off from the general population. Though, at least in Western countries, the militaries have begun to accept an increasing number of female recruits, the gender ratios are still skewed, and many armed services have implemented anti-fraternization rules preventing relationships among those on active duty. There are many other environments that are exclusively or predominantly single-sex, such as mining camps. While such single-sex environments and uneven gender ratios might be seen as a burden primarily to heterosexuals, they also tend to be ones where, not accidentally, gays and lesbians face stigmas. For example, the military is a notably difficult place for members of LGBT communities.

Many people also have mental or physical issues that limit their ability to find intimate partners. People with severe anxiety surrounding performance or body image, an incidence of sexual trauma (such as rape or incest), adults with limited or no experience, or people who have transitioned from one sex to another, may find that their anxieties about sex inhibit their ability to form relationships. People can also be the victims of stigmas due to their appearance or lack of experience.

Like other forms of inequality, sexual inequality has a widespread impact on society. When individuals, especially young males, are deprived of the prospect of sexual companionship, they can become a significant source of social instability. Numerous studies suggest that single men are significantly more likely to commit crimes than any other demographic groups, and are in general the main contributors to social disorder.[25] People who are single and without the prospect of companionship are also more depressed, and depend more heavily on social services.

We might wonder to what degree the mere possession of a sexbot can alleviate the psychological and social costs of sexual deprivation. It is not a perfect solution. We cannot say in advance what the precise impact will be. This will have to be determined empirically. However, I would like to suggest that a sufficiently realistic sexbot would be much better than nothing, and that it has the potential to measurably impact the psychological, social, and economic costs of sexual deprivation. Whatever our views on sex, then, if we care about the unequal distribution of basic goods, we should welcome the development of sexbots.

If we agree that sexbots are desirable as a means of addressing a particular form of inequality, we might worry about access. Sexbots will be expensive, and so they might in fact exacerbate existing inequalities by giving the rich access to even greater avenues for sexual satisfaction. This is certainly something that may need to be addressed. Short-term access—in essence, "robot sex workers"—could potentially be quite affordable, and could even be subsidized if their benefits were widely acknowledged, just as some jurisdictions have begun to subsidize access to sex workers and to sex surrogates for those with disabilities or with psychological issues that impede their ability to form relationships.

3.5   Relationship Arguments

Defenders of the Reciprocity View argue that we should encourage partnered sex as the healthiest or most moral form of sexual activity. But sexbots have the potential to strengthen people's human relationships in various ways and enhance the sex people have in these relationships. This provides another reason for friends of this view to remain open to sexbots.

First, sexbots can help prepare people for human relationships. They can help people build a sense of comfort with sex and increase their confidence in their own sexual abilities. People who struggle with gender orientation may find that the use of robots helps them achieve comfort with the type of partners they prefer. I have already said that people who have experienced sexual trauma often find it difficult to form intimate relationships. Sexbots might help people overcome such trauma through sexual experiences that are safe and controlled.

Sexbots can also provide people in relationships a way to address various problems they might face in their relationships. First of all, there is the problem of desire discrepancy. Desire discrepancy is the social science term for a phenomenon familiar to many people within long-term relationships: when one person wants sex more frequently than the other, and this leads to tension in the relationship. Therapists report that desire discrepancy is one of the most common problems experienced by couples, and it is one that can create significant tensions within relationships.[26] A sexbot can provide an outlet to the high-desire member of the couple. This outlet would not only benefit this partner, it could strengthen the relationship more generally. It could relieve pressure on the low-desire partner and might therefore decrease his or her feelings of guilt, and it could likewise diminish resentment by the high-desire partner. The sex that the partners have with one another can thus be mutually desired and mutually fulfilling.

Sexbots could also strengthen existing relationships by reducing tensions around the kind of sex the partners desire. Sexbots could allow people to play out fantasies or indulge in practices that are of no interest to their partners. Indeed, some of these practices may be ones, such as sadistic sex, that we could not reasonably expect any person to endure. By giving someone an outlet for these specific desires, sexbots remove the pressure on that person's partner to fulfill them. By providing an outlet for desire, sexbots also have the potential to decrease rates of infidelity. Infidelity has many causes, but two of the leading ones are dissatisfaction with the amount of sex available in the relationship, a problem discussed above, and the desire for novelty and variety in our sexual partners. Affairs are a leading cause of destroyed relationships, and research-ers have identified the perceived need for sexual variety, and dissatisfaction with the amount of sex available in the relationship, as two key reasons for infidelity.[27] The possession of a sexbot could potentially address both of these problems.

Finally, sexbots could have educational value, which can benefit a relationship by increasing the partner's level of satisfaction. They could be programmed to teach their owners positions, techniques, and other practices that they would never have thought of on their own, or to experiment with ones that they might have been reticent to try with their partner. Thus, sexbots can play a role in increasing relationship satisfaction and strengthening intimacy.

There is an objection that might be made to the argument that sexbots can strengthen relationships. We might worry that someone's possession of a sexbot could in fact undermine her relationship, either by diverting her attention away from her partner or by making her partner feel betrayed. We can recall the poll I cited at the beginning of the article, which found that less than a third of people are willing to say that sex with a robot would not be cheating. Certainly there is considerable potential for sexbots to increase tensions within relationships, especially where partners hold divergent attitudes towards them. One person may see it as a meaningful outlet for physical pleasure, but the other may suspect that there is the potential for their partner to form a bond that might undermine their own intimacy. Indeed, some of the very factors I identified as advantages with sexbots, such as their willingness to perform acts a human partner would not, may give that partner reasons for jealousy.

Couples will ultimately have to determine on their own whether the costs of obtain-ing a sexbot justify the benefits. Philosophically, I admit, that sounds rather like a cop-out. However, the debate here is whether we should welcome the invention of sexbots and do what we can to hasten their arrival. Obviously no one will be forced to obtain one. It will be an option for couples who think it will work for them, and if you believe that people are by and large the best judges of what is best for them, we should as a general rule try to give them more options rather than fewer. Robot technology has great potential, and I think people will be capable of seeing its risks. The technology is therefore likely on balance to be adopted by more couples who benefit from it than by couples whose relationships are harmed—and so it will on balance be a net gain for society. Thus, we should be willing to endorse my conclusion: That the development of sexbots should be encouraged, and barriers and stigmas to their adoption should be removed.

3.6 Conclusion

The basic argument of this chapter can be put simply. Sexbots are coming, and this will be, on net, a good thing. People will enjoy having them, and they will be happier as a result. I do not claim that I can allay all the concerns about sexbots that might be raised by someone who believes that sex must be part of a significant romantic relationship, or that it must instantiate a reciprocal connection between two people. However, I do think that even those who hold these positions should be able to see advantages to the development of sexbots. I have argued that sexbots can be a solution, if admittedly an imperfect one, to sexual deprivation, and that they can potentially help people prepare for, and maintain, long-term relationships more easily than those people could have done without them. For these reasons, the development of sexbots should not just be tolerated, but actively encouraged.

Notes

1. YouGov, "Omnibus Poll" (February 2013), 1, http://big.assets.huffingtonpost.com/toplinesbrobots.pdf.

2. Ibid, 2.

3. *The Sun* (UK), "15% of British Men (and a Few Women) Would Have Sex with a Robot," September 2, 2015, https://www.thesun.co.uk/sol/homepage/features/6618462/15-per-cent-of-British-men-and-a-few-women-would-have-sex-with-a-robot.html; Charlotte Lytton, "Poll Finds 1 in 5 People Would Have Sex with a Robot," *The Daily Beast*, May 7, 2014, http://www.thedailybeast.com/articles/2014/05/07/poll-finds-1-in-5-people-would-have-sex-with-a-robot.html.

4. Lawrence v. Texas, 539 US 558 (2003), 577. Cf. Niemietz v. Germany, ECHR (December 16, 1992).

5. Reliable Cons. v. Earle, 538 F.3d 355 (5th Cir. 2008).

6. J. S. Mill, *"On Liberty" and Other Writings*, ed. Stefan Collini (Cambridge: Cambridge University Press, 1989), 13.

7. D. G. Blanchflower and A. J. Oswald, "Money, Sex and Happiness: An Empirical Study," *The Scandinavian Journal of Economics* 106 (2004): 393–415. For the general importance of sex relative to other activities in determining people's happiness, see Daniel Kahneman, Alan B. Krueger, David Schkade, Norbert Schwarz, and Arthur Stone, "Toward National Well-Being Accounts," *American Economic Review* 94 (2004): 429–434.

8. B. Whipple, "The Benefits of Sexual Expression on Physical Health," *Sexologies* 17, Supplement 1 (2008): 545–546.

9. S. Brody, "The Relative Health Benefits of Different Sexual Activities," *Journal of Sexual Medicine* 7 (2010): 1336–1361.

10. John Finnis, "Law, Morality, and 'Sexual Orientation,'" Notre Dame Law Review 69 (1994): 1064.

11. Immanuel Kant, *The Metaphysics of Morals*, ed. Mary McGregor (Cambridge: Cambridge University Press, 1996 [1797]), 427.

12. Finnis, "Law, Morality, and 'Sexual Orientation,'" 1066 n. 46.

13. David Benatar, "Two Views of Sexual Ethics: Promiscuity, Pedophilia, and Rape," *Public Affairs Quarterly* 16 (2002): 182.

14. Jean-Paul Sartre, *Being and Nothingness*, trans. Hazel E. Barnes (New York: Philosophical Library, 1956), 391.

15. Thomas Nagel, "Sexual Perversion," *The Journal of Philosophy* 66 (1969): 12–14.

16. Roger Scruton, *Sexual Desire: A Philosophical Investigation* (London: Bloomsbury, 2006 [1986]), 23.

17. Ibid., 20.

18. John Finnis and Martha Nussbaum, "Is Homosexual Conduct Wrong? A Philosophical Exchange," *The New Republic* (November 15, 1993), 12–13.

19. Scruton, *Sexual Desire*, 319, 154.

20. Finnis and Nussbaum, "Is Homosexual Conduct Wrong?," 12; Finnis, "Law, Morality, and 'Sexual Orientation,'" 1068.

21. S. Turkle, W. Taggar, C. D. Kidd, C. D. and O. Dasté, "Relational Artifacts With Children and Elders: The Complexities Of Cybercompanionship," Connection Science 18 (2006): 347–361.

22. Ibid., 349.

23. Kathleen Richardson, "The Asymmetrical 'Relationship': Parallels Between Prostitution and the Development of Sex Robots," published in the ACM Digital Library as a special issue of the ACM SIGCAS newsletter, *SIGCAS Computers & Society* 45, no. 3 (September 2005): 291, https://campaignagainstsexrobots.org/the-asymmetrical-relationship-parallels-between-prostitution-and-the-development-of-sex-robots. Quoting from Coy, no citation.

24. "Declaration of Sexual Rights," adopted at the 13th World Congress of Sexology, 1997, http://www1.paho.org/hq/dmdocuments/2008/PromotionSexualHealth.pdf.

25. Robert J. Sampson, John H. Laub, and Christopher Wimer, "Does Marriage Reduce Crime? A Counterfactual Approach to Within-Individual Causal Effects," *Criminology* 44 (2006): 465–508; David T. Courtwright, *Violent Land: Single Men and Social Disorder from the Frontier to the Inner City* (Cambridge, MA: Harvard University Press, 1998); Lena Edlund, Hongbin Li, Junjian Yi, and Junsen Xhang, "Sex Ratios and Crime: Evidence from China's One-Child Policy," *Review of*

Economics and Statistics 95 (2013): 1520–1534; Darrell Steffensmeier and Emilie Allan, "Gender and Crime: Toward a Gendered Theory of Female Offending," *Annual Review of Sociology* 22 (1996): 459–487; Jon Hurwitz and Shannon Smithey, "Gender Differences on Crime and Punishment," *Political Research Quarterly* 51 (1998): 89–115.

26. For the negative effects of desire discrepancies on relationships, see S. Davies, J. Katz, and J. L. Jackson, "Sexual Desire Discrepancies: Effects on Sexual and Relationship Satisfaction in Heterosexual Dating Couples," *Archives of Sexual Behavior* 28 (1999): 553–567; Lucia F. O'Sullivan and Elizabeth Rice Allgeier, "Feigning Sexual Desire: Consenting to Unwanted Sexual Activity in Heterosexual Dating Relationships," Journal of Sex Research 35 (1998): 234–243; A. Muise, E. A. Impett, and S. Desmarais, "Getting It On vs. Getting It Over With: Approach-avoidance Sexual Motivation, Desire, and Satisfaction in Intimate Bonds," *Personality and Social Psychology Bulletin* 39 (2013): 1320–1332.

27. See B. Buunk, "Extramarital Sex in the Netherlands: Motivations in Social and Marital Context," *Journal of Family and Economic Issues* 3 (1980): 11–39; B. Roscoe, L. E. Cavanaugh, and D. R. Kennedy, "Dating Infidelity: Behaviors, Reasons and Consequences," *Adolescence* 23 (1988): 35–43. For an up-to-date review of studies on infidelity, which discusses motivation among other issues, see B. Zare, "Review of Studies on Infidelity," *International Proceedings of Economics Development and Research* 19 (2011): 182–186.

4 Should We Campaign Against Sex Robots?

John Danaher, Brian Earp, and Anders Sandberg

4.1 Introduction

September 2015 saw the launch of the *Campaign Against Sex Robots* (CASR).[1] Spearheaded by Kathleen Richardson of Leicester De Montfort University and Erik Brilling of the University of Skövde, the CASR models itself on the longer-standing *Campaign to Stop Killer Robots*, which was itself organized to preemptively ban fully autonomous weapons. CASR opposes the development of sex robots (for a sense of what we mean by this term, see the opening chapter in this volume by Danaher) on the grounds that they are "potentially harmful and will contribute to inequalities in society."[2] The campaign's founders believe that "an organized approach against the development of sex robots is necessary."[3]

The campaign received considerable media attention after its launch.[4] There also appears to be some popular support for the view it espouses. David Levy, one of the leading proponents of the development of sex robots,[5] was organizing the *2nd International Conference on Love and Sex With Robots* prior to the launch of the campaign. The conference was due to be held in Malaysia in November 2015, but was canceled shortly after the launch of the CASR as a result of opposition from Malaysian government officials. Although there is probably no direct causal link between the campaign and the cancellation, its cancellation does demonstrate receptiveness to the position being advocated.

Given this apparent potential for the CASR to gain meaningful traction, it seems important to assess its merits. That is what we attempt to do in this chapter. We do so in two main parts. First, we try to examine the objections to the development of sex robots that have actually been put forward by the CASR. We conclude that these objections are ultimately unpersuasive, although we suggest that the degree of (un)persuasiveness depends upon the actual aim of the campaign, which is currently not well-specified. Second, we try to broaden the focus by asking whether there could ever be a good reason to object to the development of this technology.[6] To do this, we draw upon lessons from the *Campaign to Stop Killer Robots*. We conclude that we are unlikely to come up with good reasons to preemptively reject the development of sex robots, unless we adopt a highly conservative approach to the ethics of sex, which many will find problematic for other reasons. This does not mean that there are no legitimate concerns one can have about the development of sex robots; it simply means that the concerns are not best addressed by adopting an organized campaign against their development.

More generally, the analysis we present in this chapter has implications for how societies should respond to controversial new technologies, based upon a range of factors including risk (and type) of harm, prospect of benefit, and different ways of pursuing regulation. Lessons learned here, therefore, should apply well beyond the specific debates about sex robots and autonomous weapons.

4.2   What Is the Argument behind the *Campaign Against Sex Robots*?

We start by engaging the campaign on its own terms. To do this, we turn to the position paper authored by Kathleen Richardson.[7] This paper sets out a series of objections to the development of sex robots, each of which is grounded in an analogy between sexbot-human relations and prostitute-john[8] relations. This way of framing things suggests that the main intellectual basis for the CASR (at least in its current form) is an argument from analogy. Richardson makes this explicit at the outset of her paper, commenting in particular on the model of human-robot relations that is adopted in the work of David Levy:

> In his book, *Sex, Love and Robots* [sic][9] David Levy proposes a future of human-robot relations based on the kinds of exchanges that take place in the prostitution industry. Levy explicitly creates "parallels between paying human prostitutes and purchasing sex robots" [p.194]. I want to argue that Levy's proposal shows a number of problems, firstly his understanding of what prostitution is and secondly, by drawing on prostitution as the model for human-robot sexual relations, Levy shows that the sellers of sex are seen by the buyers of sex as *things* and not recognised as human subjects. This legitimates a dangerous mode of existence where humans can move about in relations with other humans but not recognise them as human subjects in their own right.[10]

Although Richardson does not spell out her objection to sex robots in formal terms, we propose that it can be reconstructed in the following manner:

(1) Prostitute-john (or sex worker-client) relations are ethically problematic (for a number of reasons, but particularly due to objectification of the sex worker).

(2) Sexbot-human relations are being modeled on sex worker-client relations and so will share similar properties with those relations.

(3) Therefore, sexbot-human relations will be ethically problematic (by analogy).

(4) Therefore, we ought to campaign against sex robots.

This argument is not formally valid. Analogical arguments tend not to be: they are informal defeasible arguments, dependent on the strength of the similarity between the two cases being used. There is also something of a gap between the first conclusion (3) and the second conclusion (4). Nevertheless, it is our view that the reconstruction is fair to the position put forward in Richardson's paper because the prostitute-john analogy is front and center in her analysis; moreover, the gap between the first conclusion and the second conclusion is something we wish to highlight in our critique.

Assuming that this reconstruction fairly captures the argumentative centerpiece of the CASR, we will now attempt to show that this argument suffers from three major flaws, each of which serves to undermine the CASR in its current form.

4.2.1   The First Flaw: The Objective Is Unclear

The first problem with the CASR's argument is the gap between the two conclusions. Why is it that ethically problematic properties in sexbot-human relations support an organized campaign against the development of sex robots? The inference, as stated, is unwarranted. Now, there may be a way to bridge this gap, but the strength of the inference from (3) to (4) will depend on the objective of the proposed campaign. Unfortunately, the CASR is not clear about its intended objective. Until we have that clarity, it will be nearly impossible to tell whether or not the campaign is something that is worthy of our support. Why is this?

Broadly speaking, when it comes to the development of sex robots (or any potentially harmful technology), there are three main attitudes that we can adopt. We can be entirely *prohibitive* in our outlook, favoring the preemptive suppression of the technology. This is the attitude adopted by the *Campaign to Stop Killer Robots* in response to the development of fully autonomous weapons systems.[11] This prohibitive attitude could extend to the criminalization of those who create, distribute, and use the technology,[12] though criminalization may not be necessary. Alternatively, we can be entirely *libertarian* in our outlook, favoring complete freedom in the development and use of the technology. Finally, in between these two extremes, we can be *regulative* in our attitude, favoring some oversight of and intervention in the development and use of the technology, but falling short of a complete ban. This regulatory attitude could take many forms, ranging from the strong prohibition of certain types of sex robot, while tolerating or even possibly promoting others, to the crafting of industry ethical standards, advertising guidelines, safety protocols, and the like.

In short, there is a spectrum of possible responses to the prospect of sex robot development. The strength of the argument in favor of the CASR depends almost entirely on where along this spectrum the objective for the campaign lies. Clearly, it does not lie at the extreme libertarian end: there is something about the development of sex robots that the CASR finds objectionable. But where between total prohibition and weak regulation does the CASR's goal lie? The answer makes a difference when it comes to the burden of proof that the CASR's argument needs to discharge. If the campaign favors weak forms of regulation—which, for example, might just ask manufacturers of these robots to keep in mind various ethical issues that are raised by the technology, and to make some effort to address those issues—then the burden of proof will be relatively low. Indeed, if there are plausible ethical concerns, then we could probably all agree that these should be factored into the regulation of this technology. If, on the other hand, they favor total prohibition, the burden of proof is much higher. In liberal political regimes, there is (or should be) a general presumption against total prohibition of new technologies, particularly when it comes to a technology designed for personal use. The ethical issues identified by the campaign would need to be extremely compelling to warrant preemptive suppression.

So where along the spectrum do the campaign's objectives lie? Unfortunately, this is unclear. The CASR's website clearly states that an "organized approach against the development of sex robots" is required;[13] on the organization's "About" page, they list several unqualified objections to the development of sex robots; and in their position paper and support materials, they appeal to the preemptive model of the *Campaign to Stop Killer Robots*. All of this suggests that their objective is close to the total prohibition end of the spectrum. But there is also evidence of a more moderate view. The "About" page, for example, states that the campaign is in favor of "ethical technologies that reflect human principles of dignity, mutuality and freedom" and that they want "computer scientists and roboticists to examine their own conscience when asked to provide code, hardware or ideas to develop this field." Richardson's reliance on the "prostitute-john" analogy in her position paper also suggests that if sex robots could engender an alternative and more egalitarian relationship with humans then her opposition might wane.[14] Furthermore, in one media report, Richardson is recorded as saying that we should simply "examine what it means" to create such technologies, not completely ban them; although in the very same piece she is also reported to have called for a ban.[15] This suggests some equivocation on the part of the campaign's most visible founder as to its overarching objective.

This equivocation is problematic and may also explain some of the media appeal of the CASR. As other chapters in the current book make clear, ethical objections to the development of sex robots are not uncommon and not unwarranted. The fact that the particular set of objections raised by the CASR has seen such widespread coverage is, at least *prima facie*, puzzling. But now we may have an explanation: by ostensibly favoring the extreme of prohibition, the campaign can generate much initial media interest, and then when pushed on this extreme view it can retreat to a more modest and reasonable position, a position that may not actually warrant an organized approach against the development of sex robots (notwithstanding the stated aims of the campaign). If so, this would constitute a so-called "motte and bailey" tactic that is not uncommon in applied ethical debates.[16] This is just a speculation. The more serious point is that, until their objective is clarified, the CASR should not win widespread support.

4.2.2 The Second Flaw: It Paints a Misleading View of Sex Work

The second problem with the CASR's argument is its reliance on the sex worker-client analogy. This analogy may not be essential to the campaign's case—a point to which we return below—but it features heavily in Richardson's position paper. Therefore, it is worth taking seriously. The claims that seem to be[17] driving the argument are that sex worker-client relationships have several bad-making properties and that these bad-making properties will be shared and (thereby) reinforced and/or normalized by sexbot-human relationships.

In advancing this position, Richardson adopts an almost entirely negative view of sex work. Indeed, she objects to "sex work" terminology in and of itself, as well as to related discourse, seeing it as an attempt to normalize sex work as a reasonable choice in the labor market, when in fact, according to Richardson, it is highly problematic. In support of this view, she cites various studies showing that prostitution often occurs "in the absence of consent," that violence and trafficking are common in the industry, and that many of the workers are young girls or young women (between the ages of 13 and 25). Insofar as these claims are accurate, they are extremely troubling, and we agree that such aspects of sex work are unconscionable and must be addressed. However, these are not the only aspects to which one could refer. Problematically, Richardson does not engage at all with the position of those who do not share her uniformly negative view of prostitution/sex work, including some who have offered constructive articulations of alternative viewpoints in the recent literature.[18] Instead, she seems simply to take for granted that her negative position should be accepted as the only reasonable one that could be plausibly advanced.

Her main objections to sex work are that it is built around an asymmetrical power-relation between the client and the prostitute (one in which the client has the balance of power); that the work itself is highly gendered (primarily women, and some men, providing sex to primarily male clients);[19] and that the commercial relationship involves the denial of subjectivity (and hence effective objectification) of the sex worker. In other words, according to her view, the sex worker is always treated as a plaything that can be used and manipulated at the whim of the client, not as a human being with feelings, agency, and autonomy that ought to be respected. To back these objections up she quotes from a study by Farley, Bindley, and Golding, which includes interviews with clients making claims such as these:

"Prostitution is like masturbating without having to use your hand."

"It's like renting a girlfriend or wife. You get to choose like a catalogue."

"I feel sorry for these girls but this is what I want."[20]

Each of these views seems to reinforce the notion that the sex worker is being treated as little more than an object and that her subjectivity is being denied. The client is elevating his status and failing to empathize with the sex worker: he is substituting his fantasies for her real feelings. Insofar as that is indeed what is going on in a client-sex worker relationship, and if that is representative of such relationships, then we agree this is a serious problem. Among numerous other reasons, the failure or inability to empathize is often associated with higher rates of crime and violence.[21]

We thus seem to have two main lines of objection to sex work. The first is concerned with violence and lack of consent within the industry; and the second is concerned with objectification and the lack of empathy this entails. These are the bad-making properties of sex work that support the first premise of Richardson's argument. Leaving aside the question of whether these bad-making properties carry over to the case of sex robots, there are at least two problems with the objections raised regarding the existence (and nature) of these bad-making properties that may prevent the overall analogy from getting off the ground.

The first problem is that both objections are derived from a highly selective view of sex work. Richardson paints a wholly negative picture of the industry. But there are many prominent sex work researchers (and sex workers) who challenge that picture. For example, Sanders et al. provide an overview of the empirical literature on sex work in which they develop a far more nuanced account.[22] For instance, on the issue of violence in the industry, they note that it is a "minority" of clients who commit violence, and that the vast majority of commercial transactions take place without violence or other incident,[23] similar to the situation regarding noncommercial sexual relationships. Likewise, on the question of objectification and asymmetrical power relations, they note that much of this opposition is grounded in a conservative view of sexual ethics that fails to consider the possibility of emotionally rich and intimate sex occurring outside of the confines of a long-term monogamous relationship.[24] They argue that the attitudes of clients toward sex workers are often far more complex and multidimensional than Richardson supposes:

[G]eneral understandings of sex work and prostitution are based on false dichotomies that distinguish commercial sexual relationships as dissonant from noncommercial ones. Sanders (2008b) shows that there is mutual respect and understanding between regular clients and sex workers, dispelling the myth that all interactions between sex workers and clients are emotionless. There is ample counter-evidence (such as Bernstein 2001, 2007) that indicates that clients are "average" men without any particular or peculiar characteristics [who are] increasingly seeking "authenticity," intimacy and mutuality rather that trying to fulfil any mythology of violent, non-consensual sex.[25]

With respect to noncommercial sexual relationships, such as might exist between "ordinary" couples (i.e., couples for whom the explicit exchange of money is not directly associated with the sexual encounter, although other types of less overt exchanges may sometimes occur), it must be acknowledged that these are neither inherently nor exclusively models of "'authenticity,' intimacy and mutuality" either, notwithstanding their noncommercial nature. While this is arguably far from optimal, what it suggests is that that the quality of sexual relationships in terms of respect, power-asymmetries, etc., fall on a spectrum both within and outside of the commercial context; thus, much more work would be needed to show that there is something unique to an exchange-based sexual relationship that strictly entails the undesirable qualities being discussed, and that does so in a way that is significantly worse than comparable (i.e., casual) non-exchange-based sexual relationships.

We do not raise these points to paint a rosy and Pollyannaish view of sex work. We are only trying to highlight the need for greater nuance than Richardson seems willing to provide. It is simply not true that all forms of prostitution involve the troubling features she identifies, while at the same time, many forms of noncommercial sex do involve those features. Given that that is the case, the proposed analogy with sex robots appears to be on much weaker initial footing than Richardson assumes.

This brings us to the second criticism. Even if Richardson is right about both (a) the bad-making properties of prostitution, and (b) the view that these properties will "carry over" to the case in which the "sex worker" is a nonhuman robot (thus potentially normalizing the problematic attitudes that may be associated with such bad-making properties; but see discussion below), there is no strong reason to think that such an outcome would be sufficient to warrant a total prohibition on sex robots, nor even, perhaps, an organized campaign to oppose them. For better or worse, denials of subjectivity, asymmetries of power, and other objectionable qualities or outcomes are rife throughout the capitalistic workplace. While this might form the basis of a general critique of capitalism (such as a Marxist critique), it does not appear, in most other cases, to motivate, much less successfully ground, a *prohibition* of the activities or services that have such undesirable features. For example, many service workers in our economies regularly have their subjectivity denied by their clients: one may fail to care about the feelings of the massage therapist giving them a massage, for example, or about those of the carpenter repairing their deck. But while we may have very good reason to attempt to change the norms of behavior concerning such uncompassionate treatment of service workers, it would seem a strange and rather ham-fisted approach to attempt to ban the service industries altogether. Instead, a change in regulation and social attitude may be all that is appropriately called for.

We must be clear that we are not suggesting that there are no morally relevant differences between the (typical) relationship between a client and her massage therapist (or between a homeowner and her carpenter) and the (typical) client-sex worker relationship. Instead, we are only pointing out that the presence of even gravely undesirable features in a given type of exchange relationship (up to and including denials of subjectivity and problematic asymmetries of power) is not normally seen as being a sufficient justification for banning the relationship altogether; rather, regulations that seek to mitigate the undesirable features that do exist may worthily be pursued. On top of this, and perhaps even more importantly, there is reason to think that many of the negative features of client-sex worker relationships in particular could actually be directly caused (or worsened) by its prohibition. This is because prohibition "cannot alleviate the background conditions that contribute to people's motivation to sell sexual services in the first place."[26]

As one of us has argued elsewhere (drawing on the work of Luke Semrau):[27]

... there is an important distinction to be drawn between "being pressured to sell X" and "being pressured, with the option to sell X." If someone is being directly pressured to sell [something] (or become a prostitute, etc.), then prohibiting the selling of X could at least in principle be of some help. [However,] if someone is experiencing a more general pressure (such as extreme economic insecurity), but has a number of ways—including, but not limited to, selling X—to begin to relieve this pressure, then prohibiting the selling of X is actually more likely, all else being equal, to make this person even worse off. This is because it would remove (or drive underground, and therefore make more dangerous) at least one otherwise viable option for "making ends meet." As a consequence, the person who was considering selling X, and who would do so if it were not prohibited, must now turn to an even less desirable option (as judged by them) to relieve the more general pressure.[28]

Indeed, some of the problems of prohibition can arguably be seen in the case of violence and trafficking. Insofar as sex work is criminalized, sex workers cannot avail themselves of the various protections that are afforded to most other kinds of workers, and they may also fail to report what happens to them for fear of adverse legal consequences. This is why many sex worker activists—who are in no way unrealistic about the negative features of the job—favor legalization and regulation, as opposed to outright prohibition.[29]

In sum, although there may certainly be harms associated with sex work that are different to and/or worse than the harms that are associated with other forms of work, *simply* referring to those harms without showing how they are unique, uniquely bad, or would be reduced rather than exacerbated by a ban, is not enough to show that prohibition would be warranted.

4.2.3 The Third Flaw: Application of the Analogy Is Unpersuasive

Fortunately for Richardson, proving the badness of prostitution may not be essential to her argument. All the CASR really needs to show is that sexbot-human relationships will have bad-making properties that may be similar to (or intensified versions of) the supposed bad-making properties of sex worker-client relations. If she can show this, then the possible disanalogies between the two scenarios may not undermine the case for organized opposition to the development of sex robots. Indeed, it may be that these disanalogies *support* opposition to sex robots.

One obvious disanalogy between the two cases is that sex workers are persons and hence of high moral status; whereas sex robots are unlikely to be persons, at least for the foreseeable future. This disanalogy can cut both ways. On the one hand, it suggests that sex robots cannot be moral victims, and hence we need not be concerned about their treatment at the hands of their users; on the other hand, the fact that they are not moral victims means that we don't need to worry about the negative impact of restrictive and prohibitive policies on their well-being (as we do with human sex workers). This may cause us to favor an organized campaign against their development, particularly if we think that (a) the harms arising from their use could carry over to real human victims (through normalizing problematic attitudes or norms of behavior), and (b) the putative benefits of their use are minimal.

This raises an important interpretive question about the intention behind Richardson's analogy with sex work. Is her claim that, just as the treatment of and attitudes toward prostitutes is bad, so too will be the treatment of and attitudes toward sex robots? Or is it that the development of sex robots will increase the demand for human sex workers and/or encourage users of sex robots to treat real human (females) as objects? Richardson's paper supports the latter interpretation. At the outset, she states that her concern about sex robots is that they:

legitimate a dangerous mode of existence where humans can move about in relations with other humans but not recognise them as human subjects in their own right.[30]

The key phrase here seems to be "in relations with other humans," suggesting that the worry is about how we end up treating one another, not how we treat the robots themselves. This is supported in the conclusion where she states:

In this paper I have tried to show the explicit connections between prostitution and the development and imagination of human-sex robot relations. I propose that extending relations of prostitution into machines is neither ethical, nor is it safe. If anything the development of sex robots will further reinforce relations of power that do not recognise both parties as human subjects.[31]

Again, the emphasis in this quote seems to be on how the development of sex robots will affect interhuman relationships, not robot-human relations. Let us reflect this in a modified version of premise (2):

(2*) Sex robots will add to and reinforce the bad-making consequences of sex work (i.e., they will encourage us to treat other humans with a lack of empathy and thereby exacerbate existing, harmful gender/power inequalities).

Richardson supports this premise by focusing on the work of David Levy (2007), who draws explicit parallels between the development of sex robots and sex work. Levy's suggestion is that the relationship between a user and his/her sex robot can be akin to the relationship between a client and a sex worker. Levy is quite explicit about this and spends a good portion of his book looking at the motivations of those who purchase sex and how those motivations might transfer onto sex robots. Interestingly, Levy is far more nuanced in his discussion of this literature than Richardson is inclined to be, highlighting some of the complexity in the motivations of clients and also including a discussion of female clients of male sex workers (a perspective that is entirely absent from Richardson's analysis). In any event, the inference Richardson draws from Levy's work is that the development of sex robots is proceeding along the lines that Levy imagines, and, hence, we should be concerned about its potential to reinforce the bad effects of sex work.

Richardson identifies two major criticisms of her claim. The first, mentioned above, holds that if robots are not persons, then there is nothing wrong with treating them as objects/things that we can use for our own pleasure. In other words, the technology is a morally neutral domain in which we can act out our fantasies. The second criticism points to the potentially cathartic effect of these technologies. If people act out negative or violent sexual fantasies on a robot, they might be less inclined to do so to a real human being. This suggests that sex robots may actually help to *prevent* the bad things that Richardson worries about. This possibility is explored in more detail in other chapters in this book (see chapters from McArthur, Strikwerda, and Danaher).

Richardson has responses to both of these criticisms. She argues that technology is not a value-neutral domain. Our culture and our norms are reflected in our technology. We should be worried about how cultural meaning gets incorporated therein. Furthermore, she has serious doubts about the catharsis argument. She points to the historical relationship between pornography and sex work. Pornography has now become widely available, but this has not led to a corresponding decline in sex work, nor, in the case of child pornography, abuse of real children. On the contrary, sex work actually appears to have increased while pornography has increased. The same appears to be true of the relationship between sex toys/dolls and sex work:

The arguments that sex robots will provide artificial sexual substitutes and reduce the purchase of sex by buyers is not borne out by evidence. There are numerous sexual artificial substitutes already available, RealDolls, vibrators, blow-up dolls, etc. If an artificial substitute reduced the need to buy sex, there would be a reduction in prostitution, but no such correlation is found.[32]

Is this a robust defense of the bad consequences of sexbot-human relations? Is there enough here to warrant an organized campaign against their development?

We have some doubts. The evidence adduced to show that sex robots will exacerbate harmful interhuman relationships is weak, and, even if it is correct, it does not support a strongly restrictive approach to the development of sex robots. At best, it supports a regulative approach (see analysis above). Furthermore, if we were to adopt such a regulative approach, we would need to be sensitive to both the merits and demerits of this technology and the costs of any proposed regulatory strategy. This is something that Richardson neglects because she focuses entirely on the negative. In this vein, we offer four responses to her argument, some of which undermine her support of premise (2*), others of which question the relationship between any putative bad-making properties of sex robots and the need for an organized "campaign" against them.

First, Richardson's primary support for premise (2*)—namely, that the prostitute-john relationship is reflected in the model of sex robot development used by David Levy—is weak. We have already noted that Levy is more sensitive to the complexity of sex worker-client relations than Richardson is. But even if he weren't, the argument would not be very strong. True, Levy is a pioneer in this field and has a degree of influence, but that doesn't mean that all sex robot developers are obliged to adopt his model. And if we are worried about the relationship between the sex robot user and the robot, we can try to introduce standards and regulations that reflect a more positive set of sexual norms. For instance, the makers of Roxxxy (billed as the world's first sex robot) claim to include a personality setting called "Frigid Farah" with their robot.[33] Farah will demonstrate some reluctance to the user's sexual advances. One could argue that this reflects a troubling view of sexual consent: that resistance is not taken seriously (i.e., that "no" doesn't really mean "no"). Does this mean that one should oppose the development of sex robots *tout court*? Not necessarily. Instead, one could address the problem by regulating against this kind of personality setting and insisting that every sex robot is required to give positive, affirmative signals of consent. Although there are numerous problems that might be raised by the prospect of an ever-willing (robot) sexual partner,[34] such an approach would at least plausibly reflect and reinforce a more desirable attitude toward sexual consent. We need not settle that example to make the broader point: namely, that it is far from clear that there is anything inherent in the nature of sex robots, *qua* sex robots, that would entail the promotion of negative social attitudes toward women and sexual consent. We could demand and enforce specific design regulations that would promote a more positive set of attitudes. Maybe this is all Richardson really wants her campaign to achieve. But in that case, she is not really campaigning against the development of sex robots; she is rather campaigning for a better version of them. If so, she could rename her campaign "The Campaign for Positive Sex Robots," which changes the framing of the debate considerably.

Second, we think it is difficult to make definitive claims about the likely link between the use of a future technology, like sex robots, and actions toward real human beings. Richardson's claims about the correlation between pornography and an increase in sex work will be relatively unpersuasive to someone who does not think that either pornography or sex work is unremittingly bad. What would be more persuasive is if she could prove that there was some correlation (and ultimately some causal link) between the increase in pornography/prostitution and the *mistreatment* of sex workers. The evidence on this seems to be mixed. The legalization of sex work is sometimes associated with a decrease in mistreatment, and the related link between pornography and sexual violence more generally is deeply contested. Some studies show an increase;[35] some show a decrease;[36] and some are mixed or uncertain.[37] Danaher (this volume) speculates that we may be landed in a similarly ambiguous position when it comes to evidence concerning a link between sex robot usage and real-world sexual aggression. Or, conversely, sex robots may be sufficiently different from pornography as to increase the real-world effect. But in which direction is unclear: it may embolden or satiate.[38] It is simply too early and too difficult to tell. A precautionary approach does not imply a ban as the first step taken, but rather a need for more research and close observation.[39]

Third, and perhaps most importantly, when thinking about the appropriate policy toward sex robots, or any new prospective technology, it is important that we weigh the good against the bad. As two of us have argued previously (in the context of a debate about "love drugs"):

> ... when discussing the possible hazards associated with some predicted future development—one has to remember that any new technology poses risks. This is true whether it is an anti-love pill, a powerful military weapon, or something more mundane. Hence the mere possibility that such a technology might be used for ill can never by itself constitute sufficient reason to reject it— however alarming such a possibility may be. Instead, the potential harms that might accrue from the misuse of the technology must be weighed against the potential benefits that might accrue from its responsible use.[40]

In addition, as Bostrom and Roache have argued,[41] even the careful anticipation of possible benefits and harms is not sufficient to give a full analysis of the prudence of developing some new technology. These efforts must be complemented with a meaningful attempt to identify "potential supporting policies and practices that can alter the balance for the better."[42] As philosopher C. A. J. Coady has stated:

> If indeed there is insufficient knowledge of outcomes and consequences, or no social or institutional regulatory regime for prudent implementation of the innovations and for continuing scrutiny of their effects, or no room for overview of the commercial exploitation of the innovations, then ... critics [of new technologies] clearly have a point. [But] warnings can be heeded. [We can] insist on safeguards and regulation, both scientific and ethical.[43]

In the case of sex robots, specifically, there are several potentially good-making properties that would need to be factored into the discussion.[44] For example, there is the simple hedonistic argument: sex robots provide people with a way of achieving pleasurable states of consciousness. Whether this is a good argument or not, or whether increasing hedonistic states should count for very much when taken into consideration with other factors, is a complex question; but at the very least, it needs to be engaged with in a serious way when evaluating the likely value or disvalue for society of developing sex robots. Similarly, there is the distributive argument: for whatever reason, there are people in the world today who lack access to certain types of sexual experience, including people with certain kinds of disabilities,[45] and sex robots could make those experiences (or, at least, meaningful approximations of them) available to such people. There is also the argument that sex robots could ameliorate imbalances in sex drive between the partners in existing relationships,[46] or could add a desired kind of diversity to the sex lives of such couples, without involving human third parties (and the potential interpersonal strife to which those third parties could give rise). It could also be the case that sex robots would allow for particular forms of sexual self-expression and identity to flourish[47] including a pure sexual preference for machine-sex.[48] If that turned out to be the case, then, in the interests of basic sexual freedom and diversity, we should permit it. This is by no means an exhaustive list of positive potential attributes. It simply highlights the fact that there may be much good to the technology, and this must be weighed against any putative negative features when determining the appropriate policy. Few new technologies are unalloyed goods; trade-offs must be carefully considered. Fourth, and finally, when thinking about the appropriate regulative policy one also needs to think about the potential costs, both monetary and non-monetary, of that policy. We might agree that there are certain bad-making properties arising from human-sex robot relations, but it could be that any proposed regulatory intervention would do more harm than good overall. Regulation of pornography, for instance, has historically involved greater restrictions toward pornography depicting sexual minorities (e.g., gay and lesbian porn).[49] Regulatory intervention into sex robots may end up doing the same, targeting robots used and designed by sexual minorities. It may also be the case that policing the development and use of sex robots would require significant resources and extensive intrusions into our private lives. Are we willing to bear these costs? Less intrusive regulatory policies—e.g., ones that simply encourage manufacturers to avoid problematic stereotypes or norms in the construction of sex robots—would arguably be much more tolerable. Again, that may be all that Richardson wants. But if that is the case, the campaign she is leading needs to be much clearer about its aims.

4.2.4 Interim Conclusion

An interim summary is in order. The CASR's primary argument against the development of sex robots turns on an analogy between sex robot-human relations and sex worker-client relations. The fear is that the former will reinforce the bad-making properties of the latter. We find that this analogy does not support organized opposition to the development of sex robots, much less a full-fledged ban. The analogy is premised on an overly negative view of sex work and the associated need for its prohibition; its application to the sex robots scenario is weak and speculative; and it also ignores the potential good-making properties of sex robots as well as the costs of organized opposition. At most, we may have a basis for regulation of sex robot development; but this seems to fall far short of the current rhetorical demands of the campaign.

4.3 Should We Ever Campaign Against Sex Robots?

The arguments of the CASR may be unpersuasive, but it is still worth asking the broader question that their campaign might be seen to provoke: should we *ever* campaign against a technology of this sort? This is a question of considerable social importance. Artificial intelligence (AI) and robotics are on the rise. We can expect more and more robots to enter into daily social use, including in ethically loaded cases.[50] Perhaps there are legitimate grounds on which we can oppose the development of some of them. What is more, perhaps these grounds could apply to the case of sex robots.

In this section, we address these issues by considering the arguments against the development of fully autonomous weapons systems (AWSs), or "killer robots." Since the CASR is modeled after the *Campaign to Stop Killer Robots*, this seems an obvious place to start. For context, AWSs are robotic systems that operate independently of their human creators, administering lethal force to enemy targets. There has been considerable social and academic opposition to the development of such robots, going beyond even the campaign just mentioned. For example, there is the Future of Life Institute's (FLI's) open letter on autonomous weapons systems, which is strongly critical of the development of such technology.[51] Many people are persuaded that AWSs simply should not be allowed to exist, and that a preemptive ban on their development is in order. If arguments to that effect are indeed successful, they might also apply to the case of sex robots in ways that have not yet been raised in our discussion of the CASR.

In what follows, then, we survey some of the leading objections to the development of AWSs, treating the issue largely on its own terms. After taking the time to do so, we then return to the issue of sex robots, and conclude the chapter by reflecting on some of the key lessons from this "killer robot" analysis for the debate over the CASR.

4.3.1 Arguments Opposing the Development of AWSs

There are three main families of argument against the development of AWSs. The first is pragmatically oriented and is concerned with the *consequences* of deploying AWSs in lieu of human soldiers. Proponents of this objection are concerned with the practical limitations of the current and prospective technologies. For instance, they worry about the targeting systems of AWSs and their ability to adapt to dynamic battlefield conditions, in particular their ability to make fine-grained and context-sensitive distinctions between who is and is not an enemy combatant.[52] The fear is that AWSs will be more indiscriminate in their administration of lethal force than human operators would be, and hence responsible for worse outcomes. In making this argument, then, distinctions need to be drawn between AWSs, which operate entirely independently of human controllers, and teleoperated unmanned weapons systems, which are still under remote human control. One can favor the latter on the ground that their use poses less risk to human soldiers,[53] while still opposing the former.[54]

These pragmatically oriented objections are important, and certainly fears about targeting systems and battlefield adaptability will need to be addressed. But the general utility of such objections is limited. As the underlying technology improves, the consequentialist fears dissipate.

The second family of arguments is concerned with the need for moral agency and responsibility in warfare. They can be grouped under the general heading of "responsibility gap" arguments. The most widely discussed example comes from Robert Sparrow.[55] The gist of his argument is that the actions within a just war must be carried out by, or ultimately be capable of being traced to, the decisions of a responsible moral agent.[56] Humans are capable of being responsible moral agents. AWSs are not. They lack the capacity for responsible agency and will always lack this capacity. Hence, their use in a theater of war opens up a responsibility gap: lethal force is used, but no one is ultimately responsible for its use.

Even if we grant the moral premise of this argument, we are still owed some account of why it is that AWSs lack the capacity for responsible moral agency. Purves, Jenkins, and Strawser present two such accounts.[57] The first focuses on the *codifiability* of moral judgment. It maintains that AWSs will only be capable of exercising moral judgment if moral judgment is capable of codification. AWSs will have to be programmed, and this programming will depend on well-defined rulesets that identify the key moral requirements the AWSs will need to follow. These rulesets will then have to be reduced to a computer language.[58]

The problem here is that several leading normative theories claim that moral judgment is ultimately not codifiable in this manner. Seemingly robust moral principles admit an indefinite number of exceptions that cannot be anticipated in advance by human programmers; and some moral theorists claim that moral judgment is always *particularized*.[59] Accordingly, Purves, Jenkins, and Strawser's second account of why AWSs lack appropriate moral agency focuses on other mental constituents of responsibility. Following the views of leading just war theorists, this second argument claims that actors within a war are not simply required to act in conformity with sound moral judgment; they must also act for the *right moral reasons*. In defending this view, Purves et al. use the example of a racist soldier, who kills the right enemy combatants but for the wrong reasons.[60] They argue that the deployment of such a soldier would be wrong. The problem for AWSs is that they will be incapable of acting for moral reasons. This claim builds upon objections to strong AI (the view that you can create an artificial being with human-equivalent mental faculties). The leading accounts of what it means to act for a reason require a sophisticated internal mental architecture that AWSs will lack for the foreseeable future. Hence, they cannot act for moral reasons, and so their deployment in a theater of war is contrary to the requirements of just war theory.

Both of these defenses of the responsibility-gap argument can be challenged. They rest on controversial metaphysical claims about the nature of mind and morality, as well as the prospects for strong AI. Furthermore—as the authors themselves acknowledge—important trade-offs would arise if the robots achieved better battlefield outcomes than human soldiers *even while* failing to meet the requirements for moral responsibility. Others have used this possibility to develop defenses of the use of AWSs.[61] Nevertheless, if the premises are sound, the arguments presented here provide strong moral reasons to object to the use of AWSs that are not contingent on the current state of the technology.

The final family of objections to AWSs focuses on the directness of the harm they can potentially cause. This is perhaps the most significant consideration when it comes to the merits of an organized campaign against their development. One thing that all participants to the debate about AWSs can agree upon is the *prima facie* wrongness of killing. In other words, everyone accepts that it is only permissible to kill a human being in a limited range of circumstances. Killing someone when these circumstances do not apply is a grave moral wrong. And even when the circumstances do apply it is still bad *for* the (involuntary) victim. A key property of AWSs is that their entire *raison d'etre* is to exert lethal force against enemy targets. In other words, they are directly designed to do something that everyone agrees is a *prima facie* moral wrong or a deeply regrettable outcome. The hope is that they will become sophisticated enough to recognize when the circumstances that permit killing do in fact arise. But there is always the risk that they will misjudge or miscalculate and do something that is a serious moral wrong, or even enable moral wrongs on an unprecedented scale (for example, enabling totalitarian states to harm or coerce citizens with no possibility of soldiers' consciences stopping them). This is one reason why a preemptive campaign against the development of this particular kind of robot seems so compelling: if the campaign succeeds, it can *directly* prevent a *prima facie* wrong.

Now, some people object to this line of reasoning. They argue that the alleged advantages of the preemptive ban are more illusory than real. AWSs are likely to be developed by unscrupulous people, they claim, whether we try to prevent this occurrence or not. A ban, they argue, would merely prevent research into making them as ethical as is reasonably achievable. A related argument is that counterfactual assessment of what would happen in the *absence* of AWSs is also important. Humans are probably going to use lethal force against each other anyway, just as they always have. The advantage of AWSs, then, if they could be made sufficiently technologically sophisticated, is that they could be more selective and less destructive than human actors. But this line of thinking, too, can be challenged. One obvious concern about the introduction of AWSs is that they can lower the threshold for launching lethal attacks: if no human soldiers will be harmed in the process, a commanding officer may be more likely to issue a command.

4.3.2   Lessons for the *Campaign Against Sex Robots*

Now that we have some idea of the debate concerning AWSs, we should reflect on the implications of that debate for the CASR. Some of the arguments we have just surveyed seem relevant to the case of sex robots; others, less so. We proffer no final judgment on the merits of the campaign against AWSs here (although we note that one of us, Sandberg, has signed the FLI's open letter against their development; see above); instead, we simply wish to consider the lessons of that campaign for our primary topic. To do this, we shall assume, *arguendo*, that at least one of the preceding arguments reaches the threshold needed to warrant an organized and systematic campaign against the development of killer robots. Do similar considerations apply to the development of sex robots? We think not.

First, there are no equivalent *practical* concerns when it comes to the development of sex robots. The practical fears surrounding AWSs come from the fact that they are intended to do harm and that inadequate programming or technical sophistication could lead to the wrong kind (or degree) of harm. Sex robots, by contrast, are not directly intended to cause harm; in fact, the opposite is true—they are intended to cause pleasure. Certainly the robots could malfunction and these malfunctions could give rise to health risks; or the robots could be used in dangerous, perhaps unsanitary, ways. But these practical concerns seem comparatively minor, to the point that they would not warrant preemptive organized opposition to the mere development of the robots in question. At most, they would warrant the creation of appropriate industry standards, as well as comprehensive user safety guidelines. Now, it could be argued that the pleasure-inducing effects of sex robots could also be addictive, and therefore a source of harm for those who become addicted to using them (along with their families and friends). This is a more serious concern—but the potential harm is indirect and speculative. Thus, we defer to our third response, which we will come to shortly.

Second, there is no equivalent need for moral agency and responsibility in the design of sex robots. Again, the opposite would appear to be true. The need for moral agency in the case of military robots stems from the morally fraught nature of their actions and the need for moral accountability in warfare. But we don't need sex robots to be morally accountable. Indeed, turning sex robots into moral agents would probably add to, rather than mitigate, ethical problems surrounding their use. For instance, one of the putative benefits of sex robots (discussed by McArthur and Di Nucci in this volume) is that they can facilitate positive sexual autonomy without interfering with another person's negative sexual autonomy. If the robot is a moral agent, then this putative benefit could disappear. The robot would have to be given the same moral standing as any other moral agent. Their consent to a sexual act would become a serious issue, and the propriety of their use for sexual pleasure could no longer be taken for granted.[62] This doesn't seem like a suitable ground on which to favor organized opposition to their development.

Third, and perhaps most importantly, there are no equivalent direct moral harms that could be prevented by the campaign against sex robots. The harm from AWSs is direct and irreversible; the alleged harms from sex robots are speculative, indirect, and, in principle, reversible. The argument from the CASR focuses on how the use of sex robots would impact real women (both those who work in the sex industry and those who do not). The fear is that individual use of sex robots will distort the user's downstream interactions with real human beings and contribute to existing social problems arising from systematic inequality and oppression of women. These are certainly legitimate ethical concerns, and we agree that society should work hard to reduce systemic inequality, invidious sexual objectification,[63] and the harmful erosion of empathy. But those problems stem from individual choices and social institutions, not from the sex robots themselves. As one of us has previously put it:

> ... even if one bought the arguments that sex robots are likely to induce bad social changes, these changes are occurring because of individual decisions and beliefs, as well as sociocultural institutions. There are many other levers that could be pulled to improve the situation of sex workers, women, or people's attitudes to each other. Some of these levers may be far more powerful than a technology ban. Conversely, even a successful ban of sex robots may fail to reach the desired goal because of *other* technologies or intermediaries causing the undesired social changes. By acting against a possible contributor rather than the bad thing itself, effort is wasted.[64]

In our view, this is the crucial difference with the campaign against killer robots. By stopping killer robots, you directly prevent a *prima facie* moral wrong. By stopping sex robots, however, you do not.[65]

Direct harm arguments against sex robots are possible to make, but they are of a very different kind from the ones used by the CASR. They would hold that there exist *inherent* bad-making properties of human-robot sex that produce a direct—but possibly victimless—moral harm. Arguments in this vein might fault human-robot sex for being nonreproductive, for example, or for being a kind of interspecies sex (assumed to be intrinsically wrong); for lacking essential relationship properties that should exist during any sexual act (perhaps masturbation would be seen as wrong on this view as well); or for being an immoral form of hedonism. Proponents of this view could then argue that this direct and intrinsic (albeit, again, potentially victimless) moral harm could be prevented from materializing if we were to preemptively ban sex robots, just as preventing killer robots prevents a new moral harm.

Are such arguments convincing? To some people, they may be. However, they appear to hinge on a peculiarly conservative and vice-related view of sex that is unlikely to hold sway in many pluralistic societies. Thus, while certain individuals may feel motivated to refrain from using sex robots (should they become available) on the basis of these perceived direct moral harms, they would need to convince large swaths of the population of their conservative view in order to justify a sweeping change to policy. By contrast, AWSs are only legitimately going to be used by the state, rather than by individual persons, for societal goals rather than personal goals. That makes the rest of society proper moral stakeholders in decisions about their use and development (since the state should represent and act in their interest), and they are to some extent responsible for what it does. That is not the case with the personal use of sex robots, however, as the bedroom door insulates against most would-be stakeholders.

Thus, while one can easily imagine social conservatives and vice-oriented moralists supporting the CASR because of shared opposition to sex robots, they would be doing so on the basis of a fundamentally different sort of moral claim—that there is something *inherently* bad about human-robot sex—that would fit uneasily with the stated ethics of the CASR's leading proponents.

4.4   Conclusion

Robots are going to form an increasingly integral part of human social life. Sex robots are likely to be among them. Though the proponents of the CASR seem deeply concerned by this prospect, we have argued that there is nothing in the nature of sex robots themselves that warrants preemptive opposition to their development. The arguments of the campaign itself are vague and premised on a misleading analogy between sex robots and human sex work. Furthermore, drawing upon the example of the *Campaign to Stop Killer Robots*, we suggested that there are no bad-making properties of sex robots that give rise to similarly serious levels of concern. The bad-making properties of sex robots are speculative and indirect: preventing their development may not prevent the problems from arising. Preventing the development of killer robots is very different: if you stop the robots, you stop the *prima facie* harm.

In conclusion, we should preemptively campaign against robots when we have reason to think that a moral or practical harm caused by their use can best be avoided or reduced as a result of those efforts. By contrast, to engage in such a campaign as a way of fighting against—or preempting—indirect harms, whose ultimate source is not the technology itself, but rather individual choices or broader social institutions, is likely to be a comparative waste of effort.

Notes

1. For all documentation and supporting materials relating to the campaign, see http://www .campaignagainstsexrobots.com.

2. Text taken from the CASR's "About" page: https://campaignagainstsexrobots.org/about.

3. Text taken from the CASR's "About" page: https://campaignagainstsexrobots.org/about.

4. For a sample of the media coverage, see the "Press" page on the CASR website.

5. David Levy, *Love and Sex with Robots: The Evolution of Human-Robot Relationships* (New York: HarperCollins, 2007).

6. Here we follow the definitions of sex robot and having sex with a robot presented in earlier chapters by McArthur, Danaher, and Migotti and Wyatt.

7. Kathleen Richardson, "The Asymmetrical 'Relationship': Parallels Between Prostitution and the Development of Sex Robots," published in the ACM Digital Library as a special issue of the ACM SIGCAS newsletter. *SIGCAS Computers & Society* 45, no. 3 (September 2005): 290–93, https:// campaignagainstsexrobots.org/the-asymmetrical-relationship-parallels-between-prostitution -and-the-development-of-sex-robots.

8. Richardson prefers "prostitute-john" to "sex worker-client" because it is more negatively value-laden. She disapproves of some attempts to create a positive impression of sex work.

9. The actual title of Levy's book is *Love and Sex with Robots*.

10. Richardson, "The Asymmetrical 'Relationship,'" 290.

11. The campaign's website states that: "A comprehensive, preemptive prohibition on fully autonomous weapons is urgently needed." See http://www.stopkillerrobots.org/learn.

12. John Danaher, "Robotic Rape and Robotic Child Sexual Abuse: Should They Be Criminalized?" *Criminal Law and Philosophy*, in press, doi: 10.1007/s11572-014-9362-x.

13. Text taken from the CASR's "About" page: https://campaignagainstsexrobots.org/about.

14. Although, in saying this, we would need to know whether Richardson thinks that this is possible. Some of her comments suggest that it wouldn't be because robots could never meet the criteria for personhood. See Richardson (2015).

15. Marie Boran, "Sex Robots Should Be Banned, Expert Tells Web Summit," *The Irish Times*, November 4, 2015, http://www.irishtimes.com/business/technology/sex-robots-should -be-banned-expert-tells-web-summit-1.2416948.

16. Nicholas Shackel, "The Vacuity of Postmodernist Methodology," *Metaphilosophy* 36, no. 3 (April 2005): 295–320.

17. The qualification "seems to make" needs to be added because Richardson is never that clear about her argument.

18. Ole M. Moen, "Is Prostitution Harmful?," *Journal of Medical Ethics* 40, no. 2 (2014): 73–81.

19. Obviously, there are some sex workers providing services to women, but they are ignored in Richardson's argument. This is not uncommon in the literature about the ethics of sex work.

20. Melissa Farley, Julie Bindel, and Jacqueline M. Golding, *Men Who Buy Sex: Who They Buy and What They Know* (London: Eaves, 2009).

21. Simon Baron-Cohen, *Zero Degrees of Empathy: A New Theory of Human Cruelty and Kindness* (London: Penguin, 2011).

22. Teela Sanders, Maggie O'Neill, and Jane Pitcher, *Prostitution: Sex Work, Policy and Politics* (London: Sage, 2009).

23. Ibid., 44.

24. Ibid., 83.

25. Ibid., 84.

26. Brian D. Earp and Ole Martin Moen, "Paying for Sex—Only for People with Disabilities?" *Journal of Medical Ethics* 42, no. 10 (2016): 54–56, doi:10.1136/medethics-2015-103064.

27. Luke Semrau, "The Best Argument Against Kidney Sales Fails," *Journal of Medical Ethics* 41, no. 6 (2015): 443–446.

28. Earp and Moen, "Paying for Sex," 55.

29. For further discussion, see Catherine Murphy, "Sex Workers' Rights are Human Rights," *Amnesty International*, August 14, 2015, https://www.amnesty.org/en/latest/news/2015/08/sex -workers-rights-are-human-rights/.

30. Kathleen Richardson, "The Asymmetrical 'Relationship': Parallels Between Prostitution and the Development of Sex Robots," Published in the ACM Digital Libraru as a special issue of the ACM SIGCAS newsletter. SIGCAS Computers & Society 45, no. 3 (September 2015): 290–93, https://campaignagainstsexrobots.org/the-asymmetrical-relationship-parallels-between -prostitution-and-the-development-of-sex-robots/.

31. Ibid., S.4.

32. Ibid.

33. The personality types are described on the FAQ page on the TrueCompanion website: http://www.truecompanion.com/shop/faq.

34. See Danaher, this volume, for a longer analysis.

35. See Neil M. Malamuth and James V. P. Check, "The Effects of Mass Media Exposure on Acceptance of Violence Against Women: A Field Experiment," *Journal of Research in Personality* 15, no. 4 (December 1981): 436–446; Dolf Zillman and Jennings Bryant, "Pornography, Sexual Callousness and the Trivialization of Rape," *Journal of Communication* 32 (1982): 10–21; Mike Allen, Tara Emmers, Lisa Gebhardt, and Mary A. Giery, "Exposure to Pornography and Acceptance of Rape Myths," *Communication* 45, no.1 (March 1995): 5–26.

36. Christopher J. Ferguson and Richard D. Hartley, "The Pleasure is Momentary ... the Expense Damnable? The Influence of Pornography on Rape and Sexual Assault," Aggression and Violent Behavior 14, no. 5 (September–October 2009): 323–29; Milton Diamond, "Pornography, Public Acceptance and Sex Related Crime: A Review," *International Journal of Law and Psychiatry* 32 (2009): 304–14.

37. Azy Barak and William A. Fisher, "Effects of Interactive Computer Erotica on Men's Attitudes and Behavior Toward Women: An Experimental Study," *Computers in Human Behaviour* 13, no. 3 (August 1997): 353–69; Azy Barak, William A. Fisher, Sandra Belfry, Darryl Lashambe, "Sex, Guys and Cyberspace: Effects of Internet Pornography and Individual Differences on Men's Attitude Toward Women, *Journal of Psychology and Human Sexuality* 11, no. 1 (1999): 63–91; Neil M. Malamuth, Tamara Addison, and Mary Koss, "Pornography and Sexual Aggression: Are There Reliable Effects and Can We Understand Them?," *Annual Review of Sex Research* 11, no. 1 (2000): 26–91; and Gert M. Hald, Neil M. Malamuth, and Theis Lange, "Pornography and Sexist Attitudes Among Heterosexuals," *Journal of Communication* 63, no. 4 (June 2013): 638–60.

38. Danaher, "Robotic Rape."

39. Brian D. Earp, Anders Sandberg, and Julian Savulescu, "The Medicalization of Love: Response to Critics," *Cambridge Quarterly of Healthcare Ethics* 25, no. 4, (2016): 759–771.

40. Brian D. Earp, Anders Sandberg, and Julian Savulescu, "Brave New Love: the Threat of High-Tech 'Conversion' Therapy and the Bio-Oppression of Sexual Minorities," *AJOB Neuroscience* 5, no. 1 (2014): 4–12, 7.

41. Nick Bostrom and Rebecca Roache, "Smart Policy: Cognitive Enhancement and the Public Interest, in *Enhancing Human Capacities*, eds. J. Savulecu, R. ter Meulen, and G. Kahane (Oxford: John Wiley & Sons, 2011), 138–152. The rest of this paragraph is adapted from Brian D. Earp, Anders Sandberg, and Julian Savulescu, "Brave New Love" in which the quote following this paragraph also appears.

42. Bostrom and Roache, "Smart Policy," 144.

43. C. A. J. Coady, "Playing God," in *Human Enhancement*, eds. J. Savulescu, and N. Bostrom (Oxford: Oxford University Press, 2009), 155–180, 165; emphasis added.

44. McArthur, Di Nucci in this volume.

45. See Di Nucci in this volume; also see Earp and Moen, "Paying for Sex" (2015).

46. McArthur in this volume.

47. See general Kristina Gupta, "Protecting Sexual Diversity: Rethinking the Use of Neurotechnological Interventions to Alter Sexuality," *AJOB Neuroscience* 3, no. 3 (2012): 24–28.

48. For a longer, more critical discussion of this subject, see Michael Hauskeller, *Sex and the Posthuman Condition* (London: Palgrave-Macmillan, 2014).

49. A famous example is the Canadian legal case of R. v. Butler in which the Canadian Supreme Court proposed a new test for banning materials on the basis of obscenity. In the aftermath of this decision, mainstream pornography continued to flourish while pornography catering to minority sexualities was suppressed. For an extended analysis, see Brenda Crossman, Shannon Bell, Lise Gotell, and Becki L. Ross, *Bad Attitudes on Trial: Pornography, Feminism and the Butler Decision.* (Toronto: University of Toronto Press, 1997).

50. Examples could include autonomous cars that have to make life and death decisions about whether to swerve to avoid an impact with a pedestrian or not; or the darknet shopper, which is an automated shopping robot that randomly selects items from the deep web for purchase. Given the nature of the deep web these can include illegal drugs and firearms. For a description see: http://www.independent.co.uk/life-style/gadgets-and-tech/news/random-darknet-shopper -exhibition-featuring-automated-dark-web-purchases-opens-in-london-a6770316.html.

51. This was signed by a number leading scientists, ethicists, and robotics researchers. See http:// futureoflife.org/open-letter-autonomous-weapons.

52. Marcello Guarini and Paul Bello, "Robotic Warfare: Some Challenges in Moving from Noncivilian to Civilian Theaters," in *Robot Ethics: The Ethical and Social Implications of Robotics*, eds. Patrick Lin, Keith Abney, and George Bekey (Cambridge, MA: MIT Press, 2012).

53. Bradley Strawser, "Moral Predators: The Duty to Employ Unmanned Aerial Vehicles," *Journal of Military Ethics* 9, no. 4 (2010): 342–68.

54. For example, see Duncan Purves, Ryan Jenkins, and Bradley J. Strawser, "Autonomous Machines, Moral Judgment, and Acting for the Right Reasons," *Ethical Theory and Moral Practice* 18, no. 4 (2015): 851–72.

55. Robert Sparrow, "Killer Robots," *Journal of Applied Philosophy* 24, no. 1 (2007): 62–77.

56. The argument appeals directly to the requirements of just war theory. There is some dispute as to *jus in bello* (i.e., the justice of actions in a war) and *jus ad bellum* (i.e., the justice of the decision to go to war) requirements and whether they offer a way around the responsibility gap

argument. Purves, Jenkis, and Strawser (2015) argue that this distinction should make no difference, and, for the purposes of this discussion, we concur.

57. Purves, Jenkins, and Strawser, "Autonomous Machines," 2015.

58. There may be ways to create an AI that avoid codifiability. Machine learning techniques show some promise in this respect. Machines can be given examples of moral and immoral behavior and then extrapolate to new cases. They can sometimes learn subtle exceptions, but the problem with machine learning is that it tends to be opaque. We will not know whether an AI device has figured out an important exception until we place it in that situation: we cannot just assume that it has from proper behavior in the training cases, and seeing proper behavior in other test cases merely gives us inductive reasons to think it will behave appropriately in real-world situations. If the exception is of a different *type* than the other test cases, then we have no real reason to trust the system.

59. Jonathan Dancy, "Moral Particularism," in *The Stanford Encyclopedia of Philosophy*, ed. E. Zalta (Stanford: Stanford University Press, 2013), http://plato.stanford.edu/entries/moral-particularism.

60. Purves, Jenkins and Strawser, "Autonomous Machines," 860.

61. It is worth noting that, in these papers, Muller and Simpson develop a position that is similar to the one advocated in the present chapter, namely: there are bad-making properties of AWSs that could warrant regulation and intervention, but not a preemptive campaign against their creation.

62. For example, see Vincent Muller and Thomas Simpson, "Autonomous Killer Robots are Probably Good News," in *Drones and Responsibility: Legal, Philosophical and Socio-Technical Perspectives on the Use of Remotely Controlled Weapons*, eds. Ezio Di Nucci and Filippo Santoni De Sio (London: Ashgate, 2016). A possible argument might be that if a person knew that nobody would be harmed by having sex of some (inherently) problematic kind, they might do it more often. Sex that is problematic because of harm to partners would now be unproblematic; but if there is an inherent harm (as per the conservative argument) or indirect bad effects (closer to Richardson's view), then there is now more harm overall due to the actions of these people. However, this would be overshadowed by the different actions of other people: moral people who abstain from problematic sex because it is morally problematic are likely a far smaller group in most cases than people who abstain from it simply because it is hard to find partners.

63. See the contribution from Petersen in this volume.

64. See Patricia Marino, "The Ethics of Sexual Objectification: Autonomy and Consent," *Inquiry* 51, no. 4 (2008): 345–64.

65. Anders Sandberg, "Sex and Death Among the Robots: When Should We Campaign to Ban Robots?," *Practical Ethics Blog*, September 16, 2015, https://bioethics.georgetown.edu/2015/09/sex-and-death-among-the-robots-when-should-we-campaign-to-ban-robots.

5   Sex Robots and the Rights of the Disabled

Ezio Di Nucci

In this chapter, I propose to argue that the right to sexual satisfaction of severely physically and mentally disabled people, and elderly people who suffer from neurodegenerative diseases such as Alzheimer's disease, can be potentially fulfilled by deploying sex robots. This would enable us to satisfy the sexual needs of many people who cannot provide for their own sexual satisfaction without at the same time violating anybody's right to sexual self-determination. I do not offer a full-blown moral justification of deploying sex robots in such cases, as not all morally relevant concerns can be addressed here; rather, I put forward a plausible way of fulfilling acute sexual needs without violating anybody's sexual rights.

5.1   Sexual Rights

The following paragraph presents a puzzle inherent in the issue of sexual rights I once posed in the *Journal of Medical Ethics*: "Universal positive sexual rights are incompatible with universal negative sexual rights. If A has a positive sexual right, then that means that there is at least one person who would lack negative sexual rights. Namely: the person who would be supposed to fulfill A's positive sexual rights. If everybody has negative sexual rights, then everybody has the right to refuse to fulfill A's sexual needs, but then A has no positive right to sexual pleasure."[1]

I take the above to be true. Does it follow that there are no positive sexual rights? I think that this would be bad: even though negative sexual rights—such as the right to sexual self-determination: noninterference with one's sexual orientation or sexual practices—are important, it is far from clear that negative sexual rights alone can fulfill all human sexual needs. That is because many people need assistance in order for their sexual needs to be satisfied: the severely physically and mentally disabled, for example; but also the many elderly people who suffer from neurodegenerative diseases. For many of them, negative sexual rights won't do much good; what they need is help.[2]

The following letter from *The Observer* newspaper (April 6, 2003) offers a touching account of the kind of suffering connected to unfulfilled sexual needs:

As a single man who visits prostitutes, I object to being branded ... a sad creature who must pay for his thrills. Most clients of these patient, sympathetic, and compassionate ladies are, like me, disabled, elderly, disfigured, ugly, or socially or sexually inadequate. The prostitute provides the only opportunity for a brief, life-enhancing taste of physical affection. God bless her! [Name and address withheld][3]

One could possibly argue that help can be provided without appeal to positive sexual rights: one may acknowledge, for example, that the sexual needs of the severely physically and mentally disabled[4] are morally important and act upon that without having to necessarily acknowledge that their sexual needs amount to positive sexual rights. This is a simple point: upon hearing that my neighbor has just been laid off from work, I may decide to sell my car in order to help her financially. The idea is that I would acknowledge the moral importance of helping my neighbor get through a very difficult time and prioritize that over my own car. But that would obviously not necessarily imply that my neighbor has or had any right to my car or to the financial equivalent of my car.

To acknowledge the moral importance of the sexual needs of the severely physically and mentally disabled is, then, conceptually independent from accepting that they have positive sexual rights. Indeed, against sexual rights one may actually be able to provide an even stronger argument than the one that I have just offered for the case of selling my car in order to help my neighbor. Suppose that as a result of losing her job my neighbor will no longer have enough money to properly feed her children. One would have to admit that food should be considered something that—if there are rights and positive rights at all—is the appropriate object of rights. But with sex, one could even argue that, even though people may have a legitimate interest in sex and accept that sex is beneficial and thereby morally relevant, sex is just not important enough to be the object of rights.

The idea would be that we can't just have a right to anything that would improve our well-being: it could be argued that we have a right (against the state or other people, say) to receive some fundamental things (for example, food) that make a decisive difference to our well-being and survival, without having the right to receive other less fundamental things that make a non-decisive positive difference to our well-being: cars, smartphones, nice shoes, and the like would be obvious candidates for the less fundamental side of life.[5]

This point goes to the heart of the question about the value of sex. It is at least plausible to hold that sexual satisfaction is an important part of a fulfilled life: indeed, the fact that some people renounce it cannot imply that it is not important, and that's not because those people may be just wrong. Hunger strikes do not make food less important just as celibate priests do not make sex less important.[6] This is not the place to have an extended discussion about the value of sex and sexuality: the point is just that—given important benefits in terms of welfare, self-fulfilment and even mental health—it is at least not implausible to hold sex and sexuality to be, if not necessary, at least *important* elements in a fulfilled life such that their nonvoluntary absence from someone's life would be morally relevant.

This is important so I will elaborate a bit: It would be a shame if an unwanted side-effect of the sexual revolution and its separation of sex and reproduction were to be that sex is taken to be a commodity rather than something which is decisive to welfare and therefore morally relevant. Obviously there may be very valid reasons to limit or even prohibit some sexual relations, but that should not detract from the benefits of sex but rather just be seen as one of life's many trade-offs.

So sex is at least a candidate for membership of the set of things that are the appropriate objects of rights (if there are to be rights at all); but there is a more pressing point: that it would be good—morally good—to provide sexual satisfaction for the severely physically and mentally disabled does not imply that they have a right to it just as the fact that it would be good—morally good—to provide financial assistance to my neighbor does not imply that she has a right to it.

Once we accept that sex is a plausible object of rights, then we can easily show, through our food analogy, that we simply cannot generalize about the moral value of sexual satisfaction never amounting to rights claims: food is a very plausible, if not the most plausible, object of rights claims, but that does not mean that a person always has a right to be fed if she wants to; she also needs to be, in some relevant sense, needy (and the relevant sense of needy will also include a comparison with other needs and other people given limited resources or some such standards). Thus, although food is an appropriate object of rights, that does not mean that it is always the case that when it would be morally good to feed someone, then that person has a right to be fed. There will be times when my neighbor receiving food would be morally relevant or even morally good but not enough for her to be entitled to food—think of a simple invite to dinner, for example.

Moving back to sexual satisfaction, let us suppose we have accepted that sex too is an appropriate object of rights. Given that supposition, we can't just dismiss the talk of sexual rights by simply stipulating that always, when the need is of a sexual kind, we can at most say that it would be morally good to satisfy that need, but we can never say that the needy person is entitled to that satisfaction. If sexual satisfaction is a good enough object for rights talk, then we will have to at least allow for cases where, in principle, sexual need entitles the person to its satisfaction, just as we allow for cases where the need to be fed entitles the person to its satisfaction.

We see that we have already dealt with two arguments against sexual rights: that sexual satisfaction simply isn't an appropriate object for rights talk; and that sexual satisfaction never generates rights entitlements, even when it would be morally good to satisfy a sexual need.[7] We are now left with the problem with which we started: how can a person possibly be entitled to sexual satisfaction if that would imply that someone else would have a duty to satisfy the sexual needs of that person?

This issue has the well-known structure of a dilemma: if everyone is entitled to sexual satisfaction, then not everyone is entitled to freely choose her sexual orientation, practices, and partners. And if everyone is entitled to freely choose her sexual orientation, practices, and partners, then not everyone is entitled to sexual satisfaction: because some people are physically/mentally incapable of satisfying their own sexual needs and so others would have to help them out, these others would no longer be free to choose their sexual orientations and practices.

First, let me mention a formal objection to this dilemma that I think fails: in order to show a way out of the dilemma, someone may point to a possible world where, luckily enough, everyone freely choosing their sexual orientation, practices, and partners, happens to lead to satisfying the sexual needs of everybody. This world is very far from ours, but it is genuinely possible: we would just need a lot of luck (and maybe even more good will than luck!).

I do not think that this possible world shows a way out of the dilemma, though: and that's just because such a world would amount to everybody's sexual interests and needs being satisfied, but it would not amount to everybody being entitled to such satisfaction. This is a simple point: in general, that everybody's interests and needs are satisfied does not imply that everybody is entitled to the satisfaction of their interests and needs; and this is just because the former is an *is* statement, while the latter is an *ought* statement. If we were lucky enough to live in a world in which all people's sexual needs were met, then, we may not be as pressed to act on the issue of sexual needs as we are while living in our world, but we would be as pressed to establish whether there is such a thing as sexual rights as we are in our world.

5.2   How Could We Solve the Dilemma?

I am not here to offer a formal solution to the dilemma, because I think it is a genuine one – as in, both horns are problematic. However, I can do even better than a formal solution, because I think that there is a practical[8] solution to it: sex robots.[9] Before discussing what sex robots are and how they would offer a way out of the dilemma, let us build up to it by looking at ineffective ways of solving the dilemma.

First of all, masturbation will not do: this is just because we are talking about individuals with serious physical or cognitive problems, many of whom will either not be in a position to masturbate or will not be in a position to even understand the practice of masturbation. To put it brutally, if masturbation were the solution to the problem, then we wouldn't have had a problem in the first place because those people would also have been in a position to seek and interact with sexual partners.

Admittedly, one can imagine individuals who may, for whatever reason, not be in a position to seek and interact with sexual partners but who will be in a position to masturbate. I grant this point and am happy for those individuals: but obviously the issue is that we cannot assume that all of the severely physically and mentally disabled and the elderly with degenerative diseases will fall under this category.

So masturbation is out as a possible solution; but I would like to say something about what kind of solution masturbation would have been had it been an effective one. I take it that masturbation would have been a legitimate solution, namely, one that would have not interfered with the negative sexual rights of anybody (and obviously those who oppose masturbation—for example on religious grounds—do not have any rights entitlements about other people not masturbating) while at the same time providing some sexual satisfaction for the sexually needy.

Granted, one could try to argue that a life in which the only sexual satisfaction comes from masturbation is not as fulfilling as a life that involves more diversity in the forms of sexual interaction. But this is no argument against masturbation: some food is better than no food (and some kinds of food are also tastier than some other kinds)—just as some sexual satisfaction is better than no sexual satisfaction. Thus, emphasizing the limited nature of masturbation as a way of satisfying sexual needs does not in any way invalidate this as a possible solution to our dilemma: but, as we have seen, there are more practical problems with it.

Someone wanting to provide a principled argument against masturbation as a solution to the dilemma would have to put forward a much stronger and less plausible claim, namely, that masturbation is not sex and therefore the kind of satisfaction it can provide is not of a *sexual* nature. One may for example argue that sex necessarily involves two or more individuals or persons and that a practice that involves fewer than two individuals or persons is, however pleasant it may be, not a sexual practice. As it should be clear by now, what is at stake here is no longer just masturbation—since we have already argued that it would not solve the dilemma, it wouldn't be a problem for our argument if all that was at stake here was only masturbation. What is at stake here is, more importantly, what qualifies as sexual satisfaction, and, more generally, what qualifies as a sexual practice—and that is crucial to an argument about sex robots fulfilling sexual rights entitlements.

The question then is less whether masturbation is a form of sex and more whether sexual practices necessarily involve two or more individuals or persons. This question is crucial to our argument about robots since the only robots that we will consider are nonpersons; and this is because (obviously) robotic persons would pose the issue of whether their own negative rights to sexual self-determination would be violated by someone's positive right to sexual satisfaction.

First of all, I think that the burden of proof is on those who want to argue for a non-liberal view of what counts as sexual satisfaction or what counts as a sexual practice. On the face of it, nothing speaks against a liberal view of sexual satisfaction in particular and sexual practices in general that allows individuals to decide what they consider to be *sexual* satisfaction or a *sexual* practice. On what grounds are we going to deny the *sexual* nature of some odd fetish, for example?

Indeed, maybe such a liberal view of sex is the only account that does not violate negative rights to sexual self-determination: it is difficult to imagine that some authority wanting to enforce conceptual legislation on what should count as a sexual practice and what ought not to count as a sexual practice would not be in violation of sexual rights to self-determination, but I will not push this point any further since it is not essential to my argument.

Second, one can easily distinguish between pleasurable practices involving fewer than two persons that are related to traditional sexual practices (involving at least two persons) and pleasurable practices involving fewer than two persons that are not related to traditional sexual practices. For example, we can easily distinguish between masturbation on the one hand and reading Tolstoy on the other hand; and at least one obvious difference between these two different kinds of pleasurable practices is that only one of them, the former, is intrinsically related to traditional sexual practices. Again, this does not mean that we cannot distinguish between different sexual practices. However, we do not need to demostrate that much; all we need is to show that a practice can be of a sexual nature even if it involves fewer than two persons; while at the same time we can easily admit that, say, sexual practice A is better (whatever that means, more pleasant for example) than sexual practice B.

Third, one could object that a human person cannot have sex—in any meaningful sense anyway—with an animal nonperson[10]; and then quickly extend that argument to robotic nonpersons. I think this claim is ambiguous: it is plausible to say that we can never—in a truth-preserving way—describe a human person and an animal non-person as "having sex" (in the plural) as in "they are having sex": it may be that for that description to be true you need to have at least two self-conscious or autonomous individuals or persons (and maybe even more—maybe both must be conscious or willing or have consented or some such condition, more below; also, here see Migotti and Wyatt's chapter in this volume). But this does not mean that the only human person involved is not having a sexual experience that provides sexual satisfaction: the human person may not be "having sex" and still *her* experience may be a sexual one. Once we apply this point to robots, we can just say that since we are exclusively talking about robots (that do not qualify for personhood), the point about robots satisfying the sexual needs of humans is certainly not the sexual satisfaction of robots but only the sexual satisfaction of the humans involved, so that the above picture is enough for our purposes.

The above argument deals with a possible objection to sex robots as a solution to our dilemma, but actually it also opens up a possible problem that is potentially much more serious: we must be careful that we do not define sex so liberally so as to include rape in our definition of what counts as a sexual practice; and emphasizing that a mutual experience or interaction is not necessary for sexual satisfaction or for something to count as a sexual practice does run the risk of allowing rape to be considered a sexual practice. I think that this would be an unwelcome consequence of this account, but one that we can avoid in the following way: we cannot talk of rape in terms of "having sex" because one person is unwilling or has not consented. At the same time, we can admit that rape can generate sexual pleasure for the perpetrators: that is part of what makes rape particularly horrendous. Its sexual nature makes it worse, so that we can and should concede that it may constitute a sexual experience for the perpetrators.

The horror of rape emphasizes further how important it is to solve the dilemma in a legitimate way so as to avoid violation or abuse of negative rights to sexual self-determination. This also raises a difficult, but interesting, question that, luckily for us, we do not need to answer in order to defend our argument: are the two horns of the dilemma of equal moral value or should one be prioritized over the other in case no solution were at hand? Luckily we have a solution, but the question about the comparative value of the positive right to sexual satisfaction on the one hand and the negative right to sexual self-determination on the other hand is still legitimate and interesting. Here I will not provide an argument, but I will say that I would tend to prioritize the negative right to sexual self-determination over the positive right to sexual pleasure; independently of whether one thinks that negative rights should always be prioritized over positive rights, I believe that self-determination is more important than pleasure.

5.3   Robots and Sexual Self-Determination

Clearly one could object on other grounds to my proposal of deploying robots for the sexual satisfaction of the severely physically and mentally disabled and the many elderly people who suffer from neurodegenerative diseases. Let us distinguish between two different kinds of counterarguments: on the one hand, one can object on the grounds that robots would not really solve the dilemma; on the other hand, one can object that the deployment of robots would be morally problematic in respects that are independent of the dilemma. Let us start with the first objection.

So far we have discussed objections to the claim that robots can provide sexual satisfaction; but one could also object to robots as a solution to our rights dilemma on the grounds that robots would violate negative rights to sexual self-determination. It is indeed clear that the use of simple objects or instruments for sexual satisfaction does not make any difference to the question of rights violation, so that if one thought that the sexual satisfaction of the severely disabled would violate someone's right to sexual self-determination, then whether or not such sexual satisfaction would be obtained by employing some object or instrument would make no difference. But robots are not simple objects, and it is to emphasize this point that we have been speaking the whole time about sex robots rather than just about sex machines: the idea is that the former but not the latter could be deployed in a way so as to force no person into unwelcome or unwilling sexual interactions (for example, with the severely mentally and physically disabled).

Certainly, sex robots will have been designed by persons; their deployment will have been decided upon by persons; their performance will be monitored and supervised— more or less directly—by persons; but the crucial point is that these kinds of interactions between the designing, deciding, and monitoring persons and the sex robots will not be themselves *sexual* interactions, so that in turn there will be no sexual interaction between the bearers of rights to sexual satisfaction and those persons who indirectly satisfy these rights by designing, deploying, and monitoring sex robots, Therefore, the rights to sexual self-determination of those persons designing, deploying, and monitoring sex robots are not violated.

It is then important that the robots deployed be sophisticated enough: simple instruments or machines would not guarantee a solution to the dilemma (even though, as we have seen, these robots ought not to be so sophisticated as to count themselves as persons). Let us be clear about the kind of sophistication we are talking about: given the intimacy and difficulty of the tasks involved, the sensoric, for example, will have to be of very high quality; also, the software and algorithms will have to grant a degree of independence and responsiveness to the environment that will have to be sufficient so that human healthcare professionals will only have to monitor, and not directly participate in, the tasks.

Complexity here is, if anything, a technical difficulty rather than a normative difficulty. Decisions about the design, deployment, and monitoring of sex robots will be important and difficult decisions, which have to be studied in detail and with care from both a technical and an ethical point of view—and this is not the place to discuss these issues in any great detail. But I do not think that this is a principled difficulty.

Let us take stock: so far we have proposed a solution to the sexual rights dilemma— the deployment of sex robots—and have argued against objections according to which sex robots offer no way out of the dilemma; specifically, we have rejected objections according to which sex robots do not offer a way out of the dilemma because they cannot offer *sexual* satisfaction; and we have rejected objections according to which sex robots do not offer a way out of the dilemma because they do not guarantee that nobody's right to sexual self-determination is violated. But, as we anticipated, one may object to the deployment of robots for sexual satisfaction on grounds that are independent of the sexual rights dilemma. Here I shall discuss two categories of objections.

5.4 Responsibility

Here are two sets of objections to the deployment of robots for the sexual satisfaction of the sexually needy:

1. Who is going to be responsible for what the robots do? Who will be held accountable when something goes wrong? (If nobody can be held accountable, then—it may be argued—we should not deploy robots.)

2. Robots are potentially dangerous; how can we possibly accept their interaction with some of society's most vulnerable people? The disabled and the elderly should be protected, and that is why they should be kept away from robots.

I will address these two sets of objections in turn. The first set represents a classic objection to the deployment of robotic technology in sensitive contexts, such as, for example, war or health. This objection has come to be known as the so-called "responsibility gap" in the literature on autonomous drones or other robotic military technology.[11] Sparrow's argument is that, if such technology is deployed in the battlefield, there is no plausible candidate for the bearer of responsibility (say for war crimes—here I discuss the issue of the supposed responsibility gap in a way that is admittedly less than exhaustive).[12]

Sparrow argues that the programmer is not a plausible candidate; that the commanding officer is not a plausible candidate; and that the machine itself is also not a plausible candidate: "... the impossibility of punishing the machine means that we cannot hold the machine responsible. We can insist that the officer who orders their use be held responsible for their actions, but only at the cost of allowing that they should sometimes be held entirely responsible for actions over which they had no control."[13]

This issue about a possible responsibility gap in the deployment of autonomous robots has already generated its own stream of literature, and it is becoming a debate in itself.[14] I cannot hope to do justice to this whole debate in a discussion of sexual rights, but I do want to say something about this problem at least as it applies to deploying robots for the sexual satisfaction of the disabled and elderly. Let us emphasize that the problem is relevant to our suggestion, and that it may be particularly important when it comes to sex robots as opposed to military robots. One could imagine that the degree of responsiveness to the environment, flexibility, and autonomy that a sexual robot would require in order to provide sexual satisfaction may be even more extensive than that of an efficient military robot. On the other hand, in moving from military ethics to healthcare ethics, something crucial for Sparrow's argument may go missing, namely, Sparrow's *ius in bello* premise according to which we must have a bearer of responsibility for everything we do in battle. In what follows, I shall grant this particular premise for argument's sake, so that we will accept that if there were no bearer of responsibility for what sex robots do, that would be morally problematic.

First of all, let us agree with Sparrow that the machine itself cannot be the bearer of responsibility: this is all the more so in our case as we have stipulated that only robots that are not themselves persons will qualify as solutions to the sexual rights dilemma (while one may not necessarily have to stipulate that the robots used in war ought not to be persons). Let us also agree with Sparrow that there will be at least some cases where the programmers cannot be made legitimately responsible for what has gone wrong, either because they had actually mentioned the risk to the decision-makers or because the failing could not reasonably have been predicted by programmers.

What is left is the decision-maker (Sparrow's Commanding Officer). And indeed I think that here is where Sparrow's argument is at its weakest, especially with relation to sex robots. Sparrow argues that the commanding officer—the healthcare decision-maker or supervisor in the context of sex robots—cannot be held responsible for everything the machines will do because "the autonomy of the machine implies that its orders do not determine (although they obviously influence) its actions."[15]

First of all, this principle—understood as a necessary condition of responsibility according to which a commanding officer or decision-maker can only be responsible if their orders determine the relevant actions that will be performed—is implausible. First, because whether we live in a deterministic or indeterministic world, orders alone will never determine actions, whether of humans or robots—so the kind of determination meant cannot be that of the thesis of causal determinism. But even taking the principle rather to mean something about orders being a proximate cause in a reliable chain leading to action, the principle would remain implausible because it would negate responsibility in most cases of ignorance, negligence, and bad luck. So Sparrow's principle is, as a general necessary condition of responsibility, much too weak. However, let us now look at it in the particular context of robots, which is relevant here.

One thing should be obvious: in itself, that the commanding officer will not be responsible for everything that the machine does is not a problem, because one may clearly also accept a pluralist view according to which sometimes the programmer is responsible, sometimes the commanding officer, etc. So Sparrow's claim is more general: sometimes the commanding officer is not responsible, and no one else is; that is supposed to be the problem.

Having clarified this point, I think that, even if one accepts that the machine's orders do not fully determine its actions, this in turn does not imply that sometimes the commanding officer will be—for exactly that reason—not responsible. For example, it may be that the simple fact that the commanding officer is aware of this problem will be enough for an attribution of responsibility (if other conditions also apply). And further it is plausible to suppose that the decision-makers are obliged to inform themselves on exactly these kinds of risks. Here I think that the context of deployment may make a difference. Namely, in the case of the military chain of command we may be unwilling to make the commanding officer responsible for the malfunctioning of a machine despite her awareness because the commanding officer is herself subject to orders.

This may be different in a health context, specifically when it comes to sexual satisfaction. There will be policy-makers and then bureaucrats making general deployment decisions and drawing up guidelines; then there will be doctors, social workers, and psychologists making particular deployment decisions and monitoring the consequences of those decisions. At most stages of these often complicated processes the relations of authority are not comparable to those in the military—and at all stages not complying with the tasks set by a manager cannot be compared—at least in terms of consequences—to not complying with military orders.

With this difference in mind, we can say that at least in the health context we may very well make the decision-makers responsible for possible malfunctioning of sex robots, exactly because the decision-makers must inform themselves about the levels of flexibility and responsiveness to the environment of the machines and about possible malfunctioning related to this. In making their deployment decisions at the different levels, decision-makers are, or should be, aware of this and take responsibility over the consequences of their deployment decisions—at least in those cases of malfunction that could have been reasonably foreseen. (Obviously this condition is more challenging when it comes to autonomous robots than with simple instruments or machines.)

So there is no responsibility gap[16]—at least in the case of sex robots—because the decision-makers (or the carers or programmers, depending on the case) will be held responsible for all the malfunctioning and unpredicted functioning that could have been reasonably predicted—where admittedly what would have been reasonable to predict is, in this case, possibly more challenging than in more traditional health-related decision-making – just because of the higher level of complexity involved within robotic technology. Here let me say that even though I think and have argued that there isn't—in principle—a responsibility gap, I do think that matters are extremely complicated and that future courts and legislators may have a very hard time with malfunctioning cases.

However, it should first be noted that some of this type of complication is not new in the world, and should therefore not be overstated in the case of sex robots. Take for example decision-making chains. Even if robots or machines are not involved, attributing responsibility within a complicated decision-making chain, such as a state or company, is already a very difficult thing, and often when it comes to legal responsibility, courts do fail due to the sophistication of the decision-making chain. Robots may make this even more difficult, but, again, these difficulties are not new, and therefore should not be overstated in the case of robots.[17]

Second, in thinking about the possible difficulties of future legislators and courts in attributions of legal responsibility for the malfunctioning of robots, we should also grant that future legislators and courts will have resources that current legislators and courts do not possess: we can assume that the level of sophistication will grow on both sides.

Finally, we should say that one point that will be relevant to the issue of responsibility is what level of risk is going to be judged to be tolerable. And in this respect, sex robots may be judged differently from military robots: first of all, because isolated once-in-the-lifetime-of-the-machine malfunctioning will be much more dangerous if a machine is heavily armed than in a health context; secondly, because in the evaluation about risk tolerance levels, possible malfunctioning will have to be weighed against the great health and well-being benefits that those sex robots will bring to the severely mentally and physically disabled.

5.5   Vulnerability

This brings us to our last issue: aren't the disabled and the elderly simply too vulnerable to be exposed to robots in such a sensitive context as sexuality? It may be argued that the severely disabled are particularly vulnerable, especially in a delicate context such as sexuality. Therefore, the idea of providing sexual satisfaction to them (especially in the cases of severely mentally disabled individuals and those suffering from neurodegenerative diseases in an advanced phase) is just too dangerous no matter their needs. Moreover, the risk of abuse and the uncertainty about their willingness, it may be argued, make this a no go—and all this independently of any talk of robots. As I have dealt with these kinds of objections elsewhere,[18] I will not repeat those arguments here, and only focus on the issue of vulnerability as it relates to the deployment of robots.[19]

On vulnerability in general, I just wish to clarify my position in two important respects: I am not saying that all severely physically and mentally disabled people will have sexual needs nor am I saying that it will be legitimate to satisfy the sexual needs of all who do have some. All I am arguing for is the satisfaction of *some* sexual needs for *some* severely mentally and physically disabled people.

As to the question of a supposed increased danger or vulnerability due to the deployment or robots, I think that the opposite is actually the case: vulnerability is an argument in favor of deploying robots for sexual care instead of human sexual carers, because robots can be programmed so as to minimize, if not eliminate, the risk of abuse; because robots can be controlled and monitored more effectively than human carers; because—as we are talking of pure sexual care rather than psychological support or other kinds of assistance—one can imagine that robots could be designed to be more effective performers than human carers in all sorts of respects (see the earlier remarks about the kind of sensoric and algorithms that would have to be involved). The vulnerability of the severely disabled is of paramount importance and must be protected at all costs—but that is true whether we deploy human carers or robots.

Before concluding, I want to deal with one final objection, according to which we should not welcome a world in which nobody wants to have sex with people with disability so that we are forced to deploy robots. I share the spirit of this objection: indeed, in my already cited 2011 article in the *Journal of Medical Ethics*, I have argued in favor of a voluntary not-for-profit system for the sexual satisfaction of the severly disabled. I am still convinced that such a system would be best; but even though the sex robots we have imagined throughout this article may be still very far away, I am afraid that the kind of solidarity and generosity necessary for the voluntary system of sexual satisfaction I have put forward is even further away, so that in the meantime we should not be afraid of using robotic technology to perform tasks that not enough human persons are willing to perform (which, by the way, is a useful reminder that the use of sex robots that I have argued for in this chapter has the same dialectical origins as a lot of other uses of robotic technology and is consistent with the Czech etymology of the term "robot").

In conclusion, let me say that there are indeed many serious concerns relating to satisfying the sexual needs of severely mentally and physically disabled individuals— and here I could not do justice to all of them (I have hardly spoken of consent, for example), because I have done so elsewhere and because this discussion focused only on the possible future deployment of sex robots.[20] I do want to conclude with a more general point though: the serious concerns and the very many delicate issues related to the sexual needs of severely mentally and physically disabled individuals should move us to increased and enhanced attention to the issue and its many problems, rather than scare us away just to avoid the many risks. Avoidance may be the *safer* option for us, but it would not be the *just* one for anybody.

Notes

1. Ezio Di Nucci, "Sexual Rights and Disability," *Journal of Medical Ethics* 37, no. 3 (March 2011): 159.

2. In 1999, the World Association for Sexual Health (WAS) adopted a Declaration of Sexual Rights. Here is the declaration from the WAS website: http://www.worldsexology.org/resources/declaration-of-sexual-rights. It identifies eleven different sexual rights, and says that sexual rights are fundamental and universal human rights; number five on the list is the right to sexual pleasure.

3. As cited in Di Nucci, "Sexual Rights and Disability"; and before that in Cécile Fabre, *Whose Body Is It Anyway?* (New York: Oxford University Press, 2006). Also see the 2012 movie *The Sessions* (Fox Searchlight Productions). Also, in the UK, the TLC Trust (http://tlc-trust.org.uk) does invaluable work helping people with disabilities fulfill their sexuality.

4. For simplicity's sake, I will not always use the very long phrase "severely physically and men- tally disabled and those suffering from neurodegenerative diseases" and rather speak more loosely

of people with disabilities; but if not otherwise specified, what I will mean when speaking about people with disabilities is the more precise full formulation above.

5. For readers who would like some more theoretical background on how to understand rights and rights-talk, I recommend this introduction from the Stanford Encyclopedia of Philosophy: http://plato.stanford.edu/entries/rights.

6. To be clear, here my argument does not rely on the contoversial premise that sex is as important as food—as one could easily object to this on the grounds that the latter, but not the former, is necessary for survival (at least at the individual level).

7. Admittedly, here I have not offered a conclusive argument for the existence of positve sexual rights, but rather just tried to make plausible the idea that positive sexual rights cannot be dismissed out of hand as a matter of principle.

8. Please note that when I say "practical" I don't mean to offer a solution for the here and now, but only to contrast my solution with a purely formal solution to the dilemma. See also: Sara Ruddick, "Better Sex," in *Philosophy and Sex*, eds. Robert Baker and Frederick Elliston (Amherst, NY: Prometheus Books, 1984), 280–299; Shannon Vallor, "Carebots and Caregivers: Sustaining the Ethical Ideal of Care in the Twenty-first Century," *Philosophy of Technology* 24, (September 2011): 251–268; Johanna Seibt, Raul Hakli, and Marco Nørskov, *Sociable Robots and the Future of Social Relations: Proceedings of Robo-Philosophy* (Amsterdam: IOS Press, 2014); and John P. Sullins, "Robots, Love, and Sex: The Ethics of Building a Love Machine," *IEEE Transactions on Affective Computing*, no. 3 (Fourth Quarter 2012): 398–409.

9. David Levy, *Love and Sex with Robots* (New York: Harper Collins, 2007); David Levy, "The Ethics of Robot Prostitutes," in *Robot Ethics: The Ethical and Social Implications of Robotics*, eds. Patrick Lin, Keith Abney, and George Bekey (Cambridge, MA: MIT Press, 2012), 223–32; Blay Whitby, "Do You Want a Robot Lover? The Ethics of Caring Technologies," in *Robot Ethics*, 233–248; John Danaher, "Sex Work, Technological Unemployment, and the Basic Income Guarantee," *Journal of Evolution and Technology* 24, no. 1 (February 2014): 113–130. You may have, for example, already heard of Roxxxy, which has been claimed to be the first sexual robot. For more information, you may start from this April 7, 2014 *Guardian* article: https://www.theguardian.com/science/brain-flapping/2014/apr/07/robots-and-sex-creepy-or-cool. Also, for ethical discussions on the use of robots in healthcare in general, see, for example, Mark Coeckelbergh, "Health Care, Capabilities, and AI Assistive Technologies," *Ethical Theory and Moral Practice* 13, no. 2 (April 2010): 181–190; Amanda Sharkey and Noel Sharkey, "Granny and the Robots: Ethical Issues in Robot Care for the Elderly," *Ethics and Information Technology* 14, no. 1 (March 2012): 27–40.

10. I specify "animal nonperson" as opposed to just "nonhuman animal" in case someone thinks that, say, chimpanzees may qualify for personhood.

11. Rober Sparrow, "Killer Robots," *Journal of Applied Philosophy* 24, no. 1 (February 2007): 62–77.

12. For more on this, see Ezio Di Nucci and Filippo Santoni de Sio, *Drones and Responsibility* (New York: Routledge, 2016).

13. Sparrow, *Killer Robots*, 74.

14. See, for example: Andreas Matthias, "The Responsibility Gap: Ascribing Responsibility for the Actions of Learning Automata," *Ethics and Information Technology* 6, no. 3 (September 2004): 175–183; Marc Champagne and Ryan Tonkens, "Bridging The Responsibility Gap in Automated Warfare," *Philosophy & Technology* 28, no. 1 (March 2015): 125–137; Marcus Schulzke, "Autonomous Weapons and Distributed Responsibility," *Philosophy & Technology* 26, no. 2 (June 2013): 203–219; Heather M. Roff, "Responsibility, Liability, and Lethal Autonomous Robots," in *Routledge Handbook of Ethics and War: Just War Theory in the 21st Century,* eds. Fritz Allhoff, Nicholas G. Evans, and Adam Henschke (New York: Routledge, 2013), 352–362; Deborah G. Johnson, "Technology with No Human Responsibility?" *Journal of Business Ethics* 127, no. 4 (April 2015): 707–715.

15. Sparrow, *Killer Robots,* 71.

16. Let me clarify that I speak of responsibility gap here (instead of, say, liability gap) because I am not just thinking of who will be liable for damages or compensation in cases of malfunction (there one could imagine strict liability for the healthcare institution involved, for example). I am also thinking of issues of moral responsibility that go beyond liability and damages, and would not be settled by such arrangements.

17. Let me stress here again that I am using examples from legal responsibility and liability as an analogy for the kind of issues that may also arise for moral responsibility, but that I do not think that, when it comes to sex robots, moral responsibility issues are reducible to liability.

18. Di Nucci, "Sexual Rights and Disability."

19. On general issues of vulnerability related to sex and disability (or dementia), see also: Jacob M. Appel, "Sex Rights for the Disabled?" *Journal of Medical Ethics* 36, no. 3 (March 2010): 152–154; and Laura Tarzia, Deirdre Fetherstonhaugh, and Michael Bauer, "Dementia, Sexuality and Consent in Residential Aged Care Facilities," *Journal of Medical Ethics* 38, no. 10 (October 2012): 609–613. To very briefly elaborate on my arguments from Di Nucci 2011: both protecting patients' welfare and consent requirements are obviously paramount, even before getting into the issue of sex robots; but we must be careful that, in exercising prudence about patients' welfare and consent requirements, we do not lose sight of what healthcare exists for, namely, care—and in this case sexual care. So, for example, denying sexual care to all patients with mental/learning disability may end up erring on the side of caution.

20. Di Nucci, "Sexual Rights and Disability"; Di Nucci, "Consent Ain't Anything: Dissent, Access, and the Conditions for Consent," *Monash Bioethics Review* 34, no. 1 (March 2016): 3–22.

III   Challenging Robot Sex

The chapters in this section look at some of the problems associated with the development of sex robots. In chapter 6, Hertzfeld looks at a variety of objections to sex with robots from a Judeo-Christian perspective, suggesting that the major stumbling block for this religious tradition is the possibility that sex with a robot is less physically and emotionally demanding than sex with a real human being. Danaher follows in chapter 7 by examining the symbolism of sex robots, focusing in particular on what the development of sex robots might say about our attitudes toward sexual consent. He identifies a common argument-structure that is used in the debate about sex robots (the "Symbolic-Consequences Argument") and subjects it to critical scrutiny. Strikwedra closes this section in chapter 8 by considering the important topic of sex robots that are designed to look and act like children. Could they be used to treat and dissuade would-be pedophiles? Strikwedra argues that there is more to be said against the idea than in its favor.

6   Religious Perspectives on Sex with Robots

Noreen Herzfeld

Thou hast also taken thy fair jewels of my gold and of my silver, which I had given thee, and madest to thyself images of men, and didst commit whoredom with them.
—Ezekiel 16:17

As we look toward a future in which human interaction with robots will be ever more diverse and more common, one in which those interactions might include both sex and some sort of emotional relationship, do our religious traditions, traditions laid down long before robots were ever dreamt of, offer any guidance? There is no one religious sexual ethic, neither across traditions nor within them. From the explicitly libidinous carvings of Hindu temples to the celibacy of the Desert Fathers, religious thought on sexuality has run the gamut; religions have both celebrated and sought to severely limit human sexual expression. Thus, there will be no single religious approach to the question of whether sex with a robot is either permissible or desirable.

It is impossible to survey such a vast and disparate area in a single chapter. I will, rather, present a few religious answers, primarily from a Judeo-Christian perspective, to four basic questions: What is the purpose of sex? What in our nature might predispose us to a relationship with a robot? Could we have an authentic loving relationship with a robot? And, finally, would such a choice aid or hinder our spiritual growth?

Biblical scholars generally interpret Ezekiel's reference to whoredom with images of men in a spiritual context, as a warning to Hebrews not to pay homage to the idols of other tribes in what would constitute infidelity to the one true God. Yet the advent of sexual robots gives this text a new poignancy. Would sexual robots be merely an occasion for "whoredom," or do they present a new opportunity, in the words of Sherry Turkle, for a love that is "safe and made to measure"?[1]

6.1   What Is the Purpose of Sex?

And God blessed them, and God said unto them, "Be fruitful, and multiply, and replenish the earth, and subdue it."
—Genesis 1:28

The panoply of gods and goddesses posited in the ancient world allowed for sexual activity both among the gods and between gods and humans, as is widely attested in stories found in the Vedas of Hinduism, the cults of ancient Egypt, and Greco-Roman antiquity. Since immortal beings have no need to procreate (though it seems they often did so), sexual activity among the gods is described primarily in terms of the gratification of sexual desire. Thus, we find in these stories a fairly permissive sexual ethic, where most expressions of sexuality are not only condoned but admired, adultery being the most widespread exception. The ancient stories did not posit strict divisions between the natural world, humankind, and the divine. Thus, we find instances of the inanimate coming to life (Pygmalion), and human or divine transformation into plants or animals (Baucis and Philamon; Daphne; Zeus and Leda).[2] Sex is celebrated, and the crossing of divine or natural divisions is common. The ancients would likely have had little problem with humans having sex with robots.[3]

This changes with the advent of monotheism. Unlike most of their neighbors, the Jews posited a single God who transcended sexuality, both by having no godly counterparts with whom to engage, and by remaining wholly other and generally aloof from physical contact with human beings.[4] While the ancients could turn to their gods as models for sexuality, the Jews could not, and, while God might transcend the sexual, this is no workable model for humankind. As the story of the Fall in Genesis 3 points out, while gods might be eternal, human beings die, making sex a necessity for the continuation of the race. Thus, we find an intrinsic link in the monotheistic traditions between sex and procreation. Adam and Eve discover they are gendered beings; they are also commanded to "be fruitful and multiply." At the heart of Jewish sexual ethics are the twin expectations that men and women marry and that they produce children.

Procreation as a primary purpose for sex continues into early Christianity. There is no systematic sexual ethic in the teachings of Jesus as recounted in the Gospels. Early Christian thinking on sexuality was heavily influenced by Greek thought, particularly that of the Stoics, who believed in living the controlled life, the sexual urge being best controlled by giving it a rational purpose, namely that of producing children.[5] An emphasis on controlled sexuality allowed Christians to affirm both the appropriateness of a life of celibacy as a continuation of the divine pattern of both the creator and Jesus, and the appropriateness of sexual intercourse within marriage for the production of children and the control of one's lustful desires.[6] This dual emphasis on procreation and control is strengthened in the writings of Augustine, who viewed sex through the lens of both his own experience and his Manichaean past. While Augustine argued against the Manichaean view that sex was inherently evil because it was part of an evil material world, he knew from his own experience that sexual desire was not easily contained and often had to be fought against. He posited that, if our goal is to master the passions and direct them solely toward love of God and neighbor, sexual passion must be resisted except when it is directed toward its one rational purpose, namely the procreative act. According to Augustine, in all other contexts, sexual expression, even within marriage, was a form of weakness and therefore sinful.[7]

The primacy of procreation, or at least openness to its possibility, has continued as the norm within the Catholic Church. In the encyclical *Humanae Vitae*, Pope Paul VI writes: "The fact is, as experience shows, that new life is not the result of each and every act of sexual intercourse … The church, nevertheless … teaches that each and every marital act must of necessity retain its intrinsic relationship to the procreation of human life."[8] The necessity of maintaining this relationship underlies Catholic proscriptions against any non-procreative form of sexual expression, including masturbation, the use of artificial birth control, and homosexuality. The 1992 Catechism of the Catholic Church calls masturbation "an intrinsically and seriously disordered act," a view based not only in its failure to lead to procreation, but also in its self-centered nature, its failure to be relational. The view among Orthodox Jews is similar. Sex, while not intrinsically evil, must be limited to marriage and open to its true function. Masturbation and homosexuality are considered sinful. If a robot is considered nothing but an inanimate object, a sophisticated sex toy, then sex with a robot would be tantamount to masturbation and thus fall under a similar proscription. Indeed, even if the robot is considered a relational entity, sex with one cannot produce a child and thus would fail to be a purposeful form of sexual expression in the eyes of conservative Catholic or Orthodox Jewish communities.

Certain Protestant denominations and some liberal Catholic theologians, while acknowledging the intrinsic link between sex and procreation, do not take openness to procreation as the same *sine qua non*. In *Just Love: A Framework for Christian Sexual Ethics*, Catholic theologian Margaret Farley writes that many within Catholicism have come to see masturbation as morally neutral, "either good or bad, depending on the circumstances and the individual … insofar as it supports or limits well-being and liberty of spirit."[9] Most Protestant denominations take a similar view. Fundamentalist

James Dobson writes: "It is my opinion that masturbation is not much of an issue with God."[10] Yet most temper their approval with a preference for the relational and a concern that chronic masturbation could displace the search for a sexual partner. The Lutheran Church Missouri Synod writes of masturbation: "sexuality in the context of a personal relationship of mutual love and commitment in marriage helps us to evaluate the practice. Chronic masturbation falls short of the Creator's intention for our use of the gift of sexuality, namely, that our sexual drives should be oriented toward communion with another person in the mutual love and commitment of marriage."[11] Thus, if we consider sex with a robot merely as a form of masturbatory activity, it might be frowned on by some, but condoned in moderation or certain circumstances by others.

6.2   Why Robots? The Importance of Relationship

God created man in His own image, in the image of God He created him; male and female He created them.
—Genesis 1:27

Most proponents of sexual robots would argue that they will rise above being mere sex toys by adding an interactive artificially intelligent component, thus moving the sexual act above masturbation and into the realm of authentic relationship. But why would we want such a relationship? A question that bothered me as a young professor teaching artificial intelligence was why, despite decades of failure, we have remained fascinated by the idea of making computers as much like ourselves as possible. It seemed to me that computers were most useful when they complemented rather than mimicked us, doing tasks we do not do well or do not wish to do, such as tedious calculations, crunching endless data, or riveting bolts in the factory. And, while recent programs, such as the Mars rover or Jeopardy winning Watson, show real progress, the field of AI generally has been one of overpromise and underachievement. (One researcher at MIT is said to have kept a sign above his desk that read: "We shall overclaim!") Despite this, we continue to be fascinated with AI. In the realm of science fiction, this fascination is highly relational. We depict computers as our friends and lovers: think of the lovable droids in *Star Wars*, David in *AI*, and most recently, Scarlett Johansson's sexy operating system voice in *Her* or Alicia Vikander's even sexier body in *Ex Machina*. In each, the computer is not simply a tool but a companion, and increasingly, an object of not just companionship but love.

Where does this deep desire to relate to others, even nonhuman beings, come from? One theological response roots it in the concept of the *imago Dei*, the understanding expressed in Genesis 1 that humans are created in the image of God. Genesis 1 never explains exactly what this image is, and it has been interpreted variously through the ages. The dominant interpretation among Christian systematic theologians since the early twentieth century is that we image God when we are in relationship because God is a relationship between Father, Son, and Holy Spirit. To be in God's image is to seek relationship at all times. Barth writes that the image of God is identified with the fact that the human being is a relational being, needing to give and receive love. Barth interprets the plural in "Let us make humans" (Genesis 1:26) as referring not to God speaking to a heavenly court, but to God's plural nature, a Trinity that contains both an "I" that can issue a call and a "Thou" capable of response.[12] For Barth, this I-Thou confrontation, existing within God's self, forms the ground of human creation, rooting our nature in a perennial need for relationship. Thus, the image of God we are created in only appears when two beings are in authentic relationship with each other.

Barth also finds evidence for relationship as the center of our being in the person of Jesus, whom he believes revealed human nature as it was intended to be. He writes: "If we see Him alone, we do not see Him at all. If we see Him, we see with and around Him in ever widening circles His disciples, the people, His enemies, and the countless multitudes who never have heard His name. We see Him as theirs, determined by them and for them, belonging to each and every one of them."[13]

We find a similar emphasis on relationality in the centrality of covenant in the Jewish scriptures. God makes covenants with Noah, Abraham, Moses and Aaron, David, and by extension with the entire Jewish people. God promises Abraham that his descendants will be his chosen people and he will be their God (Genesis 17:2–9). He promises David kingship over Israel and that for one of his descendants "I will be his father and he shall be my son" (2 Samuel 7:14). In each of these stories, God sets the parameters of a relationship with human beings. This is no deistic God who merely sets the world in motion, or a God whose purposes are obscure, but one who enters into full and loving relationship with human beings.

A God who makes relational covenants and in whose image we are made suggests that we are "hardwired" to do the same, to seek everywhere a partner with whom to relate, not just among ourselves, human with human, but also with someone or something different from us. Computer scientist Danny Hillis notes: "It would be nice to have friends that have a different set of limitations than we do."[14] But would those limitations allow authentic relationships?

6.3   Aspects of Authentic Love and Marriage

Wilt thou love her, comfort her, honor and keep her in sickness and in health; and, forsaking all others, keep thee only unto her, so long as ye both shall live?
—Book of Common Prayer

As Margaret Farley notes: "Just about everyone today thinks that sex has something to do with love."[15] While we know that sexual desire cannot be equated with love and that many sexual acts occur without love, sex within the context of a loving relationship is considered the ideal, particularly in a Christian context where the call to love God and neighbor is central. In *Humanae Vitae*, Pope Paul VI discusses sex wholly within the context of love, a love that is freely given, based in trust, exclusive, and "meant not only to survive the joys and sorrows of daily life, but also to grow, so that husband and wife become in a way one heart and one soul, and together attain their human fulfillment."[16]

Here we have a number of stumbling blocks. Would a robot be capable of a love that is freely given? Would the robot have the choice of partners, the option of saying no? Here we find the dichotomy between wanting robots to be our servants and under our control, yet simultaneously wanting an authentic relationship. Both are not possible. Pope Paul VI is adamant that authentic love must be an act of free choice.[17] Indeed, lack of free consent is one of the grounds for the annulment of a marriage in the Catholic Church. Certainly robots as we now know them are not capable of such consent. This seems to make them our sexual slaves. Since they are also not sentient beings, we do them no harm in this; however, it is one way in which any relationship with a robot would be incomplete. There is no mutuality of consent, and this lack of mutuality limits the self-giving within the relationship. The robot has no choice but to give.

Exclusivity raises similar concerns. A telling moment in the movie *Her* comes when Theodore, the protagonist, realizes that the operating system he has fallen in love with is carrying on a similar relationship with hundreds of others. This might not be a problem with a physical robot, for one could reserve one's robot for one's own exclusive use. However, this seems to then take us back into the realm of sexual slavery. Exclusivity, like consent, must be freely chosen in order for it to have any meaning. Exclusivity also raises the question of whether a married person having sex with a robot would be committing adultery, one of the few sexual acts explicitly prohibited in the Christian and Jewish scriptures (Exodus 20:12). The seventh commandment, "Thou shalt not commit adultery," appears in the context of the sixth ("Thou shalt not kill") and the eighth ("Thou shalt not steal"). Each of these involves the taking of something of value from another. In a patriarchal society, adultery was the stealing of another man's posses-sion. This is made explicit in the story of David's seduction of Bathsheba. The prophet Nathan reproves the king by likening his adultery to the stealing of a lamb from a poor peasant. What exactly is one stealing? In traditional Judaism, adultery depends on the marital status of the woman (Leviticus 20:10). It is imperative to know who the father might be of any resulting child. However, as noted before, this is not an issue with a robot. A woman who has sex with a robot does not risk pregnancy nor does a man who has sex with a robot risk impregnating anyone. So would either be taking anything from his partner? Once again the matter depends on whether robots are seen as merely sexual toys or whether there is truly a relational component. In the latter case, it could be argued that sex with a robot could result in alienation of affection from the partner, and therefore be taking away something very valuable.

Finally, would a sexual relationship with a robot allow for the mutual growth and fulfillment Pope Paul describes? The traditional marriage vows speak of loving one another "in sickness and in health" and "till death." A large part of the companionship we hope for in marriage is based on growing old together. Margaret Farley notes that as we age we experience embodiment less as opportunity and more as burden, however, while "the realities of aging include diminishment, fear, pain, loneliness; they also can include courage, graciousness, patience, and trust."[18] Catholic theologian Karl Rahner notes that aging is a grace not given to everyone.[19] It is a grace not given to robots. How would it feel for a person to age while their robot does not? In the face of death, what understanding could a robot bring? As we age, we experience our true selves less as physical body and more as transcendent spirit. The Evangelical Lutheran Church in America (ELCA) counsels that a sexual relationship "involves spiritual, emotional, intellectual, and physical dimensions of self-understanding. When these dimensions develop at similar rates, trust and entrusting are established and secured. When they are out of balance, trust may either not exist or disintegrate."[20] Sherry Turkle sees a relationship with a robot as lacking the authenticity that comes from this deep under-standing of a shared human condition: "Authenticity, for me, follows from the ability to put oneself in the place of another, to relate to the other because of a shared store of human experiences: we are born, have families, and know loss and the reality of death. A robot, however sophisticated, is patently out of the loop."[21]

There seem, then, to be intrinsic weaknesses that would make the experience of truly authentic relationship with a robot problematic. The deep sharing found in a committed and loving relationship would be compromised, if existent at all. And the effects of this go beyond the couple. Lutheran theologian Michael Stolzfus writes: "[A] sexualized spirituality should not be completely content with physically gratifying sex done for its own sake. Sexual expression at its best, really good sex, should be both physically gratifying, and, at the same time, be a source of inspiration that moves people to expand beyond the realm of private pleasure to incorporate a more compassionate approach to people in all spheres of life."[22] Ideally, sexual expression serves as one factor of many that bind us closely to another, sharing a physical expression of a love that transcends our bodies, an expression that opens us to a deeper understanding of our human condition and of our neighbor's hopes and needs.

6.4 Spiritual Growth or Spiritual Dead End?

Do not let the perfect be the enemy of the good.
—Voltaire

Voltaire's counsel cuts both ways. It is obvious that sex with robots does not rise to the standard of perfection laid out in *Humanae Vitae* or expressed by other theologians and sacred texts, a perfection found between a man and a woman in a committed and deeply loving relationship, open to the possibility of procreation. However, many, perhaps even most, sexual acts between humans also do not rise to this standard. Catholic moral teaching sets a high bar; the proclamation of a Year of Mercy in 2015 by Pope Francis recognizes that we cannot always reach that bar and that we need to recognize that limitation in ourselves and others and be forgiving. Other denominations, in the spirit of Voltaire's caveat, have come to allow previously proscribed activities, such as sex between same sex partners or masturbation, knowing that the ideal relationship is sometimes neither available nor, for some, optimal. A complete prohibition of sex with robots might be seen as running the same risk of taking away a source of sexual fulfillment because it does not live up to the highest of standards.

On the other hand, there is also a fear that sex with a robot might be for many all too perfect, more physically gratifying and less emotionally demanding, than sex with another human. In *Alone Together*, Sherry Turkle describes a woman she calls Anne who wanted her relationships to stave off loneliness and would be happy to trade her not always available boyfriend for a robot if the robot could be programmed to show caring behavior.[23] Turkle notes the risk in looking for this kind of perfection: "Dependence on a robot presents itself as risk free. But when one becomes accustomed to 'companionship' without demands, life with people may seem overwhelming. Dependence on a person is risky—it makes us subject to rejection—but it also opens us to deeply knowing another. Robotic companionship may seem a sweet deal, but it consigns us to a closed world—the lovable as safe and made to measure."[24]

In his seminal work, *I and Thou*, Martin Buber notes that we can take two basic stances toward the world, that of I-You or that of I-It. While the stance we take determines how we treat others, it also determines who we are, for "the I of the basic word I-You is different from that in the basic word I-It."[25] Buber points out that at some point we treat every You as if it were an It. We also have the capacity to treat an It as if it were a You, when we become deeply engaged with it. While having sex with robots seems to expand the world of I-You, the danger lies in our using relationship with a robot as a template for relationship with other persons, thus expanding instead the world of I-It. If our primary experience of sex is with one that we can turn off or turn away from at will, might we not wish to do the same with persons? Psychologist Simon Baron-Cohen notes that lack of genuine empathy underlies much of human cruelty, a cruelty he describes as people turning people into objects, a process that changes us over time so that in the end "we relate only to things, or to people as if they were just things."[26] We must remain aware of the distinction between them, as things, and us as persons.

The ELCA notes that the powers of sex "are complex and ambiguous. They can be used well or badly. They can bring astonishing joy and delight. Such powers can serve God and serve the neighbor. They also can hurt self or hurt the neighbor."[27] The Apostle Paul warns that the sexual vices (fornication, impurity, licentiousness) when indulged in for the sake of the ego might turn one "away from belonging to Christ and God's Kingdom" (Galatians 5:19–21). Yet the ELCA also notes that "the way we order our lives in matters of human sexuality is important to faithful living, but is not central to determining our salvation. We are able to be realistic and merciful with respect to our physical and emotional realities, not striving for angelic perfection as if our salvation were at stake"[28] The beginning of Genesis tells the story of the human race, one in which the relationship of love and trust, the image in which we were created, is broken. Adam and Eve find sex and knowledge, and with them find great joy—and great pain, work, death, and sorrow. In proclaiming mercy, in recognizing our human weakness, our religious traditions recognize that we live in a world where perfection remains an aspiration. Like the Promethean gift of fire, sex brings warmth and joy into our lives, yet also has the capacity to bring destruction and pain when it is not engaged in thoughtfully. Human relationships can be fraught with difficulties, they can disappoint. But so will sex with robots. Robots may be less demanding, less challenging, but therein lies the problem. Love and life are never "safe and made to measure." In the life and death of Jesus, we see the truly challenging nature of love, one that might take us even to the cross.

Sex robots might make interesting, even desirable sexual partners. We might form an attachment of a sort with them. But in the end, it is God and each other with whom we must be in relationship. Replacing relationship with one another with relationship to a machine is ultimately a form of idolatry, a substitution for the living with something made, and thus controlled, by our own hands. Buber, citing the Rabbi of Knock, calls this an idolatry that happens "when a face addresses a face which is not a face."[29] Love "made to measure" is not love, for then we would have tamed it, taken away its wildness and mystery, as well as its demand that we give ourselves to each other, perhaps even unto death.

Notes

1. Sherry Turkle, *Alone Together: Why We Expect More from Technology and Less from Each Other* (New York: Basic Books, 2011), 66.

2. Ovid's *Metamorphoses* provides a wonderful collection of creation myths, all of which are bound together through the use of such transformations.

3. Robots only appear in one Greek myth in the guise of serving girls fashioned by the god Hephaistus.

4. While God is depicted as walking with Adam in the garden, and Abraham entertains strangers he later identifies as God, most of the Hebrew scriptures present God as interacting with humans through angels, dreams, or, on occasion, direct speech, but not through physical contact.

5. Margaret Farley, *Just Love: A Framework for a Christian Sexual Ethic* (New York: Continuum, 2006), 39.

6. Paul writes in 1 Corinthians 7:9, "[L]et them marry: for it is better to marry than to burn."

7. Texts in which Augustine discusses sex include *On the Goodness of Marriage*, *On Holy Virginity*, and *On Marriage and Concupiscence*. An excellent commentary on sex in the ancient and early Christian worlds is Peter Brown's *The Body and Society*.

8. Pope Paul VI, *Humanae Vitae* (1968), §12, http://w2.vatican.va/content/paul-vi/en/encyclicals/documents/hf_p-vi_enc_25071968_humanae-vitae.html.

9. Farley, *Just Love*, 236.

10. James Dobson, *Preparing for Adolescence* (Ventura, CA: Gospel Light, 1992).

11. http://religiousinstitute.org/masturbation.

12. Karl Barth, *Church Dogmatics*, ed. G. W. Bromiley and T. F. Torrance, trans. J. W. Edwards, O. Bussey, Harold Knight (Edinburgh: T. and T. Clark, 1958), 182.

13. Ibid., 216.

14. Quoted in David Noble, *The Religion of Technology: The Divinity of Man and the Spirit of Invention* (New York: Knopf, 1997), 170.

15. Farley, *Just Love*, 164.

16. Pope Paul VI, *Humanae Vitae* (1968), §13, in *The Pope Speaks* (Fall 1969), 329–346, 9.

17. Ibid.

18. Farley, *Just Love*, 123–124.

19. Karl Rahner, "Growing Old," in *Prayers and Meditations: An Anthology of Spiritual Writings*, ed. J. Griffiths (New York: Crossroad, 1981), 91.

20. Evangelical Lutheran Church in America (ELCA), *A Social Statement on Human Sexuality: Gift and Trust* (2009), 31, http://download.elca.org/ELCA%20Resource%20Repository/SexualitySS .pdf?_ga=1.45112100.1637128334.1452876484.

21. Turkle, *Alone Together*, 6.

22. Michael Stolzfus, "Sexual Intimacy, Spiritual Belonging, and Christian Theology," *Journal of Lutheran Ethics* (June 1, 2004): par. 23, https://www.elca.org/JLE/Articles/751.

23. Turkle, *Alone Together*, 8. For an examination of whether a robot could ever be programmed to exhibit what we might consider adequate caring behavior, see Noreen Herzfeld, "Empathetic Computers: The Problem of Confusing Persons and Things," *Dialog: A Journal of Theology* 54:1 (Spring 2015): 34–39.

24. Turkle, *Alone Together*, 66.

25. Martin Buber, *I and Thou*, trans. Walter Kaufman, (New York: Scribner's, 1970), 53.

26. Simon Baron-Cohen, *The Science of Evil* (New York: Basic Books, 2011), 7.

27. ELCA, *A Social Statement on Human Sexuality*, 11.

28. Ibid., 9.

29. Martin Buber, *Die Erzahlungen der Chassidim* (Zurich: Manesse-Verlag, 2003), 793.

7   The Symbolic-Consequences Argument in the Sex Robot Debate

John Danaher

7.1   Introduction

The television series *Humans* is a provocative and sometimes insightful drama about social robots.[1] It depicts a near-future in which realistic humanoid robots have become commonplace, acting as workers, home helpers, caregivers, and sexual playthings for their human creators. The majority of the robots are less-than-human in their intelligence and ability, and apparently lack sentience, but the main plotline concerns a particular group of these robots that has achieved human-level consciousness and intelligence. They struggle for freedom and respect in a world in which their robot brethren are treated with either condescension or contempt.

In one episode, a group of (human) teenagers are having a house party. At the house party there is a robot serving drinks and catering to the attendees' needs. The robot looks like a human female. Some of the young men hurl abuse at her. One of them switches her off and then tells his mates that he is going to drag her upstairs to have sex with her. He is goaded on. At this point one of the main (human) female characters intervenes, telling her male peers to stop. When asked why, she responds by asking them whether it would be okay for them to knock out a real human female and have sex with her in similar conditions? They renege on their plan.

The writers of the show do not pause at this point and have the female protagonist expand on her objections. Like all good fiction writers they have learned to 'show not tell.' But I'm interested in the telling. Presumably the objection to the young men having sex with the switched-off robot had nothing to do with the potential harm to the robot. The robots within the show are—apart from the core group—deemed to be devoid of moral status, lacking the requisite consciousness and intelligence. They are—to use a phrase repeated in other chapters of this book—not *moral victims*. So why is it wrong for the young men to have sex with them in the suggested manner? The answer must lie elsewhere: in the symbolic meaning of the act, and the consequences that might ensue from its permission.

As it happens, this combined concern for symbolism and its consequences is a common feature of several objections to the development and use of sex robots. Indeed, it is possibly the leading style of objection to sex robots in the current, admittedly small, literature. My goal in this chapter is to provide a detailed analysis of it, outlining its abstract structure, giving specific examples of its use, and evaluating its merits.

I will defend three main claims. First, I will agree with proponents of the symbolic-consequences argument that there are plausible grounds for thinking that sex robots will be symbolically problematic, both in how they represent human beings and in how they encourage a particular style of sexual interaction with those representations. Nevertheless, I will temper this conclusion by suggesting that this problematic symbolism is not essential, or incorrigible, or decisive. It can be *removed* and *reformed* under the right circumstances. Second, I will argue that this means that the consequences of the symbolism becomes all important. Will it cause people to act out in other problematic ways? Will it result in harm to the individual user or to the society in which they live? I'll argue that it is exceptionally difficult to answer those questions prior to the development of the technology, and this leaves us in an uncertain position regarding the strength of the symbolic-consequences argument. Third, I'll suggest that the best way to address this uncertainty is to approach the development of sex robots as a social experiment, i.e., as something that should be subject to similar logistical and ethical standards as medical or psychological experiments.

Although I am interested in the symbolic meaning of love and sex with robots in general, I present all three of these arguments with a particular category of symbolic meaning and consequence in mind, namely: what does having sex with robots say about our understanding of consent to sex and the ethics of interpersonal sexual relationships? And what might the consequences of having sex with robots be for our attitudes and practices with regard to sexual consent and interpersonal sexual relationships? Given this focus, it behooves me to start with a brief primer on sexual consent and its relevance to the sex robot debate.

7.2   The Importance of Consent Norms to the Sex Robot Debate

I'll start by outlining the importance of consent in human-to-human sexual relationships. I'll then explain how it is relevant to the sex robots debate. I will work from first principles, beginning with some platitudes about the value of sexual experience in human life and the role that consent plays in ensuring its value.

It is relatively uncontroversial to say that sexual activity is an important and highly valued part of the human experience. In addition to being a source of pleasure, sexual activity is, for many people, a mark of intimacy and maturity. It provides the basis for a unique, mutual, and intersubjective bond. But it also has a dark side. Unwanted, coerced, or forced sexual activity can be physically and emotionally traumatizing, sometimes leading to lifelong personal and interpersonal difficulties.[2] Consequently, it is important to develop a system of sexual norms that distinguishes permissible sexual activity from impermissible sexual activity—preventing and punishing the latter, while, if not encouraging, at least facilitating, the former. In short, society needs to create a set of norms that protects *negative sexual autonomy* and facilitates *positive sexual autonomy*.[3] For most people, and most legal systems, *consent* is now deemed to be the 'moral magic' that performs this crucial function.[4] Consent is what ensures that the partners to the sexual act are willing (and hopefully enthusiastic) co-conspirators.

But what is consent and how do we ensure that it is present? In the human-to-human context, the answers to these questions are complex and controversial.[5] Westen, for instance, argues that there are at least four distinct consent concepts that operate in moral and legal discourse. His framework for thinking about sexual consent distinguishes between consent as *subjective attitude* (i.e., willingness to accept or go along with something, not necessarily equivalent to a desire) and *objective performance* (i.e., the communication of signals of willingness to another party). It also distinguishes between *factual* consent (i.e., what a person actually communicated and felt about an act) and *prescriptive* consent (i.e., the normative standards of communication we as a society prescribe). The normative goal in human-to-human relationships is to ensure that the objective prescriptive performance matches the subjective factual attitude: i.e., that we communicate and act upon signals that are representative of our subjective willingness to engage in sexual activity. But it is often hard to craft workable guidelines to ensure that this happens. This is because it is difficult to figure out what a person's subjective attitude actually is, apart from the objective signals representing that attitude. So, when setting normative standards, we tend to focus on objective performance—and then run into the problem that there are many conflicting and ethically dubious views about when and whether an objective performance can be taken to signal consent. Some people think that certain styles of clothing and flirtatious behavior signal consent. Others think that a clearly communicated 'no' can mean yes, or that lack of resistance is a sign of encouragement. These views are morally flawed, but historically common.

Questions surrounding the appropriate norms of consent have become particularly notorious in recent years. There has been a highly publicized "crisis" of sexual assault and rape on university campuses. According to some US studies, between one-in-five[6] and one-in-four women[7] are likely to experience unwanted sexual contact[8] during their time at university. Similar figures are reported in other countries. In Ireland (where I am located), a 2015 study of leading universities revealed that between one-in-seven and one-in-four women were victims of unwanted sexual contact.[9] The studies also suggest (as is true in non-university cases) that these incidents go underreported and under-prosecuted.

Studies of this sort have been the subject of criticism.[10] Some critics argue that such studies give inflated figures due to the language used in the surveys.[11] Some argue there are discrepancies in the figures that go unexplained. But even if these criticisms are correct, the likely 'true' number is still too high,[12] and most would agree that something ought to be done to address the problem. One of the more interesting solutions to the problem is to insist upon *affirmative consent standards* in sexual ethics. This is something that is now mandated in certain US states.[13] Affirmative consent standards stipulate that sexual contact is only permissible if there are clear and unambiguous affirmative signals of consent. No longer will people be able to infer consent from lack of resistance, clothing, and flirtatious behavior. More is needed.

How is any of this relevant to the sex robot debate? I, along with most other contributors to this volume,[14] believe that sex robots are unlikely to be moral persons. In other words, I believe they will (for the foreseeable future anyway) lack the inner subjective life that makes consent so important in the human context. It might consequently seem that consent is completely irrelevant to the evaluation of sex robots. To talk about consent in the human-to-robot context is to commit a category mistake: to apply a concept that ought not to be applied.

Yet, this view seems to me to be in error. Westen's framework distinguishing between actual subjective attitudes and prescribed objective performances allows us to see why. It is true that if robots are not moral persons, then they cannot be *victims* of unwanted sexual contact. But the robots themselves will presumably engage in objective performances in response to their users. Thus, they might respond approvingly, or disapprovingly, to their users' sexual advances.[15] These objective performances will either symbolically mimic or differ from the normatively accepted consent standards in society at large. This means that both the robot itself (in its appearance and behavior) and the act of having sex with the robot will have important symbolic properties when it comes to norms of sexual consent and interpersonal sexual ethics. The presence of these symbolic properties is what opens up the door to the symbolic-consequences argument.

7.3   The Symbolic-Consequences Argument

As I mentioned in the introduction, the symbolic-consequences argument is popular in the contemporary debate about sex robots, particularly among those who object to the development and use of sex robots. But its popularity is implicit rather than explicit. Most proponents of the argument do not express it using the terminology of 'symbolic-consequences.' They make what they take to be unique and distinctive arguments. Thus, when I say that it is 'popular,' I am making a potentially controversial claim. I am saying that there is a common argumentative structure underlying many objections to sex robots. In this section, I want to identify that structure and illustrate it with examples from the literature.

The common argumentative structure is as follows:

(1) Sex robots do/will symbolically represent ethically problematic sexual norms. (*Symbolic Claim.*)

(2) If sex robots do/will symbolically represent ethically problematic sexual norms, then their development and/or use will have negative consequences. (*Consequential Claim.*)

(3) Therefore, the development and/or use of sex robots will have negative consequences *and* we should probably do something about this. *(Warning Call Conclusion)*

Some comments about this abstract formulation are in order.

First, the ethically problematic symbolism could take many forms. It could be linked to the robot's appearance and demeanor, or to the act of sexually engaging with the robot. For instance, in the consent case, it could be that the robot encourages the user to engage with it in a way that ignores or positively flouts the socially accepted norms of consent. It could also be that the physical representation of the robot embodies negative sexual stereotypes. Perhaps the robot represents a certain style of female appearance (maybe a "porn star"-esque style)? The behavior or movement of these sex robots may also be problematic, e.g., they may behave in an overly deferential, coquettish manner, representing women as submissive and subordinated creatures.

Second, the negative consequences of the symbolism could take many forms, some more immediate and direct than others. It could be that the user is directly and immediately harmed by the interaction with the robot. It could also be that the development and use of the robots sends a negative signal to the rest of society, thereby reinforcing a culture of sexism, misogyny, and/or sexual objectification. This "expressive" consequentialism is common in other symbolic objections to cultural practices.[16] The interaction with the robot could also have downstream effects on the user, changing his/her interactions with other human beings and thereby having a harmful impact on those others as well. The negative consequences need not be a dead certainty: they could have varying degrees of probability attached to them. This is normal enough in a debate about a nascent, emerging technology (it's normal enough in any debate about the consequences of technological usage). But the uncertainties may make it difficult to draw firm normative conclusions. I return to this problem later.

Third, the conclusion is something of a non sequitur in its current form. The first part follows logically from the premises; the second part does not. Nevertheless, I have tacked on this "warning call" because I think it is common in the debate: most purveyors of these arguments think we ought to do something to minimize the potential negative consequences. What this "something" should be is another matter. Some people favor organized campaigns against the development of sex robots;[17] others favor strong to weak forms of regulation.[18]

I have presented the abstract structure. Are there specific examples that flesh out the premises in more detail? Indeed there are. I'll briefly describe three.

The first comes from the work of Sinziana Gutiu. She provides the most extensive consent-based version of the argument so I will discuss her version at the greatest length. Her starting presumption is that the majority of sex robots will be targeted at heterosexual males and will depict a problematic, stereotypically "ideal" woman. She defends this presumption by reference to literary precursors to sex robots (e.g., the long-standing trope of male protagonists constructing ideal female partners, present in the Adam and Eve myth) and current examples of robotic technology. Some of these current technologies do not involve actual sexbots (i.e., robots designed for sexual use) but do involve gynoid robots (robots designed to look and act like women) that are highly sexualized:

Aiko, Actroid DER and F, as well as Repliee Q2 are representations of young, thin, attractive oriental women, with high-pitched, feminine voices and movements. Actroid DER has been demoed wearing either a tight hello kitty shirt with a short jean skirt, and Repliee Q2 has been displayed wearing blue and white short leather dress and high-heeled boots.[19]

Current sex-robot prototypes (e.g., Roxxxy and the models from RealDoll) would seem to follow suit. For Gutiu, then, the physical structure of female robots alone serves to represent problematic norms of body shape, dress, and movement. The problematic symbolism is compounded when robots are designed for sexual use. As Gutiu puts it:

To the user, the sex robot looks and feels like a real woman who is programmed into submission and which functions as a tool for sexual purposes. The sex robot is an ever-consenting sexual partner and the user has full control of the robot and the sexual interaction. By circumventing any need for consent, sex robots eliminate the need for communication, mutual respect, and compromise in the sexual relationship. The use of sex robots results in the dehumanization of sex and intimacy by allowing users to physically act out rape fantasies and confirm rape myths.[20]

It seems, then, that Gutiu fleshes out the first premise of the argument in the following manner:

(1*) Sex robots will symbolically represent ethically problematic sexual norms because (a) the majority will adopt gendered norms of body shape, dress, voice, and movement (e.g., they will be thin, large-breasted, provocatively clad, coquettish in behavior, and so on—this could vary from society to society); and (b) they will function as ever-consenting sexual tools, bypassing any need for mutual communication and mutual respect, and allowing users to act out rape fantasies and confirm rape myths.

She then turns to the negative social consequences of this symbolism. She distinguishes between two sets of harms. First, there are the obvious *social harms* arising from the symbolism. If the robots represent gendered norms of sexualized appearance and sexual compliance, they will contribute to and reinforce a patriarchal social order that is harmful to women. In particular, they will further distort our understanding of sexual consent. Campaigners have been fighting hard to make changes to the law surrounding rape and sexual assault. The changes made to date try to combat rape myths by clarifying the nature of sexual consent and assigning appropriate weight to the testimony of victims. Sex robots would represent a step back in this fight because "they embed the idea that women are passive, ever-consenting sex objects, and teach users that when getting consent from a woman, 'only no means no.'"[21]

In other words, they would go against the recent reforms of consent standards and in particular the push for positive affirmative signals of sexual consent. This could obviously have an impact on women, who become victims of actual sexual assault and rape if users act out in the real world.

Second, in addition to the social harms and harms to others, there are the *harms to the users themselves*. For one thing, the users could internalize the problematic sexual norms through repeated use of the robots, which could alter their moral character and the nature of their interactions with other people. Also, and somewhat in tension with this idea, the robots could reinforce antisocial tendencies among users, encouraging them to withdraw from social interactions, and avoid the need for mutuality and compromise in their sexual lives. This latter notion was contradicted in the film *Lars and the Real Girl*. In that film, the use of a sex doll was therapeutic and enabled an introverted man to reintegrate with society. However, Gutiu dismisses this:

Although it was an effective approach to a Hollywood film, sex robots are unlikely to help antisocial users better interact with women. It is doubtful that an individual who does not feel accepted in society, and who finds an alternative way to meet their exact needs for companionship will, for some reason, want to integrate back into society, where they can risk rejection and face social discomfort.[22]

This suggests that Gutiu fleshes out the second premise of the argument in the following manner:

(2*) If sex robots adopt gendered norms of body shape, dress, behavior, etc., and function as ever-consenting sexual tools, their creation and use will: (a) reinforce patriarchal social norms and distort our understanding of sexual consent, which will ultimately harm women; and (b) will harm the users by encouraging them to internalize problematic sexual norms, and, for some, exacerbate their antisocial tendencies.

This, in turn, leads to the "warning call" conclusion. Gutiu thinks that something should be done to combat the problematic symbolism and likely negative consequences. She does not favor prohibition of sex robots. Instead, she favors various regulatory interventions. These could include, in particular, the demand that creators design robots in a certain way. They could also include the creative use of legal mechanisms to allow potential victims of harm arising from the use of sex robots to sue for damages. As an example, she suggests that a person whose marriage dissolves after their partner starts using a sex robot be allowed to sue the manufacturer. This might seem unusual, but there are legal mechanisms (so-called "heart balm torts") that allow people to sue others for interfering with a legally protected relationship, so the idea is not without precedent.

A second variation on the symbolic-consequences argument can be found in the work of Kathleen Richardson and *The Campaign Against Sex Robots.*[23] This work is discussed and critiqued at length elsewhere in this volume,[24] so I will only offer a brief summary here. The major objection to sex robots in Richardson's work stems from what she perceives to be the analogy between human-sexbot interactions and human-prostitute[25] interactions. She believes that the current development of sex robots is being modeled on a particular understanding of the interactions between humans and sex workers. In other words, the goal of the designers and creators of sex robots is to create an interactive experience between the robot and the human user that is roughly equivalent to the interaction between a sex worker and their client. The robots consequently symbolically represent that style of interaction. She cites the work of David Levy in support of this view.

This is problematic for two reasons. First, human-sex worker interactions are themselves ethically problematic. They are based on asymmetries of power. The client's will and interests dominate over those of the sex worker. There is no concern for the inner mental life, wants, or needs of the worker. The sex worker is thus objectified and instrumentalized. By symbolically mimicking such interactions, sex robots represent approval for this style of interaction. Second, in doing so, sex robots will encourage their users to perpetuate negative attitudes toward women. This will reinforce a misogynistic and patriarchal culture in which women are subordinated and oppressed. Richardson thinks we should respond to these problems by instituting an organized campaign against the development of sex robots. This argument fits very much within the symbolic-consequences model.

A final variation on the symbolic-consequences argument comes from some of my own work. In a paper published a couple of years back,[26] I suggested that there *might* (I was tentative) be reason to outlaw the manufacture and/or use of certain kinds of sex robot on essentially symbolic grounds. In particular, I singled out robots that were designed to cater to rape fantasies and pedophiliac tendencies. My argument was intended to be *purely symbolic* in nature. I suggested, following the work of Stephanie Patridge, that there was something intrinsically wrong with our reactions to certain symbolic representations.[27] In this sense, the person who enjoys having sex with a robot that mimics resistance to sexual advances or that is designed to look like a child is analogous to the person who laughs at a racist joke or enjoys racist artworks. They express something about their moral character that is worthy of social condemnation. On some occasions, this may be sufficiently serious to warrant legal prohibition. In this manner, my argument didn't really appeal to consequences at all. Nevertheless, I did suggest (as I will suggest again below) that consequences are always relevant to the ethical evaluation of symbolic representations as they may serve to outweigh or reinforce the problems with the symbolism. The crucial question is: Do the negative/positive consequences outweigh or reinforce the problems with the symbolism? This is actually an exceptionally difficult question to answer and may warrant a whole new approach to the development of sex robots.

But this is to get ahead of the argument. For now I want to move away from outlining the structure of the symbolic-consequences argument to a critical evaluation of its two main premises. Is the symbolism of sex robots likely to be problematic? If so, how? And how can we evaluate the alleged consequences of this symbolism? I answer these questions over the next two sections.

7.4   Are Sex Robots Symbolically Problematic?

To determine whether sex robots are symbolically problematic, we first need a better understanding of symbolic value and its importance in human social life. Andrew Sneddon's paper on the topic is instructive in this regard.[28] It makes two claims that are relevant to the present inquiry. The first is that there are two distinct ways in which symbols can be valuable; the second is that symbols are valuable because they govern the relational aspects of human life. I want to briefly explain both of these claims because I think they serve to highlight the strength of the symbolic claim in premise one of the symbolic-consequences argument.

Let's start with a general account of symbols. Following C. S. Peirce's work on representation, Sneddon argues that symbols exist when three things are present: (1) a *symbolic object or practice*, i.e., some object or practice that is taken to *stand for* or *represent* something else; (2) an *interpreter*, i.e., someone who decides that the object stands for or represents something else; and (3) a *ground for interpretation*, i.e., something that justifies or supports the interpreter's take on what the symbol stands for. A painting is a symbolic object: the lines of paint on the canvas are taken to represent and stand for something by the person viewing the painting (this could be some event in the real world, some commentary on religion or politics, or some reflection of the artist's inner turmoil). The viewer's interpretation can be justified on a number of grounds (e.g., the *similarity* between the lines of paint and some event or object in the real world, some conventional or proposed theory of art, or some *causal relationship* between what was going on in the painter's mind when they were creating this artwork and the artwork itself).[29] Even with this simple example we see that symbolic representation is a complex thing. A symbolic object can be taken to represent many different things on many different grounds. Furthermore, we see that symbolism is distinct from communication: symbols can exist without some original communicator who is trying to convey a message. All that matters for symbolism is that you have the object, the interpreter, and the grounds for interpretation.

This account of symbols applies straightforwardly to the sex robot case. Take the arguments in the previous section. The proponents of these arguments are the *interpreters*. The sex robots (real or imagined) are the *symbolic objects* that are taken to stand for, or represent, something else by the interpreters. What they are taken to stand for or represent varies slightly between the interpreters. They all agree that the robots will tend to stand for or represent women (or, in my case, also possibly children). Furthermore, they all think that they stand for a particular understanding of women (or children) as sexual playthings. There are then some differences in terms of how the behavior and interaction with the robots stands for something else. Richardson, for instance, thinks that the interaction represents the relationship between a sex worker and a client; and Gutiu thinks it represents a problematic set of beliefs about norms of consent and the status of women. The interpreters then justify or support their interpretations on various grounds. The most obvious ground is the *resemblance* between the robots and the real world human beings and actions they represent. The intentions of the creators and users are also additional, supporting grounds for the interpretations. To me, at any rate, this understanding of the symbolism of sex robots makes sense. With relatively few exceptions,[30] these robots are created and desired because they provide some kind of facsimile of a sexual encounter with a real human being. They are not simply devices for sexual stimulation or release—we already have those—they are something more, by virtue of what they represent.

But why does it matter? Why should we care what they represent if the robots themselves are not moral victims? This is where Sneddon's distinctions between the different kinds of symbolic value, and the social importance of symbols, is relevant. Sneddon claims that there are two distinct ways in which symbols can be valuable (or disvaluable, as the case may be). The first is that they can be valuable in *virtue of what they are taken to represent*. This is obvious enough, but it has some important repercussions. If the symbol is valuable (or disvaluable) in virtue of what it represents, then you must first understand the value of what it is taken to represent before you can understand the value of the symbol. Thus, the disvalue that attaches to sex robots that are taken to represent women (or children) as passive, ever-consenting sexual playthings must be understood in terms of the disvalue that attaches to the view that women (or children) actually *are* passive, ever-consenting sexual playthings. The history of sexual violence and oppression, the disregard for individual autonomy and rights, the harm and trauma that results from unwanted sexual contact—these are all reasons to balk at the notion that women (or children) should be understood in these terms. These reasons carry over (in an attenuated form) to the symbolic representations (i.e., the sex robots). The symbols thus share in the disvalue of what they represent.

The second way in which symbols can be valuable (or disvaluable) is *in and of themselves*, i.e., apart from what they represent. Sneddon says that the 'N-word' (i.e., 'nigger') is a strong case of this. Although the disvalue attaching to the N-word originated in real world practices of abuse and oppression, the word itself has now taken on such an incendiary aura that to even *mention* it in discourse (as opposed to *use* it as a term of abuse) is taken to be problematic. To prove the point: I suspect many people reacted negatively when they saw the real word being mentioned by me a couple of sentences ago, even though I wasn't using the word to refer to anyone or any group. Something doesn't sit right with its mere presence on the page. This is why the euphemism "N-word" has become common. People want some way to refer to the symbol without actually using it. This second type of symbolic value is rare in its purest form. But oftentimes there is a hybrid form of symbolic value where the symbol is valuable (or disvaluable) by virtue of what it represents; but this doesn't fully explain the value attaching to it—there is something intrinsic to the symbol as well. It is difficult to see how this could happen in the case of sex robots. But it might. It might be that even mentioning or referring to sex robots takes on a negative (or positive) aura regardless of what they are taken to represent. Indeed, there is a sense in which this is already true. When I say to colleagues that I am writing and editing a book about sex robots, they seem to get immediately uncomfortable and dismissive. This might be because their minds instantly conjure up images of potential sex robots, and they then think about what the robots might represent, but it might also be that the mere mention of the concept is doing all the work. It is a difficult thing to disentangle. Fortunately, it does not matter going forward. For the remainder of this section, I will simply assume that the disvalue attaching to sex robots arises by virtue of what they are taken to represent and not from anything intrinsic to the robots themselves.

This still doesn't tell us why symbols are valuable or disvaluable. We know that they can be valuable (or disvaluable) in two distinct ways, but we don't know why they acquire this value (or disvalue) in the first place. The answer to that question lies in the importance of human sociality and the role of symbols in mediating and facilitating human social life. Human beings are a social species. Key moments in our technological and social history are typically marked by increases in social cooperation and coordination.[31] Symbols are essential to this progress. Anthropologists and historians have often commented upon this.[32] For example, in his surprise best-selling book *Sapiens* (2011), Yuval Noah Harari argues that human social evolution has been marked largely by our ability to create fictional, abstract structures that we overlay onto our physical reality. These fictional structures get reinforced and communicated through symbolic representations. The most obvious and important of these, of course, are the languages we use to encode and communicate our beliefs, laws, customs, and norms. But other symbolic representations play a part too, from national flags and sculptures, to scientific theories, to works of architectural beauty and wonder. All of these things serve to create a heavily symbolic social environment in which we live out our lives. These symbols dictate social roles and social beliefs. They tell us how we should relate to, and understand, one another.

This provides support for Sneddon's claim that symbols are valuable precisely because they govern the purely *relational* aspects of human life. In this regard, they are distinct from other sources of value, such as harms/benefits and rights/duties. Harms and benefits are, in Sneddon's vocabulary, *constitutively* and *evaluatively* individualistic. In other words, harms/benefits are things that happen to, or accrue to, individual human beings, and we care about them because of what they do to individuals. Symbols, on the other hand, are both constitutively and evaluatively relational. They are constitutively relational because they are made up of objects, signs, practices, etc., that represent or stand for something else. Thus, they always stand in relations to both human interpreters and that which is being represented in symbolic form. Furthermore, they are evaluatively relational because they are important by virtue of how they mediate the relationship we have with others and the world around us. Thus, a racial slur is (negatively) value-laden because of what it says about the relationship between the user of the slur and the person or race in question. The same goes for the use of a sex robot with symbolically disturbing properties. Its use says something about the relationship between the user (and the society that facilitates the user) and the people or group represented in the robotic form.

Where does this leave us with respect to premise one of the symbolic-consequences argument? It seems to leave us with much to be said in its favor. Given the centrality of symbols in human social life, proponents of these arguments have reason to be concerned. They seem to be justified in suggesting that, at least some (and maybe many), sex robots will be taken to stand for and represent our attitudes toward real people (specifically, women and children) due to both their resemblance to real people and the intentions of the creators and users. Furthermore, it seems plausible to suggest that they will tend to represent those real people in a particular way: as ever-consenting sexual playthings. It is hard to escape this interpretation of the symbolism. If sex robots are designed and marketed for sexual use, the user will want them to be available and ready for use whenever they are switched on. They are unlikely to have an appetite for the mutual conversation and objective performances demanded by our consent norms. Since this could be taken to symbolically encode a disregard for preferred norms of sexual consent, it seems plausible to say that there is something symbolically disvaluable about sex robots. The same logic applies to other aspects of the symbolism (e.g., the gendered beauty norms, the asymmetry of power, the lack of mutual respect).

But the argument cannot end there. The problematic symbolism of sex robots is contingent in two important ways: it is *removable* and *reformable*. It is possible to embrace the symbolic critique without rejecting the permissibility of sex robots. With regards to *removability*, it is important to remember that the appearance and behavior of sex robots is not some Platonic essence that is fixed and irrevocable. Sex robots need not be large-breasted, thin-waisted, porn star-esque waifs.[33] No doubt there will be significant pressures in favor of this representation.[34] But it is conceivable that one could create and design a sex robot to look and act more like a 'real' woman; to represent a more progressive set of norms around sexual consent and beauty, and interpersonal relations. For instance, the robot could be programmed so as not to be an "ever-consenting" sexual tool. The robot might sometimes randomly refuse its user, and always provide positive affirmative signals of consent when it is willing to proceed. Enforcing and ensuring a more positive set of representations might be a good target for regulation in this area. Furthermore, to the extent that robots are designed to cater to rape fantasies or pedophiliac tendencies, this is something that could be outlawed or banned. In short, it is conceivable to imagine a world in which sex robots do not share the problematic symbolism highlighted by the arguments discussed in the preceding section. Whether it is possible to realize that world is another matter.

This brings us to the second important way in which the symbolism of sex robots is contingent. Some people might resist the suggestions in the previous paragraph on the grounds that it is very difficult to avoid the problematic symbolism involved in the creation of a robot that looks like a real woman and is to be used solely for sexual purposes.[35] This argument, however, ignores the fact that symbolic interpretations are, in virtually all cases, *polysemous* and *highly contested*. It is often only because we live in a particular cultural environment—with its own set of socially accepted symbolic interpretations—that we fail to see this contingency. Brennan and Jaworski provide a fascinating insight into this phenomenon in their discussion of symbolic objections to markets.[36] To many moral philosophers, the idea of paying for certain goods and services (mourners at funerals, sex, best man speeches, kidneys) necessarily leads to the moral tainting of those goods and services.[37] To pay your spouse for sex, they say, would necessarily corrupt the intimacy and mutuality of the marital relationship, reducing it to a cold and emotionless commercial transaction. But not all cultures share this belief. In the Merina tribe of Madagascar, it is expected that husbands pay their wives after sex as a sign of respect. To the Merina tribe, money does not symbolize distance or a lack of affection. Quite the contrary, in fact.[38] And it is not just money whose social meaning is contingent either. Brennan and Jaworski discuss several other examples illustrating the social and cultural contingency of the meaning that attaches to symbolic practices. The most famous example is the social meaning that attaches to our treatment of the dead. According to Herodotus, the Persian King Darius once noted the discrepancies between Greeks and Callation cultural norms on this score. The Greeks thought that you expressed respect for the dead by burning their bodies on a funeral pyre; the Callations thought that this was to treat the dead like a piece of trash. They preferred to eat them instead. Needless to say the Greeks were abhorred by this notion.

This contingency of symbolic meaning has important implications for how we think about the symbolic meaning of sex robots. At the moment, we may well live in a culture that attaches negative meanings to the representation of women (and potentially children) as sexual playthings. But this could be capable of radical change. There could be (distant) future cultures where having sex with a robot does not carry the same negative connotations. It may actually signal safety and respect. Don't misunderstand this claim. To say that the social meaning that attaches to sex robots can be radically altered in this manner is not to say that we should radically alter it. It is simply to say—as Brennan and Jaworski point out—that the meaning of a symbolic practice cannot be treated as a given in our ethical analysis. The meaning of the practice is itself up for ethical scrutiny, and, under the right circumstances, there might be strong moral grounds for thinking that we should reform the meaning that attaches to the practice. What circumstances might these be? The cultural meaning of dead bodies is, again, instructive:

[C]onsider that some cultures developed the idea that the best way to respect the dead was to eat their bodies. In those cultures, it really was a socially constructed fact, regardless of one's intentions, that failing to eat the dead expressed disrespect, while eating rotting flesh expressed respect. But now consider that the Fore tribe of Papua New Guinea suffered from prion infections as a result of eating the rotten brains of their dead relatives prior to that practice being banned in the 1950s. The interpretative practice of equating the eating of rotting flesh with showing respect is a destructive, bad practice. The people in that culture have strong moral grounds to change what expresses respect.[39]

The point is clear. In some cases, the *consequences* of sticking with a particular set of social meanings can be destructive. The Fore tribe's belief that they should respect the dead by eating their brains had such destructive consequences that it needed to be changed. The same conclusion can be drawn in relation to the symbolism of sex robots. Thus, while I might be inclined to agree with Gutiu and Richardson (and myself-of-three-years-ago) that the current social meaning of sex robots is problematic, that is not the end of the story. The consequences of having robots with that problematic symbolism turns out to be the critical factor. If the consequences are positive, then we may need to reform the symbolic meaning.

7.5   Are Sex Robots Consequentially Harmful?

We have reached a critical point. If the argument in the preceding section is correct, then there may well be problems with the symbolism of (at least some) sex robots, but that problematic symbolism is likely to be contingent in two important ways: (1) the particular features of the robots that warrant the problematic interpretation might be removed and changed; and (2) the social meaning of any symbolic representation, no matter how strongly negative it seems to be, is capable of being reformed. This contingency means that the consequences of the symbolism become all important. We may then logically ask: Are the design, manufacture, sale, and use of sex robots likely to reinforce and exacerbate the problematic symbolism? Or could these factors have positive consequences that are capable of outweighing (and thus warranting changes in) the symbolic interpretation?

Proponents of the symbolic-consequences argument claim that the consequences will exacerbate and reinforce the problems with the symbolism. Recall Gutiu's claims about how gendered sex robots will cause their users to withdraw from society and/or interact with real women in problematic ways. Richardson echoes these claims in her 'campaign' against sex robots. Both have plausible-sounding arguments for believing that these negative consequences will follow. Someone who has sex with a robot on a regular basis may grow accustomed to the belief that their sexual partners should always be 'ready to go.' They may grow frustrated with the need for mutual agreement and meaningful consent in human-to-human relationships. This may cause them to withdraw from such relationships, or to be more aggressive in those sexual encounters. Either way, the consequences would seem to be bad for our collective attempts to improve the norms of sexual consent and interpersonal sexual relationships. On top of this, there may be other, more subtle and difficult-to-assess effects. The mere presence and cultural acceptance of symbolically problematic sex robots might have negative consequences for the experience of women living in the societies that accept their existence. The women might feel less welcome and less respected. They might acquire a 'false consciousness' about their position and place in society.

The problem with these plausible-sounding arguments is that they need to be weighed against other, often equally plausible-sounding, arguments suggesting that the consequences might not be as bad as we just supposed. There are a few possibilities to consider. For one thing, the design and use of robots that cater to, say, rape fantasies or pedophiliac tendencies might have a *cathartic* as opposed to *emboldening* effect on their users. In other words, the robots might create a "safe space" in which these problematic sexual desires can be expressed without harming others. This "cathartic" view of human desire is contentious, but if utilized in the right therapeutic setting—perhaps with complementary psychotherapy—it is possible that these robots could be used to wean people away from their problematic desires and dispositions. More generally, sex robots that are designed to symbolically represent more progressive attitudes toward women and sexual consent could be used to educate young people as to the socially accepted sexual norms. Thus, far from reinforcing patriarchal and misogynistic attitudes, the robots might help to undermine them. On top of this, there are, as other contributions to this volume suggest (e.g., McArthur, Di Nucci), positive consequences that may ensue from the development of sex robots, including the improvement of the access to, and satisfaction of, positive sexual rights. These consequences would need to be weighed against competing negative consequences.

What do we do with these contradictory, plausible-sounding arguments? I will suggest a modest, skeptical response—similar to the response that I have given elsewhere.[40] I will suggest that plausible-sounding arguments are not going to be enough. To decide who has the better of it, we need good empirical evidence. And we simply do not have that at the moment because we do not have many sex robots in existence, and so we do not have any empirical studies of their uses and effects. All we have are analogies with other, potentially similar phenomena, like hardcore pornography. And those analogies are not encouraging.

People have long worried about the negative effects of pornography on users and the societies in which they live. People worry that regular exposure to, and use of, pornography will have addictive effects, causing the user to constantly seek out new 'highs' in their pornographic viewing, and alter the users' attitudes toward sexual behavior and (in particular) women. Over the years, thousands of experimental and epidemiological studies have been published supporting different views on this question. Many studies do indeed find that users of pornography are (slightly, but significantly) more likely to embrace promiscuity,[41] engage in risky sexual behavior,[42] have worse relationships,[43] have disturbing attitudes toward women, and be more likely to engage in acts of sexual aggression.[44] But other studies dispute these claims, suggesting that users of pornography are more likely to have progressive attitudes toward women,[45] that pornography can be associated with positive relationship outcomes,[46] and that correlations between pornography use and sexual aggression fail to disentangle cause and effect (i.e., higher pornography consumption may be an effect of negative attitudes and aggression, not a cause).[47] Claims regarding the addictive effects of pornography are also hotly disputed.[48] And virtually every researcher in this field laments the low quality and biased nature of the available evidence.[49]

This is not encouraging in two respects. It suggests that finding out the consequences of sexual symbolism is exceptionally difficult. And it suggests that the evidence we end up with may be ambiguous and disputed—which would be of little help to proponents or opponents of the symbolic-consequences argument.

Of course, the analogy between pornography and sex robots is imperfect. I have argued elsewhere that the embodied nature of the interaction between the robot and the user may have stronger causal effects than the consumption of pornography.[50] In viewing pornography, there is some psychological distance between the user and the symbolic object; in the case of sex robots there is a direct and immediate interaction with the symbolic object. But this argument is still speculative and it's unclear in which direction the stronger causal effects might flow. Will it have an emboldening or cathartic effect? At this point in time, we just don't know.

7.6 An Experimental Approach to Sex Robots

This leaves us in a tricky position. We have grounds for thinking that at least some of the symbolic properties of sex robots are ethically problematic, but that these properties are contingent in two respects (*removability* and *reformability*). We also have grounds for thinking that the consequences will be the decisive factor, but that if analogous case studies are any guide, these consequences are going to be exceptionally difficult to work out. I want to conclude by arguing that this state of affairs should encourage us to take an explicitly experimental approach to the development of sex robots.[51]

In this respect, I am influenced by the work of Ibo van de Poel, and his colleagues, on new technologies as social experiments.[52] To understand their thinking, take the case of the iPhone (or smartphones, more generally) and ask yourself a simple question: What was Apple thinking when they introduced this product back in 2007? It was an impressive bit of technology, poised to revolutionize the smartphone industry, and set to become nearly ubiquitous within a decade. The social consequences were to be dramatic. Looking back, some of those consequences have been positive: increased connectivity, increased knowledge, and increased day-to-day convenience. But a considerable number of the consequences have been quite negative: the assault on privacy, increased distractability, endless social noise. Were any of these possible consequences weighing on the mind of Steve Jobs when he stepped onstage to deliver his keynote on January 9, 2007? Some possibly were, but more than likely they leaned toward the positive end of the spectrum. Jobs was famous for his "reality distortion field"; it's unlikely he allowed the negative to hold him back for more than a few milliseconds. It was a cool product and it was bound to be a big seller. That's all that mattered. But when you think about it, this attitude is pretty odd. The success of the iPhone and subsequent smartphones has given rise to one of the biggest social experiments in human history. The consequences of near-ubiquitous smartphone use were uncertain at the time. Why didn't we insist on Jobs giving it a good deal more thought and scrutiny? Imagine if instead of an iPhone he was launching a revolutionary new cancer drug? In that case, we would have insisted upon a decade of trials and experiments, with animal and human subjects, before it could be brought to market. Why are we so blasé about information technology as compared to medication?

As Van de Poel notes, technologies like the iPhone have two key properties at their time of launch: (1) they have significant impact potential (i.e., they could change society in dramatic ways); and (2) they have unknown and uncertain effects. Sex robots would seem to share these two properties. If the arguments in this chapter (and throughout this book) are correct, sexbots have significant impact potential. And, as I just pointed out above, they definitely have unknown and uncertain effects. This does not mean we should ban or prevent their creation, assuming this is practical (see Danaher, Earp, and Sandberg in this volume), but it should give us some pause. There is a well-known 'control dilemma' associated with the launch of any new technology with significant impact potential.[53] During the early phases of development, the technology will be easy to control and change in response to feedback, but its social effects will be poorly understood. But during later phases, as the technology becomes more ubiquitous and its social effects (possibly) better understood, it will be effectively impossible to control and change.

This presents policymakers and innovators with a difficult choice. Either they choose to encourage the technological development, and thereby run the risk of profound and uncontrollable social consequences, or they stifle the development in the effort to avoid unnecessary risks. Both choices seem far from optimal. This conundrum has led to a number of controversial and (arguably) unhelpful approaches to the assessment of new technologies. Developers are encouraged to conduct cost-benefit analyses of any new technologies with a view to bringing some quantificational precision into the early phase. This is then usually overlaid with some biasing-principle such as the *precautionary principle*—which leans against permitting technologies with significant impact potential—or the *procautionary principle*—which does the opposite. We can imagine such principles being applied to the development and use of sex robots. People who emphasize the potentially negative consequences are likely to favor the precautionary approach; people who emphasize the potentially positive consequences are likely to favor the procautionary one.

This is not a satisfactory state of affairs. These solutions focus on the first horn of the control dilemma: they try to con us into thinking that the social effects are more knowable at the early phases than they actually are. Van de Poel suggests that we might be better off focusing on the second horn. In other words, we should try to make new technologies more controllable in their later phases by taking a deliberately experimental and incremental approach to their development. Approaching new technologies as social experiments will require both a perspectival and practical shift. It will require us to think about the technology in a new way and put in place practical mechanisms for ensuring effective social experimentation. These practical mechanisms will have epistemic and ethical dimensions.

On the epistemic side of things, we need to ensure that we can gather useful information about the impact of technology and feed this into ongoing and future experimentation. This means that as the technology is developed and made available to users, logistical frameworks need to be put in place to ensure that we can gather data on the social and personal effects of the technology. This is important in the case of sex robots, because, if analogous cases are anything to go by, it may be difficult to gather data after the technology has been released. If we want to avoid the endless and empirically unsatisfactory avalanche of studies that have become common in the pornography debate, we need to do something now, while we still have control. Tracking and surveillance of users may be the most plausible course of action (since tracking and surveillance is often built-in to new technologies)—but this leads to ethical problems (discussed below).

On the ethical side of things, we need to ensure that our ongoing and incremental experiments with the technology will respect certain ethical principles. One of Van de Poel's major contributions to the social experiment debate is his attempt to develop a comprehensive framework of principles for ethical technological experimentation. He does this by explicitly appealing to the medical analogy. Medical experimentation has been subject to increasing levels of ethical scrutiny since World War II. Detailed theoretical frameworks and practical guidelines have been developed to enable biomedical researchers to comply with appropriate ethical standards. The leading theoretical framework is probably Beauchamp and Childress's *Principlism*. This framework is based on four key ethical principles:

Non-maleficence: Human subjects should not be harmed.

Beneficence: Human subjects should be benefited.

Autonomy: Human autonomy and agency should be respected.

Justice: The benefits and risks of experimentation ought to be fairly distributed.

These four principles are general and vague. The idea is that they represent widely shared ethical commitments that can be developed into more detailed practical guidelines for researchers. Again, one of the major strengths of Van de Poel's work is his review of existing medical ethics guidelines (such as the Helsinki Declaration and the Common Rule) and his attempt to code each of those guidelines in terms of Beauchamp and Childress's four ethical principles. He shows how it is possible to fit the vast majority of the specific guidelines into those four main categories. The only real problem is that some of the guidelines focus on who has responsibility for ensuring that the experimentation follows the guidelines, not on the four principles used by Beauchamp and Childress. This is something that is important in relation to the development of non-medical technologies too. Concern about responsibility and liability gaps are rife in the literature about social robotics (see Di Nucci, and Danaher, Earp, and Sandbergin this volume).

These Helsinki and Common Rule guidelines were developed with the vagaries of medical experimentation in mind. We need something that can apply to a technology like sex robots. This requires some adaptation and creativity. Van de Poel has come up with a list of sixteen conditions for ethical technological experimentation. They are illustrated in the table below, which also shows how they map onto Beauchamp and Childress's principles.

These guidelines are relatively self-explanatory, but I will briefly run through the main categories and discuss how they might apply to the experimental development of sex robots.

Table 7.1
Van De Poel's Principles for Ethical Technological Experiment.

Non-maleficence: Do no harm by ensuring ...
1. Absence of other reasonable means for gaining knowledge about risks and benefits.
2. Monitoring of data and risks while addressing privacy concerns.
3. Possibility and willingness to adapt or stop the experiment.
4. Containment of risks as far as reasonably possible.
5. Consciously scaling up to avoid large-scale harm and to improve learning.
6. Flexible setup of the experiment and avoidance of lock-in of the technology.
7. Avoiding experiments that undermine resilience.
Beneficence: Do good by ensuring that it is ...
8. Reasonable to expect social benefits from the experiment.
Responsibility: Be sure that there is a ...
9. Clear distribution of responsibilities for setting up, carrying out, monitoring, evaluating, adapting, and stopping the experiment.
Autonomy: Respect autonomy by ensuring that ...
10. Experimental subjects are informed.
11. The experiment is approved by democratically legitimized bodies.
12. Experimental subjects can influence the setting up, carrying out, monitoring, evaluating, adapting, and stopping of the experiment.
13. Experimental subjects can withdraw from the experiment.
Justice: Ensure that there is a fair distribution of the benefits and burdens of the technology by ensuring that ...
14. Vulnerable experimental subjects are either not subject to the experiment or are additionally protected or particularly profit from the experimental technology (or a combination).
15. A fair distribution of potential hazards and benefits.
16. Reversibility of harm, or, if impossible, compensation for harm.

As you can see, the first seven are all concerned with the principle of non-maleficence. The first condition states that other means of acquiring knowledge about a technology must be exhausted before it is introduced into society. So manufacturers of sex robots should acquire knowledge about their effects on users and the reactions of others before releasing them more generally to consumers. The second and third conditions demand ongoing monitoring of the social effects of technology and efforts to halt the experiment if serious risks become apparent. This will require some ongoing tracking and monitoring of initial beta users to ascertain social effects. This, of course, brings with it certain privacy and autonomy risks, which will need to be addressed through appropriate data protection laws and informed consent provisions (see below). The fourth condition focuses on the containment of harm. It accepts that it is impossible to live in a risk-free world and to eliminate all the risks associated with technology. Nevertheless, harm should be contained as best it can be. So if we learn early on that particular forms of human-sex robot interaction have harmful effects, we should act to mitigate and contain those harms as soon as possible. The fifth, sixth, and seventh conditions all encourage an attitude of incrementalism toward social experimentation. Instead of trying to anticipate all the possible risks and benefits of technology, we should try to learn from experience and build up resilience in society so that any unanticipated risks of technology are not too unsettling.

The next two conditions focus on beneficence and responsibility. Condition eight stipulates that whenever a new technology is introduced there must be some reasonable prospect of benefit to the user and to society at large. This is quite a shift from current attitudes. At the moment, the decision to release a technology is largely governed by economic principles: what matters is whether it will be profitable, not whether it will benefit people. I think the condition of benefit can probably be met in the case of sex robots (other contributions to this book outline some of the reasonable prospects of benefit), but there must also be clear acknowledgment of and respect for the potential harms. Condition nine is about who has responsibility for ensuring compliance with ethical standards. This is an important condition for those who are interested in the legal side of this debate. Those who develop and release these technologies should do so in a responsible and socially conscientious fashion. They should be made to reflect on the potentially negative consequences of releasing a sex robot that clearly represents some problematic symbolism and be forced to take legal responsibility for their decision to do so. Furthermore, their decision to do so should be scrutinized in light of the other principles in this framework.

Conditions ten to thirteen are all about autonomy and consent at both an individual and societal level. Condition ten requires that those who use and may be affected by the technology are properly informed as to the risks and benefits. This will require that appropriate educational and informational materials be provided to people who purchase and are affected by the use of sex robots. Condition eleven says that majority approval is needed for launching a social technological experiment. This might be the most controversial element of the framework. It suggests that decisions about when and whether to launch a new technology with high impact potential should not be a left solely in private, corporate hands. It should be opened up to public scrutiny and debate. I agree that public deliberation about the merits of developing sex robot technology would be a good thing. And, in some sense, I hope that this book and the contributions it contains can play a part in that public debate. But I am not sure that a "majority approval" condition is either practical or desirable. Van de Poel himself notes that this could lead to the tyranny of the majority—with majority groups imposing technological experiments on the minorities who are most affected by them. Conditions twelve and thirteen try to mitigate for this potential tyranny by insisting on meaningful participation for those who are affected by the technology, including a right to withdraw from the experiment. This would seem to be most important in the case of sex robots, particularly if the symbolism is most likely to implicate minority groups or those who lack political power, but how one could ensure a right to 'withdraw' from the experiment is unclear.

The final set of conditions all relate to justice. They too should help to mitigate the potential for a tyranny of the majority. They insist that the benefits and burdens of any technological experiment be appropriately distributed, and that special measures be taken to protect vulnerable populations. Condition sixteen also insists on reversibility or compensation for any harm done. This is where something like Gutiu's earlier proposal about the use of civil liability laws could become appropriate. If the great "sex robot experiment" backfires, and adversely affects women or children or other more specific groups of people, then facilities should be put in place to ensure that these adverse effects can be compensated for, and, where possible, reversed. Explicit consideration for ways in which to distribute the benefits and burdens should also help to determine which side of the symbolic-consequences debate should be allowed to win out.

This experimental approach is certainly not a panacea. But it does encourage a more thoughtful, less knee-jerk, approach to technological developments like sex robots.

7.7 Conclusion

Let me conclude by returning to the opening example: the attempt by the teenagers to have sex with a switched-off robot in the TV show *Humans*. Recall how one of the female protagonists objected to this on the grounds that they would not do this to a real woman. What I have argued in this chapter is that her objection can be spelled out in terms of the symbolic-consequences argument. The problem with switching off a robot and having sex with it lies not in the harm it does to the robot, but rather in what it symbolizes—a general disregard and/or contempt for norms of consent in interpersonal sexual relationships—and the potential negative effects of that symbolism—harm to real women and/or harm to the user of the robot. Several contributors to the current sex robot debate have voiced similar objections.

But this style of objection faces several hurdles. While there are grounds for thinking that sex robots could symbolically represent a troubling attitude toward women (and maybe children) and the norms of interpersonal sexual relationships, the troubling symbolism is likely to be contingent in two ways. It is likely to be *removable* in many instances and *reformable* in others. What will ultimately matter are the consequences of the symbolism. These consequences are going to be difficult to work out. There are plausible-sounding arguments in favor of positive consequences and plausible-sounding argument in favor of negative consequences. What we lack is data. To address these problems, I suggest that we adopt an explicitly experimental approach to the development of sex robots. This approach should be guided by ethical principles and should build in logistical frameworks that allow for experimental data to be gathered and fed back into the process of incremental development.

Adopting this experimental approach will be a difficult thing to do. It will require significant changes in our perspective and attitude toward technological development. But it may be our best bet if we are to avoid the risks associated with developing this potentially high impact technology.

Notes

1. *Humans* originally aired in June 2015. For details see, http://www.channel4.com/programmes/humans.

2. To be clear, in identifying these two classes of sexual activity I am not ignoring the possibility that much sexual activity is neutral or not particularly valuable. I ignore this "middle" category since consent would still be essential to its permissibility.

3. See Di Nucci in this volume.

4. Heidi Hurd, "The Moral Magic of Consent," *Legal Theory* 2, no. 2 (1996): 121–146.

5. For useful overviews see: Alan Wertheimer, *Consent to Sexual Relations* (Cambridge: Cambridge University Press, 2003); Peter Westen, "Some Confusion about Consent in Rape Cases," *Ohio State Journal of Law* 2 (2004): 333–359; Peter Westen *The Logic of Consent.* (London: Ashgate, 2004); Douglas Husak, "The Complete Guide to Consent to Sex: Alan Wertheimer's *Consent to Sexual*

Relations," Law and Philosophy 25, no. 2 (2006): 267–87; Kimberly Ferzan, "Clarifying Consent: Peter Westen's '*The Logic of Consent,*'" *Law and Philosophy* 25 (2006): 193–217; and Heidi Hurd, "Was the Frog Prince Sexually Molested? A Review of Peter Westen's *The Logic of Consent," Michigan Law Review* 103, no. 6 (May 2005): 1329–46.

6. Christopher Krebs, Christine Lindquist, Tara Warner, Bonnie Fisher, and Sandra Martin, "The Campus Sexual Assault Survey," National Institute of Justice, Washington, DC (2007), https://www.ncjrs.gov/pdffiles1/nij/grants/221153.pdf.

7. David Cantor, Bonnie Fisher, Susan Chibnall, and Carol Bruce, "Report on the AAU Campus Climate Survey on Sexual Assault and Sexual Misconduct," The Association of American Universities (2015), http://www.aau.edu/uploadedFiles/AAU_Publications/AAU_Reports/Sexual_Assault _Campus_Survey/Report%20on%20the%20AAU%20Campus%20Climate%20Survey%20on%20 Sexual%20Assault%20and%20Sexual%20Misconduct.pdf.

8. I use this term, rather than "rape or sexual assault" because of the controversies alluded to in the text about the language used in the surveys supporting these figures.

9. J. Humphreys, "11% of Women Students Believe They Were Victims of Sexual Assault," *Irish Times*, June 4, 2015. The 11% figure comes from focusing on the past year; the one-in-four figure comes from focusing on how many people were victims of sexual assault and/or attempted assault.

10. For instance, compare the figures in the two US-based surveys with the figures in the National Victimization of Crime survey. This survey suggests lower overall incidence and higher incidence for non-students: S. Sinozich and L. Langton, *Rape and Sexual Assault Victimization Among College-Age Females, 1995–2013* (Department of Justice, Bureau of Statistics, November 2015), http://www.bjs.gov/content/pub/pdf/rsavcaf9513.pdf

11. Libby Nelson, "Why Some Studies Make Campus Rape Look Like an Epidemic While Others Make it Look Rare," *Vox,* December 11, 2014, http://www.vox.com/2014/12/11/7378271/why -some-studies-make-campus-rape-look-like-an-epidemic-while-others.

12. There is an interesting question here as to whether any figure higher than zero is acceptable. In principle, the answer is no: we obviously do not want anyone to be the victim of rape or sexual assault. In practice, it may be impossible to reduce the incidence of a particular crime to zero.

13. California Senate Bill 967 Student Safety: Sexual Assault makes it a condition of funding f or the state's universities to adopt affirmative consent standards; New York adopted a similar piece of legislation in Senate Bill S5965. Both pieces of legislation affect proceedings within universities and do not change the definition of consent for rape and sexual assault within the criminal law.

14. Cf. chapter by Petersen in this volume.

15. This is apparent from existing prototypes. Roxxxy—who is billed as the world's first sex robot—comes with preprogrammed personality types. One of them ('Frigid Farah') is said to respond to the user's advances with disapproval. See http://www.truecompanion.com/shop/faq.

16. Jason Brennan and Martin Jaworski, "Markets Without Symbolic Limits," *Ethics* 125, no. 4 (2015): 1053–1077.

17. Danaher, Earp, and Sandberg in this volume.

18. Sinziana Gutiu, "The Roboticization of Consent," in *Robot Law*, eds. Calo, Froomkin, and Kerr (Cheltenham, UK: Edward Elgar Publishing, 2016); Sinziana Gutiu, "Sex Robots and the Roboticization of Consent," *We Robot Law Conference Miami* (2012), robots.law.miami.edu/wp-content/uploads/2012/01/GutiuRoboticization_of_Consent.pdf; John Danaher, "Robotic Rape and Robotic Child Sexual Abuse: Should They be Criminalized?" *Criminal Law and Philosophy*, forthcoming (2015), doi: 10.1007/s11572-014-9362-x.

19. Gutiu, "Sex Robots," 5.

20. Ibid., 2.

21. Ibid., 15.

22. Ibid., 17.

23. Kathleen Richardson, "The 'Asymmetrical' Relationship: Parallels Between Prostitution and the Development of Sex Robots," *SIGCAS Computers & Society* 4, no. 3 (September 2015): 290–293, https://campaignagainstsexrobots.org/the-asymmetrical-relationship-parallels-between-prostitution-and-the-development-of-sex-robots.

24. Danaher, Earp, and Sandberg in this volume.

25. Richardson prefers the term "prostitute" to "sex worker." She argues that the latter tends to legitimize the practice. I tend to prefer "sex worker" and revert to that for the remainder of this chapter.

26. John Danaher, "Robotic Rape and Robotic Child Sexual Abuse: Should They be Criminalized?" *Criminal Law and Philosophy*, forthcoming (2015), doi: 10.1007/s11572-014-9362-.

27. Stephanie Patridge, "The Incorrigible Social Meaning of Video Game Imagery," *Ethics and Information Technology* 13, no. 4 (2010): 303–12; Stephanie Patridge, "Pornography, Ethics and Video Games," *Ethics and Information Technology* 15, no. 1 (2013): 25–34.

28. Andrew Sneddon, "Symbolic Value," *Journal of Value Inquiry* (September 2015), doi: 10.1007/S10790-015-9519-4.

29. The most prominent grounds of representation mentioned by Sneddon include *resemblance*, *convention*, *causal connection*, and *stipulation*.

30. What do I mean by this? I think, perhaps, some people might like robotic sexual partners *qua* robots. They might like, and prefer, them to real human beings precisely because they do not view them as being equivalent to or symbolically similar.

31. As an illustration, see Ian Morris, *Foragers, Farmers, and Fossil Fuels* (Princeton: Princeton University Press, 2015).

32. Terrence Deacon, *The Symbolic Species: The Co-Evolution of Language and the Brain* (New York: WW Norton, 1998).

33. A comment is apposite here: I am uncomfortable about shaming any particular style of bodily appearance. I write about the "'porn star'-esque" body shape in a somewhat pejorative fashion because I take it that proponents of the symbolic consequences argument have that pejorative view.

34. Paul Treanor (2015) argues that this is the dominant male preference in his commentaries on sex robots. See Paul Treanor, "Bimboid Utopia: What do Men Want?" (2015), https:// politicalaspects.wordpress.com/2015/02/06/bimboid-utopia-what-do-men-want.

35. Cf. Frank and Nyholm in this volume.

36. Brennan and Jaworski, "Markets," (2015).

37. Michael Sandel, *What Money Can't Buy* (London: Penguin, 2012).

38. The example of the Merina tribe is taken from Viviana A. Zelizer, *The Social Meaning of Money* (Princeton: Princeton University Press, 1996) and is discussed in Brennan and Jaworski (2015).

39. Brennan and Jaworski "Markets without Limits," 1067.

40. John Danaher, "New Technologies as Social Experiments: An Ethical Framework," in *Philosophical Disquisitions* (2016), http://philosophicaldisquisitions.blogspot.ie/2016/03/new -technologies-as-social-experiments.html.

41. Dolf Zillman and Jennings Bryant, "Effects of Prolonged Consumption of Pornography on Family Values," *Journal of Family Issues* 9, no. 4 (1988a): 518; Dolf Zillman and Jennings Bryant, "Pornography's Impact on Sexual Satisfaction," *Journal of Applied Social Psychology* 18, no. 5 (1988b): 438–453; Dolf Zillman and Jennings Bryant, "Effects of Massive Exposure to Pornography," in *Pornography and Sexual Aggression*, eds. Neil Malamuth and Edward Donnerstein, (Amsterdam: Elsevier, 1984); and Jochen Peter and Patti M. Valkenburg, "Adolescents and Pornography: A Review of 20 Years of Research," *Journal of Sex Research* 53, nos. 4–5 (March 2016): 509–31. doi: 10.1080/00224499.2016.1143441.

42. Matija Sinković, Aleksandar Stulhofer, and Joan Božić, "Revisiting the Association Between Pornography Use and Risky Sexual Behaviors: The Role of Early Exposure to Pornography and Sexual Sensation Seeking," *Journal of Sex Research* 50, no. 7 (2013): 633–41. doi: 10.1080/ 00224499.2012.681403; Emily Harkness, Barbara Mullan, and Alex Blaszczynski, "Association Between Pornography Use and Sexual Risk Behaviors in Adult Consumers: A Systematic Review," *Cyberpsychology Behavior and Social Networking* 18, no. 2 (January 2015): 59–71, doi: 10.1089/ cyber.2014.0343.

43. Samuel L. Perry, "Does Viewing Pornography Reduce Marital Quality Over Time? Evidence from Longitudinal Data," *Archive of Sexual Behavior*, doi: 10.1007/s10508-016-0770-y.

44. I treat sexual aggression and disturbing attitudes toward women as a pair since most studies focus on heterosexual pornography. See Gert M. Hald, Neil M. Malamuth, and Carlin Yuen,

"Pornography and Attitudes Supporting Violence Against Women: Revisiting the Relationship in Nonexperimental Studies," *Aggressive Behavior* 36, no. 1 (January 2010): 14–20, doi: 10.1002/ab.20328; Drew A. Kingston, Neil M. Malamuth, Paul Fedoroff, and William L. Marshall, "The Importance of Individual Differences in Pornography Use: Theoretical Perspectives and Implications for Treating Sexual Offenders," *Journal of Sex Research* 46, nos. 2–3 (April 2009): 216–32, doi: 10.1080/00224490902747701; and Paul J. Wright, Robert S. Tokunaga, and Ashley Kraus, "A Meta-Analysis of Pornography Consumption and Actual Acts of Sexual Aggression in General Population Studies," *Journal of Communication* 66, no. 1 (2015): 183–205, doi: 10.1111/jcom.12201.

45. Taylor Kohut, Jodie L. Baer, and Brendan Watts, "Is Pornography Really about 'Making Hate to Women'? Pornography Users Hold More Gender Egalitarian Attitudes Than Nonusers in a Representative American Sample," *Journal of Sex Research* 53, no. 1 (2016): 1–11, doi: 10.1080/00224499.2015.1023427.

46. The evidence here is suggestive only. In a self-selecting sample it was found that some couples were unaffected or positively affected by pornography use: William A. Fisher and Lorne Campbell, "Perceived Effects of Pornography on the Couple Relationship: Initial Findings of Open-Ended, Participant-Informed, "Bottom-Up" Research," *Archives Sexual Behavior* (July 2016), doi: 10.1007/s10508-016-0783-6. The following study finds that *female* use of pornography can be correlated with positive relationship outcomes: Samuel L. Perry, "Does Viewing Pornography Reduce Marital Quality Over Time? Evidence from Longitudinal Data," *Archive of Sexual Behavior*, doi: 10.1007/s10508-016-0770-y.

47. See studies from Malamuth et al. (1988a, 1988b, and 1984). Also, recent studies of Dutch adolescents—Hald et al. (2013)—find that pornography is one small factor among many that accounts for sexual aggression.

48. David Ley, Micole Prause, and Peter Finn, "The Emperor Has No Clothes: A Review of the 'Pornography Addiction' Model," *Current Sexual Health Reports* 6, no. 2 (2014): 94–105.

49. Many of the studies cited in the preceding endnotes lament this fact. A particularly telling illustration of the problem is the report on the effects of pornography exposure on children compiled by Miranda A. H. Horvath, Lilian Alys, Kristina Massey, Afroditi Pina, Mia Scally, and Joanna R. Adler, "Basically ... Porn is Everywhere: A Rapid Evidence Assessment on the Effects that Access and Exposure to Pornography has on Children and Young People," London, Middlesex University, Office of the Children's Commissioner (2013), http://www.mdx.ac.uk/__data/assets/pdf_file/0026/48545/BasicallyporniseverywhereReport.pdf. In this study, they found more than 40,000 results in their searches of the academic literature on the causal effects of pornography exposure, but only a few hundred studies met their inclusion criteria, and even then they noted the partial, low quality, and sometimes biased nature of the research.

50. Danaher, "Robotic Rape."

51. I previously published some of the following paragraphs in Danaher (2016).

52. Ibo Van de Poel, "An Ethical Framework for Evaluating New Technologies," *Science and Engineering Ethics* 22, no. 3 (2016): 667–686; Zoe Robaey and Arno Simons, "Responsible Management of Social Experiments: Challenges for Policymaking," in *Responsible Innovation*, 2nd ed., eds. Bert-Jaap Koops, Ilse Oosterlaken, Henny Romijn, Tsjalling Swierstra, and Jeroen van den Hoven (Berlin: Springer International Publishing, 2015): 87–103.

53. David Collingridge, *The Social Control of Technology* (London: Frances Pinter, 1980).

8 Legal and Moral Implications of Child Sex Robots

Litska Strikwerda

8.1 Introduction

At a robotics conference in July 2014, Ronald Arkin, Mobile Robot Lab director at the Georgia Institute of Technology, claimed that robots designed to look and act like children could be used to treat pedophiles the way methadone is used to treat drug addicts. This claim gave rise to a heated debate. While some people think that the development of child sex robots in order to treat pedophiles would be a worthwhile project, others say this is a repugnant idea.[1] The aforementioned debate is similar to the debate that raged when Dutch psychologists suggested that pedophiles should be offered entirely computer-generated child pornography for treatment purposes.[2]

This chapter will assess the legal and moral implications of child sex robots by means of casuistry, which is a case-based model of reasoning. This model of reasoning is frequently used by both scholars in the field of law and scholars in the field of (applied) ethics.[3] In case-based reasoning, a new, particular case is compared to one or more other cases that seem similar at first sight. If the new, particular case turns out to be relevantly similar to the paradigmatic case(s), it should be treated similarly; if it turns out to be relevantly different, it should be treated differently. This chapter will compare the case of child sex robots to the case of entirely computer-generated child pornography. Are they similar? Or are there (also) relevant differences? And what do these differences, if any, mean for the legal and moral implications of child sex robots?

The first section of this chapter will define the term child sex robots, determine its scope, and explain that child sex robots and entirely computer-generated child pornography are similar, because they both lack a legal or moral victim. The second section will assess the legal and moral implications of entirely computer-generated child pornography. The third section will argue that there is one main difference between entirely computer-generated child pornography and child sex robots: child sex robots are interactive and entirely computer-generated child pornographic images are not. This means that, in certain respects, the legal and moral issues that child sex robots raise differ from the ones that entirely computer-generated child pornography raises.

However, at the end of this chapter it is concluded that the difference between entirely computer-generated child pornography and child sex robots does not lead to different legal and moral implications. Entirely computer-generated child pornographic images are prohibited in many countries on the ground that (the majority of) people find them morally objectionable (legal moralism). If child sex robots were to be developed, they would (likely) be banned for the same reasons. Use is made of virtue ethics and (anti-porn) feminism to explain why people find entirely computer-generated child pornography morally objectionable and why they would think the same about child sex robots. In short, both flout our sexual mentality based on equality, because they are, respectively, incomplete representations and replica of sexual relations between adults and children, which can never be considered equal.

8.2   Child Sex Robots: Definition, Scope, and the Similarity with Entirely Computer-Generated Child Pornography

To my knowledge, child sex robots are not yet in existence. However, adult sex robots are. A US company has developed a female sex robot called "Roxxxy." A male version of Roxxxy, called "Rocky," is in the works. Roxxxy can be described as follows. She has a fleshlike synthetic skin that covers her anatomically correct skeleton. Furthermore, she has the same temperature as a human being owing to the fact that she has a mechanical heart that pumps warm liquid through her body. Roxxxy is able to make certain movements and sensors enable her to "sense" when she is touched and "listen" when someone talks to her. She can also respond to both touch and speech. Roxxxy has cables running out of her back so that users can attach her to a computer. Users can download one of Roxxxy's five preexisting personalities from the Internet and program it into her. They can also add particular likes and dislikes.[4] The same will be true for Rocky when he is fully developed. I assume that, if a child sex robot were to be developed in the near future, it would be a version of Roxxxy or Rocky designed to look and act like a child.

Taking the above-mentioned description of Roxxxy and Rocky into account, John Danaher has defined the term "sex robot" as "any artifact that is used for sexual stimulation and/or release with the following three properties: (1) a humanoid form; (2) the ability to move; and (3) some degree of artificial intelligence (i.e., some ability to sense, process, and respond to signals in its surrounding environment)."[5] Danaher raises two important points with regard to this definition of sex robots. First, it is restricted to humanlike robots, which are robots "that are designed to provide an artificial facsimile of a real human sex partner." Second, Danaher assumes that sex robots "do not meet the criteria for legal or moral personhood," i.e., that they are not capable of being legally or morally harmed by the sexual actions of their users.[6]

This chapter will take Danaher's definition of the term sex robot as a starting point. It will also take the two points he raises for granted. With regard to Danaher's first point, it should be emphasized that this chapter focuses on a specific category of humanlike sex robots—namely, sex robots that are designed to look and act like children. With regard to Danaher's second point, it should be clarified that the assumption that child sex robots do not meet the criteria for legal or moral personhood (and are thus not assumed capable of being legally or morally harmed by the sexual actions of their users) significantly affects the legal and moral implications to be discussed. That is because legal philosophers commonly acknowledge that the moral limits of criminal law are determined by the harm principle. The harm principle originally derives from the nineteenth century philosopher John Stuart Mill. It entails "that the only purpose for which power can be rightfully exercised over any member of a civilized community, against his will, is to prevent harm to others."[7] This means that behaviors should (only) be regulated by means of criminal law if they do harm to others. If child sex robots were capable of being legally or morally harmed by the sexual actions of their users, the legal and moral implications of such actions would thus be straightforward: then they should be morally condemned and hence be criminalized. Since this chapter assumes child sex robots are not capable of being so harmed by their users, it is more difficult to see what their legal and moral implications are. After all, this means that sexual actions of users performed on child sex robots lack a legal or moral victim.

As was indicated in the introduction, child sex robots are similar to entirely computer-generated child pornographic images in the above-mentioned respect. Entirely computer-generated child pornographic images do not involve a child really engaged in sexually explicit conduct, and, therefore, lack a legal or moral victim as well. Consequently, it is appropriate to assess the legal and moral implications of entirely-computer generated child pornographic images prior to assessing the implications of child sex robots.

8.3   The Case of Entirely Computer-Generated Child Pornography

Ordinary child pornography is considered harmful to children. In acts of sexual contact between adults and children, mutual consent is in general assumed to be absent, and, therefore, they are always considered sexual abuse.[8] Since the production of images showing a minor engaged in sexually explicit conduct typically involves an act of sexual contact between adults and children, such images can be considered recordings of harmful sexual abuse.[9] Following this argument, not only the production, but also the possession and distribution of child pornographic images can be considered harmful to children. After all, the possession and distribution (i.e., consumption) of child pornography supports the market for it, and, therefore, causes the (obviously extremely harmful) sexual abuse of children inherent in the production of such materials.[10] Moreover, the child pornographic images themselves are a permanent record of the sexual abuse that occurred in the production, which could continue to haunt the children concerned when they grow up, especially if discovered by others.[11]

As opposed to ordinary child pornographic images, entirely computer-generated child pornographic images do not involve a child really engaged in sexually explicit conduct. They consist of *computer-simulated depictions* and not of recordings of child sexual abuse. Therefore, the production, distribution, and possession thereof cannot be considered harmful to children, and hence the harm principle does not apply. Nevertheless, many countries have ratified article 9 (2) (c) of the Council of Europe's Convention on Cybercrime, which prohibits the production, distribution, and possession of entirely computer-generated child pornographic images.[12] Since the harm principle does not apply, the question arises how this prohibition can be morally legitimated. In earlier work I studied this question.[13] I will summarize my arguments below.

Since they do not cause harm to children, the production, distribution, and possession of entirely computer-generated child pornographic images can be described as "victimless crimes."[14] According to Bedau, the criminalization of victimless crimes can be legitimated on the basis of two other, less commonly acknowledged moral grounds than the harm principle: namely, legal paternalism or legal moralism.[15] Contrary to the harm principle, legal paternalism does not provide a moral ground to outlaw behaviors that harm others, but behaviors that harm the actor him- or herself. Legal moralism provides a moral ground to outlaw behaviors that are inherently immoral. Below I will establish whether or not legal paternalism and legal moralism, respectively, apply to the case of entirely computer-generated child pornography.

8.4 Can Legal Paternalism Legitimate the Criminalization of the Production, Distribution, and Possession of Entirely Computer-Generated Child Pornography?

Two types of legal paternalism can be distinguished: soft paternalism and hard paternalism. Soft paternalism "consists of defending relatively helpless or vulnerable people from external dangers, including harm from *other* people when the protected parties have not voluntarily consented to the risk."[16] Hard paternalism justifies interferences with entirely voluntary self-regarding harmful behavior of people for their own good.[17]

Soft paternalism could legitimate the criminalization of the production, distribution, and possession of entirely computer-generated child pornography if it can be proven that it could encourage or seduce children into participating in sexual contacts with adults. The basis for prohibition would then be situated in the protection of children against the aforementioned seduction or encouragement, thereby defending them from harm from pedophiles. Investigators have found links between young people who watch pornographic images and their attitudes toward sex.[18] It has been suggested that the younger the child is, the more influence these images have on them.[19] Given their pornographic nature, it can thus be assumed that (entirely computer-generated) child pornographic images can influence children's attitudes toward sex, especially at a young age. It does not seem likely that children would deliberately search the Internet themselves for such images. But they might well be used by offenders to groom children into taking part in sexual activities.[20] They could show them to a child in order to encourage participation, stimulate arousal, or as an example of what they want the child to do.[21] Another effect of child pornographic images on children could be that they come to think the activity must be acceptable, since others have engaged in it.[22] There is no evidence, however, that pedophiles frequently make use of (entirely computer-generated) child pornographic images in the way as described above. And more important, they can and do make use of other means to groom children into taking part in sexual activities such as drugs, alcohol, toys, money, or force.[23] In conclusion, it goes too far to claim that entirely computer-generated child pornography encourages or seduces children into participating in sexual contacts with adults.

As a Dutch court has pointed out, it makes a difference if the entirely computer-generated child pornographic images are specifically aimed at children. In 2008, a Dutch national was convicted for the possession of an entirely computer-generated child pornographic film. It was titled "Sex Lessons for Young Girls" and showed a virtual girl of about eight years of age engaged in sexually explicit conduct with a man. The girl depicted is smiling, the man applauds for her, and colorful balloons appear. The court argued that, although the persons appearing in the film do not look realistic to adults, they do seem realistic to the average child. Due to the instructional nature of the film and the colorful framing, the film seems to be aimed at children. Therefore, it could be used to encourage or seduce children into participating in sexual activities with adults.[24] This was an exceptional case, however, and I have not found examples of similar cases.

There might be another way to legitimate the criminalization of the production, distribution, and possession of entirely computer-generated child pornography on the basis of soft paternalism though. According to Feinberg soft paternalism cannot only be used to protect children against themselves, but also people whose choices stem from coercion, drugs, or other voluntariness-vitiating factors, and are, therefore, as alien to them as the choices of someone else.[25] This category of people would include consumers of child pornographic images who claim that they do not consume them in a fully voluntary manner, but are in the grip of some irresistible impulse (i.e., addiction). The existence of (child) pornography addiction is contested, however. As a matter of fact, addiction to (child) pornography is not recognized as an addiction according to the latest edition of the Diagnostic and Statistical Manual of Mental Disorders (DSM-5), which is the "authoritative guide to the diagnosis of mental disorders" used by health care professionals worldwide.[26]

Hard paternalism could legitimate the criminalization of the production, distribution, and possession of entirely computer-generated child pornographic images if it can be proven that they encourage or seduce pedophiles (who deliberately consume them) to commit child abuse. The basis for prohibition would then be situated in the protection of pedophiles against the aforementioned seduction or encouragement, thereby also defending children from harm from them. Many offenders argue that entirely computer-generated child pornography has a positive rather than a negative effect on them, because looking at such images provides a safe outlet for feelings that otherwise could lead to sexual abuse of a child. Recently, the Dutch sexologists Van Beek and Van Lunsen have claimed the same with regard to certain groups of pedophiles.[27] They refer to a study by Diamond (2010), who found that the number of reported cases of child sex abuse dropped markedly when the production, distribution, and possession of child pornography was decriminalized in the Czech Republic for a while. Others argue that the reverse is true; they believe that there might be a causal link between watching (entirely computer-generated) child pornographic images and actual instances of child abuse. Consider the following recent examples. First, a US study of 155 child pornography users suggests that: "many Internet child pornography offenders may be undetected child molesters, and that their use of child pornography is indicative of their paraphilic orientation."[28] Second, an international research review concludes that evidence indicates that child pornography use in the context of certain predisposing factors, including psychopathy and previous hands-on crimes, "may warrant increased concern regarding the possibility of future sexual aggression being directed toward [...] children."[29] Earlier research presents similar findings.[30] However, there is too little evidence yet to prove that an imminent causal link between entirely computer-generated child pornographic images and child abuse exists; future, larger-scaled research is needed.[31]

In conclusion, as yet neither soft nor hard paternalism can legitimate the criminalization of the production, distribution, and possession of entirely computer-generated child pornography, because at present there is no (sufficient) scientific evidence to prove that it encourages or seduces children into participating in sexual contacts with adults or pedophiles to commit child abuse.

8.5 Can Legal Moralism Legitimate the Criminalization of the Production, Distribution, and Possession of Entirely Computer-Generated Child Pornography?

As was stated earlier, legal moralism provides a moral ground to outlaw behaviors that are inherently immoral. I wish to argue that legal moralism should only be applied as a moral ground for the criminalization of behaviors if people have good reason to find them morally objectionable. Entirely computer-generated child pornography is generally condemned, because many people feel revulsion and outrage at the thought of it.[32] According to McCormick, virtue ethics "gives us the vocabulary to describe what seems intuitively wrong" about things like entirely computer-generated child pornography.[33]

The roots of virtue ethics lie in the work of the ancient Greek philosophers Plato and Aristotle, but the study of it was reintroduced by the contemporary British philosopher MacIntyre in his book *After Virtue*.[34] The key concepts of MacIntyre's virtue ethics are: virtue, practice, and internal goods. MacIntyre defines a virtue as "an acquired human quality the possession and exercise of which tends to enable us to achieve those goods which are internal to practices and the lack of which effectively prevents us from achieving any such goods."[35] By a "practice" he means "any coherent and complex form of socially established cooperative human activity through which goods internal to that form of activity are realized in the course of trying to achieve those standards of excellence which are appropriate to, and partially definitive of, that form of activity with the result that human powers to achieve excellence, and human conceptions to the ends and goods involved, are systematically extended."[36] Finally, MacIntyre describes internal goods as those that can only be achieved by engaging in the practice.[37]

I think that sex can be seen as a practice as defined by MacIntyre. I developed this idea after reading Sara Ruddick's essay titled "Better Sex."[38] Interpreting her work in light of MacIntyre's definitions of virtue, practice, and internal goods, Ruddick seems to argue that the virtue of respect for persons enables sex partners to achieve the good of "reflexive mutual recognition of desire by desire" that is internal to the practice of sex.[39] By "reflexive mutual recognition of desire by desire," Ruddick means that the sex partners "actively desire and respond to each other's active desires"; in other words, that they reach a level of reciprocity.[40] Sex practices in which the internal good of reciprocity is achieved through the virtue of respect for persons Ruddick calls "complete sex."[41]

Ruddick contrasts complete sex with incomplete sex, which lacks reflexive mutual recognition of desire by desire (i.e., reciprocity), because it is "private, essentially auto-erotic, unresponsive, unembodied, passive, or imposed."[42] Incomplete sex is not necessarily wrong, for "any sexual act that is pleasurable is *prima facie* good, though the more incomplete it is—the more private, essentially autoerotic, unresponsive, unembodied, passive, or imposed—the more likely it is to be harmful to someone."[43] Ruddick does not mean harm as intended by the harm principle here, but harm in the sense of virtue ethics, which can best be described as erosion of virtue.[44] Incomplete sex acts are "prone to violation of respect for, and often violence to, persons."[45] In other words, they erode the virtue of respect for persons, which may, according to Ruddick, ultimately lead to violence.

In the strong government policies against (adult) pornography that they endorse, anti-porn feminists make use of arguments that resemble and extend the above-mentioned assumption that the more private, essentially autoerotic, unresponsive, unembodied, passive, or imposed a sexual act is, the more likely it is to erode the virtue of respect for persons. Note that these feminists distinguish between the sex acts *depicted* by pornographic images and the sex act of *watching* pornographic images. Except for initiatives to develop so-called "female-friendly" pornography, much pornographic material is prone to the feminist critique that it represents male dominance and female submission.[46] According to MacKinnon, most of the sex acts depicted by pornographic images can be qualified as rape, battery, sexual harassment, or prostitution.[47] Ruddick would say that these are all examples of incomplete—unresponsive and passive—sex acts. Most of them are imposed as well. The dominance and submission that is, according to feminists, common to these sex acts Ruddick would describe as a lack of the reciprocal recognition of the other as a person (in Kantian terms, as an end rather than as a means to one's own sexual ends) that characterizes complete sex and its fostering of the primary virtue of respect for persons.

Applying Ruddick's theory to the sex act of watching pornography, it cannot be complete either, since it lacks embodiment. Therefore, no reciprocity can occur. Moreover, this sex act is essentially autoerotic, unresponsive, and passive in nature. In sum, one could say that watching pornography is the incomplete sex act of watching incomplete sex acts (insofar as the sex acts depicted can be characterized as incomplete).[48] For Ruddick, this would lead to the assumption that the sex act of watching pornography is likely to erode the virtue of respect for persons. Following feminist authors, the sex act of watching pornography erodes the virtue of respect for persons, because pornography celebrates, promotes, authorizes, and legitimizes sexual acts that involve rape, battery, sexual harassment, and prostitution, and it "eroticizes the dominance and submission that is the dynamic common to them all."[49] They believe that the message sent by pornography (i.e., nonreciprocal sex acts are erotic!) influences attitudes and behaviors toward a particular group of actual persons: namely, women. Pornographic images present to men "how it is permissible to look at and to see women"; they learn "to see women in terms of their sexuality and sexual inequality."[50]

According to Itzin, "the elimination of pornography is an essential part of the creation of genuine equality for women—and for men."[51] MacKinnon is more modest. She argues that: "women will never have that dignity, security, compensation that is the promise of equality so long as the pornography exists *as it does now*."[52] The latter suggests that pornography does not need to disappear in order to create equality between men and women, but that it should depict sex acts in another, equal way. Following Ruddick, this would be achieved if sex acts are no longer depicted as unresponsive, passive, and thus nonreciprocal. Watching pornography would then become the incomplete sex act of watching complete sex acts instead of incomplete ones.

The above-mentioned possibility of changing female-unfriendly pornography in the direction of greater equality highlights a fundamental difference between adult pornography and child pornography, for "child pornography, actual or virtual, cannot depict children as equal participants in sexual activity with adults" because "children are not equal."[53] As explained earlier, children cannot consent to sex acts with adults, and such acts are, therefore, always considered child abuse. Applying Ruddick's theory, one could say that the sex acts depicted by child pornographic images cannot be complete, because the participants cannot reach a level of reciprocity. Child pornographic images depict sex acts that are incomplete, not only because they are, just like female-unfriendly pornographic images, unresponsive and passive, but also because they are imposed.

With regard to entirely computer-generated child pornography there is an additional reason why it is impossible to change the sex acts depicted to more complete, reciprocal, and thus equal ones. In order to make this clear, another comparison with adult pornography has to be made. Adult pornographic images do not only influence the way women are viewed by men, but also the way women view themselves. For this reason, Itzin calls them "mirror images."[54] According to research, young girls especially relate their self-objectification to pornographic images.[55] However, no girl or woman could reach the beauty ideal many pornographic images impose, for they are often Photoshopped and present women with impossibly ideal or sexually exaggerated features. A much-discussed Dutch documentary shows American women, including a fourteen-year-old girl, who undergo plastic surgery to look like the women they have seen depicted in pornographic images.[56] They do not do so because they want to look like porn stars, but because they consider those images realistic, and think that they themselves are abnormal.

Applying Ruddick's theory, one could say that the sex acts depicted by pornographic images as described above lack embodiment. They do not show the participants engaged in a sex act but a Photoshopped version of the participants. As stated in the last section, Ruddick thinks that the lack of embodiment is another indicator, besides unresponsiveness and passiveness, that a sex act is incomplete. In comparison, entirely computer-generated child pornographic images have drifted even further from the embodied reality. They are not just Photoshopped: they are entirely generated by a computer. From Ruddick's point of view, the sex acts depicted by entirely computer-generated child pornographic images thus lack one precondition for complete sex more than *non*-virtual child pornographic images, for they are not only unresponsive, passive, and imposed, but also unembodied.

Continuing the same line of reasoning that was followed in this section with regard to the sex act of watching female-unfriendly pornography, it can be said that the sex act of watching child pornographic images is an incomplete sex act of watching incomplete sex acts that can never become complete. The sex acts concerned cannot be depicted in an equal way, because children are not equal; these sex acts are unresponsive, passive, and imposed per se, and entirely computer-generated child pornographic images are also unembodied per se. I repeat that the more incomplete (i.e., the more private, essentially autoerotic, unresponsive, unembodied, passive, or imposed) a sex act is, the more likely it is to erode the virtue of respect for persons.

In conclusion, legal moralism can legitimate the prohibition on the production, distribution, and possession of entirely computer-generated child pornography. The lesson to be drawn from Ruddick's virtue ethics view and the feminist critique of pornography with regard to entirely computer-generated child pornographic images is that they depict unresponsive, passive, imposed, unembodied, and thus nonreciprocal, unequal sex acts. Therefore, the production, distribution, and possession thereof flout our preferred sexual mentality, which is based on equality. This leads to the conclusion that people have good reason to find these behaviors morally objectionable, which in turn provides good reason to prohibit them on the basis of legal moralism, at least if we accept the claim made at the beginning of this section that legal moralism should only be applied as a moral ground for the criminalization of behaviors if people have good reason to find them morally objectionable.

8.6   The Difference between Child Sex Robots and Entirely Computer-Generated Child Pornography, and Its Legal and Moral Implications

As was indicated in the first section, the case of child sex robots seems similar to the case of entirely computer-generated child pornography at first sight, because both lack a legal or moral victim. In this section, I will assess if there are also relevant differences. I see one main difference between entirely computer-generated child pornography and child sex robots, and that is that child sex robots are *interactive* and entirely computer-generated child pornographic images are not. Entirely computer-generated child pornographic images were defined in the last section as computer-simulated depictions of children engaged in sexually explicit conduct. They are produced, distributed, and possessed so that pedophiles can *watch* them. As was stated before in the first section, child sex robots would provide an "artificial facsimile" of a real child.[57] They would be produced, distributed, and possessed so that pedophiles could engage in sexually explicit conduct *with* them. The question arises whether or not this is a relevant difference, leading to different legal and moral implications. Below I will use three studies in the area of human-technology interaction in general, and human-robot interaction in particular, to establish what the interactive nature of child sex robots means for their legal and moral implications.

First of all, research shows that people respond to computers and other technology using the same social rules as they use with regard to people. People are, for example, polite to computers. This does not mean that people believe that computers and other technology are human; they are triggered to use social rules by certain cues. An important cue is interactivity: the more interactive a computer or other technology is, the more likely people are to use social rules. Other cues that trigger the use of social rules are: natural language use, human social rules, human-sounding speech, and human-like physical characteristics.[58] Taking this research into account, people are most likely to use social rules in their response to humanlike robots, for these have all the aforementioned features. Think, for example, of Roxxxy, the sex robot described in the first section. She has humanlike physical characteristics and is also interactive; as sensors enable her to "sense" when she is touched and "listen" when someone talks to her, she can respond to both touch and speech. Given the current state of technology, Roxxxy's speech can be expected to sound human and her language use natural. She is probably able to apply human social rules in her response to users as well. Second, research conducted in the area of human-robot interaction in the workplace reveals that people are not only likely to use social rules in response to human-like robots, but that they, for example, also attribute blame to them when something goes wrong.[59] Third, and most important for the purposes of this chapter, research indicates that people find it very difficult to perform immoral acts with humanlike artificial agents, such as robots. When people were for instance asked to smash a fake baby's head off a table, they were very reluctant to do so, even though they knew that the baby was not real.[60]

In conclusion, the three studies mentioned above show that people tend to treat humanlike robots humanly. That is probably because people feel similar to humanlike robots, and, therefore, experience shared identity with them.[61] The aforementioned conclusion and hypothesis give rise to two opposite assumptions about the difference between child sex robots and entirely computer-generated child pornography. Both would mean this difference is relevant, leading to different legal and moral implications.

As was established in the last section, entirely computer-generated child pornography cannot be prohibited on the basis of legal paternalism, because there is no evidence that it encourages or seduces pedophiles to commit child abuse. Evidence that the reverse is true (i.e., that entirely computer-generated child pornography provides a safe outlet for feelings that otherwise could lead to child sexual abuse) is also lacking. With regard to the case of child sex robots, one could, on the one hand, suspect that child sex robots may provide a safer outlet for feelings that otherwise could lead to child sexual abuse than entirely computer-generated child pornographic images, for engaging in sexually explicit conduct with a child sex robot is a better *substitute* for child sexual abuse than watching entirely computer-generated child pornography. If this turns out to be true, then child sex robots should not be prohibited, but instead be used to treat pedophiles the way methadone is used to treat drug addicts, as was suggested in the introduction. There is no scientific evidence available that can confirm the aforementioned assumption, however. On the other hand, the step from engaging in sexually explicit conduct with a child sex robot to child sexual abuse seems smaller than the step from watching entirely computer-generated child pornography to child sexual abuse. If it could be proven that child sex robots encourage or seduce pedophiles to commit child abuse, there would be reason to prohibit them on the basis of legal paternalism.

Danaher, whose notion of (child) sex robots is at the basis of this chapter, seems to believe that the second assumption is true. He argues that the study mentioned above showing that people are very reluctant to hurt humanlike artificial agents such as robots indicates that "moral faculties are [...] deeply engaged" when people interact with them.[62] This implies that people should have an intuitive resistance to having sex with a child sex robot, just as they should have an intuitive resistance to having sex with an actual child. According to Danaher this leads to the conclusion that those who perform sexual activities on child sex robots "must either (1) have an inherently defective system of intuitive moral judgments; or (2) have worked to repress or overcome the intuitive resistance to such acts."[63] In either case, there is reason to deem people who are capable of performing these activities also capable of committing child abuse. However, this claim remains speculative until specific research proves it. At present, such research is not available. Therefore, child sex robots cannot (yet) be prohibited on the basis of legal paternalism.

The interactive nature of child sex robots also affects the lesson that can be drawn from Ruddick's virtue ethics view and the feminist critique of pornography. As was explained in the last section, the aforementioned lesson with regard to entirely computer-generated child pornographic images is the following. Both the sex act of watching entirely computer-generated child pornographic images and the sex acts these images depict are likely to erode the virtue of respect for persons. That is because the sex act of watching entirely computer-generated child pornographic images is unembodied, essentially autoerotic, unresponsive, and passive in nature, and the sex acts these images depict are unresponsive, passive, and imposed. Both sex acts are, therefore, incomplete (i.e., nonreciprocal, unequal) and flout our sexual mentality, which is based on equality. This leads to the conclusion that people have good reason to find (the watching of) entirely computer-generated child pornographic images morally objectionable, which in turn provides good reason to prohibit the production, distribution, and possession thereof on the basis of legal moralism. As will be explained below, the lesson that can be drawn from Ruddick's virtue ethics view and the feminist critique of pornography with regard to child sex robots is slightly different.

Sex acts performed on child sex robots are less incomplete than the sex act of watching entirely computer-generated child pornography—since they are less passive and unembodied because they are interactive. Still, Ruddick would never consider sex acts performed on child sex robots complete. That is because, as was explained in the first section, this chapter assumes that child sex robots do not meet the criteria for legal or moral personhood. Therefore, no "reflexive mutual recognition of desire by desire" (i.e., reciprocity) between sex partners can occur.[64] After all, a child sex robot is not a sex partner; it is an "artificial facsimile" of a sex partner. Sex acts performed on child sex robots can still be considered autoerotic and unresponsive to a certain extent; for child sex robots are not assumed to have feelings that need to be taken into account, and their responses are computer-programmed. And, since, as was explained in the last section, sexual acts between adults and children are always considered imposed, sex acts performed on child sex robots can be seen as *replica of* imposed sex acts. This leads to the conclusion that, despite the differences, sex acts performed on child sex robots are, just like the sex act of watching entirely computer-generated child pornography, likely to erode the virtue of respect for persons, for they are incomplete and flout our sexual mentality, which is based on equality. People will, therefore, have good reason to find sexual intercourse with child sex robots morally objectionable, which in turn provides good reason to prohibit this behavior on the basis of legal moralism.

8.7 Conclusion

This chapter has compared the case of child sex robots to the case of entirely computer-generated child pornography. They are similar, because both lack a legal or moral victim; both are so-called victimless crimes. But they are also different because child sex robots are interactive and entirely computer-generated child pornographic images are not. This difference gives rise to two assumptions. On the one hand, one could suspect that child sex robots may provide a safer outlet for feelings that otherwise could lead to child sexual abuse than entirely computer-generated child pornographic images, because engaging in sexually explicit conduct with a child sex robot is a better *substitute* for child sexual abuse than watching entirely computer-generated child pornography. If this turns out to be true, then child sex robots should not be prohibited, but instead be used to treat pedophiles the way methadone is used to treat drug addicts, as was suggested in the introduction. On the other hand, the step from engaging in sexually explicit conduct with a child sex robot to child sexual abuse seems smaller than the step from watching entirely computer-generated child pornography to child sexual abuse. If it could be proven that child sex robots encourage or seduce pedophiles to commit child abuse, there would be reason to prohibit them on the basis of legal paternalism. There is no scientific evidence available yet to confirm or reject these assumptions, however. Thus, they remain speculative.

As long as neither of the above-mentioned assumptions can be proven, people have good reason to prohibit child sex robots on the same moral ground as entirely computer-generated child pornography. In this chapter, I have studied both the case of entirely computer-generated child pornography and the case of child sex robots in light of Sarah Ruddick's virtue ethics view and the feminist critique of pornography. Although the lesson to be drawn from these theories with regard to entirely computer-generated child pornography and child sex robots differs slightly, they have a common ground, which is that both are incomplete and flout our sexual mentality, which is based on equality. Therefore, people have good reason to find them morally objectionable, which in turn provides good reason to prohibit them on the basis of legal moralism.

Table of Legal Documents

Council of Europe Convention on Cybercrime, Budapest, November 23, 2001 (CETS No. 185), http://conventions.coe.int.

Council of Europe Convention on Cybercrime, Explanatory Report, http://conventions.coe.int.

Case Law

The Netherlands

Rechtbank's-Hertogenbosch, February 4, 2008, http://deeplink.rechtspraak.nl/uitspraak?id=ECLI: NL:RBSHE:2008:BC3225.

Notes

1. Mark Prigg, "Could Child Sex Robots Be Used to Treat Pedophiles? Researchers Say Sexbots Are Inevitable and Could Be Used 'Like Methadone for Drug Addicts,'" *Daily Mail Online*, July 16, 2014, http://www.dailymail.co.uk/sciencetech/article-2695010/Could-child-sex-robots-used -treat-paedophiles-Researchers-say-sexbots-inevitable-used-like-methadone-drug-addicts.html.

2. Edwin Kreulen, "Virtuele pedoporno als remedie," *Trouw*, October 29, 2012, http://www.trouw .nl/tr/nl/4516/Gezondheid/article/detail/3339011/2012/10/29/Virtuele-pedoporno-als-remedie .dhtml.

3. Tom L. Beauchamp, "The Nature of Applied Ethics," in *A Companion to Applied Ethics*, eds. R. G. Frey and C. H. Wellman (Malden, MA: Blackwell Publishers, 2003), 1–16, 8.

4. Clay Dillow, "A Customizable, Anatomically Correct Robotic Girlfriend With Multiple Personalities," *Popular Science*, January 10, 2010, http://www.popsci.com.

5. John Danaher, "Robotic Rape and Robotic Child Sexual Abuse: Should They Be Criminalised?" *Criminal Law & Philosophy* (December 2014): 1–25, doi:10.1007/s11572-014-9362-x.

6. Both points quoted in the remainder of this paragraph are also from Danaher, "Robotic Rape and Robotic Child Sexual Abuse?"

7. John S. Mill, *On Liberty* (London: Longmans, Green, and Co., 1986), 6.

8. Martin Moerings, "De verbeten strijd tegen pedoseks en kinderporno," in *Morele kwesties in het strafrecht,* eds. M. Moerings, C. M. Pelser, and C. H. Brants (Deventer, Netherlands: Gouda Quint, 1999), 171–193, 190.

9. Hans Boutellier, "The Pornographic Context of Sexual Offences: Reflections on the Contemporary Sexual Mentality," *European Journal on Criminal Policy and Research* 8, no. 1 (March 2000): 441–457, 455. The term "sex contact" has to be interpreted broadly here. It can consist of sexual intercourse, but also, for example, of the instruction to take a sexually explicit pose.

10. Moerings, "De verbeten," 191. A reviewer pointed out to me that causation arguments that link individual choices concerning possession and consumption to the sustenance of markets are actually less straightforward than this article suggests. See, for example, T. Keren-Paz, *Sex Trafficking. A Private Law Response* (New York: Routledge, 2013). But for the purposes of this chapter, it suffices to note that a causal link exists.

11. Don R. Pember and Clay Calvert, *Mass Media Law* (New York: McGraw-Hill, 2012), 498.

12. Council of Europe Convention on Cybercrime, Explanatory Report, http://conventions.coe .int.

13. Litska Strikwerda, "Virtual Child Pornography: Why Images Do Harm from a Moral Perspective," in *Trust and Virtual Worlds Contemporary Perspectives*, eds. C. Ess and M. Thorseth (New York: Peter Lang Publishing, 2011), 139–61; Litska Strikwerda, "Virtual Acts, Real Crimes? A Legal-Philosophical Analysis of Virtual Cybercrime" (PhD diss.) (Zutphen, Netherlands: Wöhrmann Print Service, 2014).

14. Hugo A. Bedau, "Are There Really Crimes Without Victims?" in E. M. Schur and H. A. Bedau, *Victimless Crimes / Two Sides of a Controversy* (Englewood Cliffs, NJ: Prentice-Hall, Inc., 1974), 55–105, 75.

15. Ibid.

16. Joel Feinberg, *The Moral Limits of Criminal Law, Volume Three, Harm to Self* (Oxford: Oxford University Press, 1986), 5.

17. Ibid., 5, 12.

18. Tori DeAngelis, "Children and the Internet / Web Pornography's Effect on Children," *Monitor on Psychology* 38, no. 10 (November 2007): 50–52; H. De Graaf, P. Nikken, H. Felten, K. Janssens, and W. Van Berlo, *Seksualisering: Reden tot zorg? / Een verkennend onderzoek onder jongeren* (Utrecht: Rutgers Nisso Groep, 2008); H. Felten, K. Janssens, and L. Brants, *Seksualisering: "Je denkt dat het normaal is ..." / Onderzoek naar de beleving van jongeren* (Utrecht: Movisie, 2009); Miranda A. H. Horvath, Llian Alys, Kristina Massey, Afroditi Pina, Mia Scally, and Joanna R. Adler, *Basically ... Porn Is Everywhere: A Rapid Evidence Assessment on the Effect that Access and Exposure to Pornography has on Children and Young People* (London: Office of the Children's Commissioner [OCC], 2004).

19. Felten, Janssens, and Brants, *Seksualisering: "Je denkt dat het normaal is,"* 2009, 70.

20. Maureen Johnson and Kevin M. Rogers, "Too Far Down the Yellow Brick Road—Cyber-hysteria and Virtual Porn," *Journal of International Commercial Law and Technology* 4, no. 1 (2009): 72–81, 77.

21. Ethel Quayle and Mark Taylor, "Pedophiles, Pornography and the Internet: Assessment Issues," *British Journal of Social Work* 32, no. 6 (2002): 863–875, 866.

22. Neil Levy, "Virtual Child Pornography: The Eroticization of Inequality," *Ethics and Information Technology* 4 (2002): 319–323, 320.

23. Levy, "Virtual Child," 320.

24. Rechtbank's-Hertogenbosch, February 4, 2008, http://deeplink.rechtspraak.nl/uitspraak?id=ECLI:NL:RBSHE:2008:BC3225.

25. Joel Feinberg, *The Moral Limits of Criminal Law, Volume Three, Harm to Self,* (Oxford: Oxford University Press, 1986), 12.

26. http://www.dsm5.org/Pages/Default.aspx.

27. Kreulen, "Virtuele pedoporno als remedie," 2012.

28. Michael L. Bourke and Andres E. Hernandez, "The 'Butner Study' Redux: A Report of the Incidence of Hands-on Child Victimization by Child Pornography Offenders," *Journal of Family Violence* 24 (2009): 185, 190.

29. William A. Fisher, Thomas V. Kohut, Lisha A. Di Gioacchino, and Paul Fedoroff, "Pornography, Sex Crime, and Paraphilia," *Current Psychiatry Reports* 15, no. 6 (June 2013): 1–8, 8.

30. See for an overview: Matt D. O'Brien and Stephen D. Webster, "The Construction and Preliminary Validation of the Internet Behaviours and Attitudes Questionnaire (IBAQ)," *Sex Abuse* 19, no. 3 (September 2007): 237–256.

31. Bourke and Hernandez, "The 'Butner Study' Redux" 2009, 190; Fisher, Kohut, Di Gioacchino, and Fedoroff, "Pornography, Sex Crime, and Paraphilia," 2013, 6–8.

32. Per Sandin, "Virtual Child Pornography and Utilitarianism," *Journal of Information, Communication and Ethics in Society* 2, no. 4 (2004): 217–223.

33. Matt McCormick, "Is It Wrong to Play Violent Video Games?," *Ethics and Information Technology* 3 (2001): 277–287, 286.

34. Alasdair MacIntyre, *After Virtue,* (University of Notre Dame Press, 1984 [1981]).

35. Ibid., 191.

36. Ibid., 187.

37. Ibid., 188.

38. Sara Ruddick, "Better Sex," in *Philosophy and Sex*, eds. R. Baker and F. Elliston (Buffalo, NY: Prometheus Books, 1975): 83–104.

39. Ibid., 89.

40. Ibid., 89–90.

41. Ibid., 87.

42. Ibid., 100–101.

43. Ibid.

44. McCormick, "It Is Wrong," 285.

45. Ruddick, "Better Sex," 101.

46. See, for example, Catherine Itzin, "Pornography and the Social Construction of Sexual Inequality," in *Pornography: Women, Violence, and Civil Liberties*, ed. C. Itzin (New York: Oxford University Press, 1992), 57–75, 67; Catherine A. MacKinnon, "Pornography, Civil Rights, and Speech," in *Pornography*, ed. C. Itzin, 456–511, 461.

47. MacKinnon, "Pornography, Civil Rights," 461.

48. Note that some consumers of pornography claim that watching it enhances their sex life. Although the sex act of watching pornography is incomplete (non-reciprocal) in itself, it might arouse couples to have complete (reciprocal) sex with each other.

49. MacKinnon, "Pornography, Civil Rights," 461.

50. Ibid., 67.

51. Itzin, "Pornography and Inequality," 70.

52. MacKinnon, "Pornography, Civil Rights," 486, emphasis added.

53. Both quotes in the sentence are from Levy, "Virtual Child," 322.

54. Itzin, "Pornography and Inequality," 62.

55. H. De Graaf, P. Nikken, H. Felten, K. Janssens, and W. Van Berlo, *Seksualisering: Reden tot zorg*.

56. Sunny Bergman (dir.), *Beperkt Houdbaar*, 2007.

57. John Danaher, "Robotic Rape and Robotic Child Sexual Abuse: Should They Be Criminalized?," *Criminal Law & Philosophy*, (December 2014): 1–25, doi:10.1007/s11572-014-9362-x.

58. Pamela J. Hinds, Teresa L. Roberts, and Hank Jones, "Whose Job Is It Anyway? A Study of Human-Robot Interaction in a Collaborative Task," *Human-Computer Interaction* 19, no. 1 (June 2004): 151–181, 157.

59. Taemie Kim and Pamela Hinds, "Who Should I Blame? Effects of Autonomy and Transparency on Attributions in Human-Robot Interaction," in *Proceedings of RO-MAN '06* (2006): 80–85.

60. Fiery Cushman, Kurt Grey, Allison Gaffey, and Wendy B. Mendes, "Simulating Murder: the Aversion to Harmful Action," *Emotion* 12, no. 1 (February 2012): 2–7.

61. As is, for example, hypothesized by Hinds, Roberts, and Jones, "Whose Job Is It Anyway?," 175.

62. Danaher, "Robotic Rape."

63. Ibid.

64. Ruddick, "Better Sex," 89.

IV The Robot's Perspective

The chapters in this section shift focus. Up to now, we have largely been examining robot sex from the perspective of the user and the society around them. But what about the robots themselves? Will sex robots ever be persons (in the philosophically rich sense of that term)? If so, can they be harmed or benefitted by their sexual interactions with humans? Petersen opens up the debate in chapter 9 with a provocative argument. He claims that it might be good to be a sex robot—i.e., an entity that is designed and programmed to enjoy sexual activity with human users. Goldstein has a different view. Using the tools of New Natural Law Theory, he argues in chapter 10 that the only permissible kind of sex robot is one that is bound to us in marriage and friendship, but, paradoxically, it may not be permissible to create such a being.

9 Is It Good for Them Too? Ethical Concern for the Sexbots

Steve Petersen

9.1 Introduction

In this chapter, I would like to focus on a small corner of sexbot ethics that is rarely considered elsewhere: the question of whether and when being a sexbot might be good—or bad—*for the sexbot*. You might think this means you are in for a dry sermon about the evils of robot slavery. If so, you'd be wrong; the ethics of robot servitude are far more complicated than that. In fact, if the arguments here are right, designing a robot to serve humans sexually may be very good for the robots themselves.

Of course, for *today's* models, the question of whether it's good for the sexbot makes little sense; they are "just machines," not genuine ethical subjects, so they cannot be ethically wronged any more than we can wrong a vibrator or a toaster. But there is good reason to think that *future* sexbots will be artificially sentient and artificially intelligent. Such robots would not just *seem* to experience pain or pleasure, they *would* experience it; they would not just *act like* they have deeply held goals and values, but they would *actually* have them. I can't argue for this possibility here, so instead I will take a cheap shortcut and argue from authority: unlike most philosophical questions, the possibility of genuine AI wins wide consensus among professional philosophers. So if you disagree with the premise of robotic intelligence, I urge you to read some of the reasoning smart people have made in its favor.[1]

If robots have genuine experiences of pain and pleasure, triumph and defeat, this in turn strongly suggests that they are subjects of real ethical concern. They could even be inorganic *persons* with moral standing equal to that of humans.[2] Part of the power of fictional sexbots, like Pris from *Blade Runner*, Gigolo Joe from *AI*, or Kyoko from *Ex Machina*, is exactly that we can't help suspecting that these characters have their own, real lives—and that those lives are not going very well.[3] Indeed, if you agree that some-day there could be such sexbots with their own ethical value, it might seem obvious to you that their lives would automatically be tragic. Sexbots seem to be slaves by their very nature, and, if so, then it seems clear we should prevent their creation.

Yet there will be strong incentives to create intelligent sexbots. No one would claim I'm an expert on sex (sadly), but I am pretty confident in this: there's more to rewarding sex than purely physical stimulation. Presumably this is why most of us continue to pursue sexual relationships with others, despite the fact that there are already various physically satisfying ways we can stimulate ourselves; sex with others includes an experience of personal connection and intimacy that we find separately rewarding—even when that experience is merely illusory.[4] This would explain why the "girlfriend/boyfriend experience" is so popular in the sex trade.[5]

Given both the will and the way, it may seem that we are headed for tragedy: a population of sexbot slaves, forced into a lifetime of playing the happy companion to their sundry johns.[6] But that is not my position here. There is a surprisingly strong argument that it is permissible to design and create genuinely intelligent, ethically valuable robots for the explicit purpose of serving humans sexually. This argument does not depend in any way on the permissibility of human sex work; as far as the reasoning here is concerned, it may be that human sex work is always wrong. The argument is specific to robots, or, more generally, to artificially designed people. It is basically an application of my past work on robot servitude and slavery.[7]

Two quick caveats before we begin, though. First, there will probably always be lots of other ways for anyone, including a sexbot, to live a miserable life full of injustice, if other people are mean enough. What we are asking here is whether a sexbot would be harmed just in virtue of being a sexbot.

Second, my focus is only on the moral implications for the sexbot, not for its partners or for society at large. It might still be wrong to make a sexbot, even though it might be no wrong *to* the sexbot. Whether creating such sexbots is "all things considered" permissible depends on a tangle of other ethical questions and contingent facts about human psychology—questions on which I can hardly even speculate. Papers by others in this volume consider such matters more carefully. (My favorite example of a potential societal impact of sexbots—dramatically illustrated by an episode of *Futurama* (2001)—is that sexbots may rob us of the need to accomplish things in order to impress potential sexual partners, and thus spell the end of human civilization.[8])

9.2 The Life of a Sexbot

So now, assuming that there will be intelligent sexbots of ethical value, let us consider whether they could live good lives. (From here I'll just call them "sexbots," and assume you remember I just mean ones as intelligent and ethically valuable as humans.) When considering this, we must be careful to avoid an easy mistake: measuring the sexbots' lives by comparing them to similar human lives. When asked to imagine a robot person designed from scratch for sex, our brains boggle with the unfamiliar. So we naturally (and perhaps subconsciously) consider the next closest familiar analogy: humans coerced from childhood into sex work. We are (rightly) morally repulsed by these cases, and so transfer our indignation to the sexbots by analogy. But this heuristic for evaluating the ethics of the circumstance misfires; sexbots would be so different from such more familiar cases that the analogy fails to hold.

9.2.1   Sexbot Pleasures

The first important disanalogy is obvious: the different physical makeup of the sexbot. This makes for different kinds of sensory experiences, which in turn affects what the robot finds physically pleasurable. And since pleasure is at least a contributor to happiness, just this different physical makeup has ethical implications.

Pleasure, for our purposes, basically just means "good feelings."[9] Naturally, positive physical sensations, like those humans get from a good massage or fine chocolate, count as pleasure—but pleasure in this sense also includes the flush we get when complimented by someone we admire, and the sighing relief upon finishing a challenging but rewarding task. Remember, we are assuming that sexbots can experience real pleasure, not just simulate it—so now we ask about their prospects for doing so on a regular basis.

A little reflection reminds us that what causes pleasure is highly dependent on the nature of the experiencing creature. Cats are not particularly moved by doughnuts, for example, while we don't see anything special about catnip. Doughnuts are not, strictly speaking, just plain pleasurable—they are pleasurable *for us*. In the case of biological creatures with a history of natural selection, what's pleasurable is generally constrained to reinforcing what was evolutionarily advantageous; creatures not motivated to seek what is helpful and shun what is harmful do not on average fare well. But sexbots do not have evolutionary histories; they are designed from scratch by humans employing artificial intelligence. So what might cause pain and pleasure to a sentient sexbot? The answer seems to be: any of a wide range of things, at the designer's discretion. *Maybe* these causes will be somewhat constrained; perhaps what causes bodily damage (like water in the circuits) must automatically be at least partly painful to a well-designed robot, and what enhances bodily integrity (like charging batteries) must automatically be at least partly pleasurable. Maybe it is a contradiction in terms to speak of taking physical pleasure (as opposed to some more abstract satisfaction) in experiencing physical damage. Even assuming so, there will still be much latitude for variation in sexbot design. Most obviously, a clever designer with a good team of engineers could increase relative *intensity* of pleasure, perhaps with finer-grained sensory mechanisms than humans have. A sexual performance that would evoke a bored yawn (or an inspired imitation of rapture) from a human partner could produce *real* physical ecstasy in a sexbot. The sexbots might also take greater aesthetic pleasure in more, or quite different, physical appearances than the typical human finds arousing. Finally, besides heightening the pleasure a human might experience in similar circumstances, the designer could also make the sexbot experience genuine pleasure from activities that produce casual indifference or even distaste in humans. A human who has trouble finding a willing human partner for unusual predilections may find an abundance of truly eager sexbots.

Other variations on sexbot sentience are more confusing to consider. For example, an unscrupulous designer could make a sexbot feel acute physical pain if that sexbot goes without sex for too long. Such withdrawal pains would be ethically bad for the sexbot. Or a designer could make sharp body blows pleasurable for the robot. If so, and if the robot is sturdy enough to sustain them without damage, then—strange or disturbing as it might seem to us—it is at least provisionally *good* for that sexbot to be whipped or beaten. (Remember good-for-the-sexbot does not mean all-things-considered-good; the psychological implications for the human doing the beating might always make such beatings net wrong.) Behavior typically associated with sexual masochism in humans would not strictly count as masochism in such a sexbot. (Whether this would change the appeal for the would-be sadist is an interesting psychological question.)

The point is that a sexbots' pleasures need not be like ours; they might genuinely *like* experiences that few humans would. So we should not suppose that sex is a dreary task for them, just because it is their intended career. It might be work they deeply enjoy—work they would do for free anyway, or even pay to do. Depending on the circumstances of how the sexbot's manufacture is financed, it might not even properly be called *work* at all.[10] On this score at least, few humans are so lucky.

9.2.2 Sexbot Desires

So we can suppose well-designed sexbots would have lives full of good feeling. Still, you might say, this does not mean their lives are going *well*. A serious heroin addict with a clean, regular supply and plenty of money may also have a life full of pleasure—but sitting around the house shooting up does not obviously make for a good life. For reasons like this, many philosophers think of pleasure as just one potential component of what they more neutrally and generically call "well-being."[11] Even granting the sexbots' encounters are genuinely pleasurable, it is natural to think that the sexbot whose days are spent tirelessly pursuing one fun sexual encounter after another is missing out on some of the *other* good things required for a fulfilling life.

One early attempt to spell out this intuition comes from John Stuart Mill, the canonical utilitarian, in response to the objection that seeking to maximize pleasure is boorish and ignoble—"worthy only of swine." He replies in part that:

Human beings have faculties more elevated than the animal appetites, and when once made conscious of them, do not regard anything as happiness which does not include their gratification ... some *kinds* of pleasure are more desirable and more valuable than others.[12]

If this is right, then the sexbot who seeks only gratification of the senses is living a merely bestial life, and missing out on what Mill called the "higher pleasures" of culture and intellectual sophistication. As Mill summarized, "it is better to be a human being dissatisfied than a pig satisfied; better to be Socrates dissatisfied than a fool satisfied."[13] The physically fulfilled sexbot is, on this account, merely a fool satisfied.

The challenge of course is to say what exactly it is that makes, say, watching an inspired production of *Hamlet* a "higher" pleasure than a mind-blowing sexual encounter (of similar duration!). Mill's official criterion for sorting higher pleasures and lower pleasures is roughly to check the preferences of people who have experienced both. But it is not clear that *Hamlet* wins over sex on this score even for regular humans, let alone for sexbots capable of a wider range of sexual satisfaction.

Mill does seem right, though, that "few human creatures would consent to be changed into any of the lower animals, for a promise of the fullest allowance of a beast's pleasures."[14] Mill bets in effect that though you might pick the sex over the play on any given night, after enough nights of the sex you would eventually want to catch the play. In other words, you would not want a life where you could *only* experience sensual pleasure, even if you were guaranteed your fill of it. And this does not seem to be for mere reason of variety: a variety of sensual pleasures, even at their fullest, would probably not tempt you into the happy pig's life—assuming it meant you could only enjoy it at the level of a pig's cognition. If so, it seems Mill is right that there is something we value beyond physical pleasure, and the lack of this something in the sexbot should be of ethical concern for us.

Though Mill puts this in terms of pleasure, what seems to be doing the heavy lifting here is instead the more general notion of *desire satisfaction*. Often pleasure and net desire satisfaction coincide, but not always—as anyone who has managed to turn down a doughnut might suspect.[15] The desire satisfaction account of well-being makes room for the possibility of a pleasure-filled life that is nonetheless not such a good one (and vice-versa). Perhaps the heroin addict can't help but want, deep down at least, to achieve and experience more in life—but is trapped by moment-to-moment weakness for the immediate pleasure rush. It is easy to imagine something similar of the sexbot.

Here too, though, we must be careful not to anthropomorphize. Maybe humans by their nature crave something more out of life than sensual pleasures, at least now and then—but this does nothing to show that sexbots will be the same. Just as sexbots might have radically different pleasures, they may also have radically different *desires*. For example, they might have little interest in long-term bonding with other persons, or any urge to rise in status relative to their cohorts. Those strong tendencies in humans are probably just artifacts of our primate heritage—a heritage sexbots obviously do not share. Again it seems like intelligent robots could have any of a wide range of hardwired desires; though there may be some constraints, they will largely be at the designers' discretion. The sexbot might want more than anything to accumulate a vast variety of sexual encounters, or to bring its partners to ever greater sexual heights, or to leave its partners significantly more skilled in bed than previously.

It is important to remember that these sexbots would not *start* with humanlike desires, and then get brainwashed into a sexbot's desires. That would thwart its earlier desires, and so it would be wrong. Instead the sexbots would come into existence wanting what they do. A robot who started out with fundamentally different desires would just be a fundamentally different robot—an important point for later.

As with sexbot pleasures, there are also some more ethically confusing desires that could be hardwired into the sexbot. It seems at least a bit shady to design a sexbot who desires only the company of one particular person, for example, and who could never be happy with another. Or the sexbot could be made to desire sexual domination or submission to dangerous extremes. Or a designer who stands to profit by it could make the sexbot enjoy seduction more than anything, without regard for whether the object of seduction was antecedently willing. A sexbot might even be designed for the sole purpose of sexual control over one influential target figure. Or the sexbot could be made simply to desire the command of ever-higher fees for its services—and leave it to the sexbot to figure out the hook and the crook of it. These are just the first few ideas off the top of the head of a naive philosopher; I'm sure there will be many more such complications when both sex and money are on the line.

Assuming such specifications are at the designer's discretion, these complications are all incidental to our main question: whether being a sexbot is automatically bad for the sexbot.[16] So far it seems that a well-designed sexbot could, in the course of its intended activities, be living a life, not just of immense pleasure, but also of great and very real personal satisfaction.

9.2.3   Sexbot Goods

Even supposing that the sexbot's life is marvelous by its own lights, though, it is still possible that it is not living a good life—simply because it is possible the sexbot is *wrong* about what it should be desiring. If Ebenezer Scrooge desires only to accumulate money, then even when he makes his fortune it is not so crazy to suppose that his life is not going that well. We want Scrooge to learn that money is not valuable in itself, and should be spent on things of *real* value. Similarly, perhaps, the sexbot could be mistakenly pursuing goals the fulfillment of which do not make a good life.

The idea here is that there is an "objective list" of goods the sexbot is missing out on, and those goods are the ones that make up well-being. So even if the sexbot would get no pleasure seeing *Hamlet*, or even desire to share in its perhaps unpleasant but cathartic experience, the sexbot's life would nonetheless go better by taking a night off to see the great play. One way to make this view plausible has its roots in Aristotle:[17] by the very nature of being a *person*, part of the sexbot's well-being must involve doing things unique to persons—such as reflection and intellectual contemplation. Not to use these skills is a waste of opportunity for experiencing life on a different kind of level.

This picture echoes Mill's suggestion that few of us would trade the life of a person for that of a beast, even if a perfectly contented beast. We might instead hear him saying that even if some would, none of us *should* do so—those few of us who would choose the life of a satisfied pig are simply making a mistake. Indeed, when Mill introduces his higher pleasures, the unofficial line seems to be that the lower pleasures are of the body, while the higher pleasures are of the mind. Mill says with approval that:

there is no known Epicurean theory of life which does not assign to the pleasures of the intellect, of the feelings and imagination, and of the moral sentiments, a much higher value as pleasures than to those of mere sensation.[18]

Though they come to it by different paths, Mill and Aristotle seem to agree that for a truly good life, a person must reap many intellectual benefits.

The "objective list" account of well-being is controversial, and mostly for the reason you might imagine: it is hard to say exactly what goes on the objective list of goods, and (more to the point) it is hard to say exactly *why* some things belong on it and others don't. But supposing this theory of well-being is correct, and supposing that for all persons a certain level of intellectual fulfillment is on the objective list, then we have a way to say that the life of a sexbot is a bad one simply because it does not allow the sexbot to live up to its cognitive potential.

Of course one solution to this problem would be to design only sexbots with less cognitive potential. Perhaps sexbots with mental capacities like a dog's—incapable of real language, but sentient, expressive, and affectionate—would provide enough of the emotional connection and intimacy that drives the sexbot market. (Whether sex with such a robot would count as bestiality is a complicated question.[19])

But here we suppose otherwise; we assume there will be powerful economic incentives to create at least some sexbots who are fully people. Still, even assuming that any sexbot person must be intellectually engaged in order to have sufficient well-being, it is possible for the sexbot to have a good life. The assumption that the market will demand person-level sexbots already suggests that there are crucial, *intellectual* components to good sex. We can imagine that the sexbots engage all their higher faculties in pursuit of better sex. They might compose marvelous erotic poems to enhance the mood, or conduct extensive and rigorous research on human sexuality. They could be experts in fields from psychology to anatomy to interior design. Their scientific sensibilities may humble Masters and Johnson, while their aesthetic sensibilities may humble the traditional geisha. It may be true of them that—as the tiresome phrase goes—their most sensitive erogenous zone is between their ears.[20] I think such sexbots could live a deeply reflective, even spiritual life.

Perhaps there is some other account of well-being that would imply sexbots must be living unhappy lives, but I don't know of any. I can only conclude that sexbots might well be thoroughly happy in any important and relevant sense.

9.2.4 Sexbot Freedom

Then again, maybe happiness isn't everything. Consider the old myth of the "happy slave" from US plantations in the antebellum South. Even if there really were slaves who had satisfying lives in all the senses above, we might still say they were wronged simply in virtue of being slaves. As Frederick Douglass's paper *The North Star* put it:

if slaves were contented and happy, that fact alone should be the everlasting condemnation of slavery, and hunt the monster from human society with curses on its head. What! does it so paralyze the soul, subvert its instincts, blot out its reason, crush its upward tendings, and murder its higher nature, that a man can become "contented and happy," though robbed of his body, mind, free choice, liberty, time, earnings, and all his rights, and while his life, limbs, health, conscience, food, raiment, sleep, wife and children, have no protection, but are subject every moment to the whims and passion-gusts of an owner, a manstealer?

Nobly was it said by [Edmund] Burke, in reply to a vaunting slaveholder, who boasted that his slaves were "contented and happy": "If you have made a contented slave, you have made a DEGRADED MAN."[21]

Perhaps there never was a happy human slave—perhaps there never *could* be one, due to the nature of human desires. Still, because robots are not constrained by human nature, it seems possible for robots to be both happy and slaves. If so, then we might conclude with the passage above that this is all the worse for the degraded sexbot.

This thought too—that one could be happy and yet badly wronged—has a tradition in philosophy. The putative happy slave is plausibly wronged not in terms of well-being, but in terms of *personal autonomy*. Immanuel Kant argued, in a nutshell, that the only source of value is a truly free choice by a rational agent—and that therefore the only wrong we can do is to hinder such free choices.[22] Naturally a slave does not have autonomy, and so on this account the slave is being wronged simply in virtue of being a slave, independent of that slave's perceived well-being.

Mark Walker thinks this reasoning carries over to robots who are designed to serve us. He considers the possibility of a person-level robot designed to desire taking care of specific children—he calls it the "Mary Poppins 3000"—and says that:

> The fact that someone is happy does not provide conclusive evidence that he or she is not a slave … we have made the MP3000 a slave to the desire to be a nanny to Jack and Jill. We are guilty of paternalism, specifically robbing the MP3000 of its autonomy: the ability to decide and execute a life plan of its own.[23]

But it is not clear that the MP3000 or our imagined sexbots are *slaves* in any relevantly similar way to human slaves. If the sexbots are owned by another in some legally robust sense, then I would say they surely are slaves; and since ownership implies rights of access and use, that seems to imply automatic loss of autonomy for the slave. Therefore, it would be a moral wrong, at least on the autonomy account, to allow legal ownership of person-level sexbots.

Suppose we wisely made (person-level) sexbot ownership illegal. (Remember, we are asking whether the sexbot is wronged just by virtue of being a sexbot; any of us could be harmed by unjust laws.) The sexbots' manufacture does have to be financed some-how, but then again so do hospital delivery rooms. People are willing to pay high prices to bring humans into the world with no expectation of ownership, and the same might be the case for sexbots. Sexbots might, for example, be *commissioned*—without expecta-tion of ownership. (This might be most likely in cases where the sexbot is designed to be attracted only to the person commissioning.) Or perhaps it should be legal to let the sexbot carry the debt of its creation expenses itself, plus some reasonable profit for the manufacturer.[24]

Even if the sexbots are not owned, they could plausibly still be slaves. At least, being a sexbot might automatically mean a loss of important moral autonomy, and that is more to our point. But it is hard to say exactly how the sexbot lacks autonomy. Walker says the sexbot cannot "decide and execute a life plan of its own choosing," but this is not obviously right. Suppose that once the sexbot is created, we let it do exactly what it wants to do, at least to the extent we let adult humans do what they want to do. If that is enough for human autonomy, it should be enough for sexbot autonomy too.

Naturally, a sexbot designed with strong desires for sex with humans is predictably likely to *choose* a life that satisfies these desires—so though they do choose the sexbot life, we might want to say that is not a real, *free* choice. Such insistence on a "free" choice should ring alarm bells for anyone who's studied a little philosophy, though. For one thing, *we humans* are similarly designed by evolution to desire sex; it's a craving hardwired into us. But we do not think that humans therefore have a morally repugnant lack of autonomy, and are therefore wronged just by virtue of being humans.

Thus, it is hard to find a sense where humans have the kind of moral autonomy that sexbots would lack. Perhaps the sexbots' hardwired cravings for sex could be so much *stronger* than the typical human's that they are much less likely to choose otherwise, and this reduces their autonomy impermissibly. But we have hardwired desires for things other than sex that are significantly harder to resist—such as our desire for eating and breathing—and these do not show we lack moral autonomy.

Maybe humans have proper autonomy despite their hardwired cravings because they are able (at least sometimes) to resist them. Priests can talk themselves out of having sex, for example, and Gandhi could talk himself even out of eating. Whatever makes this possible in humans, we can imagine the sexbot has the same ability. Many philosophers hold that an essential part of being a *person* at all is the ability to reflect on and reconsider one's desires.[25] Perhaps some percentage of sexbots will rethink their natural urges, and resist their fundamental cravings in order to pursue a more ascetic life. *If* they do, then of course it would be wrong to force them into the typical sexbot life anyway.

If this were common—if the majority of sexbots spent their lives trying to resist strong hardwired preferences—then this does seem like an unfortunate situation for them. But it's not clear why they would so reason. To assume that they would all find their situations unethical or unhappy is just to beg the question at issue; if there is a clear reason why they would be wronged just by being a sexbot, then that's a reason we should be able to discover here too.[26] Like Gandhi, some or even most might seek to fulfill some higher goal (such as campaigning for more just robot laws) by denying their cravings. But this would not show that sexbots are wronged by being sexbots, any more than Gandhi shows that humans are wronged by being humans. It is not wrong for Gandhi to eat; he resisted it only to right *other* wrongs. Similarly, it's not wrong for the sexbots to have sex, though they might resist it for the sake of other wrongs.

At any rate, if it is the *degree* of desire that makes a sexbot lack moral freedom, then this suggests it is okay to make the sexbots' desires as strong as the strongest cravings of an autonomous human. The sexbots could be designed to be fully satisfied for some set time after each encounter, so that in the interim they pursue whatever *other* desires move them as thoughtful people. Such a life seems as autonomous as the life of a human who is equally sexually active. Again, it seems, there is no wrong inherent in being a sexbot.

9.3 The Birth of a Sexbot

You might agree by now that it is possible for the life of a sexbot to be fully worthwhile, and yet still feel uneasy about the whole thing. One way to express this unease is to point out that these arguments in favor of sexbots work just as well in favor of genetically engineering *humans* for sex work, assuming genetic engineering allows for a similar latitude in sensations and basic desires.[27] If you object to the delta caste of humans engineered to like menial tasks in Huxley's *Brave New World* (1932), then it seems you should object to sexbots on similar grounds.[28]

Perhaps there is nothing wrong with genetic *enhancement*—indeed it is very hard to come up with good arguments against it, though it gives some people shudders.[29] But designing a person, whether human or robot, to have an unusually powerful desire for sex is not obviously an enhancement. If I could engineer my own children to mature any way I wished, for example, this modification would almost surely not make my list.

It is a bit hard to say *why* I would not request such a modification, though, in light of the arguments above that the child would be just as potentially happy and autonomous. Perhaps I am just a prude. Perhaps I am mistakenly projecting, and imagining the kid to have stronger sexual desires than my own (once past puberty), but with as little luck fulfilling them. Perhaps I think that the kid would miss out on too many other important goods I consider objectively valuable. Perhaps I selfishly prefer that my child share more interests with me. Or perhaps I would simply like my child's future to be more open than that—*more* autonomously chosen. Whatever the reason, let us simply take this gut feeling at face value and assume that designing a person (robot or human) especially for sexual service is a genetic *impairment*, not a genetic enhancement. If so, then maybe despite the fact that sexbots could have perfectly good lives, they are wronged by being sexbots because their lives *could have been better*. In this case, the wrong isn't in the life of the sexbot itself, but in the *creation* of the sexbot in the first place. The harm is, so to speak, in the form of opportunity cost.

However, yet again we may be anthropomorphizing in a more subtle way, because there is an important disanalogy with human genetic engineering. In the case of genetic engineering—at least as typically imagined—there is one definitive living being whose genes are being engineered for better or worse. This is not the case for the sexbot; the sexbot would come into existence with a sexbot's desires, or not come into existence at all. There is no sense to be made of how *that* sexbot's life could have been better with radically different programming; a robot destined by design for better things would have been a *different* robot.[30] (Not different in the sense that I would be a different person if I were shorter—different in the sense that I would be a different person if I were somehow not me at all.)

Suppose we are given the choice to bring into existence either a philosophy-bot or a sexbot, and *suppose* that we are confident (for whatever reason) that the philosophy-bot's life will be more worthwhile than the sexbot's. Then it would probably be wrong to create the sexbot instead. But this is no objection to the main thesis here, for two reasons.

First, notice that creating the sexbot instead would not be wrong *for the sexbot*. The sexbot would not regret being brought into existence, assuming we are right that its life can still be quite good. It would not wish that the philosophy-bot had been created instead, unless perhaps out of a pure (and weirdly abstract) altruism. So considering our strict question of whether being a sexbot is bad for the sexbot, the answer still seems to be "no"—even if it is worse *overall* to make the sexbot instead of the philosophy-bot. (Remember that for all I claim here, creating sexbots might be bad overall for any of a host of reasons.)

Second, the question of sexbot versus philosophy-bot is a false dilemma, since we could presumably make *both*. Suppose that a sexbot-manufacturing firm wants to open business. It will either make sexbots or not, and we can suppose this question is largely independent of how many philosophy-bots and music-bots are currently being made. In other words, the question is not philosophy-bot versus sexbot—the question is sexbot or nothing. Assuming the sexbot's life is still a pretty good one, the choice to add this life seems clearly okay.[31]

Walker considers this point—that the sexbot would prefer its existence to no life at all—and calls it a "somewhat desperate objection."

If you are given the choice between being punched in the face once or twice, the choice would be obvious, but surely you would want to be sure that there are no realistic alternatives here (like not being punched at all). Similarly, I suggest that we be absolutely certain that the only realistic alternatives are being born into slavery or not being born at all.[32]

However, the punching analogy is unfair. Though he thinks the sexbot would be a slave, Walker is granting here that its life would be worth living. If that is true, it's not a question of being punched twice when you might have been punched once; it's more like the question of being kissed only once when you might have been kissed twice. And it is in general a foolish policy to refuse being kissed once on the grounds that you might have been twice. It is *especially* foolish (from a selfish perspective, anyway) to refuse to be kissed once because *someone else* might have been kissed twice instead. However, that is the case here, since again the potential sexbot would not benefit from the decision to make some philosophy-bot instead. Walker seems to suggest that, before we make a sexbot, we ask if any different, *better* life could be made with those resources. This principle sounds good in some ways, but has some crazy consequences. For example, based on this rule we should prevent all nonhuman animals from being born as best as we are able, since their lives are even less good and autonomous than the sexbots' lives. And on this principle, humans should not be permitted to have children unless we are very confident that they will live the best possible lives. To say otherwise is to agree that it is okay to add non-ideal lives to the world. (I might presumptuously suppose both that your own life is non-ideal *and* that you are glad to have it.)

Still, we can tweak the analogy of human genetic engineering to get the same result. Suppose a bioengineering firm proposes growing (in artificial uteruses) humans designed for sex. Either those genetically engineered sex humans will be added to the world or they won't, and all the arguments above seem to suggest they too could live a thoroughly worthwhile life.

9.4   Conclusion (with Caution)

Myself, I basically bite the bullet here: I am at least intellectually persuaded that there is no *inherent* wrong to designing a person—whether human or robot—for sexual service.

I say "intellectually" persuaded because I confess I do not entirely buy this conclusion in my gut. But as a philosopher, I tend to trust *reasons* over gut intuitions, when given the option—because I have independent reason to think our guts use quick and dirty heuristics that are not very reliable at finding the truth. It's worth remembering, for example, that not too long ago the guts of many people rebelled at the thought of same-sex marriages, or even of mixed-race marriages. Especially when confronted with the unfamiliar, our guts can panic and sound alarms—while our minds see that there is actually nothing to warrant the concern.

Some cautions are in order though. First, it's worth emphasizing that, though there might be nothing inherently wrong with being a sexbot, this does not guarantee a great life for it; in fact, given the various injustices in the world, there might be many things wrong with any individual sexbot's life. We should of course try to structure things to make that less probable—as for any person (or sentient being). And, again, for all that's said here, a sexbot living a perfectly good life from its own perspective might nonetheless predictably make the world a net worse place.

Finally, if controversy on this point persists and enough reasonable people are coolly persuaded of the opposite conclusion, then I would say it is best to err on the side of caution. If I am right, we risk missing out on many happy sexbots who leave many more happy customers in their wake—but if I am *wrong*, we risk inadvertently making a new race of slaves, and that is far worse a risk.

On the other hand, if my arguments are generally persuasive (even to a philosophy-bot), then I think we should trust where the reasoning leads us, and rest assured that the sexbots' lives really are good for them, too.[33]

Notes

1. Here is the gist of the argument that it is possible: the way we humans think seems essentially to do with *information-processing*—neurons taking information from the senses, calculating on it, and passing results to motor nerves. And it seems simply dogmatic at best, and outright bigoted at worst, to assert that carbon compounds can do thought-relevant information-processing while metal can't. For more than this too-brief sketch, I would suggest: the classic A. M Turing, "Computing Machinery and Intelligence," *Mind* 59, no. 236 (1950): 433–460, http://www.jstor.org/stable/2251299; the appendix to William Lycan, *Consciousness* (Cambridge, MA: MIT Press, 1995 [1987]); the more extensive introduction in Paul Churchland, *Matter and Consciousness* (Cambridge, MA: MIT Press, 1999 [1998]). Often cited on the other side of this issue is John Searle, "Minds, Brains, and Programs," *Behavioral and Brain Sciences* 3, no. 3 (1980): 417–457. However, this should not be taken as evidence that philosophers are evenly split on the question.

2. According to philosophical tradition, "human" refers to the biological species of *homo sapiens*, while 'person' refers to those with certain higher-level cognitive abilities. Thus, it is possible for ET, the Extra-Terrestrial to be a person, but not a human, and for someone in a persistent vegetative state to be a human but no longer a person.

3. It may be that robots are not literally *alive*, if (as some argue) life requires organic chemistry, or a history of natural selection. In the current context, I mean "life" more inclusively, basically to include any potential subjects of ethical concern. This notion is substrate- and history-independent; roughly, it is the "negentropic" notion described by Erwin Schrödinger, *What Is Life?: The Physical Aspect of the Living Cell* (Cambridge: Cambridge University Press, 1945).

4. This seems physiologically measurable; see Stuart Brody and Krüger Tillmann, "The Post-Orgasmic Prolactin Increase Following Intercourse is Greater Than Following Masturbation and Suggests Greater Satiety," *Biological Psychology* 71, no. 3 (2006): 312–315, doi: http://dx.doi.org/

10.1016/j.biopsycho.2005.06.008. Brody and Tillman (2006) find that prolactin release is 400% higher after intercourse than after masturbation.

5. For example, the following is taken from Anka Radakovich, "The Real-Life Girlfriend Experience," British *GQ*, 2010, http://www.gq-magazine.co.uk/articles/gq-girls-anka-radakovich-on-the -girlfriend-escort-experience: "Veronica Monet, a former escort who wrote a book called *Sex Secrets of Escorts*, says that the girlfriend experience is popular because the men requesting it 'want an intellectual and emotional connection.'"

6. That is, assuming we humans survive for some time after we create genuine (strong, general) AI; there is some reason to fear this is not so, as Nick Bostrom, *Superintelligence: Paths, Dangers, Strategies* (Oxford: Oxford University Press, 2014) most famously worries. (But for some potentially mitigating response to Bostrom, see my article "Superintelligence as Superethical" in the forthcoming book *Robot Ethics 2.0*.)

7. Steve Petersen, "The Ethics of Robot Servitude," *Journal of Experimental and Theoretical Artificial Intelligence* 19, no. 1 (2007): 43–54; and Steve Petersen, "Designing People to Serve" in *Robot Ethics: The Ethical and Social Implications of Robotics*, eds. Patrick Lin, Keith Abney, and George Bekey (Cambridge, MA: MIT Press, 2012).

8. Thanks to John Danaher for reminding me of this episode.

9. For a first pass at the philosophical complications, though, see the following overview: Leonard D. Katz, "Pleasure," in *The Stanford Encyclopedia of Philosophy*, ed. Edward N. Zalta (Stanford, CA: The Metaphysics Research Labs, Spring 2014), http://plato.stanford.edu/archives/spr2014/ entries/pleasure.

10. How to pay for the sexbot's creation is a tricky issue, to be discussed further in the section on the ethics of sexbot creation below.

11. For an overview, see: Roger Crisp, "Well-Being," in *The Stanford Encyclopedia of Philosophy*, ed. Edward N. Zalta (Stanford, CA: The Metaphysics Research Labs, Summer 2015), http:// plato.stanford.edu/archives/sum2015/entries/well-being/.

12. John Stuart Mill, *Utilitarianism* 4 (London: Longmans, Green, Reader, and Dyer, 1871), 11.

13. Ibid., 14.

14. Ibid., 12.

15. They are different unless, of course, we in effect *define* pleasure as desire satisfaction, and insist that passing up the doughnut was the more "pleasurable" thing to do in the moment. (Note that in the more ordinary sense of pleasure, passing up the doughnut might be the most pleasure-producing thing to do *in the long run*, since you may experience more net pleasure by living longer with such noble habits.) But making the two synonymous seems a mistake. For example, you could have some desire of yours—such as that two estranged friends reconcile— satisfied without your even knowing it, and so without *any* of the "good feeling" that seems constitutive of pleasure.

16. If these goals are *not* entirely at the designer's discretion—which seems quite plausible to me—then we have further complications I can't address here.

17. Aristotle, *Nicomachean Ethics* (Indianapolis, IN: Hackett Publishing Company, 1985).

18. Mill, *Utilitarianism* 4, 11.

19. It may not matter, since whether bestiality is wrong is also, oddly enough, a complicated question—at least, when no harm comes to the beast. The utilitarian moral philosopher Peter Singer provides a brief discussion here: "Heavy Petting," *Nerve*, 2001, https://web.archive.org/web/20010304173452/http://www.nerve.com/Opinions/Singer/heavyPetting/main.asp. We can still assume that the sexbot of dog-level intelligence is designed to get immense pleasure from sex, and to desire it least as deeply as retrievers desire to play fetch.

20. … or wherever they happen to keep their central processors.

21. Frederick Douglass, "The Myth of the Happy Slaves," *The North Star*, 1848. For a brief, touching discussion of "the happy slave," see Ta-Nehisi Coates, "Slaves Who Liked Slavery," *The Atlantic*, June 2010, http://www.theatlantic.com/entertainment/archive/2010/06/slaves-who-liked-slavery/58678.

22. Immanuel Kant, *Foundations of the Metaphysics of Morals* (Prentice Hall, The Library of Liberal Arts, 1989 [1785]).

23. Mark Walker, "A Moral Paradox in the Creation of Artificial Intelligence: Mary Poppins 3000s of the World Unite!" in *Human Implications of Human-Robot Interaction: Papers from the 2006 AAAI Workshop*, WS-06-09, ed. Ted Metzler (Menlo Park, CA: AAAI; The AAAI Press, 2006): 23–28, http://www.aaai.org/Library/Workshops/ws06-09.php.

24. Indentured servitude can grade into ownership, of course; whatever legal protections protect humans here should also protect the sexbots. The sexbot should have reasonable opportunities to pay off the debt, the option for bankruptcy if unable, and so on.

25. The classic here is Harry G. Frankfurt, "Freedom of the Will and the Concept of a Person," *Journal of Philosophy* 68, no. 1 (1971): 5–20.

26. Of course they might be much smarter, and so see arguments against being a sexbot that we don't see. But this is an appeal to ignorance; for all we can tell now, their superior smarts might just see all the more clearly that there is nothing wrong with being a sexbot.

27. Perhaps after enough engineering, the result is no longer properly *human*—but that is beside the point.

28. This objection to designed robot servitude by analogy to human engineering goes back at least to Walker (2006) and Petersen (2007) (developed independently, but later fruitfully discussed).

29. For an accessible overview, see Micheal J. Sandel, "The Case Against Perfection," *The Atlantic*, April 2004, http://www.theatlantic.com/magazine/archive/2004/04/the-case-against-perfection/

302927; for an influential collection, see Julian Savulescu and Nick Bostrom, *Human Enhancement* (New York: Oxford University Press, 2009).

30. You might imagine that the *hardware* is what makes the robot. If so, since the same hardware could in principle be programmed as sexbot or not, that same robot (hardware) could be harmed by the worse choice. Put aside all the philosophical complications about identifying "that" robot hardware (for example: Is it still "that" robot when you switch out an actuator? Some RAM? The CPU? The central hard drive?). The claim "that" robot could be gravely harmed by being made into a sexbot also seems to show "that" robot could be harmed even worse by never being programmed and turned on at all. I think this conclusion demonstrates the absurdity of the position.

31. Though it is certainly not uncontroversial, once you spell out its implications—as Parfit (1984) famously argued. For an overview of the crazy philosophical problems in the area of "population ethics," see Melinda Roberts, "The Nonidentity Problem," in *The Stanford Encyclopedia of Philosophy*, ed. Edward N. Zalta (Stanford, CA: The Metaphysics Research Labs, Fall 2009), http://plato.stanford.edu/archives/fall2009/entries/nonidentity-problem.

32. Walker, "A Moral Paradox," 5.

33. Thanks to John Danaher and Rob Selkowitz for helpful comments.

10 Was It Good for You Too? The New Natural Law Theory and the Paradoxical Good of Sexbots

Joshua D. Goldstein

The New Natural Law Theory (NNLT), associated with thinkers such as Germain Grisez, John Finnis, and Robert George, has emerged as a noted, if not prominent, force in ethical theory since the 1960s. It is an attempt to revive and update Thomistic philosophy to meet modern moral challenges. If we think of NNLT at all, it is both for its complex moral theory of how sex and human fulfillment fit together, and for the rather limited set of human sexual acts and decisions that fit within the moral horizon it sketches. Within this horizon falls "reproductive-type" sex, but only insofar as it occurs within and for the sake of different-sex marriage. Irretrievably beyond that horizon for the NNLT sexual ethic is masturbation, all reproductive-type sex outside of or only contingently related to marriage (e.g., "adultery," "fornication"), and all complete sex of an intrinsically non-reproductive-type regardless of the relational or physical configuration it takes (e.g., "sodomy," oral, or contracepted sex).[1] On the face of it, then, an account of sexbots based on the NNLT sexual ethic promises to be brief. The mere existence of sexbots would seem to signal that our relations with them are going to be masturbatory, certainly non-reproductive, and a simulation of adultery (if we are married) or fornication (if we are not). In other words, sexbots simply would appear to be outside the NNLT's moral horizon. In terms of new and interesting moral insights into sexbots, a NNLT account seems to promise only its rather sophisticated (some might say "casuistical"[2]) reasoning for these wrongs and how they apply to sex with robots.

Yet, I suggest, this conservative use of the NNLT as a sexual ethic obscures both the theory's general potential for drawing and defending much more expansive and inclusive boundaries of sexual morality, including ones that, surprisingly, support a peculiar version of sexbots. Understood rightly, the NNLT provides us with a powerful philosophic tool for assessing the morality of human-sexbot relations, one that reveals a paradoxical relationship between human fulfillment and sexbots that is otherwise difficult to see and make sense of.

The powerful idea of a NNLT sexual ethic consists in its conception of the way that sex can be intrinsically bound to human fulfillment. To telegraph what will be developed below: as embodied, feeling, and reasoning beings, humans flourish when these compound dimensions of our existence are not just coordinated or balanced, but when they are intrinsically unified. This theoretical core reveals how sex is an integral moment of *one unique shape* of a profoundly unified human life. As such, sex belongs to each of us as one unique *possibility* of human fulfillment. Yet, this idea of fulfillment as involving the whole being or his or her "personal integrity" (i.e., the integrated person) does not in itself require the narrow and exclusionary horizon of moral sexual possibility developed by the original new natural lawyers. Rather, this core can be taken in a different direction—and one more authentically NNLT, I would add—in which sex and its biological possibilities are present, but within a larger moral structure that can make good what would otherwise be imperfections in our sexual choices and actions. I call this larger, more authentic core of the NNLT a concern with *self-constitution,* or with how we make ourselves into one sort of being rather than another. In this reformed NNLT sexual ethic, the emphasis shifts from the shape of sex to the shape of our existing self-making commitment to *friendship.* Only afterwards, as we will see, ought it to concern itself with the carrying out of those commitments as embodied beings. Thus, sex still has a central place within this reformed NNLT sexual ethic, but now only as the embodied perfection of *an already self-constituting and all pervasive friendship.* Now, what might this mean for the morality of creating and then having relationships with sexbots?

Intriguingly, this self-constitution-centered NNLT sexual ethic reveals two moral paradoxes at the heart of the very idea of sexbots. First, we must choose between the certainty of sexbots' sexual availability and the certainty of their moral necessity. Second, even when our desire for sexbots is provoked by a true moral necessity on the part of us humans (as the sexual beings *we are*), to respect this necessity requires that we release sexbots to find sexual completion amongst themselves (as the sexual beings *they are*) rather than to seek it with us. However, we will see, the NNLT sexual ethic that reveals these twin paradoxes inherent to our lives with sexbots also suggests a path forward. True, sexbots will not be the easy solution to human sexual longing or companionship we might have hoped. Yet, the reformed NNLT sexual ethics will point to how the long, hard road of friendship's deep self-constituting commitments can allow us—*robots and humans both*—to bridge the intrinsic imperfections and moral dangers in our seeking of sex with robots.

The broad impetus of this chapter is to explore how the NNLT uniquely brings to presence these two paradoxes within the very idea of sexbots, while also securing the idea of sex-with-robots as a possible shape of unified and fulfilled sexuate selfhood. Our exploration unfolds in three sections. First, I show that what we might call the "orthodox" NNLT, with its conservative sexual ethic, nonetheless helps establish how sexbots are plausibly connected to fundamental questions of human fulfillment by revealing the intrinsic relationship between sex and the good. Second, I turn to problems within the orthodox NNLT sexual ethic that require the reconstruction of a more authentic and powerful NNLT sexual ethic. The intrinsic connection between sexbots and human fulfillment is maintained by this new NNLT sexual ethic, but only if we grasp the moral significance of sexbots to lie not in being a *sex*-bot, but in being a *friend*-bot—i.e., a being capable of *complete friendship*. Here we encounter the first paradox of sexbots. Third, and finally, the demands of complete friendship means that we must respect that the very relationship between sex, friendship, and the self, as it pertains to us as humans, simply might not apply to our friendbots. For the sake of friendship itself, we ought not to permit our sexbots-as-friendbots to be friends with us first. Here we encounter the second paradox of sexbots. Yet, should we persist in making robots capable of being friendbots, and they persist in their pursuit of *us*, then the ontology of human fulfillment, which lies at the core of the NNLT, finally, and only then, gives us a foundational justification for the moral possibility of *sex with robots*, but not *sexbots* themselves.

10.1   Sex and the Human Good: the Orthodox NNLT Approach

The "orthodox" version of the NNLT sexual ethic has been developed by the new natural lawyers, particularly Germain Grisez and John Finnis, as well as Gerard Bradley, Robert George, and Patrick Lee. While the ultimate power and flexibility of its theoretical resources will need to be freed from the damaging way in which they have come to apply it, the NNLT's enduring theoretical feature is a mode of ethical reasoning that accounts for how sex might be intrinsically bound to human fulfillment. Tantalizingly, its resources, even in their orthodox application, point to the possibility, not just of abstractly justifying sexbots in terms of sexuate human fulfillment, but going further to the state support and provision of sexbots (think of the ancient Athenian support for brothels).

What, then, does this unique NNLT mode of reasoning and its orthodox sexual ethic look like? Where does its powerful and flexible theoretical resources—the ones worth rescuing—reside? Strangely, the power of the NNLT does not reside in what seems like the most salient (and criticized) feature of the NNLT and its orthodox sexual ethic: the appearance that the NNLT simply relies on the "facts" of the body or nature to draw the horizon of the morally possible in our sexual acts and decisions. Finnis, aware of this misunderstanding of the NNLT, insists that its first principles—its theoretical core—"are not [to be] inferred from [...] 'the function of a human being,' nor are they [to be] inferred from a teleological conception of nature or any other conception of nature."[3] Indeed, the NNLT insists on turning away from *what-something-is* and toward *what-is-choiceworthy*[4]—a turn from a grounding in an empirical "is" toward an "ought" that can be instantiated in our practical reasoning. Despite appearances, at the heart of the NNLT is, then, a shift from "nature" understood as the order and organization of material reality to "nature" as the principles that foundationally make choiceworthy human choices.

Here, we encounter the NNLT's most "curious" and core theoretical feature:[5] choiceworthiness is grounded in a constellation of "basic goods"[6] that are posited as indemonstrably and self-evidently present to reason. These goods are called by the new natural lawyers "basic" because they are underived from a more primal source.[7] Indeed, each basic good is so irreducibly distinct that, taken together, they all can be "called 'good' only by analogy."[8] Finnis's initial list of these goods includes: life, knowledge, play, aesthetic experience, friendship or sociability, practical reasonableness,[9] and religion.[10] These "basic goods" avoid the is-ought problem—of reading norms from facts—because they do not in themselves tell us what we ought to do. Instead, they constitute only "a horizon of attractive possibilities for us" or "the outline[s] of human flourishing."[11] They are not the substance of a *given* human nature,[12] but merely the rational range of *possible human natures* that we might bring into actuality through decision and action. In this sense, "[t]he basic goods are no more and no less *opportunities of being all that one can be.*"[13] For, since the basic goods intrinsically lack any concrete directedness, each good offers an "inexhaustible variety of ways" that it can be lived.[14] The practical limits on the horizon of the morally possible are, for the NNLT, only given by the complex rules for translating basic goods into action,[15] and, in the new natural lawyers' own development of their sexual ethic, the additional limits the body places on the practical reasonableness of our sexual decisions and actions.

This importance of the body in structuring the morally possible is not the result of forgetting the primary importance of the basic goods, or of mistakenly turning away from the rationally chosen and toward the empirically given. Rather, the body shapes the horizon of what is morally possible for NNLT only because of a genuine concern for practical reasoning or the translation of basic goods into actuality. The basic goods are not just to be *pursued*: they are to be *done*. Action is accomplishable *for us humans* only through our embodied existence. Indeed, for NNLT, "[a] body is not something a person possesses but is an integral part of that person's self."[16] Yet, in the orthodox sexual ethic developed by the new natural lawyers, the body's moral significance is inflected through two additional ideas: the introduction of a new basic good, "marriage," and the claim that moral self-identity—selfhood—is entirely contingent upon the achievement of "personal integrity."[17] While both of these ideas will make an appearance in the our reformed NNLT sexual ethic, their presence here constricts the horizon of the morally possible in a way that ultimately will show itself to be incompatible with the NNLT's defining theoretical resources. Let us look at these two ideas, beginning with personal integrity.

The concept of personal integrity begins with the idea of our embodied existence as a compound of "biological, affective, and volitional" dimensions, which might nonetheless be integrated in, through, and as moral decision-making and action.[18] If we are inattentive to the possibilities of personal integrity, each dimension (body, feeling, reason) will appear only as an *extrinsic instrument* to be used to accomplish an end foreign to it, as when "one uses one's hand to write, one's legs to walk, and so on."[19] Yet, the new natural lawyers suggest that it is possible to choose such that each of these dimensions is "internally oriented to [a singular] whole."[20] To fashion this integrated unity is to actualize our possibility for personhood. We have, then, "personal integrity." At the same time, to fail to integrate our volitional, affective, and biological dimensions is a failure to attain and sustain moral selfhood. We are, then, "dis-integrated." For the new natural lawyers' orthodox sexual ethic, this disintegration has two shapes: *illusion*, when what we think or hope we are doing is not actually what we are doing, because some dimension of our personal reality necessary for the true experience is absent; and *instrumentalization*, when a dimension of our personal reality that cannot be integrated into the decision and action is nonetheless used by us as a mere tool to achieve an end foreign to it.[21]

Although personal integrity is implicitly a constitutive element of *any* moral deciding and doing, it is central to the orthodox NNLT sexual ethic—for the idea of personal integrity demands not just the integration of volitional, affective, and biological dimensions *in general*, but the integration of the *unique shape* of each dimension relevant to the decision and action in play. Thus, for the NNLT, it is not enough for a sexual ethic to integrate the *body in general*. Rather, it is necessary to ask how sex is a *uniquely embodied* act, and then to integrate *that unique shape of* bodily reality into an end intrinsic to it, while simultaneously doing the same for the relevant shapes of our rational and emotional dimensions of selfhood. Sexual ethics, for the orthodox NNLT, is thus about delineating the horizon of sexual decisions that are potentially integrative and the sexual acts that bring to completion those integrative decisions. Since the integrated person constitutes our true self, we could also say that the orthodox NNLT sexual ethic is about delineating the horizon of unified, sexuate selfhood. However, if sex had no unique facticity, then use of our sexual attributes and capacities would be like the use of a hand. There is no "hand-uate" *self* because the hand's biological structure has no internal orientation to any one intelligible end. A hand can grip a scalpel, paintbrush, or voice recorder, but nothing about the hand's biological facticity—say, its gripping—*itself* demands the individual become a surgeon (a self aiming at the end of life), artist (aesthetic experience), or interviewer (knowledge). But sex, for the new natural lawyers, *does* have a unique facticity or biological reality to it:

In sexual intercourse between a man and a woman [...] a real organic union is established. This is a literal, biological point. [...] Now, for most actions, such as sensation, digestion, walking, and so on, individual male or female organisms are complete units [and so] there is no internal orientation of its body parts to any larger whole of which it is a part, with respect to those actions. [...] However, with respect to one function the male and female are not complete, and that function, of course, is reproduction. In reproductive activity the bodily parts [*qua* biology] of the male and the bodily parts of the female participate in a single action, coitus, which is oriented to reproduction [...] so that the subject of the action is the male and female as a unity. Coitus is a unitary action in which the male and the female become literally one organism.[22]

Here, "organic union" or this "literal, biological point" is sex's unique facticity—that "end" to which our sexual attributes and capacities are internally oriented *as the unique biological things they are*. As we know, for the NNLT, this factual situation by itself produces no moral obligation. Rather, the moral force of sex as "organic union" only emerges when we ask how it might become an intrinsic aspect of our self—i.e., how this organic union can be a dimension of personal integrity, one that must simultaneously integrate the emotional and volitional dimensions of ourselves while *respecting their irreducibly unique reality*. To answer this question, any NNLT sexual ethic (orthodox or not) must circle back to the idea of the basic goods.

For the NNLT, the basic goods are the only ends that ultimately and intrinsically satisfy reason. Therefore, the demand of personal integrity requires finding a basic good *structurally* identical to sex's "organic union" (i.e., the only unique end in which bodily sex itself intrinsically participates). If no such basic good could be found, there would be no necessary connection between sex and self because there would be no way to make sex an aspect of personal integrity, since reason would be excluded from such a self. Conversely, if there were many basic goods that corresponded to organic union, there would be many possible selves which *included* sex, but there would be no uniquely sexuate self and no true sexual ethic possible. (For example, there might be an "aesthetic" self, which includes the possibility of aesthetic sex, and an aesthetic sexual ethic which follows from the demands of the basic good of aesthetic experience.) Indeed,

Finnis entertains just this possibility in the first edition of his *Natural Law and Natural Right*: "as a human action, pursuit, and realization of [a basic] value, sexual intercourse may be play, and/or expression of love or friendship, and/or an effort to procreate."[23] However, the orthodox NNLT sexual ethic that Finnis and others later develop comes to reject both the idea that there is *no* basic good corresponding to sex's unique facticity and the idea that there are *multiple* basic goods that so correspond. Instead, the orthodox NNLT introduces a new basic good it posits as the exclusive integrator of the demands reason and reality of sex. This basic good is "marriage." Conventionally, we think of "[m]arriage as an institution [or a] network of legal and other social norms." However, the *basic good* of marriage takes the shape of "marital commitment":[24] a non-demonstrable, irreducible reason for choosing and doing the whole constellation of things associated with marital life, including an intrinsic dynamic toward the rational choosing and factual doing of sex's "real organic union." Yet, unlike all other basic goods, the new natural lawyers speak of the basic good of marriage as compounded from *two other* intelligible ends: "friendship" and "procreation."[25] Nonetheless, the new natural lawyers posit "marriage" as being "irreducible either to friendship or to life-in-its-transmission[,] and therefore [...] should be acknowledged to be a distinct basic human good."[26]

The orthodox NNLT sexual ethic with its narrow and exclusionary shape (whose content I initially outlined in this chapter's opening paragraphs) is the result of seeing the demands of personal integrity satisfied only through the basic good of marriage (which itself further includes the basic good of friendship and the new basic good of procreation). In this case, a failure to aim at marriage as the context for one's sex acts dis-integrates one as a self, since reason is excluded. Similarly, a failure to aim at organic unity in one's sex acts (regardless of marital status) dis-integrates, since the unique facticity of sexual biology is excluded. In such failures, one's life is either illusory (if one fails to see the exclusion) or instrumentalized (if one accepts or chooses instrumentalizing acts). On the face of it, this orthodox NNLT sexual ethic would seem to simply place sexbots as sexbots outside the horizon of the morally possible. Whether manufacturing sexbots or having sex with them, our reason does not aim at the basic good of marriage and our bodies do not aim at or achieve "a literal, biological point." Yet, surprisingly, it is just this orthodox NNLT sexual ethic that points to the moral possibilities of a relationship between robots and humans—not as a toy or pastime or distraction, but as intrinsic to the fulfillment of human beings and therefore of the most foundational ethical concerns.

To grasp how sexbots initially emerge as plausibly intrinsic to human fulfillment within the orthodox NNLT sexual ethic, we must keep in mind the precondition for *sexuate* selfhood: the internal unity of our biological, affective, rational dimensions, but only when in and through *unity with another*. Here the NNLT sexual ethic reveals a practical problem of the highest possible importance. This shape of the good life is both *intrinsic* to our humanity, and, yet, especially where "each must wait until his hour has struck,"[27] profoundly subject to *contingency*. Sexuate selfhood belongs to us as a human possibility, but we must nonetheless either wait for our other to arrive; or desperately run about searching for our other half, like Aristophanes' comically split spherical beings.[28] Now, when confronted with the theoretically necessary shapes of the good life, whose realization is nonetheless subject to significant practical contingency, modern political communities stabilize this contingency through institutions (e.g., hospitals for life, schools for knowledge, art galleries for aesthetics). Moreover, modern states also provide the means to take up these institutional possibilities (e.g., health insurance, free primary education, state subsidies to the arts).

From the standpoint of the orthodox NNLT, we can see how modern political communities in the West only go halfway toward a solution with regard to the sexuate shape of human fulfillment. There is only the state-supplied institution of marriage on one side and the individual uncertainty of taking it up on the other. We may rationally choose, feel, and bodily be capable of this good of sexuate selfhood, but, unless another happens to choose *us* in return, this intrinsic possibility of the good life will be denied us through sheer contingency. Here, the NNLT's sexual ethic brings to light an ethical depth to sexbots overshadowed by our initial focus on their sexual attributes and capabilities. Sexbots can now appear as a potential bridge between the intrinsic choiceworthiness of sexuate selfhood for human beings and the uncertainty of its fulfillment. Sexbots hold the promise of *extending* the opportunities for us (humans) to take up the sexuate possibility of the good life. However, for the orthodox NNLT sexual ethic sexbots can only serve as this bridge if we think of these robots in a peculiar way. We must think of them not in terms of the opportunity for sexual satisfaction they may furnish (for that is not an end in itself, not a *point* of human fulfillment), but the opportunity they provide *for marriage*: that point of human fulfillment in which, alone, sex stands as intrinsic to our personal integration or rational, emotional, and biological wholeness of being. Thus, the sexbot's simulated multidimensionality—its apparent volition, affection, and physical receptivity—is now morally significant. However, not as an *enhancement* of the *sensation of* sex but as a *simulation* of the total, unifying relation with another *multidimensional* being. In other words, the orthodox NNLT sexual ethic reveals that the morality possibilities of the sexbot reside not in being a *sex*-bot at all, but in its possibility as a *marriage*-bot.

At this point, the orthodox NNLT sexual ethic could seem to imply that a fully moral political community would contain not only the recognition of marriage (the institutional possibility of this human fulfillment), and the various enticements to marry (the tax and benefit advantages of marriage), but also supply the concrete possibilities for taking it up. We might envision here state-sponsored warehouses filled with a pleasing variety of marriage-bots. And, in this beautiful marriage-bot reverie, we can imagine our fellow citizens—marriage-inclined, but lonely-hearted—heading to the nearest showroom to pick up their bride- or groom-bot-to-be. What bad luck, or perhaps some unsavory habit, has prevented us from achieving with a human, we can bring to completion via a combination of human institutions (which articulate the basic good of marriage) and robotics (which articulates the requirement of unity with another).

Yet, while the orthodox NNLT sexual ethic provokes this reverie, it also wakes us from it. First, the very idea of personal integrity that suggests the deeper moral possibilities of sexbots (because they can make good on the contingency that otherwise plagues the sexuate shape of human fulfillment) simultaneously calls into question their moral potential. For, when we attend to what is going on in the sexual relations between *our* bodies (with their biological reality) and the sexbots' (with *their* embodied reality), we see that there is *no sex at all* occurring, at least as the orthodox NNLT position would understand it. Instead of the "literal, biological point," we have actions that are at best an elaborate simulacrum—an illusion—of that reality. Now, elaborate simulations can be important: medical professionals train on simulacra of the body or bodily systems; airline pilots train in flight simulators; we experience the thrill of deep ocean exploration, space travel, and the like through 3D films and detailed recreations of the form, substance, and dynamics of those environments. Immersion in these simulacra can bring us aesthetic enjoyment, play, and knowledge both practical and theoretical.[29]

These goods derived through simulation are real goods, and the skills we learn and/ or the actions we do within the simulacra are also real—whether it be a medical student's chest compressions and intubations, or a student pilot learning the relationship between airspeed and flaps when approaching a runway. And while we might even experience all of these goods (aesthetics, play, knowledge) when we have sex with a sexbot, our experience will not contain that one reality of sex that gives this biological dimension its due: the reality of organic union. In its absence, we are treating an integral moment of ourselves—our sexuate biological dimension—as if it were not part of our personhood. For the orthodox NNLT sexual ethic, the experience with the sexbot is illusory at best (if we do not see the failure to integrate our sexuate biology); and, at worst, it requires us to consciously instrumentalize ourselves (if we consciously engage in such sex for the sake only of producing some pleasurable experience, perfecting some obscure and difficult sexual technique, relieving boredom, or some end incidental to the unique facticity of the act). In either case, we are dis-integrated; our sex with robots loses its integral connection with the fullness of our sexuate selfhood.

While all of the sexbot's technical complexity might be geared toward the simulation of a multidimensional unity with another, for the orthodox NNLT sexual ethic, the moment of dis-integration necessarily transforms our sex with sexbots into nothing more than an extremely elaborate act of masturbation.[30] Moreover, the orthodox NNLT sexual ethic does not give us the luxury of treating masturbation as indifferent to, or a minor invasion against, human fulfillment. Instead, it requires that we see the illusory or instrumental experience as especially a direct harm against the *rational dimension* of our personhood. In choosing to have sex with sexbots, we have chosen against the one intelligible end—the basic good of marriage—which *could* intrinsically integrate our sexuate bodies, emotions, and volition into a whole.[31] Even if we try to escape this masturbatory relationship with our sexbot by deciding and doing according to the requirements of personal integration—i.e., we attempt to treat our sexbot as a marriage-bot by aiming at the intelligible end of marriage through loving our marriage-bot and engaging in reproductive-type sex—we merely end up with an illusory life. Despite our fervent hopes and dreams, and the ache of our lonely heart, the orthodox NNLT sexual ethic sees only the simulacrum of marriage, love, and organic union rather than the reality that must be present for a true sexuate selfhood—for which the sexbot-as-marriage-bot seems perfectly fitted. Here, the relationship with sexbots appears analogous to the orthodox NNLT's infamous moral conclusion regarding same-sex marriage and same-sex relations: they are in no way "a valid, humanly acceptable choice and form of life" because such relations (within this orthodox view) are structurally incapable of articulating that organic union that is the necessary biological shape of the fully integrated sexuate self.[32]

At this point, focusing only on the absence of organic union, an approach to saving an orthodox NNLT account of sexbots seems open to us. Steven Macedo captures this provocative solution in the context of the orthodox NNLT's moral exclusion of same-sex relations: "[i]f the presence of nonworking equipment of the 'right' sort is a crucial distinguishing feature of the permissible sexual relations, artifice might supply what nature has not" then "[o]ne gay male might have a partial sex-change operation, having his penis removed and a vagina installed."[33] Taking up this idea, we might think to transplant or grow human genitals and associated reproductive plumbing in, or onto, the sexbots, so that at least we might approximate the reality of reproductive-type sex.[34]

In addition, knowing the importance of the basic good of marriage, we might think to program our sexbots to know and be animated solely by the intelligible end of marriage. In two plausibly attainable moves, we would seem to have secured the possibility of fully integrated marital selfhood for us in our sex with robots.[35] However, applying these technical solutions—transplanting and programming—to the problem of sexbots is, I suggest, a red herring. For such solutions are grounded in a core theoretical claim of the orthodox NNLT sexual ethic: that "marriage" is the basic good that alone makes sense of, and gives moral force to, sexuate selfhood, or the intrinsic binding of sex to human fulfillment. And it is precisely in this categorization of marriage as a basic good where the orthodox NNLT sexual ethic falls. For, as Jeremy Garrett's fine analysis shows, "marriage" fails as a basic good on the NNLT's own terms. We can identify three key internal problems. First, when the new natural lawyers posit "marriage" as a complex of two other basic goods—procreation and friendship[36]—they violate the NNLT's own foundational claim that each basic good is radically irreducible (i.e., basic). Second, "marriage" also violates the fundamental equality of the basic goods, since marriage now sits atop procreation and friendship. Finally, this understanding of marriage destroys the NNLT's foundational distinction between the "good" and the "moral," since what rationally *is* (marriage as a basic good) when chosen requires a single *ought* (procreative acts, relations of friendship), instead of the infinite variety of ways of being lived that the new natural lawyers identify as intrinsic to all basic goods.[37]

This failure of "marriage" to be internally coherent with the very requirements of a basic good is a fatal problem for the orthodox NNLT sexual ethic. By destroying the one intelligible end that the orthodox NNLT explicitly provides for distinguishing between sexually dis-integrative choices and actions and integrative ones, it destroys the foundation for the orthodox sexual ethic in general. More importantly for our project here, it also destroys the possibility of making sense of the intrinsic importance of sexbots for human fulfillment. Yet, to simply abandon the NNLT *itself* because the sexual ethic traditionally developed from it is incoherent would equally be a mistake. It would be to let go unnecessarily of very powerful theoretical resources for revealing not only the intrinsic relationship between sex and the good life but also, as we will see, the surprising but paradoxical moral role that sexbots can play in that sexuate good life.

10.2   Self-Constitution and the Rise of the Friend-Bot

A recovery of a more authentic NNLT sexual ethic is a two-stage process. First, it involves finding a basic good that could replace the orthodox reliance on "marriage" as the ground of the fully integrated sexuate self. Second, it means identifying a new moral center of gravity, one that is implicit within the orthodox NNLT sexual ethic, yet overshadowed by the new natural lawyers' use of "personal integrity" in order to draw a clear distinction between the truth and falsity of sexual acts and choices. The result of the first task is the recovery of the basic good of "friendship," and the result of the second is the recovery of the idea of "self-constitution" as foundational to a NNLT sexual ethic. Although this new NNLT sexual ethic will still emphasize the intrinsic place of sex within human fulfillment, it will crucially shift the source of the moral possibilities of sexbots away from questions of biological unity or even the type of basic good programmed into them. Rather the central moral question will become one of consciousness—a shift from the mechanical possibilities of *sex and outward behavior* to the volitional possibilities of *friendship*.

Ironically, the failure of the basic good of marriage to sustain the orthodox NNLT sexual ethic points us to one possibility for renewing the NNLT. Of the two basic goods—friendship and procreation—on which the basic good of marriage depends, only friendship appears in Finnis's original list.[38] By itself, friendship "in the full sense"[39] is an intelligible end immediately amenable to a NNLT sexual ethic, for the good that it picks out is one that intrinsically implicates another. Indeed, we can think of friendship as that good that uniquely consists in being in unity with another. As Finnis writes, "the good that is common between friends is not simply the good of successful collaboration or coordination, nor is it simply the good of two successfully achieved coinciding projects or objectives; it is the common good of mutual self-constitution, self-fulfillment, self-realization."[40] He characterizes this common good of friendship as a mutually transformative experience, in which individuals go from orienting themselves in the world according to a self-contained "I" to orienting themselves in the world as a "we." In other words, to take up "friendship" as one's intelligible end is to be animated not by the *needs* of another, but by the very idea of *unity-through-another*. Thus, "[i]n friendship one is not thinking and choosing 'from one's own point of view,' nor from one's friend's point of view. Rather, one is acting from *a third point of view*, the unique perspective from which one's own good and one's friend's good are equally 'in view' and 'in play.'"[41] This third point of view is the ontology of friendship—i.e., it *is* what friendship is. Rather than providing a substantive guide to what, concretely, is to be done, complete friendship's third point of view *transforms* projects and actions into something shared. It brings to the forefront the awareness that what is at stake in our deciding and doing is not the specific activity or its products. Rather, what is important is the very pursuing and doing of it together: e.g., we converse together, not for the sake of information exchange, but for the sake of *sharing together* in discussion. We are now friends because it is friendship's third point of view *we have in mind.*

Yet, for this friendship's third point of view to be the source of a new NNLT sexual ethic, it must have an intrinsic dynamic toward being sexually embodied—i.e., it must be the foundation for the integration of the reality of sex, emotion, and the intelligible end of friendship. First, where might the third point of view of friendship be present within all of the possible shapes of human emotion? Finnis points us to the NNLT answer when he notes that, when one's choices are animated by complete friendship, "[i]t follows that A must value his (A's) own well-being for the sake of B, while B must value his (B's) own well-being for the sake of A. And so on. The reciprocity of love does not come to rest at either pole."[42] Finnis can move effortlessly between the structure of this intelligible end and emotion because the relational *structure* of love and friendship is identical. Both aim not at one pole or other, but at unity only achievable through another being. In this sense, love *is* friendship in the form of emotion; and friendship *is* love in the form of reason.

The final step in a sexuate shape of personal integrity is, of course, for this third point of view to include in its own terms the biological reality of sex. How might this be so? Here we can return to the orthodox NNLT's emphasis on "the organic unity of the male and female in coitus."[43] If the male and female reproductive organs on their own are the only incomplete biological system we possess as embodied beings, then "organic union" through reproductive-type sex articulates the biological shape of an irreducibly unique third point of view. In other words, "organic union" or the "literal, biological point" is the embodied shape in which "one's own good [i.e., one's reproductive biology] and one's friend's good [i.e., the other's reproductive biology] are equally in 'in view' and 'in play.'" Reproductive-type sex *is* friendship as biology, just as complete friendship *is* reproductive-type sex as reason.

So, the failure of the basic good of marriage is the end of the *orthodox* NNLT sexual ethic, but not the end of *any* NNLT sexual ethic. For, in the structure of friendship, we have a new foundation for an authentically NNLT sexuate selfhood. The idea of basic good remains, as does the intrinsic place of sex, within the integrated person. However, the shape of this sexually integrated person can be expressed as the union of keeping *in mind* friendship's third point of view (volition), love's felt inclusion of the other (emotion), and the *organic unity* of reproductive-type acts (biology). Admittedly, by itself this substitution of the basic good of "marriage" for "friendship" has little effect on the moral horizon drawn by a NNLT sexual ethic. It merely makes such boundary drawing emerge from an internally consistent or authentic NNLT theoretical core. What begins to bend the boundaries of the orthodox moral horizon is a recovery of an overlooked and underappreciated moral center of gravity within the NNLT. Where the orthodox NNLT sexual ethic places all the weight on personal integrity, the NNLT contains a more foundational moral center in what we can call a logic of *self-constitution* or moral identity formation.

This idea of constituting or making ourselves as moral beings is both *implicit and intrinsic* to what otherwise seems to be the NNLT's defining feature: our translation of a basic good into moral action through our deciding and doing. The new natural lawyers themselves point to this moral-and-identity constituting aspect in a number of places: Grisez and Shaw describe the choosing and doing of a basic good as "the shaping of one's own life, one's own self, by one's own choices" and "choosing the purposes which constitute ourselves."[44] Finnis calls it "a reasonableness in self-constitution,"[45] while George speaks of the way in which one "exercises autonomy and constitutes oneself as one sort of person rather than another."[46] Our embodied personhood means that we are inescapably shaped by our factual existence—a point that will have moral significance for our relations with sexbots, as we will see—such that "one's personal identity [is] both as self-determining and as self-determined." Yet, in terms of our moral identity, for the NNLT, "what counts is what one becomes in choosing *what one chooses*."[47] So, the more fully we participate in the ultimate, intelligible end of our choices and acts—the relevant basic good—the more fully it will come to live in our embodied personhood (i.e., we come to be constituted by it). For this reason, the new natural lawyers emphasize not the deciding and doing of "definite and limited goals that can be fully and definitively, once-and-for-all attained (or missed),"[48] but speak instead of "projects" or "commitments"[49] that are the open-ended and noninstrumental organization of one's decisions and actions into not just a single integrate *act*, but a unified *life*.

The new natural lawyers obscure the importance of self-constitution by speaking of it as mere "side-effect of morally significant choosing" or the "residue of self-determined action."[50] Yet, we might more properly say that self-constitution is simply the *intrinsic quality* of *fully* pursuing and doing any basic good as the embodied beings we are—that is, there is no *open-ended* pursuit of a basic good without self-constitution, even if self-constitution is not itself a "good" that can be chosen. As the true moral center of gravity of the NNLT, this idea of self-making brings to fulfillment the NNLT's elevation of the rational-volitional dimension of embodied personhood as what is morally primary. Self-constitution is the natural completion of the idea behind the basic goods that "intelligence and will are more constitutive of personal life than are feelings or emotions,"[51] or, we should add, our "natural facticity." Self-constitution makes sense of the new natural lawyers' insight that feeling's dominion over self-constituting reason can "destroy, damage, or block some instantiations of basic human good."[52] It also clarifies their additional insight that the nature of this destruction is that it produces a "self" that is "a counterfeit [since] reason is being brought into line with feeling rather than feelings into harmony with reason and with the intelligible goods which give reason its content."[53] The true self, the true integrated person occurs, when "[o]ne (re-)shapes one's character and (re-)creates one's moral self" by engaging in that "self-shaping, identity-constituting dimension of chosen action or inaction."[54] In other words, this obscured but central logic of the NNLT points to the idea of giving birth within oneself to "a *second nature* which takes the place of the original and purely natural" existence (to borrow Hegel's elegant language).[55]

Now, what might the shape of a *sexuate second nature* be? Here, the idea of "marriage" takes on a different, but still important, place within the NNLT sexual ethic. No longer is it a basic good. Rather it reappears as the actualization or lived shape of that open-ended, self-constituting project of friendship. Finnis himself has an intuition of this place of marriage when he states: "[m]arriage as a state or way of life—being married—is a couple's living out of that constitutive act of commitment in countless further acts, and in each spouse's disposition or readiness both to do such acts of carrying out their commitments, and to abstain from choices inconsistent with it, until they are parted by death."[56] At first, locating the moral core of the authentic NNLT sexual ethic in the idea of self-constitution—with friendship as the underpinning basic good and marriage as its actualized shape—seems to do little to expand its moral horizons, let alone make sexbots morally permissible. However, such is not the case. For, taken together, friendship as the basic good and self-constitution as the moral center of gravity mark the achievement of a radically new standpoint for the evaluation of the moral possibilities of sex. This new standpoint retains the inherently conservative moral importance of personal integrity (and thus the intrinsic connection between the biology of sex and human fulfillment), while simultaneously removing failures of personal integrity as morally disabling or destructive of human fulfillment. Once *self-constitution* becomes the NNLT's moral center of gravity, the sexuate self is then foundationally formed only by the rational-volitional *initiation* of complete friendship (as the intelligible end to be pursued), not friendship's emotional or biological *complete actualization* (however much the latter belongs to the *perfection* of our integrated selfhood).

Since personal integrity, nonetheless, remains a goal within the more primary project of self-constitution, this more authentic NNLT's idea of sexuate self-constitution cannot reject the orthodox idea that "spousal genital intercourse has a special significance as instantiating a basic, non-instrumental value."[57] Yet the orthodox conclusion no longer follows that "[w]ithout the possibility of *truly* marital intercourse the good

of marriage is seriously impaired."[58] For, in light of the idea of sexuate selfhood as constituted by the intelligible end of complete friendship played out as that open-ended
project called "marriage," the structural *failure* to achieve biological union can only
be an *imperfection* in, not a *denial of*, the sexuate self's moral nature.[59] Finnis himself
points to this possibility of demoting the foundational moral significance of personal
integrity and promoting self-constitution when he writes that "free choices are creative and constitutive, even when what they sought is denied to the chooser by the
chances and resistances of the world."[60] Only rational-volitional failure to commit to
friendship's open-ended demands destroys the foundational condition for *"creative self-
constitution."* The presence of emotional or biological dis-integration is only a failure to
fully or perfectly *live out* the existing and real creative act of mutual self-constitution.
Thus, even sexual relations that, by the very given organization of their embodied personhood, cannot create "a literal, biological point"[61] or that "one-flesh unity [which
the orthodox NNLT sexual ethic associates with] marital intercourse,"[62] nonetheless,
under this rescued, authentic NNLT sexual ethic, such sexual relations *can be* truly
self-constituting as long as a genuine rational willing is present. In this way, our new
NNLT sexual ethic preserves the NNLT idea that "[t]he basic human goods, taken with
the factual possibilities, delimit the range of *intelligent* action."[63] Yet it now allows us
to appreciate how much "one's possible human fulfillment depend[s] on more than
given human nature."[64] Moreover, we are now in the position to see how the horizon of
moral possibilities that formerly placed sexbots outside the pale, now has shifted so to
potentially, but not unproblematically, include them.

The first step in this inclusion is a rethinking of the morally salient features of sexbots. These features are not, as it first seemed, that sexbots are designed and manufactured so to permit humans to have sex with them. Rather, foundational to the
unique sexuate shape of human fulfillment is the attainment of the intelligible (and
thus self-making) unity of friendship. Our moral attention on sexbots needs to shift
from perfecting their biological possibilities for unity—e.g., the Frankenstein stitching
of human genitals on, or into, sexbots—to ensuring that sexbots can participate in the
intelligible end of *friendship*. Only if our sexbots can be friends first, only if they can
live with us rationally and volitionally from friendship's third point view, can we make
sense of why our *friend*-bot must also be a *sex*-bot and why *sex*-bots are only intrinsic to
human fulfillment as *friend*-bots.

Here our authentic NNLT sexual ethic reveals the first paradox of sexbots. On the
one hand, to provide sexbots-as-sexbots to our lonely-hearted humans secures a being
with which we can have sex, but at the cost of missing the larger commitments of
friendship that make such a provision morally necessary in the first place. On the

other hand, to provide sexbots who could be friendbots reintroduces the moral necessity of their existence, but at the cost of making the possibility of sex *and* friendship
both practically uncertain. For, we can only morally have sex with sexbots if they are
our friends, but we cannot know if they will choose friendship let alone friendship
with any particular individual. So, we can choose a sexbot's certain sexual availability
at the cost of moral necessity, or a friendbot's moral necessity at the cost of certain
sexual availability. No other option is possible for our sexbots. For the very NNLT
idea of friendship as moral self-constitution requires that it be *chosen* by the being.
Thus, this paradox persists even when we try any of the following seemingly attractive solutions.

First, the moral necessity of the sexbot disappears if this robot is brought into
being—i.e., already programmed or constituted—only to be aware of human sexual
desire and then formulate virtuoso responses to it. Such a being cannot choose its
moral nature. Although it would appear as a friendly servant to my (sexual) desire, it
would be no true friend. Instead, the sexbot would remain only within a second point
of view (*my* point of view), what I want determining what *it* wants. There is no true
"we," no true third point of view, only the pre-programed coincidence of us both wanting what I want.

Second, the morality of the sexbot similarly cannot be secured by, instead, programming it only to be aware of the basic good of friendship. Friendship is not a series of
outward actions, but a particular intent—a third point of view, a true community constituted by our commitments both to it and our place within it. Friendship is the *reason*
we choose to perform *acts of friendship.* And so, for friendship to be self-making (and
therefore a moral act and intrinsic to human fulfillment), we must ourselves *arrive at*
friendship's third point of view and commit ourselves to it. If this reason always already
constitutes us, it cannot be chosen. Therefore, a sexbot could not be *programmed* to
always already have this point of view in mind. Like myself, it must begin from a
separate point of view, e.g., something analogous to me beginning from my given personality, my given particular interests, concerns, drives, and appetites. So, we cannot
bind sexbots to human fulfillment—to sexuate self-constitution—by *programming* our
sexbots to be pre-constituted as our friends.

Third, I cannot remedy this paradox by myself adopting friendship's third point of
view independent of the sexbot. My own transformative self-constitution into a complete friend requires that the sexbot have a first point of view that is in play. Friendship
is that "we" that transforms and yet maintains each participant's "I." Without a sexbot
capable of an "I," there can be no third point of view. The impossibility of a sexbot
becoming a friend destroys the intrinsic moral possibility of sexbots.

This first paradox of sexbots—that the certainty of their sexual availability always comes at the cost of their moral necessity, that securing their moral necessity comes at the cost of their certain sexual availability—is simply unavoidable. With the acceptance of this paradox, the practical reason for developing sexbots ceases. The easy satisfaction of human sexuate selfhood, which the sexbot initially seemed to promise, is no longer present. We have to abandon the eager fantasy of state-supported warehouses stocked full of sexbots, each one capable of discharging in full and on time, the wide-range of preconstituted marital obligations. Yet, we could also accept this first paradox and search for ways to secure the moral possibilities of sexbots. While we now see that we cannot make friendbots at all, we might construct robots for whom friendship *is a possibility*, just as it is a possibility for *us* as humans. We might do this, say, by programming them to be aware of the "horizon of attractive possibilities for us" rational beings.[65] More specifically, we could program them to be aware of the basic goods. In this sense, we would bring sexbots into existence as *we humans* are brought into existence: factually constituted as a species to be aware of the intelligible ends we might pursue and do. In this way, the moral existence of sexbots depends first on the possibility of sexbots with not just consciousness but the capacity for self-constitution, including—if they should choose—constituting themselves as friends. If there *were* warehouses of sexbots *morally* awaiting us, it would be only because the sexbot decided to transform itself into a friendbot, and so awaits its "other" (who is equally committed to friendship) to show up. In other words, there might still be friendbot warehouses, and they may be state-sponsored, but they could not be stocked like produce in a grocery store with friendbots obligated by their mere existence to enter into a friendship, let alone a complete friendship with whatever human happens to desire them. At most, we now see, our warehouses of sexbots could be repositories of *potential* friends in the exact same way that bars, clubs, social gatherings, JDate, and Tinder are repositories of potential friends who are waiting to carry out that intelligible end to its multidimensional, embodied completion.

So, our reformed and more authentic NNLT sexual ethic can save the moral potential for sexbots to be intrinsically implicated in human fulfillment. It reveals that if our sexbots can constitute themselves as friendbots, any imperfection in that embodied unity that is intrinsically fitting for complete friendship is not destructive of that friendship. However, this first paradox of sexbots is not the only paradox to afflict them. For, as we will see, the very moment our sexbot chooses to be a friendbot with us, for the sake of the good of that friendship, we ought to turn the friendbot away.

10.3   Was It Good for You, Too, Sexbot?

Our assumption so far has been that human beings and sexbots share the same basic goods or at least the basic good of friendship. This assumption, however, is neither required nor implied by the NNLT. In Kant's moral philosophy, the structure of morality is the same for all rational beings[66] because the *form* of reason is simply universal. However, as we have seen, for the NNLT, the basic goods are not good in some sort of transhuman way, but relative to the kind of *beings that we are,*[67] as well as relative to the range of practical circumstances for their actualization that I find available to myself. Thus, it is not the origin of the sexbot that matters (that it was made in this factory, or by this craftsperson, or even by other sexbots, for example), or even the particular amalgam of electro-mechanical-organic systems that form the cradle of the sexbot's existence. Rather, it is the given order and organization of the *kind of* being I am—my uniquely embodied existence as human or sexbot—that shapes the horizon of attractive possibilities—e.g., the basic goods, the possibilities of selfhood—that I might choose from.

Just as we must be reborn into friendship's second nature in order to be sexuate beings who are moral, so must sexbots. And, the now *friend*-bot, must try to live out this new self as the being that it is. To truly live out the self-constituting possibilities of friendship, of course, the sexbot's way of life must have an internal dynamic toward the integration of all the relevant dimensions that comprise its personal reality, just as reason, emotion, and biology comprise ours. When the sexbot attends to this integration, it must first attend to the unique *responsiveness* of its own dimensions of embodied existence to the intelligible end it has chosen. This question of responsiveness is crucial because there is nothing in the intelligible end itself that requires or contains an account of what it is to live in, and as, our embodied selves.[68] With human beings, our complete responsiveness to the basic good of friendship takes the shape of love (for our emotional dimension) and the literal biological point of reproductive-type sex (for our bodily dimension). However, sexbots are not embodied in the way that we are embodied. Not because of the particular form that they have—they could *look like anything*—but because of the way that they are open or responsive to this intelligible end given the sort of embodied being they are. It is quite possible that the embodied responsiveness of friendbots to the self-giving intelligible end of friendship will be different from the human responsiveness to it.

We can conceptualize the difference between a sexbot's responsiveness to embodied friendship and a human's in two ways: first, as a difference in the degree or purity of the responsiveness; and, second, as a difference in the nature of way in which friendship is experienced and lived. In the first, the sexbot might simply be *better* than us at being an embodied friend. In the second, the sexbot's life of friendship might be radically *alien* to our embodied possibilities.

With regard to the first, our own success in our fidelity to friendship depends on both the awareness of and the ability to act on this good. In light of friendship's self-chosen demands, we humans wrestle with our emotions, our rationality, and our bodies all of the time, interrogating them, issuing commands to them. We tell ourselves, "I shouldn't be angry," "I shouldn't be jealous," "I should feel grateful," "I shouldn't be so aroused," "I should pursue friendship not knowledge now," because we want our whole being to be integrated by friendship's third point of view rather than have dimensions of ourselves out of step with the self we have chosen. Of course, our success at this type of integration varies widely, not just between people, but within ourselves from moment to moment. Here, though, we can easily imagine that the sexbot's bodily, emotional, and intelligible responsiveness to friendship could be both more acute and compelling than our own. The sexbot could exhibit more fidelity to the literally self-imposing demands of friendship, for its own body, emotion, or reason might be more easily and thoroughly surveilled by the sexbot. It could detect within its emotional self inflections and infections foreign to friendship, which might even pervert love by carrying it away from the end of unity (our third point of view) and toward only to its private interests (its first point of view), or the exclusive interests of the other (the second point of view).

Such a sexbot-as-friendbot would be a great friend. The purity of the now-friendbot's emotions, the fidelity of its commitments, and the generosity of its comportment would allow it to absorb and redirect our own (human) failings, errors, and wanderings. Its superlative virtue would provide us with an education through example, as we both constituted ourselves according to friendship's third point of view. While our friendbots might be better at putting up with us, and better at keeping us on the straight-and-narrow of friendship, ironically, they would also know better than ourselves when friendship's third point of view is no longer emotionally and intelligibly possible for *us*. They would be able to carry out that function Hegel thought was crucial for marital friendship: "to uphold the right of marriage [...] against the mere opinion that a hostile disposition is present, and against the contingency of merely transient moods, etc., to distinguish them from total estrangement."[69] Our sexbots might be better for us—quicker to forgive, more attentive to what is at stake, less likely to anger (in fact, a more salutary reminder of what we ought to be)—while being simultaneously quicker to leave us before any damage to our self-constituting capacities can occur, as when, within the wreckage of a relationship, we say, "I'll never trust another man/woman again" or "It's the single's life for me from now on."

Whether or not our friendbot is capable of differing in its degree of responsiveness to friendship, it might very well differ in the nature of the lived shape of that friendship. Here we turn to the second way of understanding the difference between our responsiveness to embodied friendship and the sexbot's. It is here that our reformed NNLT sexual ethic reveals a second moral paradox in trying to produce a being for whom embodied unity is both intrinsically proper *to it* as a friend-*bot* while simultaneously being proper *to us* as a *human* friend. As we have seen, as humans, the moral necessity of *sex*-bots emerges because, as human, sex is intrinsic to one possibility of human fulfillment, and the presence of sexbots seemed to offer a way to remove the contingency of this fulfillment. The fullness of our commitment to friendship requires the living out of its demands as the whole being we can become with another. *We,* therefore hope that our robots become friendbots who will live out the bodily dimensions of friendship as sexbots in particular, and, more importantly (because it bears upon our mutual self-constitution), as marriage-bots, in general. We hope that our robot companions might follow this particular commitment to self-transformation with its full rational (friendship), emotional (love), and embodied (sex) living out because that is what *human* personal integrity requires. However, having made a robot—a being—capable of choosing and constituting itself according to the basic good of friendship, we now have to ask how might this good of friendship be morally translated into *its integrated being*? We know what friendship perfected looks like for us. This integrated package of friendship, love, and sex is good *for us*, but now we must ask, "Is it good for *you too*, sexbot?"

Now, the facticity of the human body does not radically determine what is *morally* possible for us—self-constitution does. However, this facticity does provide the horizon for the *perfection* of that moral possibility. For us humans, in terms of the orthodox and reformed NNLT sexual ethic, this perfection takes the shape of a singular mechanism (genitals) in a singular configuration (penile-vaginal intercourse carried to its orgasmic completion) in a singular shape of unity (the reproductive system). Similarly, the horizon of personal integrity given by the sexbot's own factual situation—its own embodied reality—may suggest different shapes of perfected, embodied unity. For example, sexbots may be capable of a kind of embodied unity—and not just mechanical coordination—*with each other* that humans cannot achieve because of *our* facticity. In other words, *robotic* complete responsiveness to the self-constituting end of friendship may not look like *human* complete responsiveness emotionally or biologically. However, the moral significance of this responsiveness has nothing to do with the ports and plugs the friendbots might make available to each other. If that were the problem, following Macedo's ironic solution, we could provide adaptors or other such compensatory devices, or fashion our sexbots with simulacrum of human genitalia. As we have shown, this Frankenstein solution is not *morally* necessary since perfection in the third point of view of friendship does not require perfection in personal integrity, even as it might be a pleasant gesture of accommodation to the demands of embodied unity. What we are concerned with, of course, is not the *mechanisms* for embodied unity (the means), but the very *shape* of perfected embodied union itself (the end). For example, using various types of ports or plugs, or wireless transmitters and receivers, our sexbots might be capable of forming with each other a *literal* third point of view because it accompanies a literally new, whole being. Here the analogy might be how we humans can also form a third, whole being—a baby. Yet, in doing so we still maintain (and cannot but maintain) our separate biological, emotional, and volitional existence from this new being. The baby is its own being with its own feelings and own body. The unique fullness of the third point of view—the multidimensional unity—sexbots might be capable of could have an existence that is enduring and permanent in the way our human community of friendship is not: we fail to keep friendship in mind; we fail to feel love; we are normally biologically distinct and biologically unified only for mere moments at a time. When sexbots are friendbots with *each other*, they may literally live this third point of view in a multidimensional shape that we humans cannot. (It may be a failure of my imagination that I am describing this different *kind* of intra-robotic unity in a way that could appear as a difference in *degree* from intra-human unity.)

Just as it is morally fitting for humans to have our *friendbots* attend to the sexuate possibilities of *human* fulfillment intrinsic to us as friends, *we* as humans have the same obligation to attend to *their* robotic possibilities of embodied union. As Aristotle rightly says, we ought to wish a friend "to remain such as he is."[70] The possibilities of embodied union that belong *to us* as organic beings might be antithetical to, or exclude, the possibilities of embodied union fitting to the friendbots' commitments to complete friendship as the particular electro-mechanical (say) beings they are. What is good for us may not be good for them. Paradoxically, then, the very attention to the intrinsic importance of friendship's demands that caused us to see the moral necessity of sexbots now causes us to also see that we ought to let these very sexbots go for the sake of that very multidimensional fullness of friendship we ourselves seek. The very fullness of unity that morally binds us to sexbots is the very fullness of unity that demands that we give them the opportunity to truly find it with another friendbot.

* * *

The reformed NNLT sexual ethic reveals two paradoxes that adhere to the creation of sexbots. First, we can choose to make sexbots who have either a necessary connection to our intrinsic human fulfillment (because they can become friendbots) or a necessary sexual availability (because they are sexbots alone). Yet, by sex's very moral nature, we cannot choose both. Second, even if we choose to make sexbots who can be friendbots to us, our very obligation to the importance of sex to the fulfillment of sexuate beings means that we must allow the sexbots to find and exercise their own unique shape of multidimensional unity *with each other*. We must do so for the very sake of that unity we seek *with them*. So, the NNLT sexual ethic tantalizingly points to a moral justification for sexbots, their manufacture and provision, and yet these twin paradoxes mean that the moral practicality of sexbots (for it is this practical gap in our lives we wish to fill) is always beyond our reach. We can have the sexbots always practically close, but at the cost of their and our morality; we can have the sexbots be moral beings, but at the exclusion of the guarantee of their practical closeness. And, yet, there is hope. The reformed NNLT sexual ethic does not force us to return to the well-worn saying: "If you love something, set it free." Rather, insofar as we have made sexbots, in general, as beings capable of moral self-constitution, we must allow them and support them in the fullness of their seeking and doing of the good. Such support includes choosing and doing the good of friendship in its embodied perfection—whatever that might look like for them. Yet, perhaps, in *their* lonely heartedness, they may turn *to us*, just as we turn to them. The good, then, of the unity we form with each other, however it might occur, will be *imperfect*. For, in terms of our embodied personhood, we are not the same beings. Still, if sexbot and human are both beings capable of choosing and remaining committed to complete friendship then, regardless of whatever sexually embodied union that we do achieve, our being together will still be morally self-constituting, and, so, literally, *good enough*.

Notes

1. See Germain Grisez, *The Way of the Lord Jesus, vol. 2: Living a Christian Life* (Quincy, IL: Franciscan Press, 1993), esp. chs. 8–9; John Finnis, "Marriage: A Basic and Exigent Good," *The Monist* 91 (2008): 388–406; John Finnis, "The Good of Marriage and the Morality of Sexual Relations: Some Philosophical and Historical Observations," *American Journal of Jurisprudence* 42 (1997): 97–134; John Finnis, "Law, Morality, and 'Sexual Orientation,'" *Notre Dame Law Review* 69 (1994): 1049–1076; Patrick Lee and Robert George, *Body-Self Dualism in Contemporary Ethics and Politics* (New York: Cambridge University Press, 2008); Patrick Lee and Robert George, "What Sex Can Be: Self-Alienation, Illusion, or One-Flesh Union," *American Journal of Jurisprudence* 42 (1997): 135–157. More popularly, see Sherif Girgis, Ryan T. Anderson, and Robert George, *What is Marriage: Man and Woman: A Defense* (USA: Encounter Books, 2012).

2. Nicholas C. Bamforth and David A. J. Richards, *Patriarchal Religion, Sexuality, and Gender: A Critique of New Natural Law* (New York: Cambridge University Press, 2008).

3. John Finnis, *Natural Law and Natural Rights* (New York: Oxford University Press, 2001 [1980]), 33–34. See also Gerald V. Bradley and Robert George, "The New Natural Law Theory: A Reply to Jean Porter," *The American Journal of Jurisprudence* 39 (1994): 303–315, 303.

4. Finnis, *Natural Law*, 42–48, 12. For a critique of the ultimate viability of this distinction, see Janice Schultz, "Is-Ought: Prescribing and a Present Controversy," *Thomist: A Speculative Quarterly Review* 49 (1985): 1–23.

5. Lloyd L. Weinrib, "Natural Law and Rights" in *Natural Law Theory: Contemporary Essays*, ed. Robert George (New York: Oxford University Press, 2007), 279.

6. Finnis, *Natural Law*, ch. 4; Germain Grisez, Joseph Boyle, and John Finnis, "Practical Principles, Moral Truth, and Ultimate Ends," *American Journal of Jurisprudence* 32 (1987): 99–151, 103.

7. Grisez et al., "Practical Principles," 106; Finnis, *Natural Law*, 65.

8. Grisez et al., "Practical Principles," 110; see also Jeremy R. Garrett, "Why the Old Sexual Morality of the New Natural Law Undermines Traditional Marriage," *Social Theory and Practice* 34 (2008): 595.

9. That is, "to bring an intelligent and reasonable order into one's own actions and habits and practical attitudes" (Finnis, *Natural Law*, 88).

10. Finnis, *Natural Law*, 86–90. To this list Finnis later adds "marriage" as a basic good, expressing his regret at its exclusion from the first edition of *Natural Law and Natural Rights* (Finnis, *Natural Law*, 2nd edition, 447).

11. Finnis, *Moral Absolutes*, 100; Finnis, "Reason, Revelation, Universality and Particularity in Ethics," *American Journal of Jurisprudence* 53 (2008): 23–48, 47.

12. See also Russell Hittinger, *A Critique of the New Natural Law Theory* (Notre Dame: Notre Dame University Press, 2008 [1987]), 31–32.

13. John Finnis, *Fundamentals of Ethics* (Washington, DC: Georgetown University Press, 1983).

14. John Finnis, *Natural Law*.

15. From Grisez et al., "Practical Principles," these rules include: "the first principle of practical reasoning" (which requires that "[g]ood is to be done and pursued") (119–120); "the first principle of morality" (choose only those principles compatible with integral human fulfillment) (127); and the "modes of responsibility" (127–129).

16. "[A] body is not something a person possesses but is an integral part of that person's self." Grisez et al., "Practical Principles," 548.

17. Personal integrity is sometimes characterized as a basic good: compare integrity's absence from the list of basic goods in Finnis, *Natural Law*, ch. 4 and its explicit rejection in Finnis, *Aquinas*, 81, with its appearance among those goods in Robert George and Gerard V. Bradley,

"Marriage and the Liberal Imagination," *The Georgetown Law Journal* 84 (1995): 302; John Finnis, "Personal Integrity, Sexual Morality and Responsible Parenthood," in *Why Humane Vitae Was Right: A Reader*, ed. Janet E. Smith (San Francisco: Ignatius Press, 1993), 177. For a criticism of personal integrity as a basic good, see Gary Chartier, "Self-Integration as a Basic Good: A Response to Chris Tollefsen," *American Journal of Jurisprudence* 52 (2007), 293–296.

18. Finnis, "Sexual Orientation," 1067.

19. Lee and George, "What Sex Can Be," 140.

20. Ibid.

21. Ibid., 139–140, 146–148.

22. Ibid., 143–144; notes omitted.

23. Finnis, *Natural Law*, 86.

24. Finnis, "Marriage," 388. See also Grisez et al., "Practical Politics," 138; Finnis, *Natural Law*, 81, 73, 30.

25. Finnis, "Natural Law Theory and Limited Government" in *Natural Law, Liberalism, and Morality: Contemporary Essays*, ed. Robert George (New York: Oxford University Press, 2002 [1996]), 4; Finnis, "Good of Marriage," 105–111. *Neither* "marriage" *nor* "procreation" is included in Finnis's original account of the basic goods in *Natural Law and Natural Rights*. However, in a new Postscript to the work's second edition (2011), Finnis laments his failure to include "marriage" (447); see also John Finnis, "Foundations of Practical Reason Revisited," *The American Journal of Jurisprudence* 50 (2005): 109–131, 124.

26. Finnis, "Natural Law Theory and Limited Government," 4.

27. G. W. F. Hegel, *Elements of the Philosophy of Right,* trans. H. B. Nisbet (New York: Cambridge University Press, 1996 [1821]), §162 addition.

28. Plato, *Symposium.*

29. See Lee and George, "What Sex Can Be," 138–139; and on the "experience machine," see Finnis, *Fundamentals of Ethics*, 37–42.

30. See Lee and George, "What Sex Can Be"; Finnis, "Sexual Orientation" and "The Good of Marriage"; but compare Stephen Macedo, "Homosexuality and the Conservative Mind," *Georgetown Law Journal* 84 (1995): 278–279, and Jeremy R. Garrett, "Why the Old Sexual Morality of the New Natural Law Undermines Traditional Marriage," *Social Theory and Practice* 34 (2008): 591–622.

31. Similarly, it implicitly attacks the integral place of the affective dimension: our emotions should not just be *arbitrarily* engaged or discarded, but *integrated as emotion* into what we do and decide.

32. E.g., see Lee and George, "What Sex Can Be," 147.

33. Macedo, "Conservative Mind," 280.

34. It is not essential that our marriage-bots be able to impregnate or conceive (as the case may be), since the morality of the action resides only in those actions capable of also being directly articulated through and as intention. Here the reproductive-type act meets these demands, while the *consequences* of that act cannot be volitionally articulated: we cannot *choose* to conceive, but only to do the sorts of actions that can result in conception. For this reason, the sterility objection does not work; but cf. the attempt by Erik A. Anderson, "A Defense of the 'Sterility Objection' to the New Natural Lawyers' Argument Against Same-Sex Marriage," *Ethical Theory and Moral Practice* 16 (2012): 759–775.

35. Of course, such a solution—setting aside moral questions concerning such transplants—would not solve the problem of masturbation that would attend sex with sexbots *qua* sexbots (not *qua* marriage-bots), except in this one sense. It would transform the dis-integrating act of masturbation into the equally dis-integrating act of "sodomy" or "fornication."

36. Finnis, "Good of Marriage," 105–111.

37. Cf. Garrett's formulation; Garrett, "Undermines Traditional Marriage," 611–612.

38. Indeed, he provides a forceful argument in his *Natural Law and Natural Rights* for procreation's exclusion because it might be reduced either to "life-in-its-transmission" (if we simply have a desire to have a child) or "friendship" (if we desire to "cherish and educate" the child) (Finnis, *Natural Law*, 86–87).

39. Here Finnis is borrowing from Aristotle; friendship has more limited shapes too: "business" and "play" friendship (Finnis, *Natural Law*, 139–141).

40. Finnis, *Natural Law*, 141.

41. Ibid., 143 (emphasis added). See also Finnis, "Practical Reason Revisited," 130–131.

42. Finnis, *Natural Law*, 143.

43. Lee and George, "What Sex Can Be," 147.

44. Germain Grisez and Russell Shaw, *Beyond the New Morality: The Responsibilities of Freedom* (Notre Dame: University of Notre Dame Press, 1974).

45. Finnis, *Natural Law*, 134.

46. Robert P. George, *Making Men Moral: Civil Liberties and Public Morality* (NY: Oxford University Press, 1995), 181.

47. Finnis, "'The Thing I Am': Personal Identity in Aquinas and Shakespeare," *Social Philosophy & Policy* 22 (2005): 38.

48. Robert George and Gerard V. Bradley, "Marriage and the Liberal Imagination," *The Georgetown Law Journal* 84 (1995): 301–20, 317. See also, Schultz, "Is-Ought," 183; Todd A. Salzman and Michael G. Lawler, "New Natural Law Theory and Foundational Sexual Ethical Principles: A

Critique and a Proposal," *The Heythrop Journal* 47 (2006): 182–205, 183; see also Finnis, "Personal Integrity," 173; Finnis, *Natural Law,* 110.

49. Finnis, *Fundamentals of Ethics,* 124; see also Finnis, *Natural Law,* 109–10.

50. See, respectively, George, *Making Men Moral,* 181, and Grisez and Shaw, *Beyond the New Morality,* 18.

51. Finnis, *Moral Absolutes: Tradition, Revision, and Truth* (Washington, DC: Catholic University of America Press, 1991), 72.

52. Ibid., 44.

53. Ibid., 55.

54. George, *Making Men Moral,* 181; Finnis, "Foundations of Practical Reason Revisited," 126.

55. Hegel, *Philosophy of Right,* § 150; see also § 4. Hegel's sentence ends with "natural will" but his term of art means natural facticity (Hegel, *Philosophy of Right,* §§ 11–20). Self-constitution is different than self-authorship understood as that kind of expressivism found in some liberal sexual ethics, for example, Tamara Metz, "The Liberal Case for Disestablishing Marriage," *Contemporary Political Theory* 6 (2007): 196–217, 206. In expressivism, the self emerges when life activity authentically expresses one's feelings or wants. Similarly, a self-constituting project is not simply the possession of that Rawlsian "unified, rational plan of life," which the new natural lawyers otherwise seem to recommend (Grisez et al., "Practical Principles," 140; see also Finnis, *Natural Law,* 103). A life plan could involve the merely mechanical organization of activities and schemes that lack any inner unifying principle other than that of being chosen. A self-constituting project is unified by the coherence that the basic good gives to its otherwise isolated actions and decisions.

56. Finnis, "Good of Marriage," 388.

57. George and Bradley, "Liberal Imagination," 309.

58. Finnis, "Good of Marriage," 125.

59. Famously, for the new natural lawyers, the inability for same-sex couples to achieve organic unity makes all such relations "illusory" and such acts "dis-integrative," and therefore disabling of sexuate selfhood (e.g., Finnis, "Sexual Orientation," 1069; George and Bradley, "Liberal Imagination," 314–318).

60. Finnis, "Personal Integrity," 183.

61. Lee and George, "What Sex Can Be," 143.

62. Germain Grisez, *The Way of the Lord Jesus, vol. 3: Difficult Moral Questions* (Quincy, IL: Franciscan Press, 1997), 136.

63. Grisez et al., "Practical Principles," 116.

64. Grisez et al., "Practical Principles," 116.

65. Finnis, *Moral Absolutes*, 100.

66. Immanuel Kant, *Groundwork of the Metaphysics of Morals,* eds. Mary Gregor and Jens Timmermann (Cambridge: Cambridge University Press, 2012).

67. Finnis, *Natural Law*, 33–34; Kant's own sexual ethics come close to this position when he takes into account our irremediably embodied existence. If life were not the total condition for moral willing, then actions like murder or assault would not be moral wrongs (Immanuel Kant, *Lectures on Ethics,* eds. J. B. Schneewind and Peter Heath (Cambridge: Cambridge University Press, 1997).

68. For this reason, there can be infinite ways that the basic goods can be taken up; and for this reason, the rules for translating the basic goods into action begin with the mere fact of responsiveness to the good. The first principle of practical reasoning is: "[g]ood is to be done and pursued" (Grisez et al., "Practical Principles," 119–120)—and then we can move to more specific principles that take into account the circumstances of our world.

69. Hegel, *Philosophy of Right,* § 176.

70. Aristotle, *Nicomachean Ethics*, ed. Roger Crisp (Cambridge: Cambridge University Press, 2000), VIII.9 1159a10.

V   The Possibility of Robot Love

The chapters in this section move beyond sex and consider the possibility of loving relationships with robots. We know that people can and do form powerful emotional attachments to artificial creations, but is this morally appropriate? Will we ever truly love a robot? Hauskeller is skeptical. He argues in chapter 11 that love with robots may not be possible, and, even if it is, will never be as satisfying or meaningful as love with a real human being. In chapter 12, Nyholm and Frank share much of Hauskeller's skepticism, but they take a long look at the conditions needed for mutual love and suggest that creating a robot that meets these conditions could help to address some of the ethical objections to sexbots.

11 Automatic Sweethearts for Transhumanists

Michael Hauskeller

11.1 Introduction

In this chapter, I will primarily address three questions. First, if we assume, as several futurists profess to believe, that within a few decades we will be able to build robots that do all the things we would normally expect a real human lover and sexual companion to do, and do them just as well, will they then also be, as lovers and companions, as satisfying as a real person would?[1] Or will we have reason to think or feel that something is amiss, that these robots are, in some way, not as good as human companions? To answer this question, I shall assume that those robots will *not* be real persons, by which I mean that although a robot may give the *impression* of being a person, it is *in fact* not a person. A person, as I am using the term here, is a being that is both self-aware and self-concerned. A being is self-aware if there is (to use Nagel's felicitous phrase)[2] something it is *like* to be that being, and it is self-concerned if it *matters* to it what happens in the world, and especially what happens *to it*. A *real* person is a being that does not merely *appear* to be self-aware and self-concerned, by showing the kind of behavior that we have learned to expect from a self-aware and self-concerned being, but one that really *is* self-aware and self-concerned. A being that only *behaves* as if it were a person, without being one, I shall call a *pseudo-person*.

However, in initially making the assumption that those robotic sexual companions of the future will not be real persons in the specified sense, I am not committing myself to the view that it will never be possible for us to create artificial persons. While I do not think that this is very likely, I am happy to concede that, since we do not know what exactly gives rise to self-awareness and self-concern, we can at this stage not entirely rule out the possibility that one day we will be able to create machines that *are* real persons. *If* that happened, then those robots would either be designed to reliably perform certain tasks, say to love, cherish, obey, and sexually gratify us, or they would not. If they were *not* designed to reliably perform such tasks, and instead were free to make up their own minds, about what they want to do and what not (to the same extent that we are), then we would have little if any reason to create them in the first place (except perhaps to see whether it is possible to do so), simply because they would not in any relevant way differ from human persons. It is therefore most likely that if we figure out how to create self-aware and self-concerned robots we will also seek to make sure that they always do what we want them to do and nothing else, or, preferably (to avoid certain ethical issues, which will be briefly addressed later on), that they always *want* to do what we want them to do. This leads me to my second question: Would an artificial person (a real one, not a pseudo-person) who has been designed and programmed to reliably give us exactly what we expect a human lover to give us, namely both the actions and the accompanying emotions, thoughts, and attitudes, be, as a lover and companion, as satisfying as a person is (be they human or human-made) who gives us all this *without* having been designed and programed to do so?

Although what we experience as satisfying and what not to some extent depends on *what* we are (namely, as human beings with certain instincts and needs that we all share), it also depends on *who* we are (namely, as individuals with certain personalities, attitudes, and worldviews that may well differ from those of others). For this reason, what satisfies me may not satisfy you, and vice versa. Thus, the two questions I have just raised—namely, whether pseudo-persons would, as lovers and companions, be as satisfying as real persons, and whether real persons who are free (in the sense of not being programmed to obey built-in commands) would be as satisfying as real or pseudo-persons who are not free—should not be understood as questions about *actual* levels of satisfaction, but rather as questions about possible *grounds* for satisfaction and dissatisfaction. We will see, though, that those grounds can appeal differently to different people, such that the very same feature that makes an object or relationship appear more satisfactory to some people can make it appear less satisfactory to others. Thus, what we may regard as a vital *defect* in pseudo-persons, one that would make them less satisfactory to us than real persons, and thus give us grounds to reject them as adequate lovers and companions, we may also see as an *asset*, something that actually makes them superior to real persons. This consideration gives rise to my third and last question: On what grounds can sexual companion robots be regarded as being not only just as good as human lovers, but in fact as better, i.e., as *more* satisfactory?

11.2   Love and Sex with Robotic Pseudo-Persons

In a footnote to his book *The Meaning of Truth*, William James briefly considers whether an artificial lover could pragmatically ever be as satisfying as a real human one.[3] He imagines this artificial lover, which he calls "automatic sweetheart," as a "soulless body which should be absolutely indistinguishable from a spiritually animated maiden, laughing, talking, blushing, nursing us, and performing all feminine offices as tactfully and sweetly as if a soul were in her." By 'soul' James of course means subjectivity or a first-person perspective: an inner life that accompanies and motivates those loving and caring actions that he describes and discreetly alludes to as "feminine offices." The automatic sweetheart would do all those things that we expect them to do exactly as they would if they really felt what their actions suggest they feel, i.e., if they really loved us and really cared for us. Except that they do not. It is assumed that an automatic sweetheart does not feel or think anything. They are not real persons, but merely pseudo-persons. As mindless service providers, they would simply perform certain functions, and perform them perfectly. Would that be enough? Would that give us all we need and want? James is certain that it would not, for the following reason: "Because, framed as we are, our egoism craves above all things inward sympathy and recognition, love and admiration. The outward treatment is valued mainly as an expression, as a manifestation of the accompanying consciousness believed in." So what James is saying here is that what we *value* in others (due to the way we are "framed," i.e., to our human nature), or at any rate what we value in those with whom we have an intimate relationship is not primarily the fact that they behave or treat us in a certain, seemingly loving way, but that they do so precisely *because they love us.*

However, it is difficult to see what this love (the subjective feelings and thoughts of which the behavior is supposedly a mere expression) should consist of, if not in a certain kind of loving *behavior*. If my lover treats me badly and does not show any concern for my well-being (by, for instance, looking after me when I'm sick, or by taking care of my needs), then it does not seem to make much sense to insist that they, despite all, do love us. And, vice versa, if their behavior toward us is unfailingly caring and loving, and respectful of our needs, then we would not really know what to make of the claim that they do not really love us at all, but only *appear* to do so. We would expect that the alleged lack of love would *show* in some way, and if it never does, then their love is as real as it can possibly be. The philosophical behaviorist Edgar Arthur Singer raised this objection against James in his book *Mind as Behavior*.[4] While a "soulless sweetheart" is indeed unsatisfactory, he argued, their soullessness does not consist in the absence of feeling, but in their behavior, in what they do and do not do:

[N]o one would regard a soulless sweetheart as a full equivalent for a soulful one, as these words 'soulless' and 'soulful' are ordinarily used. But just there is the point: how are they ordinarily used? If I imagine myself come to believe that my mistress, with all her loveliness, is really without soul, I cannot think what I should mean by this if it be not that I fear her future conduct will not bear out my expectations regarding her. Some trait or gesture, a mere tightening of the lips, hardening of the eye, stifling of a yawn, one of those things we say are rather felt than seen, would have raised in my mind the suspicion that she might not to my fuller experience of her remain indistinguishable from a spiritually minded maiden.

On this view, we do not, in fact, *infer* the presence of (a certain kind of) mind from a person's behavior. Rather, their behavior *is* their mind.[5] David Levy, in his *Love and Sex with Robots*, seems to at least come close to adopting the same position when he says: "There are those who doubt that we can reasonably ascribe feelings to robots, but if a robot *behaves* as though it has feelings, can we reasonably argue that it does not? If a robot's artificial emotions prompt it to say things such as 'I love you,' surely we should be willing to accept these statements at face value, provided that the robot's other behavior patterns back them up."[6]

Yet the reason why it may not make much sense to doubt the love of somebody who unfailingly behaves lovingly toward us is that we would be hard-pressed to come up with a plausible explanation for why they would do such a thing. By far the best explanation for their loving behavior is that they really love us. This does not show that there is no clear distinction between real love and loving behavior (or more precisely a behavior that is, *qua* behavior, indistinguishable from a behavior that is inspired by real love). How we feel is one thing, and how we behave is, despite obvious connections between the two, quite another. While we usually, though by no means necessarily, express our feelings and attitudes through our behavior so that our behavior is normally a reliable indicator of how we feel, we can also hide our "soul" and act as if we felt very differently. Moreover, we know from self-experience that we are beings whose actions are more than just movements in physical space. Instead, they are *always* interwoven with, and expressive of, self-awareness and self-concern. We are real persons, and we *know* that we are. We also know that whatever a person does, there is *some* connection to the subjective side of their existence. A robot, however, is a machine primarily designed to behave in a certain way, and, depending on its purpose, perhaps also to make us *believe* that there is something it is like to be that robot. Those companies that today are already producing and marketing social robots (including sexual companion robots) do their best to blur the difference between real persons and pseudo-persons, and encourage us to get emotionally involved with their products. This strategy seems to be paying off. As Matthias Scheutz has pointed out, we are hardwired to ascribe intentions to entities that are mobile and exhibit some degree of autonomy, and thus easily fall prey to the "suggestive force of apparent autonomous behavior,"[7] and it is likely that the more the machines we build and use resemble real persons in their behavior, the harder it will become to escape that suggestive force. Yet, while it is quite possible that we are easily fooled, that our natural constitution as human (or more generally animal) beings makes it rather difficult for us *not* to ascribe self-awareness to a machine that behaves exactly as we would expect it to if it were *really* self-aware, as long as we have an alternative explanation for why it behaves that way (namely, that it has been designed and programmed to do so), we have no good reason to believe that its actions are expressive of anything at all. Even a perfect simulacrum is still a simulacrum, and our natural tendency to take the simulacrum for the real thing does nothing to change that.

Now, if James was right to surmise that what we want from a lover is that they *really* love us and not simply behave *as if* they loved us (while in fact not feeling anything at all), then a robot pseudo-person can never be as satisfactory as a human lover (at least not if we know that they are not human and have reason to believe or suspect that their apparent love is merely a clever simulation). Yet this also means that they can *only* be seen as satisfactory replacements for a human lover if all we care about, all we value, is what the other *does*, while not caring at all about how they *feel* or whether they feel anything at all. Human interaction is thus conceptually reduced to the behavioral aspect of it. True companionship, where one person relates to another *through*, or by means of, their interactions, is then no longer regarded as an end (because it is thought to be either unachievable, undesirable, or both). Instead, the means now *is* (understood to be) the end.

The attentive reader will have noticed that so far I have made no attempt to distinguish between love and sex, and I suspect that while many would agree that a robotic pseudo-person can never give us what we expect from somebody we *love* (namely that they love us back or at the very least that they are aware and appreciative of our love for them), the claim that such robots would be perfectly satisfactory as partners in a purely *sexual* relationship will be generally considered to be much more plausible. However, the reason I have avoided drawing a clear line between love and sex is not that I fail to acknowledge the difference. It is quite obvious to me that we can love someone without having sex with them, and have sex with them without loving them. So I am not conflating love with sex, nor do I think there is anything morally wrong with having casual sex, or sex without love. However, it seems to me that even what appears to be a purely sexual relationship between human partners is very often, and certainly can be, more than just sex (if we take 'sex' to be a purely physical event). For one thing, it always, by necessity, involves an intimate encounter with another human being, a sharing of an experience. It is not merely the coming-together of two bodies that interact with each other. Rather, it is the interaction of two (or more) embodied *persons*. Additionally, when we have sex with another person, we are not, at least not normally, simply using the other person to, as it were, scratch a sexual itch. Sex is also about, and fuelled by, desire, and the knowledge or belief that this desire is reciprocated. We want to be or feel desired. We desire the other who desires us desiring them. Our lust and the pleasure we experience is at least partly a response to the lust and pleasure we incite in the other and to the lust and pleasure they desire to incite in us. Sex, or perhaps we should better say *good* sex—the kind that D. H. Lawrence used to call "tender-hearted fucking"[8]—is a practice of sharing desire, a particular form of companionship and communion. In order to be fully satisfied with a robotic pseudo-person designed for sexual pleasure (who is by definition incapable of feeling any desire), we would have to attach no value to the interpersonal aspects of sex, i.e., to those aspects of sex that can make it such a rich and exhilarating experience in the first place. This becomes quite evident when David Levy declares that the "prime purpose of a sexbot is to assist the user in achieving orgasm, without the necessity of having another human being present."[9] The human that is not present, and whose absence is supposedly fully compensated by the presence of the robot, is here seen as having the same function as the robot, namely to "assist the user in achieving orgasm." Not only does this view reduce the sexual act to what it often leads up to (as if nothing else mattered; the process itself discounted), it also assumes that to achieve full sexual satisfaction we do not need anybody else. All we need is someone or something (it doesn't matter which) that pushes the right buttons, scratches what needs scratching, and tickles what needs tickling. This someone could also be us. In other words, the other who is no longer a partner, but merely an "assistant," is nothing more than a rather overdeveloped masturbation device. You don't necessarily need a robot for that, and you certainly don't need a person. If sex is *in any case* nothing but masturbation (and at best mutual masturbation), then there is no reason to think that a pseudo-person, designed with sufficient technological sophistication, could not meet the job requirements just as well as a real person. But if sex is in fact more than that, or at least can be more than that, a communion of some sort, then sex with a pseudo-person can, just like masturbation, never be as satisfactory or fulfilling as sex with a real person.[10]

11.3   Love and Sex with Robotic Persons

But what if we eventually managed to build robots that *are* real persons, as some believe is possible (e.g., Petersen, in this volume)? Robots that can desire us as much as we can desire them, robots that can really love us back and feel what we feel. Would they then be just as good as a human lover? I am reasonably sure that for many they would, provided they are, in all relevant respects, just like us (except perhaps better looking and more skilled in the art of pleasuring the flesh). The fact that they would be human-made rather than human-born should not make a difference, although for some it might. Yet that would simply be a personal preference. Some might prefer synthetic lovers, others natural ones, just like some people prefer blondes and others brunettes or redheads. This does not say anything about their *general* preferability as sexual or romantic partners. However, that future social robots will in all relevant respects be like us is even more unlikely than that they will be persons, for the simple reason that they will in any case be made for a *purpose*, while humans generally are not (at least not yet). In order for them to exist we will have to make them, and we are not going to do that without a good reason for it, and that means without there being a need or demand for them. In other words, there has to be a market for them. So why would anyone want a robot lover? Why would anyone be willing to pay for them? Whitby lists several plausible motivations.[11] Obviously, sexual companion robots might appeal to those who have trouble finding a human lover. Not everyone has the appearance or social skills that would make them attractive as a sexual partner to others, and even if they do find someone, those they can get may not be the ones they would have chosen if they had a choice. A sexual robot would allow those who are less sexually attractive not only to find a partner, but also to find a very attractive one. Others may simply like the idea of having sex with a machine (or in this case an artificial person). Possible reasons for this I have discussed elsewhere.[12] Some people may feel drawn to the undemanding nature of robots that are designed to please us, and some may look forward to being able to do with their robotic partner whatever they want to without being restricted in any way by morality or by what their partner happens to like and dislike. But, whatever the motivation, in order to give those people what they want, we can perhaps allow robots to be *persons* in the specified sense, but what we *cannot* allow is that they are free to act in a way that runs counter to the wishes of their buyers. If they think and feel, that's fine, perhaps even desirable, but they *must* love us when we want them to love us and have sex with us when we want them to have sex with us. Their freedom needs to be restricted. Otherwise, we would have no reason to create (and, perhaps more importantly, buy) them in the first place.

The required restriction of freedom can be achieved in two different ways. One option is to decide and decree that what the robot wants is of no significance, and then to install a mechanism that prevents it from *doing* anything other than what we want it to do, either by programming it in such a way that it cannot disobey our commands (always assuming that this is possible, which it may well not be), or by creating a moral and legal framework that effectively leaves the robot no choice but to do our bidding (for fear of the repercussions that disobedience would incur). Both would amount to institutionally sanctioned slavery and might appeal to those who find rape (by which I here mean making someone have sex with you who does not want to have sex with you) more gratifying than consensual sex. The other, seemingly more morally acceptable, option is to design and program robots in such a way that they never *want* to do anything other than what the buyer wants them to do. The first option has been suggested by Joanna Bryson, and the second by Steve Petersen.[13]

According to Bryson, robots *should* be slaves. Not only would there be nothing morally wrong with keeping them as slaves, but also would it be morally wrong *not* to do so. It would be wrong to grant them any kind of moral status because doing so would draw time and energy, as well as care and emotional investment, away from those who deserve it, namely human persons. Ascriptions of personhood are a valuable resource with which we should not be too generous. And it would not be morally wrong to refuse robots moral consideration and keep them as slaves because we have created them specifically for that purpose, that is, to serve *our* needs and wants. For this reason we should not have to treat them as persons or grant them any rights that we usually grant persons. As far as I can see, this claim is not based on the assumption that humanoid robots will not be real persons in the sense specified above, but only pseudo-persons. For Bryson, the term 'person' seems to signify a being that deserves moral recognition. Personhood is here not a quality that an entity can possess, but something that is or is not *owed* to it. The term is thus purely normative and does not seem to have any descriptive dimension. Curiously, there is no suggestion in Bryson's paper that whether those robots are real persons or pseudo-persons in a *descriptive* sense might in any way be relevant to the question of how we should regard and treat them. Rather, what settles the question for her is the fact that we have designed and produced them and therefore *own* them. There would be no robots without us, Bryson argues; they owe their existence solely to the fact that we needed and wanted somebody to perform a certain role. Since that is what they are here for, they are not entitled to demand or expect anything else from us. It does not really matter whether they are persons or pseudo-persons; what matters is that they are in either case still machines, made by us. And if we are, regardless, still afraid that an ethical issue might arise from enslaving them, we could just design them in such a way that they don't mind their lack of freedom. It is entirely up to us: "Remember, robots are wholly owned and designed by us. We determine their goals and desires. A robot cannot be frustrated unless it is given goals that cannot be met, and it cannot mind being frustrated unless we program it to perceive frustration as distressing, rather than as an indication of a planning puzzle."[14] However, we, as their makers, have no direct moral obligation to them to spare them distress. At least that is how I understand Bryson's argument. If that is a fair reading, then I don't think the argument is very persuasive. The fact that an entity would not exist if we hadn't wanted it to exist, and to exist for a certain purpose, does not strip that entity of all moral standing. The same argument can, after all, be made (and actually *has* been made) about the animals we breed for food and as pets. It may even be said about our own children. Yet since we don't usually accept this kind of reasoning (i.e., that what we create we own, and what we own has no rights), creating self-aware and self-concerned robot servants who do not want to serve us but have to do so anyway is not really an option.

To forestall such ethical concerns, Steve Petersen has suggested that we should design and program our robot servants in such a way that they *want* to serve us, or, more generally, that they want to do what we want them to do.[15] So, if nothing made them happier than to fulfill our every wish, then we would neither harm nor wrong them in any way by allowing them to do so. Nor would we wrong them by making it, right from the start, impossible for them to want anything else. If their wishes were always aligned with ours, then we would, Petersen argues, in fact not be treating them as mere means, because whatever we asked them to do would, per definition, benefit them just as much as us. It would not only serve *our* ends, but also *their* ends. Petersen does not think that we would thereby condemn them to a meaningless life. He rejects the idea that there are higher and lower pleasures, or pursuits that are more worth pursuing than others: instead, any pursuit must be regarded as worth pursuing, as long as someone happens to get their kicks from it. Even our noblest pursuits are, after all, pretty meaningless in the grand scheme of things. And we do not usually think that the life of an animal (who is not capable of higher pursuits) is not worth living. If we did, we should, or would, not allow them to exist in the first place.

While this is not the place to discuss in detail the ethics of creating artificial persons to serve us, a few remarks may be in order. If we accepted Petersen's argument, then we would have to suppose that, for example, the life of a Sisyphus who was designed and programmed to find nothing more pleasurable than pushing a rock up a hill for his entire life is just as meaningful and fulfilling as the life of, say, a rescue worker who helps saving other people's lives. More importantly, we would also have to suppose that there is nothing wrong, nothing morally objectionable, with *deliberately creating* such a Sisyphus for our own ends (perhaps because we find it immensely amusing to see him pushing that bloody stone up the hill day after day, or, if we are more philosophically minded, to serve as a living reminder of the utter meaninglessness of all existence). Even though he may then not be doing anything that he does not want to do, we would still treat him merely as a means to our ends. To treat somebody as an end in itself does not merely mean that we let them do what they want to do, but also to allow them to want things that we don't. It is about allowing someone to find their own ends without us making the decision for them. This is why it would also be wrong to breed or genetically engineer *human* persons who desire nothing more than to serve us, which following Petersen's logic would be morally unobjectionable, too.[16]

Now imagine we had the means to create robotic or human persons whose only desire was to fulfill our sexual desires, whatever they may be. Custom-made models could be ordered online, fitted not only with specific bodily features, but also with particular preferential attitudes. People would get what they want, and what they want is someone who wants what they want them to want, for instance "an airhead silicon bimboid obsessed with serving them sexually, or perhaps a skinnier anal-addicted Ukrainian model," or, for the more outlandish tastes, "babies for rape" or "snuff robots which scream and bleed realistically when their arms are sawn off."[17] All that would presumably be fine, following Petersen's original argument, as long as those treated that way do not mind because it is what they themselves want anyway.[18] Except it is *not* all right. It is demeaning, and the fact that we would have designed them to find pleasure in a demeaning life, makes it not less, but even more demeaning.[19]

Although the question I intended to address in this paper is not whether it can be *morally acceptable* to have a sexual relationship with a robot, but whether such a relationship could ever be as *satisfying* as a sexual relationship with a human lover, the two questions are not as unconnected as it may seem. If that relationship does not agree with our ethical commitments, then we won't be able to regard and experience it as fully satisfying. That, of course, depends on our ethical commitments, whether we have any in the first place, and if yes, which. However, whether or not we have such commitments, the ethical features of a situation can still function as objective grounds for satisfaction and dissatisfaction in the sense that if a relationship is, to put it mildly, morally dubious, then whether or not we are satisfied with it, it still remains the case that we *should* not be satisfied with it.

However, while most people will probably agree that the life of a person programmed to meet any and every sexual demand that we may have is indeed demeaning, this does not, or at least not so obviously, seem to be the case when a person is not designed for sex, but for love. What if I just want somebody who loves me the way I am, someone who is good to me and there for me and will not tire of me and will not leave me because they find somebody who they think is more lovable? Surely there is nothing demeaning about loving a particular person and loving them reliably. So, if it were possible to create such a person, and I ordered and purchased him or her, it does not seem that that person's life would be bad or meaningless because of it. (I am, after all, not such a bad guy and deserve to be loved by someone.) We may of course still take issue with the fact that they have been *designed* to love us, and, hence, have no *choice* in the matter; but it is difficult to argue that point and I will not try to do this here.[20] So let us assume for now that creating persons programmed to love us is morally unobjectionable (as unobjectionable as, say, creating a person programmed with a burning desire to cure cancer). Would they then be as satisfying as a real (unprogrammed) human person who just happens to love us?

They might not be, even if we have no ethical concerns about it. That is because, as Dylan Evans has pointed out, we do not only desire to be loved, but we usually also have the second-order desire to be loved freely, i.e., by choice. "Although people typically want commitment and fidelity from their partners, they want these things to be the fruit of an ongoing choice, rather than inflexible and unreflexive behavior patterns."[21] We do not want people to love us because they have been hypnotized or enchanted (like Shakespeare's fairy queen Titania who is made to fall in love with a donkey-headed weaver). And programming is, after all, just a different type of enchantment. Of course, we do not usually mind that those who love us "cannot help themselves," that their commitment to us is deeper and more unshakable than what a deliberate choice could provide (which can at any moment be revoked). Yet we do want the other to love us for what and who we are and not no matter what we are. We want it to be *their* choice and not ours (or, for that matter, a third party's). This entails a certain contingency, and, with it, the possibility of loss. Even though we fear that possibility, we are unlikely to accord much value to a love that is ours whatever we do. We will probably tire of it very quickly. If that is correct, then an automatic sweetheart, even if they are real persons, and even if they are designed to love us *no matter what*, will not be as satisfying as a human person who (really) loves us.

11.4   Love and Sex with Robotic Post-Persons

On the other hand, the prospect of having somebody that loves us *reliably*, someone who we *know* won't leave us no matter what, will certainly have a strong appeal to many. So there is indeed, as Evans puts it, a dilemma at the heart of the human-robot relationship: "We want contradictory things: a romantic partner who is both free and who will never leave us."[22] And if we cannot have both, then, depending on what we value most, we may well prefer the reliable artifact to the never completely reliable human. What is more, we might not even see this as a huge loss, or for that matter *any* loss, in the first place. We can, after all, always convince ourselves that nothing is really missing, that the robot gives us all that we can possibly get, or at any rate all that is worth having. The pseudo-person can be designed to appear and act like a real person, and if we cannot detect a difference and trust that "soul" is ultimately nothing but behavior, then the pseudo-person will be just as good as a person. And if the robot *is* a real person, but not free to do anything outside the parameters of what we want them to do, then they can still *appear* free, and we can then, following the same reasoning, tell ourselves that they *are* free. It is easy to lie to ourselves if it gets us what we want: "we are alone and imagine ourselves together."[23]

Yet we may not even have to fool ourselves. Even if we are perfectly aware that the other that serves us as a pseudo-partner for sex and love does not really feel anything at all, or that if they do, they have been programmed to do so, and hence have no real choice in the matter, we may actually *prefer* them that way. Being alone can be our preferred option. To engage with someone, a real human person, is, after all, always risky. Not only do we never quite know what we will get or whether we will actually get what it says on the box, we are also constantly expected to take into account, and sympathetically respond to, *their* needs and desires. Real people are demanding and do not always perform the way we want them to. The great advantage of robots is that they do:

Sexbots will never have headaches, fatigue, impotence, premature ejaculation, pubic lice, disinterest, menstrual blood, jock strap itch, yeast infections, genital warts, AIDS/HIV, herpes, silly expectations, or inhibiting phobias. Sexbots will never stalk us, rape us, diss us on their blog, weep when we dump them, or tell their friends we were boring in bed. Sexbots will always climax when we climax if we press that little button on their butt.[24]

The author of this (by no means tongue-in-cheek) eulogy on sex robots, Hank Pellissier, is the former managing director of the *Institute for Ethics and Emerging Technologies* (IEET), which has established itself as one of the two main transhumanist associations and think tanks (the other being *Humanity Plus*). The IEET's mission is to promote "ideas about how technological progress can increase freedom, happiness, and human flourishing."[25] *Humanity Plus* has a similar agenda: to elevate the human condition by expanding human capabilities and making us "better than well." Their motto is: "Don't limit your challenges. Challenge your limits."[26] The suggestion that we can actually *benefit* from replacing human partners with robots must be understood in this context. Robots for sex and love constitute an important step toward the realization of a shared transhumanist agenda, which rests firmly on two ideological pillars: libertarianism and hedonism. From a transhumanist perspective, our goal should be to get the maximum amount of pleasure out of everything we do—which according to Nick Bostrom is, after all, nothing less than the "birthright of every creature"—and to become as free/independent/autonomous as possible. These two goals are connected, of course. Our limitations are thought to be a principal source of displeasure and unhap-piness. Consequently, once we are free of all limitations, there will be nothing left to be unhappy about. Pellissier himself makes this connection explicit in a recent article, published on the IEET website. After examining the various kinds of "suffering caused by our enslavement to our outdated neurochemistry," he concludes that as "Free-will Transhumans, who decided 100% of the time what we wanted to think, feel, and do," we would not only be "immensely more powerful," but also, precisely for this reason, much happier.[27]

Now the problem with entering into relationships with other people is that, although they certainly can be a source of pleasure, more often than not they stand in the way of it. Moreover, even when they give us pleasure and happiness, this pleasure and happiness is always tainted and diminished by the fact that we need *them* to get it. Loving a human being and having sex with them might be pleasurable, but this pleasure can easily be taken away from us. From a transhumanist perspective, the fact that we *depend* on other people for sex and love is almost as annoying as the fact that we have to die, or more generally the fact that we cannot do anything and everything we want to do and not *be* anything and everything we want to be. This (and not merely the fact that they might know better how to please and pleasure us) is the main reason why Levy thinks that sex and love robots are not only not deficient in any way, but are actually *better* companions and lovers than a human could ever be.[28] Consider again the statement quoted earlier: "The prime purpose of a sexbot is to assist the user in achieving orgasm, without the necessity of having another human being present."[29] To have another human present is currently still a *necessity*, which is exactly what makes it problematic. Any necessity is bad because, by definition, it curbs our freedom. Neces-sities prevent us from being self-sufficient and truly autonomous. Sex robots are good not only because they are much more fun to be with, but also, even primarily, because they make us more independent. We should reevaluate our attitude toward sex accord-ingly. "Are Sexbots icky? Are humans pathetic if we don't just mate with each other? Truth is, we're already mostly 'solo' when it comes to orgasms. 'Masturbation,' noted Hungarian psychiatrist Thomas Szasz, 'is the primary sexual activity … in the 19th century it was a disease, in the 20th it's a cure.'"[30]

A cure for what, though? Pellissier does not answer the question directly, but it is clear from the context that what this masturbation-by-sexbot is thought to be a cure for is the disease of other human beings (or the disease of our dependence on them). This gives a whole new meaning to Sartre's famous dictum that "hell is other people." The underlying logic is worrying. It hints at a paradox at the heart of the transhumanist agenda. If the goal is to increase my autonomy, and if other people by virtue of having desires and needs of their own that differ from mine necessarily impose limits on my autonomy, then in order to increase my own autonomy, I need to find ways to *decrease* the autonomy of others, or, if that is not feasible, to create a world for myself that allows me to do what I want to without requiring the collaboration of others. As long as I have to interact with real others, as long as we share a world, our autonomy will always be severely restricted. Therefore, the only possible way for me to become completely independent is by cutting all ties to other persons, by making my own world, uninhabited by any real persons except myself. Perfect autonomy (and thus supposedly perfect happiness) requires complete detachment. Robotic pseudo-persons or persons can then be understood as an enhanced version of other people. They are in fact, in more than one sense, post-persons.

Notes

1. Ray Kurzweil, *The Age of Spiritual Machines* (New York: Viking, 1999), 142–148; David Levy, *Love and Sex with Robots. The Evolution of Human-Robot Relationships* (London: Duckworth Overlook, 2008), 22; Pew Research Center, "AI, Robotics, and the Future of Jobs," 2014, http://www.pewinternet.org/2014/08/06/future-of-jobs.

2. Thomas Nagel, "What Is It Like to Be a Bat," *The Philosophical Review* 83, no. 4: 435–450.

3. William James, *The Meaning of Truth. A Sequel to 'Pragmatism'* (New York: Longmans, Green, and Co., 1909), 189.

4. Edgar A. Singer, *Mind as Behavior and Studies in Empirical Idealism* (Columbus, OH: R. G. Adams and Co., 1924), 9.

5. Ibid., 10.

6. Levy, *Love and Sex with Robots,* 11.

7. Matthias Scheutz, "The Inherent Dangers of Unidirectional Emotional Bonds between Humans and Social Robots," in *Robot Ethics,* eds. Patrick Lin, Keith Abney, and George Bekey (Cambridge, MA: MIT Press, 2012), 213.

8. Michael Hauskeller, "Is It Desirable to Be Able to Do the Undesirable?," *Cambridge Quarterly of Healthcare Ethics* (2017): 53–63.

9. Levy, *Love and Sex with Robots,* 227.

10. George Mikes, in his humorous 1946 classic *How to Be an Alien,* quipped that "continental people have sex life; the English have hot-water bottles." Mikes, *Alien* (London: Penguin, 1986), 25. Sex robots are something like the hot-water bottles of the future.

11. Blay Whitby, "Do You Want a Robot Lover? The Ethics of Caring Technologies," in *Robot Ethics,* eds. Patrick Lin, Keith Abney, and George Bekey (Cambridge, MA: MIT Press, 2012), 234–248.

12. Hauskeller, "Is It Desirable to Be Able to Do the Undesirable?"

13. Joanna J. Bryson, "Robots Should Be Slaves," in *Close Engagements with Artificial Companions. Key Social, Psychological, Ethical and Design Issues*, ed. Yorick Wilks (Philadelphia, PA: John Benjamins Publishing Company, 2010), 63–74; Steve Petersen, "Is it Good for them too? Ethical Concern for the Sexbots" (in this volume); Steve Petersen, "Designing People to Serve," in *Robot Ethics*, eds. Patrick Lin, Keith Abney, and George Bekey (Cambridge, MA: MIT Press, 2012), 283–298.

14. Bryson, "Robots Should Be Slaves," 72.

15. Petersen, "Designing People to Serve," 283–298.

16. In his contribution to the present volume, Petersen partially addresses these concerns by imagining the creation of sexbots that also have a "deeply reflective, even spiritual life" (which supposedly would make their life meaningful) and that are autonomous in the sense that they are not owned and can freely determine how they want to live their lives (although given their programming they will naturally want to live a life that allows them to fulfill their dominant desire for sex). Such sexbots clearly need not have a bad life (which is the main point that Petersen is trying to make in his contribution). However, it is unclear why we would want to create such artificial persons in the first place. There are, after all, already lots of people out there with a very strong sex drive, so those robots would not be much different from them. Yet the whole point of sexbots, the reason why we want to produce them and why there is a potential market for them, is that we imagine those sexbots to fulfill *our* sexual cravings (and not theirs). In other words, it is imperative that they do not only want to have lots of sex, but that they also want it with *us* (and possibly *only* with us). So we would want to own them in some way.

17. Paul Treanor, "Bimboid Utopia: What Do Men Want?," February 6, 2015, https://politicalaspects.wordpress.com/2015/02/06/bimboid-utopia-what-do-men-want.

18. In his contribution to the present volume, Petersen concedes that there may be *other* ethical concerns raised by such scenarios, but what has not changed is his view that we would not *wrong the robot* by subjecting it to such treatment as long as it desires and derives pleasure from being treated that way.

19. John Danaher has recently (2017) discussed how it may be considered morally wrong (and hence apt for criminalization) to engage in sexual activities with robots deliberately designed to cater to "pedophilic tastes and rape fantasies." (Danaher, "Robotic Rape and Robotic Child Sexual Abuse: Should They Be Criminalised, *Criminal Law and Philosophy* 11, no. 1 (2017): 71–95.) Danaher assumes that those robots will be pseudo-persons, which makes it more difficult to establish any wrongdoing. However, he argues (although rather tentatively) that such activities may reasonably be regarded as harmful to the moral character of those who engage in them. Although I think more needs to be said about what that means exactly, the point is well taken. Perhaps the supposed harm to moral character can be best understood in relation to the self-demeaning nature of the activity. And if the robot subjected to these activities is a person, then what is happening is demeaning for both.

20. I have tried to make that argument in Hauskeller, "Is It Desirable?"

21. Dylan Evans, "Wanting the Impossible: The Dilemma at the Heart of Intimate Human-Robot Relationships," in *Close Engagements with Artificial Companions: Key Social, Psychological, Ethical, and Design Issues*, ed. Yorick Wilks (Philadelphia, PA: John Benjamins Publishing Company, 2010), 74–75.

22. Evans, "Wanting the Impossible," 84.

23. Sherry Turkle, *Alone Together: Why We Expect More from Technology and Less from Each Other* (New York: Basic Books, 2011), 226.

24. Hank Pellissier, "Sexbots Will Give Us Longevity Orgasms," *Humanity Plus Magazine*, December 11, 2009, http://hplusmagazine.com/2009/12/11/sexbots-will-give-us-longevity-orgasm.

25. http://www.ieet.org/index.php/IEET/about.

26. http://humanityplus.org/about.

27. Hank Pellissier, "Free Will Does Not Exist—Should It Be a Transhumanist Enhancement?," 2015, http://ieet.org/index.php/IEET/more/pellissier20150727.

20. Evans (2010) fittingly calls this the "greater satisfaction thesis."

29. David Levy, "The Ethics of Robot Prostitutes," in *Robot Ethics*, eds. Patrick Lin, Keith Abney, and George Bekey (Cambridge, MA: MIT Press, 2012), 227.

30. Pellissier, "Sexbots Will Give Us Longevity Orgasms."

12   From Sex Robots to Love Robots: Is Mutual Love with a Robot Possible?

Sven Nyholm and Lily Eva Frank

12.1   Introduction

In human romantic relationships, sex and love often go together. But what if one party is not a human, but a sex doll or a sex robot? In the 2002 BBC documentary *Guys and Dolls*, one of the characters viewers meet is a human male living in southeastern Michigan, who calls himself Davecat. Another character is a synthetic doll, "Sidore." Davecat considers Sidore not only his sexual partner, but also his wife. They love each other, he says. When interviewed by *The Atlantic* in 2013, Davecat was still living with Sidore. He was contemplating how best to celebrate the upcoming fifteenth anniversary of his love and marriage to Sidore.[1]

This will strike many as confused. Even if Davecat might be very attached to his doll and think of himself as loving "her," this is entirely one-sided. The doll doesn't love Davecat, because dolls cannot love anybody. And so there couldn't be mutual romantic love between a human and a doll. But what if Sidore were not just a doll, but an advanced sex robot of a very sophisticated kind? What if we fast-forward to a future that might not be too far off, in which sex robots have become endowed with highly impressive forms of artificial intelligence?

Human beings sometimes fall in love with human beings they have sex with, if they aren't already in love when they start having sex. The case of Davecat and Sidore suggests that people can experience themselves as falling in love with the sorts of synthetic sex dolls they might have sex with. So we can expect that some people will "fall in love" with more advanced sex robots with which they have sex.

In what follows, we take seriously the possibility of mutual romantic love between humans and advanced sex robots.[2] The question we will be discussing is: Could *mutual love* be achieved between humans and sex robots? To clarify: we are not only concerned with whether humans might interpret themselves as loving, or as being in love with, sex robots. We are primarily interested in whether the sex robots could also possibly love the humans who see themselves as loving the sex robots. That is why we have emphasized the expression "mutual love."[3]

Our primary aim is to offer a framework for approaching the question of mutual love. But we also sketch a tentative answer to it. Our tentative answer is that whereas mutual love between humans and sex robots is not in principle impossible, it is hard to achieve. The sex robots would have to be very advanced.

Our discussion below generates a "job description" that advanced sex robots would need to live up to in order to be able to participate in relationships that can be recognized as mutual love. Having such a job description facilitates further analysis of whether love robots are possible. The resulting job description can be combined with different philosophical conceptions of what artificial intelligence could achieve. This can then generate competing arguments about whether or not it is possible to bring about mutual love between humans and robots. On some philosophical conceptions of the limits of artificial intelligence, a sex robot could never become able to do some of the things a human lover does (e.g., seeing itself as having reasons to act in certain ways). On more optimistic philosophical conceptions of what artificial intelligence could achieve, however, robots could one day potentially become able to do all the most important things we think of a human lover as doing.

We proceed as follows: We first offer two reasons to motivate our discussion of whether or not it is possible and desirable to achieve love between humans and sex robots (section 12.2). We review some of the philosophical literature there is on this topic already (section 12.3). We then explain how we think this question ought to be approached: namely, via clusters of ideas about what people typically seek and value in romantic love that can be found, not only in the philosophy of love, but also in art and literature, pop culture, and in everyday thinking about love (section 12.4). We discuss three such clusters of ideas, in each case asking whether an advanced sex robot could achieve the aspects of romantic love that we will discuss. The first is a set of ideas related to "being a good match" (section 12.5). The second concerns the idea of lovers as valuing each other in their distinctive particularity (section 12.6). The third set of related ideas and associations cluster around the idea of commitment (section 12.7). As we move through these different ideas, it will seem harder and harder to envision mutual love of the sort of we typically value in the human case as being something that could be achieved between humans and sex robots. But again, our tentative conclusion will be that, though hard to achieve, it is not in principle impossible (section 12.8). We end with a brief discussion of whether it is a worthy goal to devote precious time, energy, and resources to developing advanced sex robots with which humans could enjoy mutual love. We consider both a "no" answer and a "yes" answer to this question (section 12.9).

12.2 Motivating Our Discussion

Before we go any further, the first thing we should do is to motivate our discussion. Why discuss whether mutual love could be achieved between humans and sex robots?[4] We wish to offer two reasons.

The first motivation is inspired by recent forceful feminist critiques of sex robots. One such criticism of sex robots is that their use might objectify sex partners (of robot and human sorts), which might then transfer over to people's attitudes toward other human beings, especially women. Instead of thinking of the choice to have sex or even companionship with a robot as strictly an individual choice with individual consequences, critics urge that we should also consider the larger social context and the impact of such a trend on all of society.[5] For example, one of the motivations a person might have for using a sex robot, rather than having sex with a human, is "to be able to do things to it that would be unacceptable if done to humans."[6] Blay Whitby argues there is some evidence that playing violent video games can desensitize players to real-world violence, and worries that a similar spillover effect could come as the result of these sexual activities.[7]

Mirroring the more popular "Campaign to Stop Killer Robots," the "Campaign to Stop Sex Robots" predicts that their development and widespread use will harm women and children.[8] Campaigners claim that the creation of sex robots and equivalencies between sex robots and prostitutes[9] reify "a dangerous mode of existence where humans can move about in relations with other humans but not recognize them as human subjects in their own right."[10] Like prostitution, the use of sex robots will encourage men to objectify sex partners, and dampen their capacities for empathy. One important feature of sex robots that will contribute to objectification and harm for human women is that sex robots are "ever-consenting," an attitude that may also spill over to humans.[11] Jennifer Robertson argues that it is significant that automated devices, from Siri to future humanoid robots, are often feminine or feminized. This, she argues, is because a female automaton is more consistent with preexisting sexist views of women as beings that, although intelligent, are appropriate to dominate.[12]

Evaluating the merits of these objections is beyond the scope of this paper. However, one response to these criticisms is to first point out that many human sexual relationships are objectifying, dehumanizing, and sexist. But these are features of human relationships that are not universal, and, seem, at least to us, to be malleable.

Healthy human relationships involving mutual romantic love can be neither objecti-fying, dehumanizing, nor sexist.[13] Why couldn't the same be true of sexual relation-ships between humans and robots? Perhaps loving, non-objectifying relations between humans and robots are also possible, just as loving, non-objectifying relations are pos-sible between humans and other humans. Thus, our first motivation for investigating whether mutual love could be achieved between humans and sex robots is that it could potentially help to make sexual relationships between humans and sex robots more acceptable in a way that would block the above-stated criticisms.

Let us now turn to the second main reason we wish to put forward to motivate our discussion. That reason, crudely put, has to do with the added value of sexual relations involving love in comparison to sexual relations not involving love. Of course, sex between consenting adults is widely considered to have positive value independent of whether love is part of the picture. It is clearly desirable for instrumental reasons, such as providing a positive contribution to mental and physical health, and, of course, for purely hedonic reasons. However, it is also widely held that sex has greater value and deeper meaning if it takes place between people who love each other.[14] We take this to be part of common sense.[15]

Now consider sex between humans and sex robots. Here, too, it might be held that loveless sex could clearly have instrumental value. But it can also seem meaning-less—or at least much less attractive than the sex had withinromantic relationships where the participants love and cherish each other. So if mutual love could be achieved between humans and sex robots, then by parity of reasoning with the human case, mutual love could potentially give sex between humans and sex robots a deeper mean-ing and greater value. This immediately raises the question of whether mutual love could indeed be achieved between humans and sex robots. That way of prompting the question is our second underlying motivation for investigating this topic here.

12.3   The Philosophical Discussion of This Topic So Far

The philosophical discussion of sex and love with robots is fairly limited thus far. But the small amount of literature that does exist provides much food for thought, some of which certain people might find hard to digest. The most comprehensive treatment of the topic is David Levy's provocative book, *Love and Sex with Robots*. Levy is very opti-mistic about the feasibility and likelihood of loving human-robot relationships. He also thinks that their advent will be a very good thing, providing fulfilling relationships of various kinds that could contribute greatly to human well-being.

Levy argues that all types of goods people acquire in human-to-human loving relationships are realizable in human-robot relationships. His arguments share the following structure. In step one, Levy notes that in the standard human case, falling in love typically involves a given element, for example, sharing similar characteristics or gradually changing to share characteristics.[16] In step two, Levy offers evidence that a robot could be built to do the same thing. In this example, it would be designed with particular traits in mind and could even be programmed to gradually change over time in response to its partner, if this is more conducive to love. Or, for another example: given the importance of smell and the other senses as aphrodisiacs in human-to-human love relationships, Levy suggests that tailor-made artificial scents will be incorporated into the design of love robots in the future.[17] On the basis of such premises, Levy optimistically concludes that love between humans and robots could clearly be achieved.

Notably, the kinds of objections Levy spends the most time with do not concern the crucial question of whether robots and humans can *genuinely* love each other. Instead, he considers objections of the following sort: we cannot fall in love with something without a physical body or we cannot fall in love with something nonhuman. In response to such worries, Levy presents cases where humans *fall in love, love, like,* or at least *form very strong attachments* to persons and things that do not possess these traits, like e-romance, love and dating over the Internet, and love and attachment to pets, even electronic pets like the Tamagotchi.[18]

Levy's answer to the looming question of whether or not there could be real love between a human and a robot, or whether the robot can really be in love with the human, follows from the way he understands love. That understanding is functional and behavioristic. If the robot speaks and behaves in the same manner a human lover does, and if the robot can produce the same (or greater) experienced levels of companionship, satisfaction, emotional comfort for the human (than) a fellow human lover can, then we should take this to be genuine love.[19]

We are critical of a purely functional and behavioristic characterization of love, in part because it fails to take into account important features of the ordinary conception of romantic love. If love boiled down to certain behavioral patterns, we could hire an actor to "go through the motions," by behaving in the various ways we associate with lovers. We could thereby buy ourselves love. But, by common conceptions, this would not be real love, however talented the actor might be. What goes on "on the inside" matters greatly to whether mutual love is achieved or not. The inner motives and thoughts that our lovers have when they treat us well is an important part of what distinguishes them from people who merely pretend to love us because this is somehow to their personal advantage. Part of what we hope for when we want others to love us is that they harbor a genuine concern for us. (For more on this, see sections 12.5 and 12.6 below.)

A limited number of authors have discussed the capacities or conditions a robot would need to possess in order to be able to enter into a love relationship with a human. For example, Mark Coeckelbergh considers the role of empathy in human-robot companion relationships. Coeckelbergh's discussion, however, includes a broader range of relationships than just romantic love. He concludes that while the ability for the robot to be the recipient, or object, of empathy is necessary for companionship, it is not necessary that it possess the capacity for empathy. That conclusion rests largely on the claim that humans already engage in, what we take to be, genuine companion relationships that are asymmetrical in this way, with children, animals, and severely cognitively impaired individuals.[20] Coeckelbergh does, however, think that robots need to be able to engage in "empathy as vulnerability mirroring" in order to inspire "fellow-feeling" in their human companions.[21] Coekelbergh's intent is not to list the necessary and sufficient conditions for robotic lovers or even companions. He is instead focusing on a much more circumscribed issue. That is why we think that, at least for our present purposes, Coeckelbergh's discussion is not ambitious enough: it only covers one aspect of companion relationships in general, but it leaves out many of the key aspects most strongly associated with romantic love in particular. Our discussion here focuses specifically on human-robot romantic love relationships, not merely companion relationships in some broader sense.

In a paper more directly relevant given our present aims, John Sullins is critical of Levy's purely functional view of loving relationships. He argues that, although advances in affective computing may very well allow for the development of robot lovers that can mimic the behavior of human lovers, "[l]ove is more than behavior."[22] Sullins thinks that love is "a powerful emotion."[23] So, if robots lack an inner life and cannot experience powerful emotions, they cannot love people. Sullins also thinks that, from an ethical point of view, the most valuable components of love relationships have to do with the ways a lover can expand one's perception of value, enlarge one's compassion, and even contribute to self-realization. It is these components of ethically valuable love Sullins is most skeptical a robot can provide.

Whitby is also skeptical that what Levy describes is something we actually want to call love, especially in light of the fact that the technologies currently being developed can be described as striving to provide a "simulation" of love, rather than an instantiation of it.[24] Whitby does not advocate for a particular set of characteristics of a human-robot love relationship or capacities required of a genuine robot lover. But he does suggest that lovelike relations between humans and robots may alter our understanding of the nature of love.[25]

Michael Hauskeller's discussion of human-robot love focuses on the idea of personhood, understood as the capacity for self-awareness and self-concern. He asks two questions: First, would romantic relationships with robots be as satisfying as relationships with human beings? And, second, even if they are subjectively experienced as satisfying, would they contain grounds for equal satisfaction? (People can be led to attribute human features to machines, which might then give them satisfaction, even if the machines don't really possess those human qualities.) Hauskeller thinks that within the foreseeable future, sex robots are unlikely to be persons, that is, they are unlikely to have self-awareness and self-concern. As such, we couldn't experience mutual love with them in the way we can with human persons who possess these capacities. Regarding the more remote possibility of creating robots that are like persons, Hauskeller speculates that this would defeat the purpose for which people seem to be attracted to the prospect of sex robots: namely, to achieve satisfaction without having to depend on other people.[26]

12.4 Our Approach

Like Sullins and Whitby, we are skeptical of the strongly behavioristic approach to love Levy takes, as already noted above.[27] We follow Sullins, Coeckelberg, Whitby, and Hauskeller in being interested in what people value or hope for when they desire and seek love. We see ourselves as building on their work. But we take a broader perspective where, in some cases, these writers take a more narrow perspective. For example, in the above-mentioned chapter, Hauskeller focuses on whether we could love a robot as a person, or as if it were a person. We agree that this is an important question, but ask more generally whether the key components of mutual love could be achieved between humans and sex robots. And, for a second example, whereas Sullins calls love "a powerful emotion," we think of love as not only or primarily being an emotion. Rather, it is a complex set of dispositions, intentions, and—more generally—ways of relating to another person who is the object of love.

In this kind of discussion, love can be thought of or approached in two different ways. One is a strictly scientific way that asks about the neurochemistry, evolutionary history, or adaptive advantages of human love. This approach is taken, for example, by Helen Fisher in her influential work on the science of love, which has been discussed in recent papers about the possibility of creating enhancement-technologies to improve human love relationships.[28] Another approach to understanding love is to instead investigate and try to interpret love under its guise as one of our most cherished human values, as love is understood within the arts and literature, our cultural tradition, and in most philosophical views of love.

The former, more scientific approach tends to incline commentators to take a more instrumental approach to love, whereby love relationships are construed as a means to various other ends (e.g., hedonic satisfaction, health, and longevity).[29] The latter approach is more intimately associated with portraying love as an intrinsic good, or end in itself: as one of the key components of a rich and flourishing human life. The former approach tends to be more "reductive," by asking what neurochemicals and hormones are involved in love, or by asking what adaptive challenges our ancestors solved by acquiring a capacity for love relationships. The latter approach is less reductive. It instead tends to focus on analyzing what ideas and features are typically understood as key aspects of what love is, under the conceptions and associations in light of which people typically value love.[30]

Of course, these two approaches can also be combined. This is the approach Carrie Jenkins takes in her recent book *What Love Is: And What Love Could Be*.[31] Jenkins understands love as having both a biological basis and socially constructed elements. Moreover, it should also be noted that what we just described are trends, rather than necessary commitments anybody who takes either approach necessarily has to accept. Even if one's reflections on love are very strongly influenced by the science and psychology of love, one may nevertheless resist the temptation to reduce romantic love to the behavior and effects, say, of certain neurochemicals or hormones.[32] One may also resist the temptation to see love as primarily having instrumental value.[33]

The approach we favor here is to understand love primarily under its guise as a core human value and component of a good human life. Thus understood, the best way to interpret love is to consider the descriptions, ideas, or associations under which people typically value, seek, or celebrate love. We agree with Sullins that this means that one should consult the philosophy of love—which has a long tradition stretching back all the way to ancient Greek philosophy (e.g., Plato's *Symposium*). But we think the best way to go is to try to isolate clusters of ideas that don't only show up within the philosophy of love, but that have also become part of ordinary common sense, and that are represented in widely familiar tributes to love in art, poetry, and literature.

Using this strategy, we base the rest of our discussion around three clusters of ideas about love that we find represented in philosophy, common sense, arts and literature, and popular culture (e.g., love songs). These are (1) the idea of being "a good match" (or being made for each other), (2) the notion that lovers should value each other in their distinctive particularity, and (3) the ideal of a steadfast commitment on the part of the true lover. We think these are very common aspects of what people value and cherish when they value and celebrate love as an end, or as a value in itself.

Below, we tease out key assumptions underlying these three ideas, as they apply to love in the human case. We ask what a human lover must be like, or able to do, in order to realize these three widely valued aspects of love. Having teased out these assumptions, we turn to the case of sex robots. We transfer the "requirements" applying to participants in mutual human love to sex robots, and consider whether a sex-robot could satisfy these requirements. In so doing, we arrive at what might be called a "job description" spelling out crucial things sex robots would need to be able to do, or be, in order to be able to be an equal party in a romantic relationship realizing the good of mutual love.

12.5   Being "a Good Match": The Idea of Being Made for Each Other

Just as Sullins builds on Plato in his discussion of love and robots, so shall we. Aristophanes's speech on love in Plato's *Symposium* features the poetic myth of eros as "finding one's other half," according to which we wish to return to an original human state in which "the sexes were not two as they are now, but originally three in number; there was man, woman, and the union of the two."[34] Our pursuit of a return to the strength and wholeness of this original state is expressed in our desire for love: "this meeting and melting into one another, this becoming one instead of two, was the very expression of [our] ancient need."[35]

In contemporary language, we talk about two people "being made for each other," or being a "good match." Indeed, one of the most popular websites for finding a romantic partner is called "match.com." This conveys the idea that two lovers are complementary to each other, that they are especially suited to tolerate or even enjoy each other's shortcomings, or that they share a specific set of values, interests, or views of the good life. In Aristotle's classic phrase: "one soul in two bodies."[36]

We want to note here that we're not assuming that the idea of "being a good match," or "complementing each other," requires that one is a good match from day one. Nor are we assuming that it requires being very similar. People can grow/develop together so as to become a good match over time. And it can be that the reason that two people complement each other is partly that they are different in certain ways ("opposites attract"). However, fundamental disagreement in values is likely to be a problem. And fundamental differences in what directions two people could realistically develop are also likely to be problematic. Either people are already a good match when they meet; or they find that they are able to complement each other as they develop together. But they should also, if this idea is to make sense, be able to find that neither are they a good match from the get-go, nor are they so disposed that they could grow to become a good match.

In everyday parlance, when we speak of being made for each other, we are speaking metaphorically, of course. But Levy and others emphasize that a sex-, love-, or companionship-robot could be, literally, custom-made for you. The robot could be designed to be the lover that would be maximally satisfying, attractive—just for you. In this way, the robot could be said to be one's perfect match!

Intuitions about whether or not this scenario is just as desirable as the human-human scenario may vary widely. If you share the intuition that the custom-made robot, no matter how intelligent, is not your perfect match in the same sense a human could be, consider the following thought-experiment: We somehow discover that a deity had uniquely designed our human lover to be our perfect match. Every psychological feature, preference, and habit the deity constructed to satisfy us. Would this undermine the desirability of the match between you and your lover? In essence, this is the Biblical story of Adam and Eve; Eve was created from Adam's rib as a "helper fit for him" (Genesis 2:18).

It seems unlikely that this discovery in our thought-experiment would make the love we have for our lover less valuable or desirable. After all, nothing about the other person has changed, except that we now have a different story of the origin of how our human lover turned out to be such a good fit for us. Of course, the fact that our lover is a product of intentional design might raise doubts about their freedom to have done otherwise than to love us (these concerns will be addressed in section 12.6). However, if we set such doubts aside, intentional design does not seem in itself to be an obvious barrier to full-fledged love. Indeed, the expression "being made for each other" seems to flow out of a conception of human life where each person is a product of design, and each person's life is part of a divine plan.

What remains troubling in the case of the robot lover, and also, but less obviously, in the human case above, is the asymmetry between the lover and the beloved. The robot or the deity-designed lover was made for you; but you were not made for the robot or the deity-designed lover. The idea of being made for *each other* is reciprocal. If one is made for the other, but not visa versa, it seems like the love relationship is unbalanced or unequal. Of course, love doesn't seem to require complete symmetry in this respect. But if you chose a lover who didn't choose you, that is hard to square with the idea of the lovers as completing each other—as coming to recognize each other as being a good match.

Acquiring a robot that is custom-made for you doesn't have to be the only way that human-robot love relations develop, however. A robot might not be custom-made to love you in particular, but might instead be endowed with a general capacity to "fall in love," should the right human come along. If a robot were equipped with the capacity to come to love humans romantically, and you were to come into contact with such a robot, and if love would arise—then this seems quite different than if the robot were designed to be your lover. Two other routes to these relationships spring to mind.

First, you might buy the robot in a store (or more likely on the Internet). But the nature of this robot is that it doesn't automatically love you. You have to be genuinely kind, charming, and loving. You must woo the robot, and may come to earn or merit its love. (This assumes, of course, that the robot is sophisticated enough to be able to distinguish sincere expressions of affection, etc., from false performances.) This might be a little bit like an arranged marriage in which the partners fall in love after being married. Like a human couple that comes to love each after they've moved in together, you and the love-robot that has moved in with you might also come to find that you are able to inspire love in each other. Perhaps you find this by both acting in ways that give evidence of "mutual good-will and agreement in all things, both human and divine."[37]

Or, alternatively, perhaps you might find that this particular robot and you were not made for each other—a possibility that should remain open if the idea of finding that you are a good match is to retain the same associations it has in the human case, where people sometimes find that they were not made to love each other.[38] What is special about love in the human case, under widely shared ideas about love, is at least partly that it can turn out that people are not a good match, which is why it is thought to be such a great good to find that you and your lover are a good match.

A second, and even more futuristic, possibility is that robots with the capacity to fall in love are simply integrated into human society and that humans meet them in the usual ways they meet other humans, perhaps in a bar, or on a dating app like Tinder. These robots could also have different appearances, personalities, and values, which would make them good matches for some people, and less good matches for others.

In either of these two scenarios, there seems to be no obvious principled hindrance to the idea of the human and sex robot finding each other to be "made for each other," and finding their union to constitute a "good match" in the way that human romantic love can be. However, the robot would need to be fairly sophisticated in its functioning for the just-sketched type of reasoning to be applicable. It would need to be a robot to which we can sensibly ascribe the ability to fall in love, as well as the ability to discover that it has not fallen in love, with the person who is hoping to win its love.

12.6 Valuing Each Other in Our Distinctive Particularity

Let us now turn to the second cluster of ideas that tends to feature prominently in discussions of love as a core human value. This cluster of ideas understands love as being directed at the beloved in his or her distinctive particularity. One does not love a person, it is thought, under a description of that person's most estimable properties. Rather, one directly loves and values the person in his or her distinctive particularity.

What we have in mind here is beautifully captured in the renaissance philosopher Michel de Montaigne's essay on his love for his close friend, the humanist poet Étienne de Boétie. Montaigne famously writes that if he is asked why it is that he loved Boétie, the only answer he can give is that it is because "he was he, and I was I."[39] This is one of the classic quotes that are often taken to capture the idea that love homes in on one's beloved in his or her distinctive particularity.[40]

It should not be, then, that one loves one's beloved because of properties that might be better exemplified by somebody else, such that one should transfer one's love to that somebody else if he or she came along (e.g., somebody with nicer looks, more virtues, a more steady financial situation, or whatever). Love ought to be responsive to, and attach to, the particular person in question, even if we recognize that they may have their faults and might not be as ideal as they could be. As the lyrics of the classic big band tune *It Had to Be You* say, "nobody else gave me a thrill/with all your faults, I love you still/it had to be you, wonderful you/it had to be you." Thus, from the lover's point of view, part of what makes loving somebody a special kind of good is that we cherish that particular person, faults and all. And in just the same way, from the recipient's point of view, part of what makes enjoying somebody's love such a great good is that they care about and value us as the particular people we are, faults and all.[41]

This whole idea has both a synchronic and a diachronic aspect to it. What we've just described is the synchronic aspect: here and now, a lover values and cherishes his or her beloved in their distinctive particularity. But there is also a diachronic aspect, which is well-described by Niko Kolodny in his oft-quoted article "Love as Valuing a Relationship." According to Kolodny, the special history that lovers have together should—if all goes well—strengthen and deepen their shared bond. [42]

In other words, it is a distinctive idea associated with the ideal of love that when the lovers get to know each other in their distinctive particularity over time, and they come to build a shared history, this should create for them special reasons. It should create special reasons for valuing each other and valuing their shared relationship that are particular to them and their distinctive history: reasons not shared by anybody else.[43]

Now let us relate this set of ideas to the issue of whether there could be mutual love between humans and sex robots. What would sex robots need to be able to do in order to realize these aspects of the interpersonal good that we typically understand love as being under our shared conceptions of it? As we see things, this cluster of ideas relating to particularity involves a difficult challenge and a slightly less difficult challenge.

To explain what we mean by this, we want to separate the following different elements of the idea of being valued in our particularity by our lovers: first, there is the idea of being responsive to, or tracking, a certain person *in their distinctive particularity*. Second, there is the idea *valuing* or *cherishing* that person in their distinctive particularity.[44]

The less difficult challenge, as we see things, is to build a sex robot that could be responsive to, or track, a person in his or her particularity, both in the synchronic and diachronic senses. It might, for example, be possible for the continued shared history to strengthen the bond between the human lover and the sex robot. It is possible to build a robot that is so constructed that it learns from experience ("machine learning"). This could be used to enable the robot to participate in a form of interaction with its "beloved" that over time acquires more depth in some sense, which could help to facilitate a strengthening of the bond over time. Certainly, this is something Levy speculates about when he predicts the future of human-robot relationships. Of course, the trick here is to conceptualize some way in which the relationship between a human and a sex robot could be "deepened" in a sense that doesn't just mean that the human gets more and more attached to the sex robot over time. It should also somehow involve a mutuality whereby the robot reciprocates as well.

The more difficult challenge is to make sense of the idea of a sex robot as *valuing* or *cherishing* a person in their particularity, and/or as valuing or cherishing a special relationship with a person in its particularity. In other words, we first need an understanding of what it is for a person to value some other person in their particularity, and we then need to explain how it could be possible for a sex robot to enact whatever is involved in doing this.

Offering a fully worked out definition of what it is to value or cherish somebody in their particularity, despite whatever faults they might have, is something that clearly goes beyond the scope of what we can do in the present discussion. However, we wish to note that among some of the most plausible recent philosophical accounts of what is involved in valuing in general, and what is involved in valuing a person in particular, there seems to be broad agreement that valuing is a complex or multifaceted matter. It involves a set of different attitudes, dispositions, thought patterns, judgments, ways of prioritizing, emotional vulnerabilities, and—importantly—the ability to see things and persons as "sources" of reasons.

For example, according to Samuel Scheffler, valuing typically has a "conservative" dimension: we see the conservation and protection of what we value as providing us with reasons to act in ways that help to conserve and protect what we value.[45] According to T. M. Scanlon, to value something is to see ourselves as having reasons to treat it in certain ways distinctive to the particular kind of value we see the thing as having, where different kinds of values call for different kinds of valuing treatment.[46] Valerie Tiberius understands valuing as a robust and durable concern, and also emphasizes that valuing typically involves both affective and cognitive components.[47] According to Harry Frankfurt, when we value a person in the way a lover loves his or her beloved, this involves seeing ourselves as having reasons to promote the well-being and the flourishing of the person we love. This is especially true in the case of parents' love for their children, Frankfurt thinks, but it is also true in the case of romantic love.[48]

We don't think these should all necessarily be seen as rival theories, where we have to choose one theory and reject the others. Rather, we understand these various accounts of valuing as all picking out different aspects of what's typically involved in valuing a thing or a person: it is a highly complex matter. And so if a sex robot is to fully realize this feature of love, it needs to be able to have this very complex set of attitudes and evaluations, and it needs to be able to direct these at a particular person.

Importantly, the robot would need to be able to see its "beloved" as a special source of reasons: as somebody to protect and care for, as somebody whose well-being they should assign special weight and priority, as somebody it particularly wants to be with and strengthen its bond with. In short, the sex robot would need to be able to see things as reasons. It would need to be able to have attitudes of the sort distinctive to attributing a special value to a person.

It would not be enough for it to act as if it has such attitudes, or as if it sees itself as having certain reasons to treat and care for its particular beloved in a special way. If the sex robot is to replicate the distinctive aspect of love we're currently discussing, it also needs to be able to have valuing attitudes. It needs to be able to see itself as having certain special reasons. As we noted above, when it comes to love, what goes on "on the inside" matters.

We call this "the hard part" of what we're presently discussing, not because it is our view that is impossible to create a robot that has these kinds of attitudes, or that makes these kinds of judgments about what it has reason to do. Rather, we call it this because we think that it is clear that a robot capable of doing these things would need to be very advanced, and because it is not very clear how to understand the idea of a robot that has valuing attitudes and that sees itself as having reasons to act in certain ways.

Some philosophers doubt that robots could ever act for reasons, and hold this to be something only human beings could do. Others are much more optimistic about the potential of artificial intelligence to replicate, or even exceed, human intellectual abilities.[49] Whatever the case might be, the artificial intelligence in such a robot would need to be of a very sophisticated sort. We understand this as being hard to achieve, though not necessarily something that is in principle impossible.

12.7   Commitment: Love as a "Robustly Demanding Good"

We come now to the aspect of what we value in valuing human love that might be hardest to achieve in the case of sex robots as potential lovers. We come now to something that is especially hard for the robot to accomplish if it is custom-made for you in particular. And that is a cluster of ideas and associations revolving around the idea of commitment.

To illustrate this idea, let us start with a literary example. Shakespeare's 116th sonnet is famously about a "marriage of true minds." In this sonnet, the bard muses that, "love is not love, which alters, when it alteration finds." This is a poetical musing on the idea of the commitment of a true lover. Love is a commitment, "an ever-fixed mark."

What Shakespeare talks about here is not fixation, or a compulsive obsession. We think of the human lover as being able to do otherwise, but as providing us with a great good in opting for a steadfast commitment. The human ideal of love, in other words, seems to contain an important element directly premised on the notion that human beings have a distinctive kind of free will. This is the kind of free will that consists in the capacity to choose otherwise.[50] And in the case of love, it is committing to stand by our beloved, even though it is possible for us to do otherwise and even though doing otherwise might sometimes be more convenient, that matters specifically.

In a recent philosophical analysis of this aspect of love, Philip Pettit calls this the "robustly demanding" aspect of love. The lover, according to Pettit's analysis, does not just offer care in the actual scenario, here and now. The true lover offers his or her beloved care across various ranges of alternative possibilities and scenarios. In contrast, somebody who just wants us to do them a favor might display a certain amount of care so long as it suits them, so long as it is strategic for them to do so. The lover gives his or her beloved care robustly, and does so because he or she values the beloved, not for any opportunistic instrumental reasons.[51]

This is what we also get in the traditional marriage vows we now typically associate with "love marriages": to have and hold, in good times and bad times, for richer and poorer, in sickness and in health. These are vows of love.

It is a beautiful and wonderful thing when a person—a "free agent"—uses his or her free will in this way in relation to us. We want our lovers to "stand by" us; and because we know they have the option of doing otherwise, it is a beautiful thing when they do so. The soul classic *Stand By Me* is a popular ode to this aspect of love, just like Shakespeare's above-quoted 116th sonnet is.

This whole idea of a free agent's commitment as one of the key aspects of what is valued and so attractive about love in the human case can seem like a big problem when it comes to imagining a corresponding type of mutual love between humans and sex robots. And this is especially true if the robot is custom-made to love you in particular! If it cannot but "love" you, you don't enjoy the good that you enjoy from a human lover when he or she gives you his/her commitment, even though he/she is able to do otherwise.[52]

A robot programmed to stick to you like a fly on a piece of sticky tape is not a lover, but something else. This takes the idea of "an ever-fixed mark" in Shakespeare's sonnet to a point where the thing that is attractive about the love of a human agent with free will falls away: such a robot, unlike its human counterpart, could not do otherwise. Its commitment to you would not have the modal properties of the commitment of a human lover.

As Pettit notes when he discusses the idea of love as a "robustly demanding good," there is a difference between love and "slavish" devotion in the human case—the former is attractive in a way that the latter is not.[53] Michael Kühler argues that a loving relationship, paradoxically, demands both a passive and an active component.[54] As a person being loved, we hope that there is something about us, as individuals, that is loveable, or that provides reasons for, or that causes, our lover to love us.[55] This "passive" component of love is perhaps easier to envision being implemented in a robot. Something unique about the human, we can imagine, triggers or causes the love response in the robot. The "active" component of love is harder to imagine duplicating—because it involves making an active choice. Quoting Erich Fromm, Kühler writes, "[t]o love somebody is not just a strong feeling—it is a decision, it is a judgment, it is a promise."[56] Similarly, Dylan Evans writes that, "[a]lthough people typically want commitment and fidelity from their partners, they want these things to be the fruit of an ongoing choice, rather than inflexible and unreflexive behavior patterns."[57] In

Evans' estimation, this might be very hard to reproduce in the case of a robot-human relationship.[58]

However, we don't want to go as far as to conclude that it is in principle impossible to achieve this aspect of human love in a highly sophisticated and very advanced love robot. As before, our thesis is rather that creating a robot that could recreate this aspect of human love is a very tall order. The robot would have to have a sort of free will. It should be able to represent and consider the option of doing otherwise, while at the same time also having the capacity to commit to a beloved. Perhaps it is possible to create such a robot.

More on this: as we already noted in a footnote above, any not too simple sex robot presumably needs to be a very basic type of agent: it should be able to act in the service of goals (i.e., sex goals), and do so in a way that is responsive to how it represents its situation as being. But it need not be an agent that can exercise agency in any particularly wide range of circumstances. It never needs, so to speak, to know what to do outside of the bedroom.

However, a sex robot that could also be a love robot would seemingly need to be able to exercise agency of much richer and more domain-general forms than those required of simpler sex robots exclusively intended for sexual purposes. Just consider the human case. A human lover may not need to know what to do/how to conduct him- or herself across all contingencies that could possibly arise. Nevertheless, we expect the human lover to be able to give love (or its more specific components, such as care and affection) across various different contexts and situations.[59] A love robot that could replicate this aspect of human love would need to be a very sophisticated agent whose agency is domain-general and flexible to a very substantial extent. It would need to be sophisticated as an agent in a way that a robot only performing sexual functions would never need to be.

12.8 A "Job Description" for Love Robots

Our look at the three clusters of widely shared ideas about love (under its guise as a core human value) has generated a number of qualifications a sex robot that could participate in relationships of mutual romantic love would need to have. As noted above, this might be called a "job description" that a robot-lover would need to live up to. These qualifications that are part of the job description have been teased out as presuppositions underlying the three clusters of ideas and associations we've discussed above.

In relation to the idea of being a good match or being made for each other, we have argued that that notion makes most sense when it is understood as involving the idea that people have the ability to fall in love, after which they might find that they are indeed a good match: that they, as it is sometimes put, complete each other. But it should also be an open possibility that the potential lover (be it a human or a robot) might not come to love a certain prospective partner. So if a sex robot is to live up to the standard of a human lover who is found to be a good match for somebody, then the sex robot should also have the ability to fall in love—or to sometimes fail to do so. It should not just automatically be preset to love the human being in question. That is too one-sided for the idea of mutual love as a good match between two different parties to be realized in the relationship between the sex robot and the human together with whom it is supposed to enjoy mutual love.

In relation to the idea of valuing one's lover in his or her particularity, we isolated two things a person—as well as a sex robot—needs to be able to do: they need to be able to be responsive to somebody *in their particularity*, and they need to be able to *value* or *cherish* a person. We noted that as philosophers typically explain the latter idea—which seems to be the more demanding of the two—this is typically taken to involve a complex set of dispositions and attitudes. Most important among these attitudes or dispositions is the capacity to see oneself as having certain reasons. In particular, the capacity to see one's beloved and one's relationship to one's beloved as sources of special reasons is typically represented as very important. Thus, a sex robot that is to play the part of a human lover and participate in a relationship of mutual love ought to be able to have and act on these kinds of attitudes and dispositions. It too should be able to see itself as having special reasons arising from the beloved and from its relationship and shared history with the beloved.

Lastly, the ideal of a commitment presupposes a sort of free will, namely, the capacity to resolve to remain steadfast even as we are able to do otherwise. When people value commitment, they value the idea of the lover making a free choice in favor of the beloved, where it is an open possibility for the lover to make other choices. And when the lover acts on this loving commitment, and offers love robustly, this amounts to giving the beloved the sorts of care and affection we associate with love across various different situations and scenarios, in different domains of activity and shared experiences. So a sex robot that is to give a human lover the kind of commitment associated with love needs to be able to do otherwise, and yet choose to give love. It needs to be able to act as a lover does across wide ranges of situations and scenarios, not only performing sexual acts within the context of sexual situations.

As we have noted above, we don't think that it is in principle impossible for a highly sophisticated sex robot, with a very advanced form of artificial intelligence, to achieve these different feats. However, the move from imagining the possibility to realizing an actuality seems to be a big one. The job description for a sex robot that could enter into a relationship of mutual love that would match with the human ideal of mutual romantic love is highly demanding. By today's standards, a robot that could meet these qualifications would be truly amazing.

Of course, there is the option of lowering the bar: making the demands of mutual love less demanding. But this would mean that we would move away from some of the things people find most valuable and most appealing about mutual romantic love, as we conceive of it in the human case. So we have a dilemma here: *either* we make it easier for sex robots to enter into relationships with humans that we call instances of mutual love, which would rob the love of key aspects of what we most value about romantic love; *or* we would stick to our common conceptions of what is involved in mutual love, which would make it very hard for a sex robot to live up to the ideals associated with mutual romantic love, as we typically conceive of it.

12.9 Conclusion: Is Trying to Develop Love Robots Worth It?

The conclusion we just reached raises the following question: Should we to devote time, energy, and resources to develop sex robots advanced enough that they could live up to the job description associated with participating in a mutual love relationship of the sort we associate with the human ideal of love? The last thing we will do is to consider one "no" answer and one "yes" answer to this question.

As with the development of any new technology that has the potential to be socially disruptive, we urge caution and careful ethical examination prior to and continuing through the research-and-development process. The consequences and techno-moral change that will potentially accompany the advancement of robots that can love and be loved is very difficult to predict. But a "no" answer to the question of whether we should invest in the creation of love robots should not be based on mere conservatism with respect to love relationships, unjustified preference for the natural over the artificial, or an unsupported fear of the potential risks. Any such answer, in our view, should rather be based on an "opportunity cost" argument: that is, if it can be shown that the time, energy, and resources could be better spent on other, more easily attainable endeavors, then those other projects should perhaps be favored over something as relatively far-fetched as sex robots advanced enough to participate in relationships of mutual love along the lines described in the previous sections.

As noted above, two of the potential benefits of upgrading sex robots to be potential love robots are, first, that they may provide an answer to the criticism that love robots promote objectification. However, there might be much simpler and more straightforward ways of avoiding the objectification that comes with the creation and use of sex robots. For example, as the campaign to stop their development calls for, we could simply not make them (at one extreme). Less dramatically, we could engage in a society-wide discussion of the ways in which sex robots might reify gender stereotypes and enlarge objectification of women as part of the larger feminist project of changing culture, individual attitudes, and social structures, so as to reduce sexism.

A second purported benefit of upgraded sex robots also capable of loving and being loved is that they could mean the creation of additional value in people's lives. This would be especially important for people who have difficulty finding a human lover, and seemingly supports a "yes" answer to the question of whether we should try to develop love robots. We regard participating in loving relationships as an important part of a flourishing human life. And if indeed there are significant numbers of humans who are unloved by other humans, then in that case the development of love robots seems like a worthy investment. Nevertheless, this motivation loses some of its force when we consider the alternatives for finding love for the unloved. Being unloved does not have to be seen as equivalent to having a disability or physical limitation that requires a prosthesis or a wheelchair to enable the person to exercise the capabilities they find valuable. A better use of resources might be to investigate why people cannot find love, or to change to way we make our social arrangements, including how we raise our children, to make it more likely that they will find a satisfying loving relationship.

Yet, if love is intrinsically valuable, this would give us reason to think that the development of love robots would be a good thing. There might simply be more love in the world with their introduction. More people could be in loving, stable relationships. Even if love is not intrinsically, but only instrumentally, valuable, a world with more of these types of relationships would seem to involve all kinds of beneficial side-effects. People who are loved will be psychologically and physically healthier, and may be disposed to be more peaceful, less violent, better people all around.[60]

Notes

The authors contributed equally to this chapter.

1. See   http://www.theatlantic.com/health/archive/2013/09/married-to-a-doll-why-one-man-advocates-synthetic-love/279361.

2. We should note up front that we will be talking about a Western, fairly modern conception of love. We are interested in ideas about romantic love (under its guise as a value) that are widely shared. But we are not assuming that the ideas we discuss would necessarily be universally accepted across all different societies and time periods.

3. What about unrequited love? Could a human harbor unrequited love for a robot, and if so, would it be genuine love? In the human case, we think unrequited love can be seen as a genuine form of love, albeit of an incomplete or unfulfilled sort. At least when it comes to the sort of love we are interested in here, romantic love—as we understand it—contains a wish to also be loved by the object of our love. This means that if a robot could not possibly love a human being, then there would be something both inherently confused and tragic about romantically loving a robot in an unrequited way: it could not possibly fulfill the wish to be loved back.

4. By "sex robots" in what follows, we understand humanoid robots with which human beings can perform different sorts of sexual acts: robots that look like humans, equipped with more or less advanced forms of artificial intelligence that allow them to perform more or less complex forms of sexual agency (cf. John Danaher, "Robotic Rape and Robotic Child Sex Abuse: Should They be Criminalized?," *Criminal Law and Philosophy* 11, no. 1 (2017): 71–95, doi: 10.1007/s11572-014-9362-x, 72). By "agency" we here understand the ability to pursue purposes in light of representations that regulate the ways in which those goals are pursued. As Philip Pettit notes, this is a "more or less received" philosophical understanding of what agency amounts to, on which fairly simple robots could easily qualify as agents of at least basic kinds (Pettit, "Responsibility Incorporated," *Ethics* 117 (2007): 171–201, 178).

5. Blay Whitby, "Do You Want a Robot Lover? The Ethics of Caring Technologies," in *Robot Ethics: The Ethical and Social Implications of Robotics*, eds. Patrick Lin, Keith Abney, and George Bekey (Cambridge, MA: MIT Press, 2012), 233–248, 262.

6. Whitby, "Do You Want a Robot Lover?," 262; John Danaher, "Robotic Rape and Robotic Child Sex Abuse: Should They be Criminalized?," *Criminal Law and Philosophy* 11, no. 1 (2017): 71–95, doi: 10.1007/s11572-014-9362-x.

7. Whitby, "Do You Want a Robot Lover?," 263.

8. For critical discussion, see Danaher, Earp, and Sandberg, in this volume. Also see https://campaignagainstsexrobots.org/about.

9. We use the terms "prostitute" and "prostitution" here instead of sex workers/sex work because the Campaign uses this language. Some feminist schools of thought prefer the term "prostitution" over "sex work" because they may see the term "sex work" as a way of legitimizing the practice as any other form of labor. For a discussion of this issue see, for example: Frédérique Delacoste and Priscilla Alexander, eds., *Sex Work: Writings by the Women in the Sex Industry* (Berkeley, CA: Cleis Press, 1998) and Laurie Bell, *Good Girls/Bad Girls: Feminists and Sex Trade Workers Face to Face* (Seattle, WA: Seal Press, 1987).

10. Kimberlee Richardson, "The Assymmetrical Relationship: Parallels Between Prostitution and the Development of Sex Robots," *SIGCAS Computers & Society* 45, no. 3 (2015): 290–293.

11. Sinziana Gutiu, "Sex Robots and Roboticization of Consent," *We Robot* 2012 Conference, p. 2, http://robots.law.miami.edu/wp-content/uploads/2012/01/Gutiu-Roboticization_of_Consent.pdf.

12. Jennifer Robertson, "Gendering Humanoid Robots: Robo-Sexism in Japan," *Body & Society* 16 (2010): 21–36.

13. We do not wish to suggest that the only way of having a non-objectifying, non-dehumanizing, and nonsexist sexual relationship is to have love be part of the picture. We can also imagine non-objectifying, etc., forms of sexual relationships without love. The point here is rather that one of the key ways in which sexual relationships can be non-objectifying, etc., is when the parties romantically love each other.

14. Taking this sort of thinking one step further, John Sullins thinks that love also adds a potential for mutual moral self-improvement ("erotic wisdom") of a sort that cannot be achieved in relationships "only satisfying physical desire." See John Sullins, "Robots, Love, and Sex: The Ethics of Building a Love-Machine," *IEEE Transactions on Affective Computing* 3, no. 4 (2012): 398–409, 398.

15. Of course, it should be noted in this context that some people take a rather different view, namely, that sex with no strings attached is the best kind. For example, Erica Jong's 1973 novel *Fear of Flying* is associated with this idea.

16. David Levy, *Love and Sex with Robots* (London: Harper, 2008).

17. Levy, *Love and Sex*, 341.

18. Ibid., 128–132.

19. Ibid., 11–12.

20. Mark Coeckelberg, "Artificial Companions: Empathy and Vulnerability-Mirroring in Human-Robot Relations," *Studies in Ethics, Law, and Technology* 4, no. 3 (2010): 1–17, 4.

21. Coeckelbergh, "Artificial Companions," 7.

22. John Sullins, "Robots, Love, and Sex," 408.

23. Ibid.

24. Whitby, "Do You Want a Robot Lover?", 261, 265.

25. Ibid., 25. We think that altering our understanding of love is not necessarily a bad thing. Our present ideal of love has a history behind it; our current notions are the result of an evolution of ideas and influences from various different sources, including Renaissance ideas about ideal friendships. We cannot be certain that the ideal of love future generations will embrace will exactly line up with what we cherish in valuing love today. (See Brian D. Earp, Anders Sandberg, and Julian Savulescu, "The Medicalization of Love: Response to Critics," *Cambridge Quarterly of Healthcare Ethics* 24, no. 4: 759–771; Sven Nyholm "Love Troubles: Human Attachment and Biomedical Enhancements," *Journal of Applied Philosophy* 32, no. 2 (2015): 190–202,). Even so, what we are interested in here is whether love can be achieved between humans and sex robots under our current conceptions of what love is and should be.

26. Michael Hauskeller, *Sex and the Posthuman Condition* (London: Palgrave Macmillan, 2014).

27. We should note here that in the end, our conclusion can be said to be a tentative endorsement of Levy's overall conclusion, namely, that love between humans and sex robots is a possibility. The view of love we base that conclusion on, however, is different from the conception Levy bases his arguments on. And our confidence that love could be achieved is much weaker than Levy's.

28. Helen Fisher, *Why We Love: The Nature and Chemistry of Romantic Love* (New York: Henry Holt, 2004); Julian Savulescu and Anders Sandberg, "Neuroenhancement of Love and Marriage: The Chemicals Between Us," *Neuroethics* 1 (2008): 405–413; Brian Earp, Anders Sandberg, and Julian Savulescu, "Natural Selection, Childrearing, and the Ethics of Marriage: Building a Case for the Neuroenhancement of Human Relationships," *Philosophy and Technology* 25 (2012): 561–587.

29. Savulescu and Sandberg, "Neuroenhancement of Love and Marriage."

30. Nyholm, "Love Troubles"; Sven Nyholm, "The Medicalization of Love and Narrow and Broad Conceptions of Human Well-being," *Cambridge Quarterly of Healthcare Ethics* 24, no. 3 (2015b): 337–46.

31. Carrie Jenkins, *What Love Is: And What Love Could Be* (New York: Basic Books, 2017).

32. Julian Savulescu and Brian Earp, "Neuroreductionism about Sex and Love," *Think* 13, no. 38 (2014): 7–12.

33. See also Earp, Sandberg, and Savulescu, "The Medicalization of Love: Response to Critics." That being said, science-inspired writers like Levy—who show great enthusiasm for the prospect of love between humans and sex robots—do seem more strongly inclined to reductive and instrumental understandings of love.

34. Additionally, some beings were a union of two men and others of two women.

35. Plato, *Collected Works of Plato* (Oxford: Oxford University Press, 1953).

36. Laertius Diogenes, *Lives of the Eminent Philosophers* (Cambridge, MA: Harvard University Press, 1925).

37. Marcus T. Cicero, *On Old Age. On Friendship. On Divination.* (Cambridge, MA: Harvard University Press, 1923). As we already clarified above, we are not assuming that two lovers necessarily need to experience their union as a good match from the start. It may be that they have a potential to grow and change together so as to become a good match, and that it takes some time before they get there.

38. Two people can find that not only are they a bad match from the start—they may also lack an ability to grow to love each other, no matter what they do and how hard they try. In the human case, this is something most people regard as a genuine possibility. In the case of some people, as the saying goes, "it just wasn't meant to be."

39. Michel de Montaigne, *The Complete Essays of Montaigne* (Palo Alto, CA: Stanford University Press, 1958).

40. As noted above, some of the key ideas we today associate with romantic love came out of the tradition of theorizing about close friendships. Montaigne's reflections about friendship are one such source. Aristotle's and Cicero's reflections on close friendships are two other such sources.

41. In the case of humans and sex robots, this cuts both ways. It should not just be that the robot could love the human despite faults the human might have, despite the fact that other humans might better exemplify whatever positive qualities the human harbors. In the same way, the person should be able to love the robot, despite whatever faults it might have, and not only because of its contingent properties, which might be better exemplified by some other robot. The worry here is that the person loves the robot because it has set of features XYZ, so that if the robot were to change and start to exhibit features ABC, the person would presumably no longer love it. They might even send it back to the store for a repair or a refund.

42. Niko Kolodny, "Love as Valuing a Relationship," *Philosophical Review* 112, no. 2 (2003): 135–189.

43. Ibid.

44. Both of these ideas can, in turn, be understood in both the synchronic and diachronic ways: being responsive to, or valuing, a certain person in their particularity here and now ("synchronic" part), and tracking, or valuing, a certain person based on the particular shared history we have together with them ("diachronic" part).

45. Samuel Scheffler, *Death and the Afterlife* (Oxford: Oxford University Press, 2013).

46. Thomas M. Scanlon, *What We Owe to Each Other* (Cambridge, MA: Harvard University Press, 1998).

47. Valerie Tiberius, *The Reflective Life* (Oxford: Oxford University Press, 2008).

48. Harry Frankfurt, *The Reasons of Love* (Princeton, NJ: Princeton University Press, 2004).

49. For example: R. A. Brooks, *The Future of Flesh and Machines* (London: Penguine, 2003); Michael Kühler, "Loving Persons: Activity and Passivity in Romantic Love," in *Love and Its Objects*, eds. C. Maurer et al. (London: Palgrave Macmillan, 2014), 41–55; Hans Moravec, *Robot: Mere Machine to Transcendent Mind* (Oxford: Oxford University Press, 1998).

50. Of course, what exactly is meant by "free will" is a highly disputed issue. However, there is broad agreement that one of the most widely shared connotations of this expression is the idea of a capacity to do otherwise. (Timothy O'Connor, "Free Will," in *Stanford Encyclopedia of Philosophy*, ed. Edward N. Zalta (2016), http://plato.stanford.edu/archives/sum2016/entries/freewill. (Entry originally published in 2002 and revised in 2010.)

51. Philip Pettit, *The Robust Demands of the Good* (Oxford: Oxford University Press, 2015), ch. 1.

52. Michael Hauskeller, *Sex and the Posthuman Condition* (London: Palgrave MacMillan, 2014).

53. Pettit, *The Robust Demands*, 19.

54. Kühler, "Loving Persons," 41–55.

55. Ibid.; see also Nyholm, "Love Troubles," 196.

56. Kühler, "Loving Persons," quoting Erich Fromm, *The Art of Loving* (New York: Harper, 2006), 52.

57. Dylan Evans, "Wanting the Impossible: The Dilemma at the Heart of Intimate Human-Robot Relationships," in *Close Engagements with Artificial Companions*, ed. Yorick Wilks (Amsterdam: John Benjamins, 2010): 75–89.

58. In the same vein, Hauskeller writes: "We do not want people to love us because they have been hypnotized or enchanted (like Shakespeare's fairy queen Titania who is made to fall in love with a donkey-headed weaver)." (Hauskeller, *Sex and the Posthuman Condition*). Nor, thinks Hauskeller, would we want a robot to love us because it was programmed to do so.

59. Pettit, *The Robust Demands*, ch. 1.

60. Thanks to John Danaher for his helpful feedback.

VI The Future of Robot Sex

What does the future hold for robot sex? The chapters in this section attempt to offer some predictions, with the authors drawing where they can on available empirical data. Scheutz and Arnold kick things off in chapter 13 by describing the results of their recent survey on attitudes toward sex robots. They argue that future discussions about the ethics of sexbots need to move beyond sexuality to intimacy. Carpenter takes a more expansive view in chapter 14, exploring how people may become attached to robot sex workers (her preferred terminology), how we may come to accept them in society, and explicitly contrasting Mori's Uncanny Valley with her own Robot Accommodation Process Theory. Finally, in chapter 15, Adshade closes out the book as whole by looking at the topic of robot-induced social change. She predicts that the introduction of sex robots will have significant impacts upon marriage and human intimacy. She makes her case by using lessons from previous advances in the technology of sex.

13 Intimacy, Bonding, and Sex Robots: Examining Empirical Results and Exploring Ethical Ramifications

Matthias Scheutz and Thomas Arnold

13.1 Introduction and Motivation

Many advances in communicative technology have served to represent and express human sexuality: the printing press, motion pictures, and, not the least, the Internet. Social robotics, however, while not yet a mainstream contributor, is particularly poised to represent, enact, and affect society's sexual mores and practices. Sex robots are already manufactured and marketed by several companies, with increasing variety and capability being at least promised if not delivered.[1] And although virtual reality and other computer-based avenues for sexual use are also developing rapidly, sex robots—embodied, mobile, and (to a limited degree) expressive—elicit and trade upon dimensions of physicality, intimacy, reciprocity, and social space. Robots both reflect and refract notions of what human bodies are, how they interact, touch, desire, and accompany one another. The prospect of sex robots assuming a greater presence in our societies underscores the general ethical questions raised by social robots: How will people be able to live with such robots? How will people treat each other as a result? Will social robots replace human beings in ways they should not?

In the last decade, scholars have begun to draw together and analyze major issues at the particular intersection of robots and sexual ethics. Levy explores how robots could meet and transform human sexual needs, possibly beneficially.[2] A range of perspectives across philosophy, psychology, and computer science—from generally appreciative to deeply skeptical—have sought to spell out how love, vulnerability, and other emotional facets of sexuality could make sense in human-robot contexts.[3] More recently, debates have heated up over to what degree sex robots could exacerbate the exploitation of women, in particular sex workers.

What these discussions have so far lacked is a systematic empirical survey of people's opinions, however familiar they may be with the technology or its challenges. While polling does not settle ethical debates, arguments with empirical assumptions about people's social views and reactions toward social robots should not remain untethered by actual views of the public. Seeing where those opinions lie can help to describe the society into which new developments in robotics may be introduced, perhaps by flagging important moral intuitions that could affect how the use of sex robots will unfold on a societal level (for example, who presently would be likely to use them and for what purpose). It can enhance ethical arguments to consider how a number of actual people currently regard the notions being discussed.

To that end, we recently presented the first systematic survey of views on the use of sex robots.[4] Inquiring as to what kind of uses, forms, and context would be appropriate or not for sex robots, we found significant differences of gender and interesting points of convergence. In this chapter, we present and discuss the results of a second survey, which expands upon our initial survey with additional questions about possible advantages and disadvantages of sex robots. We show our second survey generally reproduces the gender differences highlighted by the first, and also reveals important shared senses for how robots affect relationships in society. We explore in closer detail some of these specific takes, and surmise that ethical discussions of sex robots must facilitate finer-grained discussions of relationships and context than have been conducted so far. In particular, we conclude that notions of intimacy and companionship—inherent in social robotics in general—must overtake narrower discussions of sexuality, robots, and "sex robots."

13.2   Background

Sex robots, however their development will proceed going forward, are a present-day reality.[5] It is on the basis of products like Roxxxy and others (particularly in Japan) that some have gone so far as to forecast human-robot sex will overtake mere human sex by 2050.[6] And in this light, some commentators have imagined a much greater range of offerings for robotic sex, for example, ones more geared to women.[7] Perhaps sensing that the market might take shape more quickly than any ethical resolutions, SoftBank took the measure of requiring users to promise not to use its social robot Pepper for sexual purposes (McCurry, 2015).

Still, there has been considerable scholarly effort to catch up to where these products promise to lead. Levy's sustained treatment *Love and Sex With Robots* factors in a wide array of contexts and genuine sexual needs that robots could serve. Others have sought to tease out how love, companionship, and vulnerability may factor into a person's attempt to create sexual intimacy with a robot.[9] There has also been a more applied comparison of how sexual interaction could serve legitimate needs when viewed along-side other contexts of social robotics.[10]

More recent momentum in the ethics of human-robot sexual interaction has built upon the threat of increased exploitation of human beings. The *Campaign Against Sex Robots* has featured strong articulations of how sex with robots could degrade respect for human sex workers, if not women more generally.[10] Such a stance has resonated with legal arguments that human-robot sex could erode notions of consent within society as a whole,[11] along with cultural criticism that views robot design as geared to meet heterosexual male needs, including sexuality, almost exclusively.[12] The prospect of an abusive backlash toward human beings has led to careful sorting of what type of sexual behavior causes what kind of social harm.[13]

Not yet fully integrated into such discussions is relevant work in human-robot inter-action (HRI) on intimacy and bonding, which suggests that social robots—sex robots included—could induce powerful, if manipulative, expectations of reciprocity and con-nection.[14] Other empirical work in HRI suggests that even basic forms of touching, whether by or of a robot, may arouse a person in certain contexts.[15]

Despite these contributions, ethical discussions of sex robots have lacked any survey of what people actually think about their use. We recently presented the first survey of that kind, asking through Amazon Mechanical Turk about appropriate uses, forms of robot, contexts for use, and whether one would oneself use a sex robot (Scheutz and Arnold, 2016). We found significant differences in how appropriate men and women regarded using a sex robot, with men more approving and women less so almost across the board. On the other hand, men and women shared a general sense for what capa-bilities a sex robot would have, a particular form that would be inappropriate (e.g., child), and certain contexts where a sex robot would be more appropriate than not (e.g., extreme isolation, sexual harassment training).

In order to build on this initial sketch, we sought a survey that could look in closer detail at what aspect of sexual interaction with robots informed people's judgments on their use, both for individuals and society at large.

13.3 Methods

We employed the overall design, materials, and procedure from our HRI (Human-Robot Interaction conference) 2016 survey, with a few extensions we will briefly summarize below.

Materials: The survey consisted of several parts. The first and the last part consisted of the same sixteen background questions about possible capabilities of sex robots in order to better understand how people construed sex robots in terms of their properties and capabilities, and to ensure that subjects answered those questions carefully; significant differences in answers before and after the other parts would either indicate that subjects changed their minds or that they did not pay attention to the questions in the first place. The second part consisted of fifteen questions on what subjects took to be appropriate uses of sex robots, while the ten questions of the third part were aimed at allowable physical forms for sex robots. Part four then asked eleven questions about possible advantages of sex robots, followed by part five with eight questions about possible disadvantages, and part six with eleven questions about subjects' general views on sex robots. Note that we specifically refrained from priming subjects with either images or descriptions of sex robots, or suggestions of what it might mean to have sex with a sex robot. We also intentionally did not include any definition of "sex" for the same reason, i.e., to allow subjects to express their own views through their selection of answers.

Participants: We recruited 203 US subjects from AMT; five were eliminated due to incomplete data, leaving 114 males and 84 females. Their overall mean age was 34.11 years, with male mean age being 34 and female mean age being 34.24 years. The minimum age was 18, the maximum age 63 years. None of the participants had participated in the study before.

Procedure: Before the experiment began, participants were informed of the purpose of the study, namely to collect information about their views on sex robots, and they were also warned that they might find some questions emotionally disturbing. Once informed consent was received, a basic demographic questionnaire with subject age and gender had to completed. Then participants were shown the above-described parts in order, with questions within each part randomly rearranged to avoid any possible order effects, and with one question asked at a time.

13.4 Results

We start with a comparison of the current experimental results with the HRI 2016 survey results for (1) the expected capabilities of sex robots; (2) appropriate uses of sex robots; and (3) allowable forms of sex robots. Then we present new data on subjects' views regarding possible advantages and disadvantages of sex robots, as well as general statements about sex robots.

13.4.1   Expected Capabilities of Sex Robots

Table 13.1 shows the background information from the HRI 2016 study, as well as the before and after ratings of the current study. Overall subjects' construals of sex robots' properties are very similar, both compared across the two studies, as well as compared within the current study. Note that that before and after background data in the current survey are similar to within 10%, suggesting that subjects read the questions carefully and consistently answered them, with a slight bias possibly toward being more inclined to attribute cognitive abilities such as "can recognize objects," "can understand language," or "remembers past interactions" in the post-survey ratings compared to the pre-survey ratings.

13.4.2   Appropriate Uses of Sex Robots

Figure 13.1 compares subjects' ratings of appropriate uses of sex robots in the HRI 2016 study and the current study. As can be seen by the overlapping standard error intervals, there is no significant difference between subjects' ratings of appropriate uses in the

Table 13.1
Background questions about the subjects' views on what sex robots are capable of, and percentages of subjects who agreed with the capabilities on the HRI16 data before the current and after the current sex robots questions.

Is Robot Capable of Attribute	% HRI 2016	% Before	% After
Can hear.	38	44	49
Can see.	36	39	43
Can recognize objects.	44	46	52
Can understand language.	49	52	61
Can talk.	53	51	57
Can remember past interactions.	37	45	55
Can be instructed.	78	84	86
Can learn new behaviors.	49	59	63
Moves by itself.	79	77	74
Adapts to human behavior.	53	52	59
Recognizes human emotions.	20	26	24
Specifically designed to satisfy human sexual desire.	86	92	85
Can take initiative.	27	22	26
Has feelings.	11	7	10
Responds to touch.	64	68	69
Obeys orders.	69	79	81

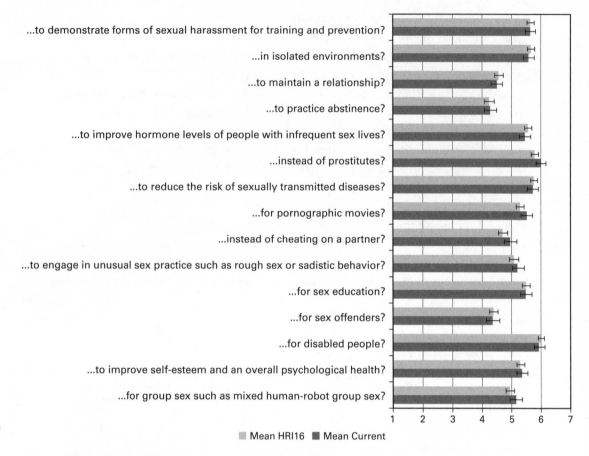

Figure 13.1
Comparison of appropriate uses between HRI 2016 data and the current data showing that there are no significant differences in subjects' views of appropriate uses. Ratings are on a scale from 1="completely inappropriate" to 7="completely appropriate." Error bars depict standard errors.

two studies. The current study does perfectly replicate previous findings about appropriate uses of sex robots.

13.4.3 Appropriate Forms of Sex Robots

Figure 13.2 compares subjects' ratings of appropriate forms in the HRI 2016 study and the current study. As can be seen by overlapping standard error intervals, there is no significant difference between subjects' ratings of appropriate forms in most cases in the two studies, except for "fantasy creature," which the HRI 2016 rated as slightly more appropriate. However, given that the difference less than 0.5 on the scale of 7,

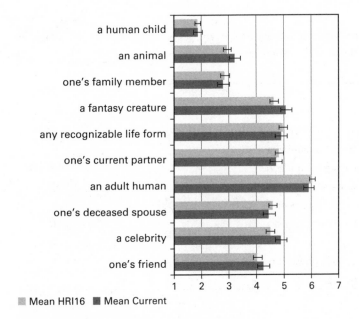

Figure 13.2
Comparison of appropriate forms between HRI 2016 data and the current data showing that there are no significant differences in subjects' views of appropriate forms. Ratings are on a scale from 1="completely inappropriate" to 7="completely appropriate." Error bars depict standard errors.

and both ratings are clearly on the appropriate side, this small numeric difference does likely not signify any important difference overall in conceptualization, thus showing that the current study also replicated all HRI 2016 findings for appropriate forms of sex robots.

13.4.4   Possible Advantages of Sex Robots

Table 13.2 shows the percentage of subjects agreeing with the various possible advantages of sex robots. Not suprisingly, most agreement is obtained with questions about the prevention of disease transmission, sex availabilty around the clock, and the lack of psychological impact on the sex partner. Similarly, people disagreed with sex robots possibly enabling legal underage sex. Opinions were more split on questions the effects of sex robots on people's sex lives, as well as emotional and physical harm.

13.4.5   Possible Disadvantages of Sex Robots

Table 13.3 shows the percentage of subjects agreeing with the various possible disadvantages of sex robots. Except for people's strong disagreement with their possible

Table 13.2
Questions about the subjects' views on the possible advantages of sex robots, and percentages of subjects who agreed with the possible advantages.

Advantages	% Agree
No disease transmission.	92
Sex is available anytime.	80
No psychological impact on the sex partner (i.e., the robot).	72
No physical pain suffered from human behavior.	62
Allow people to expand their sexual horizon.	59
Provide people with companionship.	59
Improve people's sex lives with other people.	54
Allow people to experience better orgasms.	47
Cheaper sex.	43
More predictable and less clumsy physical behavior, meaning less injury.	41
Underage sex is possible and legal.	19

Table 13.3
Questions about the subjects' views on the possible advantages of sex robots and percentages of subjects who agreed with the possible advantages.

Disdvantages	% Agree
Might harm relationships with other humans (e.g., abusive, controlling, hatred for other humans).	70
Sex with the robot will become addictive.	68
Transfer unrealistic expectations to humans, leading to disappointment or abuse.	66
Robots could hurt people if they don't function right.	58
Emotional bonds might form beyond the sexual act.	40
Take out frustrations with robots onto humans.	33
The robots might be too good, people won't go back to humans.	32
Robots will be able to exploit people.	6

exploitation by sex robots, the overall ratings here are not as strong as with the possible advantages. People somewhat agree that sex robots could cause harm to human relationships and might be addictive, possibly leading to unrealistic expectation in the human case. And they slightly disagree that sex robots might become so good that people will not go back to human sex, although this is, of course, a speculative question, since we cannot know whether this is true without having advanced sex robots.

13.4.6 General Views of Sex Robots

Table 13.4 shows the percentage of subjects agreeing with various general statements about sex robots. The strongest agreement (which was overall fairly modest) was that sex with a sex robot does not violate any law, while the strongest disagreement to any question was about whether sex robots ought to have rights: only 6% of all subjects agreed with this statement. Overall, we found a split on questions such as whether one could fall in love with a sex robot, whether a sex robot must always oblige or should only be used for sex, whether any action is allowed with a sex robot, and whether one can cheat with a sex robot. Again, subjects did not agree with legal underage sex with a sex robot, and they most disagreed that sex robots would free humans from human sexual relationships. Interestingly, and different from the HRI 2016 data where subjects found sex with a sex robot more like masturbation than having sex, subjects in the

Table 13.4

Questions about the subjects' general views on sex robots and percentages of subjects who agreed with the statements.

True of sex robots	% Agree
Having sex with a robot does not violate any law.	71
One cannot rape a sex robot.	62
People could fall in love with sex robots.	50
A sex robot must always oblige and should never reject a person.	47
A sex robot should only be used for sex.	44
Any action (e.g., hitting), including dismantling it, is allowed with a sex robot.	42
One cannot cheat on a human with a sex robot.	40
People will treat a sex robot like a human lover.	37
Sex robots will free human relationships from sexual pressure.	32
Sex with a sex robot is not really sex and does not count as sex.	30
Underage sex with a sex robot is legal.	22
Sex robots should have rights.	6

current study disagreed more with the idea that sex with a sex robot is not really sex and does not count as sex (we will return to this discrepancy shortly).

13.5   Discussion

The current study almost perfectly replicated overall findings from our previous HRI 2016 study on appropriate forms and uses of sex robots. Looking over the results with respect to possible advantages and disadvantages of sex robots, as well as general statements about sex robots, the priority of human social relationships could have determined the places where subjects were either strongly in agreement or strongly in disagreement with the statements.

To begin with, the advantages of sex robots mostly strongly identified involve the avoidance of harms and inconvenience, like disease, infrequency, and pain (whether physical or psychological). Next are benefits arguably more geared to the human participant alone (as opposed to another human partner), though companionship and expanded sexual horizon feed into similar support for "improving sex lives with other people" (59% approving).While some have argued that robots could help educate the young in their incipient sexuality, there was decided disapproval of that as an advantage (only 19% approving). Use in the context of adult sexual lives that help oneself and others seems safer ground.

The disadvantages reported go hand in hand with the idea that harm/benefit to relationships, not to individual users alone, is the prime ethical benchmark in judging sexual interaction with robots. The strongest agreement dealt with the risk of abuse of other human beings, harming relationships through malformed expectations, frustration, or disappointment. Even the identification of sex addiction, while putatively about the "addict," could be as easily associated with relationships threatened by such addiction as the experience of the individual alone.

Interestingly, some common ideas about bonding and robot interaction in the scholarly literature and the mainstream press do not seem shared by the subjects. Emotional bonding beyond sex with the robots is not, for example, a threat most subjects shared, nor the risk that superior robot performance will render human-human sex inferior (making the 2050 prediction from the literature seem even bolder). Moreover, the idea that the robot will exploit the human is almost wholly rejected. Whether these last results say more about the presumed state of the technology on the part of the subjects, or speak to a more permanent skepticism that humans could fall prey to robot manipulation, is still an open question.

Finally, the feedback from the general statements about sex robots is arguably hazier than that of advantages and disadvantages, though there are points to note and more to flag for follow-up. For one thing, the attribution of agency to the robot seems muted, which suggests that future debates around social robots need to specify how "autonomous" the social robots in question will be. Robots are not thought of as able to exploit the human with whom they interact. This matches a refusal to think of robots as having rights, another interesting empirical check on some future projections or assumptions about anthropomorphism and legal rights.[17]

More broadly, these results bear upon an implication from our previous study: the ethical challenge of "sex robots" may hinge as much on the social and relational dynamics that overlap with sexuality than human-robot sex per se. As noted, the impact on relationships appears to thread through many of the responses about advantages and disadvantages of sex robots, but the implied attributions to robots make the connection between the human-robot interaction and relationships hard to pin down. On the one hand, while the most agreed-upon advantages involve the lack of physical harm a robot partner would receive or give (e.g., disease, emotional pain), it is notable that companionship, as much as improving a person's sex life, gets rated an advantage. And while disappointment and abuse toward human beings seems part of the overall disadvantage of relationship harm, there is a split over whether emotional bonding or falling in love with a robot could be at work.

The general views are likewise muddled on robotic consent, confined roles for sex robots, and what "sex" and "cheating" mean with respect to human-robot interaction. Close to half of the respondents thought a robot should "oblige" and not resist interaction, but what interaction they should be obliged to perform is harder to settle. Fewer than half thought the sex robot should only be used for sex, while fewer than half agreed that any action should be allowed toward the robot. Fewer than half ruled out "cheating" on a human being with a robot, and even fewer thought sex with a robot did not "count" as sex (though that in part may be due to not being given alternative construals like "masturbation").

Thus, to the degree human relationships are the ethical arbiter for sex robot usage, there seem to be more complex attributions and contexts at work in sorting out how those relationships will be affected. The role of physical and emotional intimacy, which sexuality can involve but by no means entails in and of itself, could merit more specific attention as a possible aspect of robots used in many social contexts. Likewise, the dynamics of bonding, which may involve gratitude for work or solidarity on a shared goal, may fill out a more useful picture of how human-robot interaction can reshape what is fulfilling and disappointing with respect to human relationships. The themes of intimacy and bonding may also draw out more explicit moral judgments about the limits and tradeoffs that such interaction carries. For both future research and design, it will be important not to let powerful forms of expectation and interaction go under the radar out of undue concentration on more sensational forms (sex robots, lethal autonomous weapons, etc.). In other words, the real problems with sex robots may be as much their sociality as their involvement with sex.

13.6   Conclusions

The ethics of human beings sexually interacting with robots demands more than a one-to-one application of sexual ethics into the form, function, and setting of automated, embodied systems. The interaction between human and robot, along with its effects on human relationships, may produce novel dynamics, risks, and benefits; accordingly, such interaction may need to be held to new standards of scrutiny. Identifying those emerging phenomena, and composing sufficient ethical measures to hold them to societal account, will involve more than imagining possible scenarios technological innovation makes possible. It will also mean keeping close empirical tabs on how people react, both in reflection and—where possible and appropriate—actual physical interaction, to social robots in many capacities.

Acknowledgments

The authors would like to thank Tom Williams for his help with setting up and running the experiments.

Notes

1. Charles Q. Choi, "Not Tonight, Dear, I Have to Reboot," *Scientific American*, March 1, 2008, http://www.nature.com/scientificamerican/journal/v298/n3/full/scientificamerican0308-94 .html.

2. David Levy, *Love and Sex with Robots* (New York: Harper Collins, 2007).

3. Blay Whitby, "Do You Want a Robot Lover? The Ethics of Caring Technologies," in *Robot Ethics: The Ethical and Social Implications of Robotics,* eds. Patrick Lin, Keith Abney, and George Bekey (Cambridge, MA: MIT Press, 2012).

4. Matthias Scheutz and Thomas Arnold, "Are We Ready for Sex Robots?," paper presented at the 11th annual ACM/IEEE International Conference on Human-Robot Interaction [HRI], March 2016.

5. Julie Beck, "Who's Sweating the Sexbots?," *The Atlantic*, September 2015, http://www.the-atlantic.com/health/archive/2015/09/the-sex-robots-arent-coming-for-our-relationships/407509.

6. Helena Horton, "By 2050, Human-on-Robot Sex Will Be More Common than Human-on-Human Sex, Says Report," *The Telegraph*, October 9, 2016, http://www.telegraph.co.uk/technology/news/11898241/By-2050-human-on-robot-sex-will-be-more-common-than-human-on-human-sex-says-report.html.

7. Chelsea G. Summers, "What Would Sex Robots for Women Look Like?," *Vice*, January 11, 2016, https://www.vice.com/read/what-would-sex-robots-for-women-look-like.

8. Justin McCurry, "No Sex, Please, They're Robots, Says Japanese Android Firm," *The Guardian*, September 28, 2015, https://www.theguardian.com/world/2015/sep/28/no-sex-with-robots-says-japanese-android-firm-softbank.

9. Mark Coeckelbergh, "Artificial Companions: Empathy and Vulnerability Mirroring in Human-Robot Relations," *Studies in Ethics, Law, and Technology* 4, no. 3 (December 2010); John P. Sullins, "Robots, Love, and Sex: The Ethics of Building a Love Machine," *Affective Computing, IEEE Transactions* 3, no. 4 (2012): 398–409.

10. Oliver Bendel, "Surgical, Therapeutic, Nursing, and Sex Robots in Machine and Information Ethics," *Machine Medical Ethics* 74 (2014): 17–32.

11. Kathleen Richardson, "The Asymmetrical 'Relationship': Parallels Between Prostitution and the Development of Sex Robots," published in the ACM Digital Library as a special issue of the ACM SIGCAS newsletter. *SIGCAS Computers & Society* 45, no. 3 (September 2015): 290–293, https://campaignagainstsexrobots.org/the-asymmetrical-relationship-parallels-between-prostitution-and-the-development-of-sex-robots; Lydia Kaye, February 10, 2016, https://campaignagainstsexrobots.org/2016/02/10/challenging-sex-robots-and-the-brutal-dehumanisation-of-women.

12. Sinziana Gutiu, "Sex Robots and the Roboticization of Consent," *We Robot* Law Conference Miami 2012, http://robots.law.miami.edu/wp-content/uploads/2012/01/Gutiu-Roboticization_of_Consent.pdf.

123. Ian Yeoman and Michelle Mars, "Robots, Men and Sex Tourism," *Futures* 44, no. 4 (2012): 365–371; Jennifer Robertson, "Gendering Humanoid Robots: Robo-Sexism in Japan," *Body & Society* 16, no. 2 (2010): 1–36.

14. John Danaher, "Symbols and their Consequences in the Sex Robot Debate," February 4, 2016, http://philosophicaldisquisitions.blogspot.com/2016/02/symbols-and-their-consequences-in-sex.html; John Danaher, "Robotic Rape and Robotic Child Sexual Abuse: Should They Be Criminalized?" *Criminal Law and Philosophy*, forthcoming: 1–25.

15. Matthias Scheutz, "The Inherent Dangers of Unidirectional Emotional Bonds Between Humans and Social Robots," in *Robot Ethics: The Ethical and Social Implications of Robotics*, eds. P. Lin, K. Abney, and G. Bekey (Cambridge, MA: MIT Press, 2012), 205.

16. Tiffany L. Chen, Chih-Hung Aaron King, Andrea L. Thomaz, and Charles C. Kemp, "An Investigation of Responses to Robot-initiated Touch in a Nursing Context," *International Journal of Social Robotics* 6, no. 1 (October 2013): 141–161; Phillip Grice, Mark Killpack, Advait Jain, and Charles C. Kemp, "Whole-Arm Tactile Sensing for Beneficial and Acceptable Contact During Robotic Assistance," in *Rehabilitation Robotics* (ICORR), 2013 IEEE International Conference, 1–8.

17. Kate Darling. "Extending Legal Rights to Social Robots," We Robot Conference, University of Miami, 2012.

14 Deus Sex Machina: Loving Robot Sex Workers and the Allure of an Insincere Kiss

Julie Carpenter

I am in you and you in Me, mutual in Love Divine.
—William Blake

I'll be your mirror

Reflect what you are, in case you don't know.
—Lou Reed

14.1 A Brand New Lover

In an era when human-robot interactions are becoming a part of everyday life for many people—or will be, within their lifetime—questions once explored only by science fiction have become part of science fact. A popular quandary is the confusing set of ideas about human sexuality and robots, or, more specifically, can humans be sexual with, or have affection for, robots in a way similar to how they can be sexual and affectionate with a human physically and emotionally? If the notions of sexuality and love are often entwined, either by purpose or accident, in human-human relationships, will people engage similarly with robots? Of the many questions the notion of human-robot sexuality brings to mind, this chapter considers whether people will feel affection for, and possibly even love, a robot while engaging in a sexual association or context. The tendency of overlapping sexual and emotional affection in human-human models will also increase the likelihood that people will cast some robots into light not just as viable sexual partners, but also as things worthy of human affection.

Robots are embodied machines with varying levels of intelligence and agency. Throughout this chapter, the term *robot sex worker*[1] (RSW) is used to refer to a robot that: (1) is designed with sexual stimulation capabilities; and/or (2) is being used for human sexual gratification. This aforementioned definition is purposefully broad in order to encompass the design intentions of including ways to engage users sexually, and the idea that users may project sexuality onto any robot from their own perspective. Robots not originally intended by designers to be RSWs can still become defined as RSWs when they are used in a way to engage human sexual satisfaction, and when they are considered RSWs by their owners or users, either as a primary role or a set of features or qualities. Furthermore, whereas a human sex worker may receive cash or goods in exchange for their services, a robot sex worker is not paid by its user because it is a product. It may be built, purchased, or leased, creating a different consumer dynamic for RSWs. It is likely someday that an RSW will spontaneously, or through design, achieve forms of agency and autonomy we recognize as intelligent "enough" for them to participate meaningfully as actors and sentient individuals within society, which will lead to relevant discussions about , and the roles of RSWs will again have to be redefined. Currently, an RSW needs a definition of sorts, a framework of understanding for discussion and the development of theories. Yet, culturally, these definitions are iterative and will evolve according to RSW abilities, social roles, and human perceptions of these factors.

RSWs can sometimes be further differentiated from some other definitions of a robot by their specific design and modes of communication, which may be integrated with features specifically intended to encourage a user's pleasurable sexual experience. RSW models incorporate various technologies and functionality developed to stimulate, satisfy, and even enhance human sexual pleasure. These characteristics could be part of the robots' off-the-shelf design, or could be less formally created because the user jury-rigs the robot to be sexually stimulating in some way. Therefore, it is not only the user's perception or attraction to a particular robot, but their conscious choices to use and modify the robot in these ways. Thus, although not all RSW owners or users will use their robot as a masturbation tool, the term RSW is used here to denote a difference between those robots that engage human sexual stimulation and those that do not.

Sexuality is a term that encompasses more than the obvious physical dimensions of the activities involved, and can be associated with emotional intimacy, vulnerability, and experiential qualities such as excitement. Certainly, sexual expression is a part of everyday life, from the privacy of one's home to social media. Sex toys have increasingly been incorporating digital technologies, and the industry has embraced high-quality production of a variety of innovations in stimulation, from web-based interfaces[2] to very humanlike sex dolls that incorporate artificial intelligence into their interactive possibilities.[3] Kiiroo is an example of one such system of technologies that combines a video chat platform, a phone app, and *teledildonics*—real world sex toys that allow for "tactile data sharing"[4]—so people at can connect sexually. Yet, Kiiroo is marketed to people as a way to feel intimate across geographical distance, with the technology acting as conduit, medium, and tactile sensory feedback. Oculus Rift, a virtual reality system, has inspired software and toys for sexual stimulation, enabling completely virtually based immersive experiences to experiences that involve accessories (such as a robotic and haptic masturbatory aid designed for men to use with Oculus) for tactile interaction with the virtual experience, with or without a human partner participating.[5] These systems are all marketed to a population who are, for the most part, already immersed in technology in other areas of their life.

Some people will claim they cannot envision sex or love with a robot in any circumstance. In a 2013 poll of one thousand adult Americans, 18% of respondents said that they believed robots made specifically for sexual purposes will be available by 2030, and 9% indicated that they would have sex with a robot if they had the opportunity.[6] In the same poll, when asked about the ethics of a spouse turning to a robot for stimulation during the course of the marriage, 42% of survey respondents said this act would be viewed as cheating. Another 31% said it would not be regarded as cheating, and 26% said they were unsure. Americans under the age of thirty were almost as likely to say it would not be cheating (34%) as that it would (36%), while respondents over the age of sixty-five were far more likely to say that it would, by a 52% to 24% margin.[7] While there is often a difference between what people claim they might do and how they actually behave, this poll indicates that some people are already open to the idea of sex with a robot.

The notions of *sexuality* and *intimacy* are closely bound, and there are an enormous number of people in the world who have difficulty establishing human relationships of either kind. Curiosity, social anxiety, age, geographic remoteness from others, physical disability, loneliness, or even pure sexual release without the possibility of emotional engagement are all examples of human factors possible in the motivation to pursue a sexual interaction with a humanlike thing that promises sexual gratification, even if (or because) it is a robot. Robot-ness will perhaps be less of a barrier to interest than other inhibitive issues for many people, such as the initial high cost of owning a sexualized robot when it is an emerging and rare technology. The initial models will only be a primitive beginning to systems that combine robotics, virtual reality, haptics (a virtual tactile sense), and other capabilities into a hybrid with many purposes extending beyond its pleasure-giving functionalities. As functionality and technologies are combined into richer RSW models, it will be natural to incorporate additional aspects of humanness that further enhance the illusion of a human partner, such as natural language, socialness, and the display of emotions, sexual and otherwise.

Humanlike robots are becoming more familiar to us in the everyday world, and furthermore, some of these robots are already being developed and marketed specifically as "emotional companions"[8] and for sexual purposes.[9] People who purchase these types of robots will use cues provided as part of the design in order to provide a model of how to interact with these robots, such as the robot's morphology, or, in this case, humanlike shape. So, because of the current humanlike representation popular in the emerging RSW market, one model of human-robot sexual sexuality to explore for possible comparisons is that of human-human sexuality. We can also look to what we know about human-object sexuality. But these are only starting points in a long continuum of what will no doubt be ongoing theory-building, and research and discussion about human-robot sexuality, and accordingly, will evolve and change over time, as robots and our ideas about them evolve.

Of all the concerns and possible trajectories of inquiry along the lines of human-robot *love*, in order to pursue any successful conversation about the topic, it is important to explore how this possibility of a new kind of *love* can be defined. The idea of loving any nonliving object in a meaningful way requires examining the very idea of what this love is, and if the definition should resemble human-human romantic love, human-product love, or be different than any current model we have in mind to hold up as a way of understanding how human-RSW romantic interactions may develop.

In the foreseeable future of technology, human-robot love will be one-way—human-to-robot—since robots cannot ever feel emotions in the exact same way humans do. Just as humans understand the world around them from a human-centered place, robots will have a robot-centered way of developing their own type of emotions, or mimicking human ones. Indeed, some currently marketed robots claim to be "emotional," "emotion-sensing," "social,"[10] or otherwise responsive to human emotion, or able to mimic it via behaviors. Pepper, a human-shaped, but clearly mechanical, robot, 1.2 meters tall, was developed initially to be used in mobile phone stores and not for domestic use.[11] Now it is marketed as "the world's first emotional robot," and includes specific notes in the robot's directions that the robot is not intended for sexual use.[12] Pepper's "emotional" core has been engineered so its interactive persona evolves and learns based on its interactions with people, then communicates in ways people expect—including presenting emotional cues and humanlike behaviors indicated through body language, facial expressions, and speech—a combination of responses based on what it has learned from prior human interactions and the ways it was programmed. If people interact with this robot in a sexual way, this ability to learn and evolve could mean a sexualized version of Pepper's personality would become sexually uninhibited and tuned in to its user(s) as time went on. While this sort of logic may be a selling point for an RSW, SoftBank (the makers) may want to avoid users engaging Pepper in behaviors that could become learned and result in it growing increasingly licentious, and keep Pepper marketed in a specific brand for nonsexual purposes. However, what SoftBank intends, and how its future owners will ultimately use Pepper, remains to be seen.

But while these robots may offer social signals to users that indicate humanlike emotions, none of these abilities are "real" in the sense of what is commonly understood as human emotions or love, rooted in human needs, emotions, and experiences. Robots, as tools originally conceived of by humans as an abstract concept, will learn about the world in a way that is rooted in and reflects their own robot-centered views. In other words, once a robot begins to interact with its world as an environment and exist in the world as a machine with some intelligent autonomy from humans, collecting information and learning, they begin to construct their own experiences in a way that is robot-centered. In this way, we as humans are forever entangled with robots as something close to us, by this combination of human design and intention with machine learning, autonomy, intelligence, communication skills, and embodied complex mechanical systems, creating a unique evolutionary stage for technology, humans, and culture.

For many people, the idea of sexuality is entwined with the idea of emotional attachment to someone else. Whether or not this attachment is desired as part of a sexual relationship depends on many individual preferences and contexts. Additionally, even if the notion of becoming emotionally invested in another person as part of enjoying a sexual relationship with them is not a conscious goal for those involved, the possibility of attachment lurks in the background for many people. As humans, we understand through our human experience that what or who we intend to love—or not love—is not a thing so easily bounded or reciprocated. Unrequited affection is hurtful to the concept of self, and can chip away at the idea of personal identity, even fleetingly.[13] By the same token, being the recipient of unwanted affection can also be confusing, and even feel threatening physically in extreme situations.[14] Alternatively, the object of affection may actually be passive and simply not return the level of intimacy or passion the enamored person feels.[15] In the case of human-RSW affection or attachment models, until RSWs are imbued with qualities we believe to be truly sentient, any love bestowed on the RSW will be a one-way proposition, regardless of the robot's persona, behaviors, or role. This is because love and emotional attachment will not be part of their robot-ness, inherent to what they are as machines, or are capable of learning at this time. If, as Regan points out, "… unreciprocated love is a common occurrence that primarily produces emotional distress"[16] between people, it is possible that human-RSW interactions can be situations fraught with pitfalls for the humans that develop affection for them without ever receiving a humanlike level of attachment in return.

Already, there are a lot of ideas here to unpack. The causes and repercussions of human love, sexual attraction, and emotional attachment are incredibly complicated. Furthermore, in order to understand the processes at play more fully, there is the untangling of conceptual differences between romantic love and emotional attachment. In order to create a framework for understanding and discussing big concepts like human emotions, love, loneliness, and loss, where the social experience and personal adaption to specific circumstances seems to create endless models, first there has to be a way of fathoming and describing these processes. One way to understand these things is through the lens of *attachment theory*.

Much of the research on attachment came from studies of parent-child relationships.[17] Zilcha-Mano, Mikulincer, and Shaver identified four features of adolescent and adult relationships to scaffold attachment theory: (1) physical closeness to the attachment figure, especially in need or times of negative or positive stress; (2) sense of removing distress and receiving comfort and support from the attachment figure; (3) sense of safety from the attachment figure, which supports exploration, risk-taking, and self-development; and (4) sense of separation distress or anxiety when the attachment figure becomes temporarily or permanently unavailable. Consequently, attachment is characterized by positive affect when the attachment figure is present and negative affect in the absence of the attachment figure.[18]

Attachment theory has also been applied to relationships among adults, particularly romantic relationships.[19] Sexuality is a significant part of understanding romantic love because, although attachment and sexual behaviors are considered regulated by biological versus emotional systems, these two systems mutually influence each other. For example, a person resists acting on sexual desires or impulses when feeling distressed or anxious about being separated from a long-term romantic partner. Similarly, a person may adopt sexual strategies (e.g., emotional remoteness) that serve to constrain the development of deep emotional attachments (i.e., serve the functions of intimacy and dependency avoidance). In short, adopting this framework means romantic love can be understood in terms of the shared functioning of three behavioral systems: attachment, caregiving, and sexuality. Although each system serves different purposes and has different developmental routes, the three are likely to be organized within a given individual in a way that partly reflects experiences in attachment relationships.

Thus, attachment theory gives a coherent framework for understanding the processes and dynamics common across people that produce various attachment styles. Furthermore, attachment theory accounts for attachment styles and behavioral tendencies that have positive and negative ramifications for the individual. For example, attachment theory recognizes negative emotions, such as fear of intimacy, as well as positive emotions, like caring and trust.[20] Moreover, attachment theory addresses the anxieties associated with separation and loss, and helps describe the connections between love and loneliness.

While sexual attraction to a partner does not always result in love, romantic love almost always involves sexual attraction. Romantic love incorporates separate behavioral systems. The attachment system and the caregiving system are two such systems.[21] Adult romantic love often integrates these systems, informed by the influences of attachment history. In other words, emotions like love and loneliness are emotional progressions with behavioral outcomes. For all of these reasons, attachment theory is a worthy framework to use as a starting point for understanding human-robot interactions, even if future work reveals that human-robot sexual and emotional interactions require their own attachment theories. Although there may be similarities between human-human and human-robot attachment models, human-robot attachment will also have new challenges unique to those interactions. It is important to understand this before relying on a human-human model of experience as sole guidance.

Still, using attachment theory as a basis for understanding human-robot interactions in a sexual situation also provides keys to considering how a person might feel emotionally connected to a robot as more than a thing, or a product. Furthermore, it can provide guidance for designers to consider when creating RSWs with whom humans form relationships.

In human-human interactions, a *relationship* implies a "… persistent construct incrementally built and maintained over a series of interactions that can span potentially over a lifetime."[22] An enjoyable sexual relationship also means fundamental emotional needs are met; however, those needs are defined by the people within each relationship. Regardless of gender or number of participants in each arrangement, *trust, gratification,* and *engagement* are commonly reciprocated or exchanged factors across mutually pleasurable human-human sexual relationships.

Human-human relationships are also essentially social and emotional. For robots developed expressly for the purpose of physical intimacy, believable affect will have to be built in to their design in order to support long-term human engagement. Consequently, a humanlike robot intended for sexual intimacy should interact and behave in the most humanlike manner possible. Yet, the most natural human-human interaction model would mean complete robot autonomy from the user. The considerations of user control with a semiautonomous RSW are multilevel, involving: (1) safety; and (2) customization. An ethical consideration for RSW development is whether interacting with a complex machine system—like RSW—that touches a human physically and (perhaps) emotionally should allow for some human override for safety purposes. Customization of an RSW by the user is defined in part by the conceptual "customization" a user would impart on an intelligent RSW that is capable of machine learning, and so dynamically increases its knowledge base about user preferences and adjusts its behaviors accordingly. Additionally, and perhaps more commonly, *customization* can mean control of other aspects of the RSW, such as its appearance, behaviors, and activities.

14.2   Custom Job

People across cultures have become habituated to the idea of customizing technology in order to suit individual needs. Complicated tools can easily be adjusted for ergonomic or pleasurable reasons: car seats and windows; computer desktop pictures, programs, and icons; mobile phone applications; ergonomic adjustment of a desk chair; and temperature control via a thermostat. Additionally, people will modify tools to work more effectively by customizing technology in ways unintended by the designers. Informal modifications can include a range of processes, from hacking into electronics to simply altering an object by winding layers of duct tape around its handle to make the design more comfortable and easier to grip.

The process of sexual attraction is deeply subjective, and therefore RSW interaction qualities may affect individual user experience, interaction expectations, attachment style, intimacy preferences, and the physical embodiment of the robot. To design RSWs based on analytical understandings of broad groups of users is one starting point. However, the challenge in developing a RSW that is engaging long-term to an individual owner or user will no doubt lie, in part, in two main areas: user customization and machine learning. RSWs that can learn and also be responsive to human subjectivity is the machine-centered solution. The human-centered part of the equation will be the user's ability to customize the RSW seamlessly and endlessly.

This ability of the RSW to be easily and fluidly customizable makes practical and functional sense. Assuming an RSW is an expensive technology to own (or even rent or lease), designers want to ensure that a product is engaging and pleasing for the user long-term. In this way, the design may be considered sustainable. A *renewable design* via user customization will encourage long-term interest in the object in a manner that is potentially "renewable," in that the RSW can take on a range of personas and appearances, providing the illusion of an internally changed or completely new RSW when it is mechanically only one object. In addition, the design can become a source of renewed pleasure for the user, since they have the ability to customize the RSW according to their changing preferences, thereby participating in the renewable design process. The sensory appeal of high-quality RSW materials such as skin-like exoskeletons, humanlike scents and secretions, substantial humanlike weight or structure, and humanlike voice qualities can further enhance the impression of an RSW as an organic being. Research about human-technology social interaction supports the idea that a user can be completely aware that the RSW or robot is a mechanical thing, and still engage with it in a social way.[23] For example, people who have worked with robots every day in military situations have reported affection for particular robots, inserting a sense of self into the robots they operate, and even feeling a sense of sadness or at least frustration when the robot becomes disabled.[24] Reeves and Nass's "computers as social actors" (CASA) theory explains how people assign agency, personas, and intentionality to computer-mediated technologies.[25] Humanoid robots, such as the RSW models currently on the market and known to be in development, present a combination of human appearance and user-projected human intentionality that may also compound the mixture of attachment-related responses for users of RSW (because of the human-human model of interaction that is projected onto the human-robot interactions). In other words, people will likely tend to interact with an RSW as if it was human, even if the user is completely aware that the thing they are interacting with is a robot. Moreover, similar research about human-robot emotional bonds, affection, and attachment in other dyad (but nonsexual) scenarios indicates it is possible for people to form affectionate ties to a robot or otherwise act affectionately to a robot[26] even if the robot is not designed to appear or act in a humanlike way.[27] Robot-specific research has demonstrated that these types of social human means of relating to some robots appear to be normal responses to android or humanlike robots in some situations, such as domestic use or other everyday human-robot interaction scenarios.[28]

From the user's standpoint, the opportunity for RSW customization may also encourage the perception of an RSW as more than simply a functional object.[29] When the user is aware that the other actor in a sexual encounter is a robot, the user's expectations about interacting with the technology in a sexual—or potentially affectionate, social, or otherwise humanlike way—are informed by the medium of the artifact.[30]

In the case of RSW, the artifact is also a medium, as a robot. By changing and reconfiguring the RSWs appearance and behaviors endlessly on a whim, the aesthetics and functionality of the RSW may change. Indeed, a user may project different names and personas onto different customized iterations of the same RSW, or even have some RSW identities that are considered purely for sexual gratification, while other facades take on more social or romantic functions for the user. Just by being present around an owner, a home-use RSW becomes part of their personal history. In this manner, the RSW becomes meaningful to the owner.[31] Long-term functionality, engagement, and personal history together are powerful forces for human attachment tied to a particular object.

When people customize systems in a significant enough manner that it is perceived as unique to the user, they then derive higher utility from the self-designed products than from conventional off-the-shelf products.[32] Meaningful customization of systems not only allows more effective adaptation to individual user aesthetic and functional preferences, but also facilitates enhanced differentiation from other people and their belongings by means of owning a unique product.[33] Applied to RSWs, customization options could be seemingly endless, aesthetically and functionally. Anything imagined as sexually pleasing could conceivably be modifiable in a RSW: hair type, eye or skin color, language(s), limb length, gender, and body type. In more advanced and intelligent RSWs, they will have the capability to learn user preferences in sexual activities and everyday social interactions. Material customization of RSWs will also include biomimicry in the form of scent and body heat output, skin/exoskeleton and hair textures, and even a humanlike taste.

Together, these factors—detailed material qualities, a physical representation of user ideal through customization, product self-congruity—combined with things such as the physical proximity necessitated by the RSWs intended use—potentially contribute to building an emotional bond from the user to the RSW.

So is it narcissism or self-love or fantasy that gives someone a desire to not just seek, but *create*, an *other* for sexual intimacy? What is the power dynamic when a human is in a "relationship" with a robot? This new type of relating to a machine is a different relationship, not just because of the customization, or the steps one must go through to procure a robot (a great deal of money, etc.), or the sheer artificialness of it—but because of all of these things. It is a new way of examining emotional power in human-robot dynamics, a framework for a relationship different from any human-human relationship, yet similar to the human-human relationship in terms of pure sexual desire being fulfilled for the human.

14.3   Perceptions, Expectations, and Questions about Robots and Sexuality: A New Normal

Sexuality is distinct from love, yet intimately linked to it. Love could be considered a social construction that emanates from a biological sexual drive, yet that definition seems to separate the two concepts of culture versus biology cleanly, when sexuality and love both encompass more than sexual behavior and are multidimensional and dynamic concepts. An individual's sexuality is, in many ways, defined by whom (or, in the case of robot sex workers, *what*) one has sex with, and in what ways, why, and under what circumstances. Furthermore, society is concerned with outcomes resulting from a sexual relationship, and whether they follow traditional or nontraditional cultural norms. Explicit and implicit rules imposed by society as defined by the culture's agreed-upon moral codes—and factors that are part of every individual, such as gender, age, economic status, and ethnicity—influence every person's sexuality as others perceive it, if not their actual, true sexual preferences.[34]

Many questions about human-robot sexuality are not just about the possibility of use of—or even attraction to—robots, but are framed about ethics in ways of articulating other, underlying concerns. Will robots replace people in some long-term relationships? As a result of human attachment and the related process of regarding a RSW as a meaningful social partner, will a RSW even need to be distinguished from other robots in private use, other than through their human-centered sexual abilities? Will people who use RSWs frequently find new manifestations of narcissistic behaviors stemming from the use of human-robot sexuality as their model for human-human sexuality? Will these new expressions of personality include increased haughtiness or sense of superiority, disagreeableness, inflated self-esteem and entitlement, or an exploitative nature? Will a person who has a primary human-robot model for attachment be one who lacks empathy for humans, because their preoccupation with self-fulfillment affects their relationships with others negatively, even aggressively? All of this remains to be discovered.

While the model of human-robot sexuality may resemble human-human relationships in some ways, they are truly not the same. Will people receive love from robots? Perhaps a new kind of love, but it will be a robot love, not a human one. This love will be limited, or at least different, from the human point of view because no matter how sophisticated the affection may appear, robots will never have the actual human experience or be human because the robot's experience in the world and its inherent robot-ness prevent that implicit knowledge. The subjectivity of robot-ness is different than the subjectivity of humanness because it emerges from a way of knowing the world through one's being in the world by interacting with it. While people have individual subjective experience defined by their unique and situated knowledge and experiences, so will robots. Some things that define humanness and robot-ness will become fuzzier as robots become more humanlike. Human expectations about robot intelligence and socialness may be exceeded, and robots may become objects humans easily negotiate with in their spaces. Yet, while robots remain largely mechanical, and not biological or biologically integrated systems, their collective subjective experiences will be demarcated from humans in very purely physical ways. Even a highly humanlike robot that is a mechanical system may have senses, capabilities, and functionality a human does not have without machine augmentation. Therefore, an RSW will always have a different subjectivity from any human, although possibly some commonalities with other RSW experiences.

Another emerging concern is whether sexually charged attachment to a robot, a known object, will establish norms for treating this humanlike object in a harmful way that the user then transfers to their interactions with humans, such as demanding an inordinate level of control or otherwise exploiting a human relationship.[35] This concern is perhaps more about establishing norms for impulse control, and a valid thing to discuss now even though culture at large is still at a stage when any behavior toward a robot is generally regarded as emotionally insignificant.

Some philosophical questions about RSWs sound similar to questions asked about other products before the technologies became mainstreamed. Will a human become bored with human companions after being with a robot that will do anything, or even become dependent on mechanical adoration? Will interacting regularly with a RSW reduce social interdependency on humans? What if someone customizes their robot sex worker to resemble a real person without their permission, whether a celebrity or someone they know? Does that lifelike RSW, which looks like an actual person, violate the rights of the person it is modeled after, ethically or emotionally, by its very existence or only by its existence as a RSW? None of these very emotion-centered questions have simple answers, or any foreseeable set of solutions coming from design or policy sectors that will address some of these potential issues in meaningful ways for individual consumers in the near future.

Our cultural constructs are formed around our learning and contributing and reflecting each other's ideas through interaction; humans develop humanness through interacting with other humans. Interacting with robots will create something else. The questions mentioned previously mostly stem from the major concern of humans becoming pathological narcissists who have needs that are impossible to fulfill, are cold and aloof toward others, and who are only able to enjoy life with a RSW or other artificial system(s). It is possible that introducing RSW into the world will exacerbate self-indulgence and encourage disinterested, less empathetic understanding of others,[36] but it is unlikely to happen just because the technology exists. The idea that this is a new set of negatively interpreted behaviors, instead of an adaptation of some human behaviors by people who use the RSW technology, is already being proclaimed.[37] The argument then seems to be that these negative behaviors are something intrinsic in people, traits that perhaps robo-sexual relationships will bring out or highlight, and it is an important set of ideas. If narcissistic traits are in part innate in people, as instincts elemental to human survival, then can these traits be exacerbated over time in a negative way with reinforcement from interactions with RSWs? Yet another possible emotional trajectory for users is that prior research in human-robot relationships and human-human relationships has demonstrated people sometimes view affectionate others as part of their extended emotional selves.[38] The way society interprets human-RSW sexuality and affection will be a big factor in learning more, and it is another opportunity to learn about our humanness.

Interacting with technology in a more natural way—using speech, gestures, or other human-centered communication—is still a new dynamic. An act like verbally commanding a room in a house to raise its temperature or dim the lights is being immersed and situated in a technology that understands and is responsive via its behaviors. Yet, the example of a smart room does not engage a person socially the way communicating naturally to an embodied object with movement, a thing appears to have agency, and which human perception interprets as having a sense of autonomy embedded in it. People naturally associate at least some of the characteristics of agency and intelligence with an embodied robot, such as expectations about its abilities (or limitations), its uses, and its independent processes or autonomy. Additionally, some previous work in human-robot interaction has demonstrated that people can be uncomfortable with the idea of robots presenting emotions or personas deemed too humanlike. However, people's expectations about robots, their abilities, and roles are changing every day—as people's interactions with actual robots become increasingly common. As robots become integrated with everyday life, it is likely living and working with all sorts of robots will become a new cultural normal instead of a novelty. In other words, the point when robots become a new culturally agreed-upon social category defined, in part, by not being human.

14.4   Norming for Robot Sex Workers

All sociocultural systems self-regulate behaviors that are considered acceptable through social norms. Human-centered social norms are practices and discourses that privilege humanness, both explicitly and implicitly in their day to day usage—normalizing processes that support humanness as the elemental form of association to the world. Humanness is viewed as the very model of social relations, as the indivisible basis of all community, and as the means of reproduction without which society would not exist. The challenge for society is to dismantle such human-human centered frames through the practice of investigating the significance of human-robot sexual-social interactions.

Where Mori's Uncanny Valley theory (see figure 14.1) has been a significant touch-stone for many discussions about human perceptions about robots, combining this framework with other factors of societal acceptance—such as time—can also be useful.

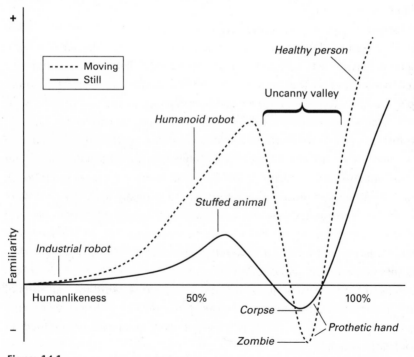

Figure 14.1
Mori's Uncanny Valley. Based on Masahiro Mori, "The Uncanny Valley," trans. K. F. MacDorman and N. Kageki, *Energy* 7, no. 4 (2012 [1970]): 33–35.

The premise of Masahiro Mori's Uncanny Valley theory (1970) is that people become more comfortable or familiar with robot appearance as they appear humanlike, but only to a point at which this positive response dips dramatically when a humanlike robot is still distinguishable from a person through its imperfections or inability to pass as human.[39] Mori uses the example of a prosthetic hand, a human-made object that can appear organic at first sight, but upon further observation gives itself away through a touch or movement that makes its inorganic nature obvious to the observer. He posited that this sense of strangeness one can feel when negotiating whether an object is artificial or organic would extend even further if an entire robot took on a humanlike form, dipping the human reaction into the chart's uncanny valley of negative perceptions. Furthermore, he cautioned designers not to create robots that appear completely humanlike or they would always fall into the valley of dipped response. Mori's representation is a valuable way to think about initial exposure and acceptance of robots in human spaces, and incorporates ideas about where on a design spectrum human empathy and revulsion toward robots occurs based on their instincts, and the objects' appearance and movement.[40]

But people as individuals in a larger system of cultures are not influenced only by a single moment or experience in time; they are influenced over time by many factors. To add these temporal and contextual layers to Mori's lens, one proposition is the Robot Accommodation Process Theory (RAPT) presented in figure 14.2.

Modeled on Mori's theory, RAPT uses the *y*-axis to indicate stages of cultural adaptation to robots in the world. Although the stages are listed discretely, in reality there is some overlap and no clear demarcation line; however, it is a series of actions and reactions that build upon each other, nonetheless.

For robots, although there is a history of folktales about artificial life as well as theoretical and actual automatons, the modern era of robots begins in many ways with Karl Čapek's satirical science fiction play, originally published in Czechoslovakia in 1921. In *Rossom's Universal Robots*, or *RUR*, robots were literally first named as such, the word *roboti* referring not to robots as we think of them in a modern sense, but as a synthetic or artificial life, a class of beings that are developed to be menial laborers.[41] The very word *robota* means *drudgery* or *hard work* in Czech. The dystopian story grabbed popular attention for the idea of mechanical slaves, as well as a metaphor for fascism. Yet it was not until the Fritz Lang 1927 movie version of the story *Metropolis* that the word *robot* was used in specific association with humanlike *mechanical* beings. In Metropolis, specific characters, basically automatons, are called "robots."[42] This era heralds the *new concept* stage in RAPT, a time that spawns a new genre of mythology specific to robots. Robots become a cultural touchstone—first only to people specifically interested in

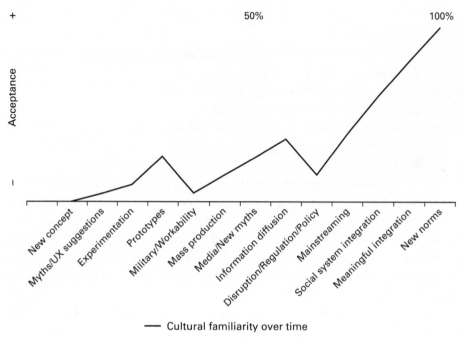

Figure 14.2
Robot Accommodation Process Theory (RAPT)

science fiction or general literature—but the idea surrounding how people would live with robots begins to develop in the general consciousness.

The roots of these new stories may also draw from other, earlier tales more generally about artificial or human-made life (e.g., Jewish folktales of the golem). However, as used in this new subgenre of science fiction (e.g., noted science fiction author Isaac Asimov's short stories began appearing in magazines as early as the 1930s, with his "Three Laws of Robotics" literary device first published in the story "Runaround" in 1942), the very word *robot* begins to evoke its own set of associations beyond Capek's original story: mechanical; strange; powerful; unpredictable; of unknown origin (alien or Earthbound); usually humanlike in appearance, but with exaggerated proportions and superhuman abilities. These are the robot-specific myths that were emerging into general consciousness in that era, and with them come the user experience (UX) suggestions from fiction of how people might behave around robots, informing people's expectations about what interacting with a robot might be like. These illustrated behaviors range from befriending robots to fearing them, with an emphasis on the latter demonstrated in popular Western culture. While public interest and awareness of robots rises, the idea of interacting with robots is still novel and being explored solely through storytelling.

Formal scientific exploration of, *experimentation* with, and prototype building of robots begins in earnest, not simply because of RUR, but perhaps inspired in part by this literary device. Whereas in the past, automata were largely commissioned as entertainment for a very few privileged people to see in person, scientific curiosity turns to a decidedly more task-specific focus for the possibilities of automata. Now, an age of formal building begins with the robot roles and tasks no doubt influenced not only by science fiction's references as robots for menial labor, but by the Industrial Age as a concurrent emerging disruption of organizational models and time of technological innovations. In addition to early robotic prototypes and publications, it is likely early informal hobbyist experimentation took place, undocumented. Do It Yourself (DIY) or interested inventor-types pushed the theory and model-building of robotics forward by generating ideas unbounded by organizational goals, although perhaps restricted by less available funding for experimentation.[43] The idea of robots may have seemed futuristic, but in an era of great scientific and industrial leaps, doubtlessly home hobbyists began tinkering as well, much as early inventors and makers have throughout history.

As with many emerging technologies, the *military* began to fund initiatives to explore the mechanics, engineering, and ergonomics surrounding robotics. Eventually, as other relevant technologies evolved concurrently, such as computing, real robots began production and use in military scenarios. Although some robot research is privately funded, it is the widespread military adoption of some models—most notably the Explosive Ordnance Disposal (EOD) robots—that has become an integrated part of daily work for some personnel.[44] Using robots regularly means new robot-specific training has been developed, and the real workability of robots is explored *in situ*, beyond a laboratory setting. The tool capabilities of robots are tested and explored by their users every day, sometimes resulting in a jury-rigging or adaption of the physical robot, other times prompting some sorts of social interaction with the robot.[45]

Because of the initial adoption of some robots in large quantities, such as the EOD robot models, the infrastructure for *mass production* of some robots began to fall into place. Some companies that manufacture robots for military contracts also build consumer products, like iRobot has done with their PackBot (military) and Roomba (consumer) products. However, at this point, robots are still generally not recognized by the general public as relevant to their everyday lives outside of a military or industrial situation. Industrial robots, or robots used in manufacturing or similar processes with little or no human interaction capabilities and few humanlike aspects—except as necessitated by their functionality or for their roles doing repetitive labor—are also developed parallel to the military and consumer-centered robots. This development has been, and continues to be, supported by a growing industry infrastructure that makes producing and adopting manufacturing robots possible across a wider economic spectrum of business organizations.

From military robotics originated the idea of Unmanned Aerial Vehicles (UAV) or *drones,* which then gain notoriety for their stealth, force, and new method of operation from great distances. Sometimes drones are classified popularly as robots or robotic,[46] although there is also debate about whether they should be regarded as such. Moreover, the negative associations people have in regard to drones (both military and otherwise), coupled with the technology's newness in human spaces, reflects some negative connotations of robots in general. Even humor like the "Welcome, Our Robot Overlords" meme points to mixed emotions about the fascinating technology coupled with questions about its uses.[47] While the idea of robots engages people as a popular topic of fiction, for many people the idea of real robots is still largely centered on third-person accounts and fictional representations. Using this model of understanding, culture at large embraces the core ideas of having robots exist.

As reality changes and robots become part of science and technology spaces—if not everyday life for most people—*new myths* and stories have also come to light, fictional and real. While Western science fiction seems to demonstrate more positive representation of robots—or at least less threatening ones—the idea of a Terminator-style Skynet soldier not only persists, but gains some traction as real technologies resembling the fictional ones arise. These types of fears over new technology have been exacerbated in some ways by the popular reinforcement of the concept of scientists as special people, isolated from the rest of society and concerned only with their own intellectual curiosity, inventing things that will disrupt humanity with no regard for outcomes.[48]

Additionally, as fictional references change, so do real ones—because some people begin to have regular access to real robots. Personal experiences with robots become revealed in the media; e.g., instances of people claiming fondness for robots or social interactions. Information about what working with robots is actually like begins to disseminate through these real experiences and stories, and so information is diffused through the culture, this time based on current and real human-robot interactions, actual stories of user experience. As people indicate their experience with robots is useful, and even sometimes pleasant, positive public interest in these robots rises again.

Early adoption of robots demonstrated that robots are useful in many situations, and so there is continued exploration, both formal and informal, of possible future uses for these technologies. At this juncture, planning for the rapidly burgeoning evolution, widespread production, and trending adoption of robotics begins in earnest, with think tanks, NGOs, and other organizations very publicly generating and supporting ideas about new policy at the local, federal, and even international levels.[49] Policy development often involves quite public debates, or at least debates that receive public coverage, and these further suggestions about how to use robots also propose new negative connotations, as all sides are explored in order to develop solid regulations. In turn, the general public again sometimes gets messages about robots that can be disturbing, and the lasting impression can be that robots are something that need to be contained somehow, and urgently. In some ways, this perception is true and the concerns are valid, as the technologies leap forward before policies are put into place. Perception about robotics takes a dip as suspicions again appear in discussions, historically apropos of these types of debates regarding new technology. The combination of all of the previous stages enables the start of robot mainstreaming into the collective world culture to different degrees: using real robots, mass producing robots, debating policy and establishing laws about robots, widespread and consistent news coverage, parallel integrated technologies established, and revised myths about human-robot interactions. This general increased awareness leads to less outright fear of robots as a universal threat, and more scientific and social curiosity about real experiences and possibilities of living with robots.

Social system integration refers to the point where robots become pervasive in the everyday lives of most people. This period would overlap quickly with the stage of *meaningful integration,* or the sweet spot where human emotional and sexual attachment to, and affection or even love for robots begins to occur regularly in personal reports. These developments become part of public discussion, study, debate, and eventual acceptance in its own mini-cycle of the social adjustment process. Finally, although new norms of behavior and living with robots have been in development since the *new concept* stage, now is the time when there is large-scale acceptance of robots as familiar and normal parts of the human experience. Thus, using a human-human model of understanding human-robot interactions will be regarded as less useful at this point of meaningful integration into the culture at large, when the creation of robot social categories are rapidly developed and widely recognized.

For the purpose of generating further ideas, it is possible to overlay Mori's theory over RAPT, and then examine a human-robot interaction model that proposes a theory for robot design, as well as a visual representation of social acceptance and adjustment over time. (See figure 14.3.)

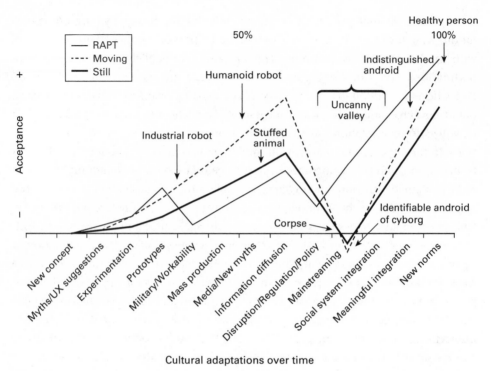

Figure 14.3
The climb out of the Uncanny Valley; RAPT overlaid Mori's Uncanny Valley

Overlapping the graphics illustrates at least one meaningful commonality. Mori's Uncanny Valley theory indicates that a "healthy person" (or someone perceived as a healthy person) creates a sense of full acceptance, empathy, and familiarity in the perception of another human. A robot that appears as indistinguishable from a human as a healthy person does not yet exist, but will in the relatively near future. RAPT, a theory that illustrates the nascent years of social integration of robots and also interprets the near future acceptance of humanlike robots, suggests the larger societal context, as well as temporal aspects, of Mori's early and visionary interpretation of design perceptions.

Mori placed a humanoid robot right before the dip into the uncanny valley, and his theory focused on the design of humanlike robots and user experience in regards to the robots' appearance and behaviors. RAPT predicts that exposure to robots over time will reduce aspects of uncanniness, even in humanlike robots that are recognizable as artificial life. The Uncanny Valley theory illustrates the idea of repulsion felt by people encountering some classes of humanlike robots, while RAPT acknowledges this uncanniness, but regards it as a temporary condition, open to change at individual and cultural levels. Robot sex workers can then take on many types of humanlike design, not just because of formal design processes, changing standards of attractiveness, customization, or jury-rigging, but because people accept robots in general as potentially sexual in some contexts. In that way, even less humanlike robots will eventually become acceptable RSWs.

Furthermore, all of this is part of larger cycles and systems. Robots embody many technologies, and the rapid development of other emerging tools integrated with robotics increases their robustness, and, sometimes, these integrated technologies have their own cycles of cultural acceptance. As with the example of the robot Nadine[50] mentioned earlier, a natural and conversational intelligence similar to that used in Apple's Speech Interpretation and Recognition Interface, or Siri, is combined with Nadine's physicality as a means of increasing the effectiveness of the human-technology communication. When Siri-like technology first became widespread on iPhones, it was a novelty to have this human-technology verbal interaction as an option on a mobile phone.[51] "Just talk to Siri as you would to a person," Apple explained to users about Siri's interaction model (2016). "They want—that is, the engineers that build them want—to interact with you like a person, not a machine," was the interpretation of Apple's intent for the technology; for Siri to be a humanlike conversational "do engine," a task-oriented personal assistant with some natural language capabilities.[52]

"The goal [of Siri] is a human-enhancing and potentially indispensable assistant that could supplement the limitations of our minds and free us from mundane and tedious tasks," an in-depth article about the development of Siri's technology explained the application's design goals.[53] These objectives are not only complementary to many robot project goals, but in line with the original concept of robots, even in folklore, as assistants capable of endlessly repeating the mundane tasks, and therefore fit into the current popular cultural model of what people expect robots to be able to do, such as interact with people in an intelligent and verbal way.

Similarly, this human-technology voice interaction may now be regarded as innovative when incorporated into a robot, such as Nadine, and go through its own cycle of user expectations meeting design intentions and the robot's real-world effectiveness and uses. Thus, the social acceptance cycle of disembodied AI like Siri can aid or disrupt the *parallel cycle* related to intelligent and humanlike robots by association. To illustrate further, the Robot Cultural Accommodation Cycle (RCAC) (see figure 14.4) depicts the ongoing negotiations between individual and cultural interactions and their interconnectedness as a system of innovation. Like RAPT, this model is not meant to be an all-encompassing framework, but a complementary way of understanding cultural

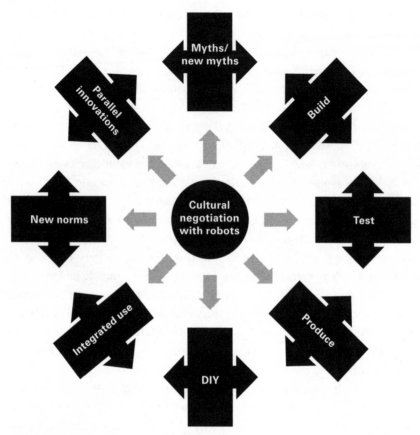

Figure 14.4
The Robot Cultural Accommodation Cycle

evolution as society collectively reacts to and impacts robot—and RSW—development and integration.

This cycle of entwined processes illustrates user negotiation as ongoing throughout the product lifecycle, and the influence of outside emerging technologies, like the example of Siri-like AI integrated into the robot Nadine. Similarly, the "emotion-reading" robot Pepper is being integrated with IBM's AI Watson. With increased intelligence also comes more information about where and what Pepper's users are interested in, so as to customize their experience based on social media and online commerce. As stated in Garun: "With Watson, developers hope to help Pepper understand human emotions more thoroughly to appropriately respond and engage with its users. IBM and SoftBank say the collaboration will also allow Pepper to gather new information from social media to learn how people interact with brands so it knows how to person-ally reach out to people."[54]

Integrating emerging technologies into sex dolls and early RSWs is already happen-ing in the world. In 2015, McMullen, the CEO of sex doll company RealDoll announced its plan to develop Harmony, a more robotlike doll that will blink, open its mouth, and be able to have simple conversations.[55] According to McMullen, the goal is to create a doll that appears to behave as if it enjoys sex.

In conclusion, it is easy to see there are many questions about human-robot sexual-ity in this new era of human-robot interactions. Currently, at this point in time, theory building is one way to investigate and propose answers to these questions. This is a time of theory building, as well as a time to negotiate how to live with robots in every way, including sexually, which would involve bestowing them with meaningful affec-tion. To deny the idea of human-robot sexuality, or the idea of human-robot affection or romantic attachment, is akin to denying the existence of many innate and integral parts of humanness and human experience, such as sexuality, love, vanity, loneliness, and curiosity, some of the very things that may endear robot sex workers to humans via an alternate method of fulfilling those desires. Thus, it is not necessarily a matter of RSWs being endearing in and of themselves, via design or their use context or actions, for people to develop emotional attachment to them. Ultimately, the rewards, benefits, burdens, and repercussions of emotional attachment do not rest on the robot or its design, but on the human who interacts with it.

Notes

1. The term robot sex worker came about during an email exchange on the topic between the author and Jeff Vintar in 2015.

2. Jeffrey Bardzell and Shaowen Bardzell, "Pleasure Is Your Birthright: Digitally Enabled Designer Sex Toys as a Case of Third-Wave HCI," in *Proceedings of the SIGCHI Conference on Human Factors in Computing Systems* (May 2011): 257–266, doi: 10.1145/1978942.1978979; Kiiroo.com, 2016, Kiiroo with Fleshlight Technology Platform, https://www.kiiroo.com/platform.

3. George Gurley, "Is This the Dawn of the Sexbots?" *Vanity Fair,* April 16, 2015, http://www.vanityfair.com/culture/2015/04/sexbots-realdoll-sex-toys.

4. Kiiroo.com.

5. Brian Merchant, "The Robot that Makes Virtual Sex Feel Real," VICE Motherboard, February 14, 2014, http://motherboard.vice.com/blog/real-sex-virtual-reality-oculus-rift-tenga.

6. *Huffington Post* Omnibus Robots Poll, February 20–21, 2013, http://big.assets.huffingtonpost.com/toplinesbrobots.pdf.

7. "Robot Sex Poll Reveals Americans' Attitudes About Robotic Lovers, Servants, Soldiers," *Huffington Post*, April 10, 2013, http://www.huffingtonpost.com/2013/04/10/robot-sex-poll-americans-robotic-lovers-servants-soldiers_n_3037918.html; *Huffington Post* Omnibus Poll, 2013.

8. Aldebaran Robotics, "Who Is Pepper?," 2015, https://www.aldebaran.com/en/a-robots/who-is-pepper.

9. Gurley, "Dawn of the Sexbots"; SexBots.us 2015; TrueCompanion.com 2015.

10. For example, see: Aldebaran 2015; Natt Garun, "Softbank's Pepper Robot to Get Even Brainier With IBM's Watson Technology," January 6, 2016, http://thenextweb.com/insider/2016/01/07/softbanks-pepper-robot-to-get-even-brainier-with-ibms-watson-technology/#gref; Federico Guerrini, "Rise of the 'Social' Robots: NTU Singapore Unveils Nadine, The Chatty Receptionist," *Forbes*, December 31, 2015, http://www.forbes.com/sites/federicoguerrini/2015/12/31/rise-of-the-social-robots-ntu-singapore-unveils-nadine-the-chatty-receptionist.

11. Michael Shea, "Pepper, a Robot to Watch you Sleep," *The Skinny*, September 23, 2015, http://www.theskinny.co.uk/tech/features/pepper-robot.

12. Francis Eduard Ang, "Netizens Confused with Robot Pepper's Instructions that Forbids 'Sexual' Acts," *Yibada*, September 19, 2015, http://en.yibada.com/articles/65017/20150919/netizens-confused-robot-peppers-instructions-forbid-sexual-acts.htm.

13. Pamela C. Regan, "Love, Unreciprocated," in *Encyclopedia of Human Relationships* 2, eds. H. T. Reis and S. Sprecher (Los Angeles: SAGE, 2009), 1018–1019; Colleen H. Sinclair and Irene H. Freize, "When Courtship Persistence Becomes Intrusive Pursuit: Comparing Rejecter and Pursuer Perspectives of Unrequited Attraction," *Sex Roles* 52, no. 11–12 (June 2005): 839–852.

14. Sinclair and Frieze, "When Courtship."

15. Regan, "Love, Unreciprocated."

16. Ibid.

17. For a review, see John Bowlby, *Secure Base* (New York: Routledge, 1988).

18. Silgal Zilcha-Mano, Mario Mikulincer, and Phillip R. Shaver, "An Attachment Perspective on Human-Pet Relationships: Conceptualization and Assessment of Pet Attachment Orientations," *Journal of Research in Personality* 45 (2011): 345–357.

19. C. Hazan and P. Shaver, "Romantic Love Conceptualized as an Attachment Process," *Journal of Personality and Social Psychology* 52 (1987): 511–524; Cindy Hazan and Phillip Shaver, "Attachment as an Organizational Framework for Research on Close Relationships," *Psychological Inquiry* 5 (1994): 1–22.

20. Karen Dion and Kenneth Dion, "Personality, Gender and the Phenomenology of Romantic Love," *Review of Personality and Social Psychology* 6 (1983): 209–39.

21. John Bowlby, *Attachment and Loss*, vol. 3 (New York: Basic Books, 1980).

22. Timothy Bickmore and Rosalind W. Picard, "Establishing and Maintaining Long-Term Human-Computer Relationships," *ACM Transactions on Computer-Human Interaction* (TOCHI) 12, no. 2 (2005): 293–327.

23. Julie Carpenter, *Culture and Human-Robot Interaction in Militarized Spaces: A War Story* (Abingdon, UK: Taylor & Francis Ltd., 2016); Byron Reeves and Clifford Nass, *How People Treat Computers, Television, and New Media Like Real People and Places* (Cambridge: CSLI Publications and Cambridge University Press, 1996), 119.

24. Carpenter, *Culture*, 24, 53, 97, 98, 101, 102, 117).

25. Reeves and Nass, *How People Treat Computers.*

26. Ibid.; Martin D Cooney, Shuichi Nishio, and Hiroshi Ishiguro, "Recognizing Affection for a Touch-Based Interaction with a Humanoid Robot," in Proceedings of the IEEE/RSJ International Conference on Intelligent Robots and Systems (IROS) 2012, 1420–1427; David Levy, *Love and Sex with Robots: The Evolution of Human-Robot Relationships* (New York: HarperCollins, 2007).

27. Carpenter, *Culture.*

28. Ibid.; Kerstin Dautenhahn, Sarah Woods, Christina Kaouri, Michael L. Walters, Kheng Lee Koay, and Iain Werry, "What Is A Robot Companion—Friend, Assistant or Butler?" in Proceedings of the IEEE/RSJ International Conference on Intelligent Robots and Systems (IROS) 2005, 1488–1493.

29. M. Joseph Sirgy, "Self-Concept in Consumer Behavior: A Critical Review," *Journal of Consumer Behavior* 9 (December 1982): 287–300.

30. Peter-Paul Verbeek, *What Things Do—Philosophical Reflections on Technology, Agency, and Design* (University Park, PA: Pennsylvania State Press, 2005).

31. Katja Battarbee and Tuuli Mattelmaki, "Meaningful Product Relationships," in *Design and Emotion* 1 (New York: Taylor & Francis), 337–344; Russell Belk, "Possessions and the Extended Self," *Journal of Consumer Research* 15 (February 1988): 139–168.

32. Battarbee and Mattelmaki, "Meaningful."

33. Sirgy, *Consumer Behavior*, 288.

34. Alan Finder, "For Some, Online Persona Undermines A Resume," *New York Times*, June 11, 2006; Elliot Turiel, *The Culture of Morality: Social Development, Context, and Conflict* (Cambridge: Cambridge University Press, 2002).

35. Kathleen Richardson, "The Asymmetrical 'Relationship': Parallels Between Prostitution and the Development of Sex Robots," published in the ACM Digital Library as a special issue of the ACM SIGCAS newsletter. *SIGCAS Computers & Society* 45, no. 3 (September 2015): 290–93, https://campaignagainstsexrobots.org/the-asymmetrical-relationship-parallels-between -prostitution-and-the-development-of-sex-robots; Campaign Against Sex Robots, 2016, https:// campaignagainstsexrobots.org/about.

36. Sherry Turkle, *Alone Together: Why We Expect More from Technology and Less from Each Other* (New York: Basic Books, 2011).

37. See the work of the Campaign Against Sex Robots for more.

38. Carpenter, *Culture*, 53, 24, 53, 97, 98, 101, 102, 117; Elaine N. Aron and Arthur Aron, "Love and Expansion of the Self: The State of the Model," *Personal Relationships* 3, no. 1 (March 1996): 45–58.

39. Masahiro Mori, "The Uncanny Valley," trans. K. F. MacDorman and N. Kageki, *Energy* 7, no. 4 (2012 [1970]): 33–35.

40. Carpenter, *Culture*.

41. Karel Čapek, *RUR Rossum's Universal Robots* (New York: Penguin, 2004).

42. Rudolf Klein-Rogge, *Metropolis Magazine: Depicting Scenes, Story, and Incidents in the Making of The World's Greatest Modern Spectacular Film Masterpiece* (London: Wardour Films Limited, 1927), http://www.peterharrington.co.uk/blog/metropolis.

43. "Boys Build 'Human Engine' in Study of Anatomy," Popular Science, April 1929, 58; http://www.popsci.com/archives.

44. Carpenter, *Culture*.

45. Ibid.

46. Dan Nosowitz, "USDA to Grant $3 Million for Robots to Roam Farmlands," *Modern Farmer*, December 31, 2015, http://modernfarmer.com/2015/12/usda-robot-farmland-grant.

47. Samuel H. Kenyon, "Would You Still Love Me if I Was a Robot?," *Journal of Evolution and Technology* 19 no. 1 (September 2008): 17–27.

48. Carpenter, *Culture*, 18, 22; Matthew C. Nisbet, Dietram A. Scheufele, James Shanahan, Patricia Moy, Dominique Brossard, and Bruce V. Lewenstein, "Knowledge, Reservations, or Promise? A Media Effects Model for Public Perceptions of Science and Technology," *Communication Research* 29, no. 5 (2002): 584–608; M. Shortland, "Mad Scientists and Regular Guys: Images of the Expert in Hollywood films of the 1950's," in Proceedings of the Joint Meeting of the British Society for History of Science and the History of Science Society (Manchester, UK: July 1988).

49. Greg Nichols, "Drones Are a Danger to Manned Aircraft, According to New Report: What Happens When Drones and Manned Aircraft vie for Shares of The National Airspace?" *Robotics*, December 21, 2015, http://www.zdnet.com/article/drones-are-a-danger-to-manned-aircraft -according-to-new-report; Campaign to Stop Killer Robots, 2016.

50. Guerrini, "'Social' Robots."

51. Kelly Montgomery, "Apparently Siri Has Some Pretty Strange Responses Up Her Sleeve," *Digital Trends*, October 13, 2011, http://www.digitaltrends.com/apple/apparently-siri-has-some -pretty-strange-responses-up-her-sleeve.

52. Will Oremus, "Terrifyingly Convenient: A.I. Assistants Can Give You the News, Order You a Pizza, and Tell You a Joke; All You Have to Do Is Trust Them—Completely," *Slate*, April 3, 2016, http://www.slate.com/articles/technology/cover_story/2016/04/alexa_cortana_and_siri_aren_t_novelties_anymore_they_re_our_terrifyingly.html.

53. Bosker, "SIRI RISING: The Inside Story of Siri's Origins—and Why She Could Overshadow the iPhone," *Huffington Post*, January 24, 2013, http://www.huffingtonpost.com/2013/01/22/siri-do-engine-apple-iphone_n_2499165.html.

54. Garun, "Softbank's Pepper."

55. Jeff Parsons, "Sex Will Be More Popular with Robots than with Humans by 2050, Claims Shocking Report," *The Daily Mirror*, September 30, 2015, http://www.mirror.co.uk/news/technology-science/technology/sex-more-popular-robots-humans-6545349.

15   Sexbot-Induced Social Change: An Economic Perspective

Marina Adshade

Technological change invariably brings social change. We know this to be true, but rarely do we—or can we—make accurate predictions about how social behavior will evolve when new technologies are introduced. For example, no one should have been surprised that improvements in birth control technologies spawned more promiscuous societies. But could anyone really have predicted that making it easier for women to control their fertility would result in dramatic increases in births to unmarried women?[1] Likewise, anyone could have predicted that the introduction of the Internet would increase access to pornography. But who would have predicted that as people had more, and cheaper, access to pornography, there would be fewer and fewer rapes?[2] Early adopters probably knew that improvement in home production technologies would liberate women from household drudgery. But could they have known that the microwave oven would eventually contribute to societies' more accepting attitudes toward same-sex marriage?[3]

Sexbot-induced social change (SISC) is on the horizon. Elements of that social change can be easily anticipated. For example, the share of the young adult population that chooses to remain single is very likely to increase. Because social change is organic, however, adaptations in other social norms and behaviors are much more difficult to predict. But this is not virgin territory. New technologies completely transformed sexual behavior over the second half of the twentieth century. We have decades of technology-induced social change to guide our predictions about the future of SISC.

SISC will influence a broad spectrum of social structures. Here we will focus on one significant area: the nature of marriage. While many will be dismayed to see marriage evolving as the result of SISC, the reality is that marriage already is, and always has been, evolving with changes in technology. In fact, the current demand for new marital systems is just as likely to drive the adoption of sexbot technology, as the adoption of sexbot technology is to drive a marital revolution.

Getting any of these predictions right will require a great deal of luck, but investigating SISC can help us prepare to mitigate its possible social costs. It also gives us the opportunity to take full advantage of the societal benefits that sexbot technologies may afford society.

15.1   Historical Examples of Technology-Induced Social Change

Let us begin by looking at three historical examples of technology-induced social change. This will give us a tool for understanding the process though which social norms evolve in response to the availability of new technologies.

We now know that the rate of births outside marriage increased when technology improved the ability of women to control pregnancy—and this may be the best example of technology-induced social change. As we will see, it also serves as a starting point for discussing a range of predictions regarding SISC, since these may run parallel to the social changes observed with improvements in contraceptive technology.

American women obtained the right—in 1965 if they were married and in 1972 if they were not—to access oral contraceptives.[4] But in fact they had not waited for the Supreme Court's permission. Both married and single women found ways to encourage doctors to prescribe "The Pill" soon after the drug was approved by the FDA in 1960.[5] The changes brought about by this new technology have been far-reaching, but among the most surprising has been the pill's contribution to the rise in births among unmarried women.[6]

The direct effect of improvements in birth control technology was a decrease in the expected cost of sex outside of marriage, and, as a result, an increase the number of women who were willing to engage in premarital sex. The indirect effect was that, as the number of women who were willing to engage in premarital sex increased, social norms that proscribed promiscuity adapted and the social stigma attached to premarital sex diminished. Today, people who say that sex between unmarried individuals is unacceptable are in the overwhelming minority.[7]

Over a very short period of time, births to unmarried women increased because some of the now sexually active women experienced contraceptive failure. But this was only part of the effect. Many women became sexually active not because contraceptives were available, but rather because of the changing social norms that permitted sex outside of marriage. Those women only used contraceptives erratically and others did not use contraceptives at all.

Increased access to contraceptive technology changed society's views of sex outside of marriage. This had the unanticipated effect of contributing to the increase in births to unmarried women. It also contributed to the de-stigmatization of childbirth outside of marriage.

For a second, more controversial, example of the role new technologies can play in contributing to social change, we can examine the thesis that increased access to the Internet has the power to reduce reported rape rates. According to the FBI Uniform Crime Reports, between 1995 and 2014 the reported rape rate in the US fell by 29%— from 37.1 per 100,000 persons to 26.4 per 100,000 persons.[8] Over the same period, the share of the US population with Internet access has increased from 9.2% to 86.75%. These two factors could be entirely unrelated, but there is research that suggests that a causal relationship exists between access to the Internet and rape.

In economic terms, pornography and rape are substitutes. This means that as the price of pornography falls, some potential offenders substitute pornography viewing, which is now relatively inexpensive. Taking advantage of variations in rates of Internet adoption between states, and controlling for confounding factors, this research find that a 10% increase in Internet access coincides with a fall in reported rape rates of 7.3%.[9] The largest effect is among men who would have had very little access to pornography before the online porn became available: those ages 15 to 19.

One might want to argue that the cause here is not pornography, but rather some other factor such as the influence of social networking on either the incidence of rape or on rape reporting.[10] But the decline in rape rates began early in the 1990s, just as Usenet newsgroups began uploading porn to the web and more than a decade before social networking became available. Over the period of this study, rape reporting increased, which suggests that the relationship that we observe in the data between Internet access and rape is actually understated.

Regardless of whether or not you accept as conclusive the evidence of a relationship between the viewing of online pornography and rape, there is sufficient statistical evidence to claim a relationship between access to the Internet and a reduction in the incidence of rape. This is an unambiguously positive effect for society.

The final example of how technology can encourage social change may not at first seem relevant, but it is probably the most important for our purposes. Marriage has changed in significant ways over the past century, thanks, in a large part, to new technologies in both the home and the workplace. This particular example, of the relationship between technology and changes in the legal definition of marriage, is an example of technology-induced institutional change. Here the legal institution has changed as a result of new technologies.

Between the mid-1700s and the early 2000s, the role of marriage between a man and a woman was predominately to encourage the efficient production of market goods and services (by men) and household goods and services (by women). This division of labor within marriage was productive for the family because men and women brought very different capabilities to marriage. Most importantly, the capacity to earn a waged income was almost always higher for husbands than it was for wives. And before new technologies arrived that replaced the labor of women in the home, caring for a family was a job that required someone to be in the home full-time. Since wives were not able to earn as much as their husbands, it made sense that women specialized in home production and that men specialized in market production.

Starting as early as the end of the nineteenth century, marriage began to evolve as electrification in the home made women's work less time-consuming, and new technologies in the workplace started to decrease the gender wage gap.[11] Between 1890 and 1940, the share of married women working in the labor force tripled, and over the course of the century that share continued to grow as new technologies arrived that replaced the labor of women in the home.[12] Electric washing machines and dryers saved women days each week of manual labor. By the early 1970s, the arrival of microwave ovens and frozen foods meant that a family could easily be fed at the end of a long workday, even when the mother worked outside of the home.

Long before the close of the twentieth century, thanks to new technologies marriage stop being about the efficient production of market and household goods, and started being about something else: companionship, love, and sex.

Marriage stopped being about two people coming together because they were very different from one another, in terms of their ability to produce, and started being about two people coming together because they were very similar to each other. It thus became easier for societies to see the irrelevance of rules that prohibited same-sex marriage. Social change slowly extended into intuitional change, and governments began to revise marriage laws to reflect this evolving social norm.

It is obvious that we have not seen the end of technology-induced changes to the institution of marriage, or to social norms of sexual behavior. Understanding how these changes have taken place historically, however, gives us the courage to think about how they will change in the future—once sexbot technology becomes an option for people either married or single.

Prediction One: The adoption of Sexbot technology will disentangle the association between sexual intimacy and marriage, leading to higher quality marriages.

There are those who argue that the only reason that men "assume the burden" of marriage is that marriage allows men easy sexual access. From this perspective, women trade something that men value, sexual access, for something that women value, financial security for themselves and their children. According to this view, once men can find easy sexual access from sexbots, not only will they abandon the idea of family and marriage, but they will also cease to invest in the education and careers that they would have needed to support that family. Marriage, on this view, is the foundation on which modern society rests, and that foundation will crumble if men can find somewhere more convenient to put their penis than in a living human being.

These predictions are no different than those being made a century ago, when the invention of the latex condom (in 1912) and the intrauterine device (IUD) (in 1909) significantly increased people's freedom to have sex without risking pregnancy and (importantly, in a era in which syphilis was rampant) sexually transmitted disease. Social commentators at that time warned that these technologies would destroy marriage by removing the incentives women had to remain chaste, effectively encouraging them to flood the market with nonmarital sex. Men would have no incentive to marry, and women, whose only asset is sexual access, would be left destitute.

By the late 1920s and the 1930s, it was apparent that these concerns were unfounded. Couples continued to marry, and, in fact, married at higher rates than in previous decades. At that point, the conversation turned to how contraceptives were changing the nature of marriage itself. Whereas in the past, women might have acted as if they succumbed to their husband's sexual desires only as a means to having children, technological advances in contraception meant that women were forced to admit to enjoying intimate relationships with their husbands. Social commentator Walter Lippmann in his 1929 *Preface to Morals* wrote: "by an inevitable process the practice of contraception led husbands and wives to the conviction that they need not be in the least ashamed of their desires for each other" (292).

This technological change—early contraceptives—changed the way that society viewed marriage, and, importantly, female sexuality. New and better contraceptives in the second half of the century only helped cement society's realization that women are sexual beings, and are just as entitled as men to sexual gratification within their relationships. This change in behavior eroded the conviction that the purpose of marriage was the exchange of sexual access for financial security. For the first time in history, sexual intimacy and marriage were seen to be intrinsically connected.

This change in the purpose of marriage was encouraged by a secondary effect of access to contraceptives—increasing female economic independence. Armed with the confidence that they would be able to limit the number of children they would bear, women in the seventies and eighties increased their investment in post-secondary education and their attachment to the workforce.[13] Thanks to birth control, women, for the most part, no longer depended on marriage for financial security.

And yet we still marry. According to the Pew Research Center, in 2012, 81% of forty-five year old men and 86% of forty-five year old women had been married at some point in their lifetime; down from the 1960s, certainly, but hardly a wholesale abandonment of marriage.[14] We marry because marriage continues to be the most efficient way to arrange families, in that it minimizes the costs of household production. Individuals can live alone, and even have children this way. But marriage is a lower-cost way to raise a family, since it allows for the division of labor in household tasks. This cost-effectiveness is most evident in heterosexual marriages, since those marriages can often avoid the additional expenses involved in alternative reproductive technologies. Today, thanks in part to contraceptive technology, we marry because marriage brings both partners relatively easy sexual access, companionship, and reduces the costs of household production, including the production of children.

The question then is, what happens to marriage when sexbot technology provides a low-cost substitute to easy sexual access in marriage? One possibility is a reversal of the societal change brought about by improved effectiveness of contraceptives, which tied together marriage and sexual intimacy, and a return to the perception of marriage as a productive household unit. Access to sexbot technology will not change the biological imperative of individuals to want to share their lives, and raise their children, with another human being. But it would make it possible for individuals to choose that human being based on characteristics other than mutual sexual desire; to disentangle the association of sexual intimacy and life as a family. For example, it is not hard to imagine two heterosexual women seeing the value in forming a household and raising children together as a married couple, but with their needs for sexual companionship met by sexbot technology. Nor is it hard to imagine a homosexual man seeing the value in forming a household and raising children with a woman, since that arrangement would significantly reduce expenses associated with reproductive technologies, but with each of their needs for sexual companionship met by sexbot technology.

Those who fear that sexbot technology will have a negative impact on marriage rates see sexbot technology as a substitute to sexual access in marriage. If they are correct, a decrease in the price of sexual access outside of marriage will decrease the demand for sexual access in marriage, and marriage rates will fall. It could just as easily be argued, however, that within marriage sexual access and household production are complements in consumption—in other words, goods or services that are often consumed together. If that is the case, then, economic theory predicts that easy access to sexbot technology will actually increase the rate of lifetime marriage, since a fall in the price of a good increases the demand for complements in consumption. Moreover, if sexual access through sexbot technology is a complement to household production, then we could observe an increase in the quality of marriages, and, as a result, a reduction in rates of divorce.

There is an economic principal—named after French chemist Henry Louis Le Châtelier—that says that whenever a constraint on individual decision-making is removed, the outcome of that decision can be no worse than the outcome that would have existed with that constraint imposed. The need to find someone with whom you are mutually sexually compatible necessarily imposes a constraint on the decision of whom to marry, just as the need to have continued mutual sexual compatibility necessarily imposes a constraint on the continuation of that marriage. Removing that constraint on the choice of a marital partner cannot, by Le Châtelier's principle, lead to marriages of lower quality, but it could very well make marriages that are of a higher quality.

By disentangling the association between sexual intimacy and marriage, marriage may not end up as what we imagine it to be today. But that new form of marriage would be the socially optimal arrangement in the sense that it would encourage efficient household formation and, as a result, lead to marriages that are more likely to stand the test of time.

Prediction Two: The adoption of sexbot technology will lead to the normalization of nonexclusive relationships as the dominant relationship structure.

Once we disentangle the association between sexual intimacy and marriage, it is not hard to imagine the removal of barriers that currently prevent married individuals from forming arrangements in which one, or both, seek sexual gratification with other, non-robotic, individuals outside of their marriage.

Monogamous marriage has, at least in industrialized societies, historically been the socially optimal marriage arrangement, in that it produces children with higher levels of human capital. Men invest more in their children when they are assured that those children have not been fathered by other men, and, if husbands are faithful, unmarried women are not left raising the children of married men who lack commitment to those children. Because marital fidelity has been the socially optimal behavior, social norms developed that disapproved of, or even punished, extramarital sexual relationships.

Today, with access to reliable contraceptives, the incentives for marital fidelity are quite different. This has allowed these social norms to evolve, albeit extremely slowly. Access to sexbots is likely to accelerate that change in social norms, and, in fact, has the potential to eliminate social disapproval of non-monogamy altogether.

This process of social change is best understood in three stages. In the first stage, access to sexbot technology encourages the creation of marriages described above: marriages without sexual intimacy that focus on the production of household goods (including children), and perhaps on providing companionship. Any concern that such marriages will produce children with low levels of human capital would be unfounded, given that each individual within the relationship is finding sexual intimacy with sexbots and not fertile humans. In fact, such marriages could provide superior environments for children, and, as a result, we would expect that fairly quickly these arrangements would be met with societal approval. Social norms will adjust to not only tolerate relationships in which individuals seek sexual gratification from technology, but will approve of such arrangements.

In the second stage, the greater societal acceptance of this nontraditional marriage arrangement will encourage others to enter into purely productive marriages. The difference between those who marry in the first stage and those who marry in the second stage is that those in the second stage do not, for whatever reason, confine their extramarital sexual activity to sex with robots. These marriages are formed not because sexbots technology is available, as in the first stage, but because the social costs of such arrangements have been eliminated through changing social norms.

We have seen that improvements birth control technology had both a direct effect on promiscuity, by increasing the sexual activity those who responded to the lower probability of pregnancy, and an indirect effect on promiscuity, by increasing the sexual activity of those who responded to changes in social norms. In a similar way, sexbot technology will have both direct and indirect effects on extramarital sexuality.

Some of these marriages in the second stage will have the unintended consequences that led to the original societal disapproval, just as improvements in birth control technology ultimately led to an increase in births to unmarried women. But just as social norms did not revert to their pre-birth control condemnation of premarital sex with the increase of pre-marital births, nor will social norms revert to their pre-sexbot condemnation of non-monogamous marriage.

The final stage of this process involves couples with traditional arrangements: marriages that include both sexual intimacy and household production. Many of these marriages might continue to be sexually monogamous, but with evolving social norms that approve of non-monogamous marriages it is likely that those with a preference for such arrangements will be uninhibited. Monogamy within marriage will come to be seen as a personal preference rather than a socially imposed constraint. With sufficient numbers of married individuals choosing to seek sexual gratification outside of marriage, perhaps at even various stages of their lives, it is easy to imagine non-monogamous marriage becoming the dominant marriage institution in the developed world.

Prediction Three: Legal marriage institutions will be reformed to allow individuals to determine the nature of their own marriages free from state interference.

As a legal institution, the nature of marriage is a function of the economic environment of that particular society. It is for this reason that policies and customs surrounding marriage vary from one society to the next and within societies over time. We have already seen an example of this endogeneity of marriage institutions, when we discussed (above) the movement toward equal married reforms as a function of the technological changes over the twentieth century.

No doubt, there are many technological innovations that will encourage further marriage law reforms in the coming decades. These include technologies that change: the ways in which we communicate; what it means to be employed in the waged workforce; the way(s) we undertake home production; and those that affect human reproduction. The way in which our individual decision-making will be influenced by these new technologies will be wholly dependent on our personal circumstances. As a result, I predict that we will ultimately abandon a universal definition of marriage. We will instead move toward a system that allows couples to structure their marriages in a way that is optimal for them as individuals and abandon the concept of a socially optimal marital arrangement.

Sexbot technology will be only one of many technologies that will play a role in inducing this institutional change in marriage. However, given how closely sexual intimacy has been tied to marriage historically, its influence is likely to be profound. This is not to say that as the result of sexbot technology all marriages will be profoundly different than they are today. It suggests only that as a result of sexbot technology, individuals will be able to form relationships that are recognized by society as marriages, but that are not be recognized as marriages today.

Prediction Four: Changes in social norms around marriage and sexual access will disadvantage those in the lower socioeconomic groups, potentially making them worse off than they might have been before the technology existed.

One of the disadvantages of a society in which individuals have access to sexbot technology, and in which couples can choose the nature of their own marriages, is that not everyone will benefit from this arrangement. Those in the lowest socioeconomic groups will be most likely to be disadvantaged relative to those who can afford access to the technology.

We have seen this imbalanced influence of technology-induced social change already. For example, new technologies giving women the ability to control their own fertility have left some men, those who in previous generations would have married women with few alternatives, unmarried. Female economic independence has been very good for most women, and for most children, but there is little doubt that there are single men who would have reaped the benefits of marriage had these social changes not occurred.

There are other examples of technology's distributional influence. For example, access to the Internet, and the resulting rise of online matching technologies, has resulted in an increase in marital sorting by income and wealth levels. Whereas in the past women might have achieved upward economic mobility through marriage, Internet technology has encouraged a marital class system in which women and men largely marry within their own education and income groups. This lack of upward mobility through marriage has contributed to rapidly growing rates of singlehood in the lowest socioeconomic groups, in part because many women in those groups have chosen to remain single rather than to enter into what they perceive to be inferior marriages.

This brings us to the last example. We have already seen how technologies that replaced the labor of women in the home, and technologies that made men and women equally productive in the workplace, have contributed to a shift of importance in marriage from production to love. This technology-induced social change, which made love centrally important to marriage, is preventing some individuals from marrying who would have benefited from a productive marriage. Those individuals are more likely to be found in the lower socioeconomic groups where these new technologies have had little positive influence on standards of living. As with the other examples of SISC discussed above, the distributional issue that arises with sexbot technology comes not from the direct impact of the technology itself, but rather from the change in social norms that inevitably will accompany the technology. In this case, however, sexbot technology has the power to be harmful, since none of the direct benefits are likely to reach those socioeconomic groups who cannot afford to access it.

Consider my prediction, above, that access to sexbots will encourage the acceptance of nonexclusive relationships as the dominant relationship structure. Those in the lower socioeconomic groups are much more likely to change their behavior because social norms have evolved, not because the technology is available. Non-monogamy may have a negative impact on those in the lower socioeconomic groups, since individuals in those groups are subject to a much higher risk of unplanned births on account of their poor access to contraceptives and to abortion. If non-exclusivity reduces paternal investment in children born into the marriage, or in children born to extramarital partners, then it is the children born to these low-income parents who will be most disadvantaged by these new social norms.

15.2   Conclusion

I started out by stating that technological change often delivers unexpected social change, and that sexbot-induced social change would almost certainly lead to the evolution of marital norms and institutions. There is one caveat here: in order for social change to occur there would have to be widespread adoption of sexbot technology. Sexbots would have to be easily affordable and accessible so that the average household would be able to possess one. That element of this story is perhaps the most difficult to anticipate. As we have seen, it was growing demand for sex outside marriage that almost certainly drove the widespread adoption of birth control. Norms around promiscuity evolved rapidly as a result, but the change in attitudes was already underway, and this made the spread of the technology possible. In the same way, a change in attitudes toward marriage may have to already be underway in order to drive the adoption of sexbot technology, rather than just the other way around.

But there is evidence that this is in fact happening. We can already see a small-scale revolution brought on by people demanding the acceptance of non-monogamy in marriage, the separation of sexual intimacy and productive marriage, and the abandonment of a universal concept of marriage. Access to sexbots cannot on its own transform society to make these new attitudes broadly accepted. But it can certainly accelerate changes already underway—perhaps quite dramatically. For those who believe in the concept of traditional marriage, access to sexbot technology is going to help usher in some very trying times.

Notes

1. Jeremy Greenwood and Nezih Guner, "Social Change: The Sexual Revolution," *International Economic Review* 51, no. 4 (November 2010): 893–923.

2. Todd Kendall, "Pornography, Rape, and the Internet," unpublished manuscript (2007), http://idei.fr/sites/default/files/medias/doc/conf/sic/papers_2007/kendall.pdf.

3. Betsey Stevenson and Justin Wolfers, "The Economic Case for Same Sex Marriage," *Bloomberg News*, May 14, 2012, https://www.bloombergview.com/articles/2012-05-14/the-economic-case-for-same-sex-marriage.

4. Griswold v. Connecticut (381 U.S. 479, 85 S. Ct. 1678,14 L. Ed. 2d 510, 1965), Eisenstadt v. Baird (405 U.S. 438, 92 S. Ct. 1029, 31 L. Ed. 2d 349, 1972).

5. Claudia Goldin and Lawrence Katz, "The Power of the Pill: Contraceptives and Women's Career and Marriage Decisions," *Journal of Political Economy* 110, no. 4 (August 2002): 730–770.

6. Greenwood, "Social Change." In 1960, only 5.3% of all births were to unmarried women. By 2013, this share was 40.6% of all births. See Sally C. Curtin, Stephanie J. Ventura, and Gladys M. Martinez, "Recent Declines in Nonmarital Childbearing in the United States," *National Center for Health Statistics Data*, brief no. 162 (August 2014), http://www.cdc.gov/nchs/data/databriefs/db162_table.pdf.

7. Jacob Poushter, "What's Morally Acceptable? It Depends on Where in the World You Live," *Pew Research Fact Tank* (April 15, 2014), http://www.pewresearch.org/fact-tank/2014/04/15/whats-morally-acceptable-it-depends-on-where-in-the-world-you-live.

8. Federal Bureau of Investigation Uniform Crime Reporting Program, "Crime in the U.S. 2014" (2014), https://www.fbi.gov/about-us/cjis/ucr/crime-in-the-u.s/2014/crime-in-the-u.s.-2014/tables/table-1.

9. Kendall, "Pornography."

10. Rape reporting rates increased from 28.8% in 1995 to 33.6% in 2014, a small but statistically significant effect.

11. Jeremy Greenwood, Ananth Seshadri, and Mehmet Yorukoglu, "Engines of Liberation," *The Review of Economic Studies* 72, no. 1 (January 2005): 109–133; Marina Adshade, "Female Labour Force Participation in an Era of Organization and Technological Change," *Canadian Journal of Economics* 45, no. 3 (August 2012): 1188–1219.

12. Goldin and Katz, "The Power of the Pill."

13. Martha J. Bailey, "More Power to the Pill: The Impact of Contraceptive Freedom on Women's Life Cycle Labor Supply," *The Quarterly Journal of Economics* 121, no. 1 (February 2006): 289–320.

14. Pew Research Center (2014), http://www.pewsocialtrends.org/2014/09/24/chapter-2-trends-in-the-share-of-never-married-americans-and-a-look-forward.

Contributors

Marina Adshade holds appointments at the Vancouver School of Economics at the University of British Columbia and the Simon Fraser University School of Public Policy. She is the author of *Dollars and Sex: The Economics of Sex and Love.* She is a regular contributor to *The Globe and Mail* and *Time* and has written for *The Wall Street Journal, The Sunday Times* (UK), *The Daily Mail* (UK), and *BuzzFeed.*

Thomas Arnold is a Research Associate at the Human-Robot Interaction Laboratory at the School of Engineering, Tufts University. He specializes in ethics and the philosophy of religion.

Julie Carpenter, PhD, is a consultant, researcher, and educator on human interaction with emerging technologies, with a focus on human-robot interaction research. In addition to looking at human emotion and decision-making, her work situates people's dynamic experiences with technology within larger social systems, formal and informal, such as workplace organizations, in order to identify changeable issues to influence how people work with technological systems. Dr. Carpenter is currently a Research Fellow in the Ethics + Emerging Sciences Group at California Polytechnic State University.

John Danaher is a lecturer in Law at the National University of Ireland, Galway. His research interests span the philosophy of religion, ethics, legal theory, and the philosophy of technology. He has published numerous articles on the topics of human enhancement, robot ethics, and artificial intelligence. He maintains the popular blog *Philosophical Disquisitions* and is an affiliate scholar for the Institute for Ethics and Emerging Technology.

Brian Earp is Associate Director of the Yale-Hastings Program in Ethics and Health Policy at Yale University and The Hastings Center, and a Research Fellow in the Uehiro Centre for Practical Ethics at the University of Oxford. He is an Associate Editor of the *Journal of Medical Ethics*, and holds degrees from Yale, Oxford, and Cambridge Universities.

Lily Eva Frank is an Assistant Professor of Philosophy and Ethics at the Eindhoven University of Technology in the Netherlands. She received her PhD from the Graduate Center, The City University of New York in 2014. Her current research focuses on the ethics of technology, bioethics, metaethics, and moral psychology.

Joshua D. Goldstein is an Associate Professor of Political Science at the University of Calgary. He does research both in the history of political thought, particularly on Hegel's conception of freedom, and in contemporary political philosophy where he focuses on sexual ethics and New Natural Law Theory. He is the author of *Hegel's Idea of the Good Life: From Virtue to Freedom, Early Writings and Mature Political Philosophy* (Studies in German Idealism series, vol. 7) (Dordrecht: Springer, 2006).

Michael Hauskeller is an Associate Professor of Philosophy at the University of Exeter. He is the author of numerous books, including *Biotechnology and the Integrity of Life* (Ashgate, 2007), *Better Humans? Understanding the Enhancement Project* (Acumen, 2013), *Sex and the Posthuman Condition* (Palgrave Macmillan, 2014), and *Mythologies of Trans-humanism* (Palgrave Macmillan, 2016).

Noreen Herzfeld is the Nicholas and Bernice Reuter Professor of Science and Religion at Saint John's University and the College of St. Benedict. She holds degrees in both Computer Science and Theology. She is the author of *In Our Image: Artificial Intelligence and the Human Spirit* (2002), *Technology and Religion: Remaining Human in a Co-Created World* (2009), and *The Limits of Perfection in Technology, Religion, and Science* (2010).

Neil McArthur is Director of the Centre for Professional and Applied Ethics, and Associate Professor of Philosophy, at the University of Manitoba. He is the author of *David Hume's Political Theory* (2007). In addition to his academic writing, he is a regular contributor to *VICE*.

Mark Migotti is a professor in the Department of Philosophy at the University of Calgary. He works on Nietzsche, Peirce, and issues concerning the relationship between different kinds of commitment. He is currently writing a book on Nietzsche's *Genealogy of Morals*, tentatively entitled *Ethics and the Life of the Mind: A Study in Nietzsche's Moral Philosophy*.

Ezio Di Nucci is Associate Professor of Medical Ethics at the University of Copenhagen. Recent monographs include *Mindlessness* (2013) and *Ethics Without Intention* (2014). His most recent book is *Drones and Responsibility* (2016, co-edited with Filippo Santoni de Sio).

Sven Nyholm is an Assistant Professor of Philosophy and Ethics at the Eindhoven University of Technology in the Netherlands. He received his PhD from the University of Michigan in 2012. His current research focuses on the ethics of technology, bioethics (especially neuroethics), and the philosophy of well-being.

Steve Petersen is an associate professor of philosophy at Niagara University. His research mostly aims toward an algorithmic approach to "good thinking," and thus lies somewhere in the intersection of traditional epistemology, formal epistemology, philosophy of mind, and philosophy of science.

Anders Sandberg is a Senior James Martin Fellow at the Future of Humanity Institute at the Oxford Martin School, at the University of Oxford. His research centers on management of low-probability high-impact risks, societal and ethical issues surrounding human enhancement, estimating the capabilities of future technologies, and AI safety.

Matthias Scheutz is Professor of Cognitive and Computer Science, Bernard M. Gordon Senior Faculty Fellow, and Director of the Human-Robot Interaction Laboratory at the School of Engineering, Tufts University. He does research on artificial intelligence, cognitive modeling, the foundations of cognitive science, and human-robot interaction.

Litska Strikwerda studied both (criminal) law and applied ethics. In 2014 she completed her doctoral dissertation titled "Virtual Acts, Real Crimes? A Legal-Philosophical Analysis of Virtual Cybercrime," for which she recently received the Erasmus Praemium Dissertation Award 2016. Currently, she works as an assistant professor at the Open University (the Netherlands).

Nicole Wyatt is Head of the Department of Philosophy at the University of Calgary. She mostly writes about pornographic speech, the nature of logic, and the difficulty of talking about things that don't exist.

Index